THE A  TION

For Jan Fairley (1949–2012)

The Art of Record Production
An Introductory Reader for a New Academic Field

Edited by

SIMON FRITH
Edinburgh University, UK

SIMON ZAGORSKI-THOMAS
London College of Music, University of London, UK

ASHGATE

Published by
Ashgate Publishing Limited
Wey Court East
Union Road
Farnham
Surrey, GU9 7PT
England

Ashgate Publishing Company
Suite 420
101 Cherry Street
Burlington
VT 05401-4405
USA

www.ashgate.com

British Library Cataloguing in Publication Data
The art of record production : an introductory reader for a
  new academic field. – (Ashgate popular and folk music series)
  1. Sound – Recording and reproducing. 2. Sound – Recording
  and reproducing – Case studies.
  I. Series II. Frith, Simon, 1946– III. Zagorski-Thomas,
  Simon.
  781.4'9–dc23

Library of Congress Cataloging-in-Publication Data
The art of record production : an introductory reader for a new academic
field / edited by Simon Frith and Simon Zagorski-Thomas.
    p. cm. — (Ashgate popular and folk music series)
  Includes bibliographical references and index.
  ISBN 978-1-4094-0562-7 (hardcover) — ISBN 978-1-4094-0678-5
(pbk) 1. Popular music—Production and direction. 2. Sound
recordings—Production and direction. I. Frith, Simon, 1946–
II. Zagorski-Thomas, Simon.
  ML3470.A77 2012
  781.49—dc23

2012001679

ISBN 9781409405627 (hbk)
ISBN 9781409406785 (pbk)
ISBN 9781409449331 (ebk)

MIX
Paper from
responsible sources
FSC
www.fsc.org
FSC® C018575

Printed and bound in Great Britain by the
MPG Books Group, UK.

Contents

General Editor's Preface

The upheaval that occurred in musicology during the last two decades of the twentieth century has created a new urgency for the study of popular music alongside the development of new critical and theoretical models. A relativistic outlook has replaced the universal perspective of modernism (the international ambitions of the 12-note style); the grand narrative of the evolution and dissolution of tonality has been challenged, and emphasis has shifted to cultural context, reception and subject position. Together, these have conspired to eat away at the status of canonical composers and categories of high and low in music. A need has arisen, also, to recognize and address the emergence of crossovers, mixed and new genres, to engage in debates concerning the vexed problem of what constitutes authenticity in music and to offer a critique of musical practice as the product of free, individual expression.

Popular musicology is now a vital and exciting area of scholarship, and the *Ashgate Popular and Folk Music Series* presents some of the best research in the field. Authors are concerned with locating musical practices, values and meanings in cultural context, and draw upon methodologies and theories developed in cultural studies, semiotics, poststructuralism, psychology and sociology. The series focuses on popular musics of the twentieth and twenty-first centuries. It is designed to embrace the world's popular musics from Acid Jazz to Zydeco, whether high tech or low tech, commercial or non-commercial, contemporary or traditional.

Professor Derek B. Scott
Professor of Critical Musicology
University of Leeds

List of Figures and Music Examples

Figures

Music Examples

List of Tables

List of Contributors

Professor Andrew Blake is Associate Dean of the School of Humanities and Social Sciences at the University of East London. An occasional saxophonist and composer, his writings include *The Music Business* (1992); *The Land without Music: Music, Culture and Society in Twentieth-Century Britain* (1997); the edited collection *Living through Pop* (1999); and *Popular Music: The Age of Multimedia* (2007). He is also the author of books on sport, fiction, and consumer culture, including *The Irresistible Rise of Harry Potter* (2002).

Alexandrine Boudreault-Fournier completed her doctoral studies in social and visual anthropology at the University of Manchester and the Granada Centre for Visual Anthropology, and then undertook two postdoctoral studies at the Université de Montréal and then Université Laval, York University and the CÉLAT (Canada). She recently produced the film *Golden Scars*, in part funded by the National Film Board of Canada (www.goldenscars.com). This film presents an intimate portrait of the realities facing young musicians in Cuba, offering an exclusive look into the unique stories of two young rappers born in Santiago de Cuba.

Jerry Boys started his career in 1965 at the world-famous Abbey Road Studios. He moved in 1968 to Olympic Studios and in 1969 to Sound Techniques. He was chief engineer at Sawmills Studio from 1975 and then joined Livingston Studios in 1982 as studio manager. He has had many roles at Livingston over the years including at one time co-owner but now limits himself to being one of their biggest clients. He has also worked at many studios around the world including Ocean Way, Capitol Studios, Abbey Road, Angel Studios, Egrem Habana Cuba, Studio Bogolan Mali and Xippi Senegal and several un-named remote corners of the world. Jerry has worked on numerous gold and platinum records including the world famous Buena Vista Social Club series for World Circuit Records. He has also won four Grammys and been nominated for many more. He also has considerable experience in recording and mixing music for film and video and also orchestral recording.

George Brock-Nannestad graduated in electronics and signal processing in 1971. He became a European patent attorney in 1989, involved with the School of Conservation of the Royal Danish Academy for Fine Art from 1991 to 1998. In this latter role, George was responsible for research and tuition in preservation and restoration of carriers for sound, moving images and data. Since 1997 George has worked as a private consultant for Patent Tactics specializing in patents, restoration concepts and the history of AV technology. He is a member of AES, Acoustical

Society of America, ARCS, AFAS, Newcomen Society, ICOM and the Danish Musicological Society. After 25 years he retired from the Technical Committee of IASA.

Richard James Burgess PhD has produced, recorded and performed on many gold, platinum, and multi-platinum albums. He was the producer and the project director for *Jazz: The Smithsonian Anthology*, a seven-year project chronicling the history of jazz. Burgess authored *The Art of Record Production in 1997* and the second and third editions entitled *The Art of Music Production* in 2001 and 2004. He has received awards as a producer and musician from *Music Week*, the British Arts Council, the Greater London Arts Association and the Park Lane Group.

Jan Butler is a lecturer in Popular Music at Oxford Brookes University, and also editorial manager for the journal *twentieth century music*. She is an active member of the International Association for the Study of Popular Music and the Association for the Study of the Art of Record Production, and her research has been funded by the Society of Music Analysis, the Arts and Humanities Research Council and the Royal Musical Association. Jan's immediate research area is the development and effects of the ideology of authenticity in 1960s American rock music, and she has recently completed her PhD thesis entitled 'Record Production and the Construction of Authenticity in the Beach Boys and late 60s American rock' under the supervision of Professor Adam Krims at the University of Nottingham. She intends to turn this into a monograph in the near future. Her other research interests include music journalism and criticism, cover versions, music in film, the analysis of music production and the institutional structures that effect the creation and reception of recorded music.

Maureen Droney is Los Angeles senior executive director of the Producers & Engineers Wing of the Recording Academy (Grammys). She began her career in the music recording industry as an assistant engineer at the legendary Automatt Studios in San Francisco, where she trained with such notable producers and engineers as Fred Catero, Jim Gaines, Leslie Ann Jones, David Kahne, Mitchel Froom and Ron Nevison. She went on to engineer projects for George Benson, Whitney Houston, John Hiatt, Tower of Power, and Santana, among many others (including Santana's GRAMMY-winning album *Blues For Salvador*). She holds a degree in Broadcast Communication Arts from California State University, San Francisco, and has taught seminars in the theory and practice of audio engineering for facilities including ABC Television and Radio, CBS Television, and Deluxe Film Labs Post Production. Prior to joining the Recording Academy, Droney was general manager of the Kiva Family of Studios, which included the House of Blues Studios in Los Angeles and Memphis and East Iris Studios in Nashville. The Los Angeles editor of *Mix* magazine for more than 10 years, she is the author of *Mix Masters*, a popular recording textbook published by Berklee Media, and is also a regular contributor to numerous audio and performing arts publications.

Jan Fairley is an ethnomusicologist, a Latin Americanist and Honorary Fellow at the Institute of Popular Music at the University of Liverpool. From 1995 to 1997 she was director of the Edinburgh International Book Festival. She has enjoyed a long career as a freelance journalist, music writer, broadcaster and editor. She has taught in Chile, Spain and the UK and carried out extensive research in Cuba. She was International Chair of IASPM (the International Association for the Study of Popular Music) from 2009–11.

Simon Frith is Tovey Professor of Music at the University of Edinburgh. He was a founder member of IASPM and a founding editor of *Popular Music*. His *Sociology of Rock* (1978) was one of the earliest academic studies of popular music and his latest book, *Taking Popular Music Seriously* (2007) is a selection of his essays from the last thirty years. He has had a long career as a music journalist, including stints as a columnist for *Melody Maker* and *Village Voice* and rock critic for the *Sunday Times* and the *Observer*. He chairs the judges of the Mercury Music Prize.

Phil Harding started in the music industry aged 16 at the Marquee Studios in 1973. His engineering credits from that period include The Clash, Killing Joke, Toyah and Matt Bianco. At the start of the 1980s, Phil started working for Stock, Aitken and Waterman and engineered and mixed hit singles for Dead or Alive, Mel & Kim, Bananarama, Rick Astley, Depeche Mode, Erasure, Pet Shop Boys and Kylie Minogue. In the early 1990s he left PWL to set up his own production facility with Ian Curnow at the Strongroom Studio complex in Shoreditch, London where they produced hits for East 17 (including the Christmas No 1 'Stay Another Day'), Deuce, Boyzone, 911, Caught in the Act and Let Loose. Phil is currently chairman of JAMES (the Joint Audio Media Education Services organization set up by the Music Producers Guild, UK Screen and the Association of Professional Recording Services) and regularly participates in JAMES Masterclasses / Accreditations and Course Planning.

Associate Professor Mike Howlett joined Gong as bass player in 1973 and in 1977 formed the short-lived Strontium 90 (with Sting, Stuart Copeland and Andy Summers of the Police). He then turned to production, working on Top 10 hits for the likes of Martha & the Muffins, Orchestral Manoeuvres in the Dark, Blancmange, A Flock of Seagulls and China Crisis, and international top-selling albums for Joan Armatrading, The Alarm, Gang of Four, Berlin and Fisher-Z among others. In 1982, he received a Grammy award for his work on A Flock of Seagulls' track 'DNA'. He was also a founding member of the Record Producers Guild (later the Music Producers Guild). Recently Mike has been recording and touring with Gong and House of Thandoy and in 2009 took up a position as Head of Music and Sound at the Queensland University of Technology, teaching production.

Katia Isakoff began her professional music career as a singer, songwriter, studio owner and music producer, with album releases through Mute and EMI Records. Her compositions and performances have been featured internationally in TV shows and adverts and she is currently managing director of the Altersonic Sound Company (record label) and Hairpin Management (artist/producer representation). For a full biography and artist roster list please visit www. thealtersonicsoundcompany.co.uk. In addition to being a practitioner Katia has designed, led and delivered numerous music production and business undergraduate and postgraduate modules and is presently a visiting lecturer at the University of Glamorgan where she leads and delivers the final year BSc module in Music Production. Katia is also a member of the JAMES (Joint Audio Media Education Services) Academic Advisory Committee, joint editor-in-chief of the *Journal on the Art of Record Production*, director of the Art of Record Production (Conferences and Journal) and an executive committee member of the Association for the Study on the Art of Record Production.

Michael Jarrett is Professor of English at Penn State University, York Campus. He is the author of *Drifting on a Read: Jazz as a Model for Writing* (SUNY Press, 1999) and *Sound Tracks: A Musical ABC* (Temple University Press, 1998); he has essays in both *The Other Side of Nowhere*, ed. Fischlin and Heble (Wesleyan University Press, 2004), and *Representing Jazz*, ed. Gabbard (Duke University Press, 1995).

Phillip McIntyre has worked professionally as a record producer, songwriter and musician. He has also directed and edited videos for national broadcast and has co-produced a radio documentary series. His period as a music journalist saw him writing feature stories on a range of internationally acclaimed musicians. His doctoral research investigated the creative process of songwriters as cultural producers and his ongoing academic interest is in communication, creativity and cultural production. He is head of the Discipline of Communication and Media at the University of Newcastle NSW.

Robin Millar is one of Britain's most successful-ever record producers with 150 gold, silver and platinum discs and 44 No 1's to his credit, including Sade's iconic *Diamond Life* album. His productions have sold well over 55 million copies, earning the UK over £400 million in foreign income and have won almost every major global music award including Brit and Grammy Awards. In 2010 the Brit Awards Voting Academy nominated *Diamond Life* as 'one of the best 10 British albums of the last 30 years'. Robin has owned and run businesses in and out of the music industry for 25 years, including Power Plant, Maison Rouge and Whitfield Street Studios, Rent-a-Ferrari, Scarlett Group PLC and Arts Media. He was awarded a CBE in the 2010 Queen's Birthday Honours and is an honorary professor at the London College of Music (University of West London) and patron of the Music Producers Guild.

Paul D. Miller, aka DJ SPOOKY, is a composer, multimedia artist and writer. His written work has appeared in *The Village Voice*, *The Source*, *Artforum* and *The Wire*, amongst other publications. Miller's work as a media artist has appeared in a wide variety of contexts such as the Whitney Biennial; The Venice Biennial for Architecture (2000); the Ludwig Museum in Cologne, Germany; Kunsthalle, Vienna; The Andy Warhol Museum in Pittsburgh and many other museums and galleries. Miller's books include *Rhythm Science* (MIT Press, 2004) and *Sound Unbound* (MIT Press, 2008). His interest in reggae and dub has resulted in a series of compilations, remixes and collections of material from the vaults of the legendary Jamaican label Trojan Records. Other releases include *Optometry* (2002) and *Dubtometry* (2003) featuring Lee 'Scratch' Perry and Mad Professor. Miller's latest collaborative release, *Drums of Death*, features Dave Lombardo of Slayer and Chuck D of Public Enemy, among others. He also produced material on Yoko Ono's recent album *Yes, I'm a Witch.*

Allan Moore is Professor of Popular Music at the University of Surrey. He has published widely, most recently editing Ashgate's *Critical Essays in Popular Musicology*, and is series editor for their multi-volume *Library of Essays in Popular Music*. He was founding co-editor of *twentieth-century music* and is on the board of *Popular Music*. He is particularly interested in the hermeneutics of recorded popular song, and is still an active performer.

William Moylan is Professor of Music and Sound Recording Technology at the University of Massachusetts Lowell, where he established and leads the Sound Recording Technology program and served as Chairperson of the Department of Music. He has been active in music and recording industry and academic communities for over 30 years, with extensive experience and accomplishments as a record producer, recording engineer, composer, author and educator. His most recent book, *Understanding and Crafting the Mix: The Art of Recording* (2nd edition, Focal Press, 2007) is unique in its focus on the artistic and creative aspects of the recording process, and on how the unique aspects of sound controlled by the recording process can shape music. Moylan's writings have become influential in the academic circles of music analysis, recording analysis, and in studies of how the recording process shapes the artistry of music.

Bob Olhsson trained at United Sound in Detroit in 1962, learning his trade on sessions with artists such as George Clinton, Johnny Taylor and Barbara Lewis. He then got a job with Motown Records where he worked during the golden years of the late 1960s and early 1970s. When Motown moved to Los Angeles, Bob moved to San Francisco and worked on a wide range of rock albums and then branched out to include everything from classical albums for Harmonia Mundi to Quicksilver Messenger Service and the Grateful Dead. Since 1991, Bob has been working in digital sound, mastering and motion-picture post-production and surround sound.

Tony Platt started at Trident Studios in London before moving to the now legendary Island Records Basing Street Studios where he mixed the 'Catch a Fire' album for a hitherto unknown Jamaican artist Bob Marley and recorded and mixed his 'Burnin' album. This led to work with several other notable reggae artists such as Toots & the Maytals, Harry J's All Stars and Aswad. Becoming freelance he recorded demos that prefaced deals for Thin Lizzy and the Stranglers before becoming engineer for Mutt Lange and working on the AC/DC albums *Highway to Hell* and *Back in Black, Foreigner – '4'* and Boomtown Rats – *Fine Art of Surfacing*. As a producer he has recorded a range of artists from Iron Maiden, Motorhead and Gary Moore to Buddy Guy, Soweto Kinch and The Bad Plus. He continues to enjoy working with artists from many genres. http://www.platinumtones.com.

Steve Savage is an active producer and recording engineer and has been the primary engineer on seven records that received Grammy nominations, including CDs for Robert Cray, John Hammond, The Gospel Hummingbirds and Elvin Bishop. He works primarily as a mix and mastering engineer in the San Francisco Bay Area but has made records in Los Angeles, New York and Denmark. His book, *The Art of Digital Audio Recording* was published by OUP in 2011 and he completed his PhD in Musicology at the Royal Holloway College, University of London in 2009. He is currently a lecturer at the San Francisco State University and was one of the co-hosts of the 2011 Art of Record Production conference at SFSU.

Susan Schmidt Horning is Assistant Professor of History at St. John's University in Queens, New York. She is a cultural historian of twentieth-century America, American technology and sound studies, with particular interest in media, the arts and popular culture. She is completing her first book, *Chasing Sound: Technology, Culture, and the Art of Studio Recording in America*, which traces the evolution of the recording studio and explores the interplay between technology, creativity, musical culture, engineering, labour and business in the American recording industry during the first century of sound recording. Her work has appeared in *Music and Technology in the Twentieth Century* (Johns Hopkins, 2002), *The Electric Guitar: A History of an American Icon* (Johns Hopkins, 2004), and the journals *Social Studies of Science* and *ICON*. Susan is also a former musician and amateur recordist who played with the 60s all-girl rock band The Poor Girls, and the 1970s trio, Chi-Pig, whose 'Apu, Api (Help Me)' (Stiff Records, *The Akron Compilation*, 1978; Chi-Pig Records, *Miami*, 2004) Susan recorded on a TEAC 3340.

Paul Théberge is the Canada Research Chair in Technological Mediations of Culture at Carleton University, Ottawa. His research interests range from issues relating to music, technology and culture, music and globalization and the uses of sound in film and television. His work has appeared in encyclopaedias of music, *The Canadian Journal of Political and Social Theory, New Formations*,

Social Studies of Science, the *Canadian Journal of Communication* and various edited collections. His monograph *Any Sound You Can Imagine* won book awards from the International Association for the Study of Popular Music (1998) and the Society for Ethnomusicology (2000).

Alan Williams holds a BM in Third Stream Studies from the New England Conservatory of Music, and an MA and PhD in Ethnomusicology from Brown University. For many years, he worked as a recording engineer and producer, primarily with singer-songwriters such as Dar Williams, Patty Larkin, Lucy Kaplansky, and Jennifer Kimball. Currently, he is an Assistant Professor of Music at the University of Massachusetts Lowell, where he teaches courses in recording aesthetics, popular music history, world music, and is the coordinator of the music business program. He is also a songwriter and performer with his band Birdsong at Morning. Their debut release from 2011 was a four-CD box set entitled *Annals of My Glass House*.

Sean Williams is based at the University of Edinburgh and teaches on the Sound Design MSc and Sound Recording undergraduate courses. An active performer using live electronics, he is a member of several ensembles including Intuitive Music Edinburgh and the Monosynth Orchestra playing original compositions, improvisations and existing pieces by Stockhausen, Subotnik and others. He also enjoys playing records whenever and wherever the opportunity arises and has produced a weekly radio show called 'Voice On Record on Resonance FM'.

Simon Zagorski-Thomas is a senior lecturer in Music and Music Technology at the London College of Music (University of West London), and the programme leader for the MA in Record Production. He is a director of the Art of Record Production Conference and is chairman of the Association for the Study of the Art of Record Production. Before becoming an academic he worked for 25 years as a composer, sound engineer and producer with artists as varied as Phil Collins, Mica Paris, London Community Gospel Choir, Bill Bruford, The Mock Turtles, Courtney Pine and the Balanescu Quartet. He is, at present, conducting research into the musicology of record production and the cognition of rhythm and groove in popular music.

Albin Zak III is Professor of Music at the University at Albany (State University of New York). His research specialties are popular music studies and the history of sound recording. He is the author of *'I Don't Sound Like Nobody': Remaking Music in 1950s America* (University of Michigan Press) and *The Poetics of Rock: Cutting Tracks, Making Records* (University of California Press), and editor of *The Velvet Underground Companion: Four Decades of Commentary* (Schirmer). His articles and reviews are published in the *Journal of the American Musicological Society*, *Journal of the Society for American Music*, *Current Musicology*, *Notes*, and several volumes of collected essays.

Acknowledgements

This book would never have happened without the Art of Record Production Conference and the many people who have supported, contributed and hosted it during its first seven years. Simon Zagorski-Thomas's co-director of the conference, Katia Isakoff, has obviously been a key player in this. The various hosts and their institutions should also be mentioned: Mark Irwin and Andy East at the London College of Music, UWL, Alan Fisher at the University of Westminster, Nicholas Cook at Royal Holloway College, Simon Frith at the University of Edinburgh, Andy Arthurs, Donna Hewitt and Julian Knowles at the Queensland University of Technology, William Moylan at the University of Massachusetts Lowell, Jim Barrett and Andrew Gwilliam at the University of Glamorgan, Justin Morey at Leeds Metropolitan University and Scott Patterson and Steve Savage at San Francisco State University. The contributors listed before this section not only deserve our thanks for their hard work but provide a fine example of the way that the Art of Record Production projects have brought together academic and industry figures to help define and refine this emerging discipline.

Simon Zagorski-Thomas would like to thank Natalia and Alex for their love and support. He would also like to thank the many conference participants for their stimulating and enlightening conversation at the social events in and around the conferences and via email.

Chapter 1
Introduction

Simon Frith and Simon Zagorski-Thomas

The first Conference devoted to the Art of Record Production (ARP) was held in London in 2005, the second in Edinburgh in 2006, with subsequent meetings in Brisbane (2007), Lowell, Massachusetts (2008), Cardiff (2009), Leeds (2010) and San Francisco (2011). And ARP has established its international profile not just by bringing together scholars and practitioners in particular cities at particular times, but also with an online journal (http://arpjournal.com), a formal association (the Association for the Study of the Art of Record Production: http://artofrecordproduction.com) and through that nebulous but essential academic support mechanism, an informal network of people who share practical, pedagogical and research concerns. This book, which brings together papers first presented to ARP conferences, marks another step in the development of a new academic subject: it lays out the scope and principles of recording studies for classroom use.

The book is designed as an introductory reader, a textbook for students on degree courses concerned with the technical, cultural and creative processes involved in the production of recorded music. The aim is to introduce students to the variety of approaches and methodologies that have so far been developed by scholars in this field. The book is therefore divided into three parts. In the first, recording is examined historically, with reference to how and why recording practice has changed over time. In the second, recording is examined theoretically, with reference to such issues as musical meaning, acoustic meaning and technique. In the third, case studies of particular occasions, recordings and technologies exemplify the various ways in which historical and theoretical methods can be conjoined. There are also three interludes of commentary from leading record producers and other industry figures on the chapters that have gone before. These industry professionals were asked to reflect on the relations between the studio and the academy, between the different ways in which practitioners and scholars make sense of recording practice.

This structure reflects the principles of ARP as a project – cross-disciplinary, designed to foster a dialogue between academics and practitioners, open minded as to what 'the study of record production' might involve – but also the realities of the organization of higher education. The ARP Conferences and online journal have been remarkably successful in bringing academics from analytical and practice-based areas of the university system together with industry professionals to explore the ways in which this field of research and teaching should progress and, if nothing else, this collection should give students a broad overview how disparate threads of intellectual activity are combining to produce a new area of study. What is less clear, though, is how the study of recording is being placed in academic departments and degree courses. This issue was discussed at both the 2010 and 2011 ARP conferences, where it was agreed that recording usually fits rather awkwardly in its obvious home, departments of music. Recording students may work closely with student performers and composers but the traffic tends to be one way: audio students record performers and performances; neither performers nor composers study recording. Meanwhile in musicology classes, in courses in music theory and analysis, the focus is still the score; the study of the recording as a material or musical object has largely been left to media or cultural studies modules.

There are obvious parallels here with the development of popular music studies (also difficult to integrate into conventional music departments) and a key point to make is that the study of record production (like the study of popular music) is not in itself a discipline, a field of study with its own clearly defined methodology, but is, rather, a cross-disciplinary project. Recording, that is to say, is a field of study that has to be approached with a range of methodologies. One of the most striking aspects of the first Art of Record Production Conference was the variety of the scholars who turned out to be active in this field: musicologists, sociologists, anthropologists, cultural theorists, ethnomusicologists, psychologists, historians, electrical engineers, psycho-acousticians, literary theorists, historians of science and more. The contributors to this book come from departments of music, cultural theory, anthropology, conservation, English, communication and media, sound recording and history, and this range of backgrounds reflects one of our aims in compiling the book: to show the different conceptual approaches with which recording can be approached.

In establishing the study of recording as a university subject, though, it is not enough simply to encourage a thousand flowers to bloom. This collection is also designed to show that the variety of approaches is not just interesting but necessary: to understand the historical, cultural and aesthetic importance of recording we have to understand it in all its aspects, and students of recording should be familiar with all approaches. From this perspective music does seem to be the best home for recording studies, if only because the academic study of music is not confined to a single discipline either. Music education necessarily involves a relationship between performance, composition and analysis, and most university music departments are organized around a combination of theory and practice. And even from an academic perspective, the study of music is necessarily cross-disciplinary. The most traditional, classical music-oriented departments are these days quite likely to employ staff whose training has been in history, psychology, sociology, acoustics, sound design or film studies, as well as in musicology as such, just as newer, commercial music-oriented departments employ people to teach cultural and media studies, new technologies and business skills as well as music itself. The problem of the study of recording, in short, is not its multidisciplinarity or concern for the combination of theory and practice, but, rather, the way it challenges long-established assumptions (both inside and outside the academy) as to *how* music works, culturally and aesthetically, and therefore how it should be understood.

To study recording is to draw attention to two aspects of musical practice that conventional music studies tend to ignore: technology and commerce. It is also to raise questions about two of the shibboleths of everyday musical understanding: the importance of the individual musical creator and the sacred nature of 'the musical work'. The study of recording, to put this another way, can be seen as an affront to the central tenet of classical music studies, that great music is the work of genius, and a threat to the usual academic hierarchy of high and low music. It's worth noting in this context that the first ARP conference was co-hosted with CHARM, the Centre for the History and Analysis of Recorded Music, the first ever funded project in the UK on classical music recording.[1] As Andrew Blake shows in his chapter in this book, to study classical music recording is necessarily to address arguments about what music is *for*.

This question hovers over all the chapters here and if every contributor answers it in their own way, we can pull out some shared assumptions.

Technical, Aesthetic and Musical

In the studio technical decisions are aesthetic, aesthetic decisions are technical, and all such decisions are musical. As we have already remarked, ARP is organized around a dialogue between scholars and practitioners but this is to suggest a distinction that may be misleading. Ten out of the 16 chapter contributors to this book have experience of professional practice in record production. Conversely, several of the industry practitioners contributing to the interludes are also engaged in academic activity of various kinds. In other words, many of the people involved in the analysis of recording write from a position of considerable hands-on knowledge and experience, while many practitioners have felt it useful to teach and reflect on what they do. This is to be expected but the assumption that there are people who do recording and other people who think about what it means is surprisingly commonplace pedagogically. The majority of existing textbooks in the field, for example, are determinedly practical, covering recording techniques, mixing techniques, processing techniques and business techniques as if they were somehow quite apart from musical judgements. The few theoretical books seem, by contrast, to be written for music students without concern for technical procedures. None of the writers here would accept such separate spheres.

In his keynote speech at the 2010 ARP Conference, the producer Steve Albini discussed the ways in which technologies influence creative practice. He suggested that digital audio systems are about the manipulation of sound after it

---

[1] N. Cook, E. Clarke, D. Leech-Wilkinson and J. Rink (eds), *The Cambridge Companion to Recording* (Cambridge: Cambridge University Press, 2009).

has been recorded while analogue systems are about capturing the sound in the first place. From this perspective, analogue recording is a kind of 'service industry' to the creative practice of musicians whilst digital systems encourage the creative practice of manipulating and distorting musical performances. Paul D. Miller's speech at the same conference similarly stressed the new creative possibilities that digital systems offer but also drew attention to the historical predecessors to this editorial approach to art.

Several of the chapters in this book examine the complexities of this issue. Sean Williams, in his discussion of King Tubby's dub mixing practice, is at pains to avoid technological determinism and instead points to the ways in which creative practice in the studio extends beyond the intended use of technology into what Andy Keep in a paper at the 2005 ARP Conference described as 'creative abuse'.[2] Alan Williams, equally keen to reject over-simple accounts of causation, shows how for some musicians headphones are a disconcerting inconvenience, for others a creative boon. Equipment becomes 'technology' only in its human use.

Attention to Detail and Context

The study of recording must pay attention to both the smallest (in studio) detail and the broadest (out of studio) context. All the chapters in this book illustrate the complexity of questions about perspective and levels of description. Allan Moore argues for a holistic approach to musical analysis (as opposed to a separate study of record production) but focuses exclusively on reception – the effect of the musical output on the listener. Albin Zak, by contrast, studies the method of production as well as the musical output but treats production as a single feature of that output. Simon Zagorski-Thomas studies a relatively small period and limited styles of music but looks at a broad range of influences on that microcosm – studio architecture, technology, economics, musical and social history, the training and practice of sound engineers, musical ideology and so on. Susan Schmidt-Horning, by contrast, looks at the single feature of studio acoustics but does so across a range of decades and styles.

The Interplay of Art and Commerce

The interplay of art and commerce in recording shapes and is shaped by power relations, by struggles over who gets to make sound decisions. In Chapter 13, Simon Frith expands on a point made by Dave Laing in the early days of rock

---

[2]   A. Keep, 'Does "Creative Abuse" Drive Developments in Record Production?', Proceedings of the First Art of Record Production Conference, University of Westminster, London 2005. [Online]. Available at: http://www.artofrecordproduction.com/content/view/141/ [accessed: 26 April 2011].

to argue that 'the recording studio is the place in which the relationship of art and industry is articulated, through the relationship of musicians and producers; it is the setting in which music – of all kinds – takes on commodity form'. The changing nature of that place and that relationship is examined in different ways in the five 'historical' chapters of this book, which also illustrate the changing economic and artistic relationships that musicians and producers have enjoyed through the recording process, something first documented in a pioneering article by Edward Kealy.[3] Since Kealy wrote, developments in digital technology have further complicated matters. On the one hand, the 'democratizing' effect of desktop technology has been accompanied by a marked decline in the financial returns from recording. On the other hand, the commodification of domestic production technology and the seemingly huge expansion of choice have been typified by a move towards 'preset culture' and the flattening of difference through correctional signal processing and editing. In general historical terms the effects of economic change on both the politics and aesthetics of production are clear enough, whether we look at real estate prices and a surplus of redundant performance venues in the 1940s and 1950s, the huge profits from the audio leisure industry boom in the 1960s and 1970s, or the cheapness of digital signal processing technology relative to acoustic recording technology in the 2000s.

Recording Is Both a Musical Activity ...

It is obvious enough that recording is a social activity through which music is made, an activity that can therefore be illuminated by ethnographic study (see, for example, Porcello[4] and Meintjes[5]) but, as Robin Millar suggests in his interlude comment here, there is surprising little work on the psychology of record production (psychologists of music have tended to concentrate on music learning and perception). Alan Williams' chapter does discuss musicians' different attitudes and reactions to technologies like headphones and talkback and Jan Butler shows how Brian Wilson's personality affected his studio use of both people and equipment, but most empirical work on studios foregrounds the collective practices involved. Recording scholars are, on the whole, wary of reproducing musicological accounts of individual genius, of substituting Phil Spector and George Martin for Beethoven and Mozart in narratives of innovation. Deciding who is responsible for what in the studio is still a matter for record-by-record investigation (much of which remains to be done) rather than, for example, genre

---

[3]   E. Kealy, 'From Craft to Art: The Case of Sound Mixers and Popular Music', *Sociology of Work and Occupations*, vol. 6, no. 1 (1979): 3–29.

[4]   T. Porcello, *Sonic Artistry: Music, Discourse and Technology in the Sound Recording Studio* (unpublished PhD thesis, University of Texas, Austin, 1996).

[5]   L. Meintjes, *Sound of Africa! Making Music Zulu in a South African Studio* (Durham NC: Duke University Press, 2003).

generalization. We need to consider groupings and communities as often as we refer to individual producers or engineers. Phillip McIntyre's chapter here on systems theory provides a good example of an analytical tool that looks beyond the mythology of the creative genius to develop a framework for examining the social and economic forces that provide the context for individual creativity.

... and a Musical Event

It is commonplace nowadays to distinguish live music (which happens in a particular time and place) from recorded music (which doesn't). In the recording process performances don't need to be completed in a single 'take' and players can make several attempts at a piece, record it in sections, repair errors and even drop in for a single note. Furthermore, multitrack recording means that performers don't ever have to be together physically; ensemble pieces can be created without the players ever having met. And, of course, recording lacks another element of the concert experience: visual spectacle. Perception involves all the senses and the fact that we can't see the performers when we listen to a record means that we hear the music differently than when we can see it being made as well.

These arguments, though, relate primarily to the activity of listening to recordings (to which we will return). The activity of making records needs to be considered differently. On the one hand, record makers are concerned to make something that will be heard as an event so that, for example, many of the historical developments in record production can be examined in relation to how they exaggerate features of a sound that might normally rely on visual cues for their interpretation. Equalization is thus used to highlight the formants of human speech and so compensate for the record's lack of 'lip reading' cues. On the other hand, recording itself does take place at a time, even if a time often (though by no means always) spread over a much longer period than a live performance, and in a place, the studio, in which music making is tied up with architectural decisions, visual cues and, as many of the essays here show, a remarkably powerful sense of space.

The Record is a New Sort of Musical Work

To create the album *Bitches Brew*, its producer, Teo Macero, edited together many, many fragments of Miles Davis and his band's improvised performances. Macero worked without Davis being present and one of the other musicians involved, hearing the record, remarked, 'I was on that record. Is that what we did?' The recording process necessarily involves collaboratively constructed performances and as recording technology has developed, musicians have been increasingly willing to hand over control of the elaborate editorial process to others. One result of this is a new kind of music decision-making hierarchy. With live performance the creative management of the event is, for the most part, undertaken by one of the participants: the musical director, the artist, the conductor. The role of the record producer involves a different approach: the capture of completed recorded elements and the exercise of editorial control over them. It is a manufacturing process rather than a preparatory process (and comparisons can be made to the film-making and the relation of director and film editor).

Listening to Records is a New Way of Listening to Music

It is an academic irony that records have been an essential tool for scholars exploring how listening works according to aesthetic and cognitive theories in which it is assumed that recordings are simply an inferior representation of the real thing. Traditional musicologists thus theorize ways in which musical devices (as indicated in musical scores) elicit aesthetic or interpretative responses and illustrate this by playing students records. Ethnomusicologists and folk music scholars make field recordings of 'authentic' songs and performing practices that are being displaced by the 'artifice' of the recording process. Social and cognitive psychologists gather 'scientific' data about the listening process by playing records to wired-up subjects in labs. Such work begs two kinds of question that are of concern in recording studies. The first is simple to ask but difficult to answer: how has the rise of recording changed listeners' experience of music (and thus music itself)? If classical music producers, as Andrew Blake shows in his essay, have attempted to relate concert and domestic listening ideologically (while being fully aware of the differences acoustically), pop music producers have also been concerned with both the social and acoustic circumstances in which their records will be heard. (Will this sound good in a car? On the radio? At a party? In a club? On an iPod?) As the French sociologist Antoine Hennion argued long ago, there may not be a real audience in the recording studio but the potential audience is ever-present in producers' minds.[6]

The second question concerns the soundscape and how the ubiquity of recorded music has shifted conventional sound meanings, not simply as a matter of musical meaning but also in terms of what one might call sound design. The sound of the 'phone voice' in contemporary R'n'B is, for example, a marker of youthful communication and community; its use in the 1960s and 1970s was as a sign of distance and separation.

The Right Methodology

To choose the right methodology for the study of recording we have to decide what it is we are studying. The range and variety of approaches to the study of

---

[6] A. Hennion, 'An Intermediary between Production and Consumption: The Producer of Popular Music', *Science Technology and Human Values*, vol. 14, no. 4 (1989): 400–424.

record production in this book (and elsewhere) are exemplified by the range and variety of research methods used. The choice of what to study determines the method of study whilst, conversely, the method of study determines what you can find out (and, therefore, what you study). In 'traditional' musicology the studied text is generally the musical score and so, it would follow, in studying record production and recorded music, the text must be the recording itself. But just what is the recording? There is the final mix. There are the component tracks that are mixed together to produce it. In recent years there are the computer files that store much of the information about how these component tracks were processed and mixed together. Beyond the final mix, there are the various commercial products that were released after the audio mastering (a further bout of audio processing after the final mix): the shellac disc, the vinyl album, the compact disc, the data compressed MP3, MP4, AAC and other digital formats. And what of single and album mixes? Twelve-inch dance mixes and other remixes?

This bewildering array of texts leads to a further research problem. The obvious starting point is to listen to the recorded artifact (of whatever variety) but this has been further complicated by the advent of digital audio. There are now a multitude of possible visual representations of digital files that can be used to create graphic interpretations of audio phenomena: waveforms, spectrograms, chromagrams, onset detection, inharmonicity detection – the list is endless and relates specifically to features that you may want to study. But that is the key: the methodology for textual analysis relies on identifying and measuring given features in the text. This is true of both quantitative and qualitative analysis although the latter may require a broader definition of measurement (and perhaps even identification). Thus we may assess and describe the effect of dynamic compression on a recording of a drum performance by measuring and analysing the data in a digital file or through a subjective interrogation of our response to the recording's playback.

Both approaches are adopted in this book. In Chapter 14, Jan Butler uses textual analysis through listening to support assertions drawn from interview evidence about the making of *Pet Sounds*. In Chapter 5, by contrast, Simon Zagorski-Thomas uses spectrographic representations of audio files to support his claims about differences in sound between UK and US recordings.

In the same way that organology provides a more general backdrop to the study of composers and works in traditional musicology, the study of studio technology is essential background to studies of recording. And just as organology overlaps with performance studies, composition and orchestration, so does the study of technology inform our understandings of the process of recording that is our research object. In Chapter 2, George Brock-Nannestad thus uses both the original technical specifications produced by manufacturers and his own practical experience of using the technology to describe the cultural significance of early, direct to disc recording, while William Moylan, in Chapter 9, draws on the science of acoustics and electronic engineering to explore the limitations that technology can impose on attempts to create spatial effects in recorded music.

The process of record production, in short, needs to be understood both from the performer's perspective and in terms of how the recording technology is used. The ways to research this are well established in other fields of study. Data collecting methods can be boiled down to observation, participation and interviews with one or more participants. Aside from observing the process at the time, we can also observe the vestiges of process after the fact: photographs, track sheets, record company and studio records, product catalogues and manuals, and so on. For example, in Chapter 3, Susan Schmidt Horning combines participant interviews with photographs and other documentation to build up a picture of studio usage in the 1950s. Alan Williams (Chapter 8), Phillip McIntyre (Chapter 11), Jan Fairley and Alexandrine Boudreault-Fournier (Chapter 16) by contrast, rely on the observation and participant observation techniques of ethnomusicology and anthropology.

If the object of study is the meaning of recorded music, different methodological questions arise – meaning for whom, captured how? In Chapter 7, Allan Moore draws on traditional musicological, formal analysis and yet his approach is rooted in a much broader understanding of the listening process; he uses both the ecological perceptions of Eric Clarke[7] and the cognitive linguistics of George Lakoff and Mark Johnson.[8] By contrast, in Chapter 9, William Moylan considers listening in terms of psychoacoustics while still paying attention to more subjective and aesthetic questions about spatial and musical interpretation. An alternative, more sociological way of defining the issues here is through an examination of the discourses in which recording has, over time, come to be understood. Thus Simon Frith (Chapter 13) and Albin Zak (Chapter 4) make extensive use of journalistic commentary while Paul Théberge (Chapter 6) uses a statistical approach, drawing on government and industry figures, to identify broader trends in society.

And this brings us to our final point. While we have been arguing that the organized study of recording is something new in the academic curriculum, discussion of recording has a history as long as that of recording itself, and long established ways of making sense of what happens in the recording studio implicitly inform even the most systematically self-conscious modern scholarship. As Peter Doyle noted at the 2009 ARP Conference, recording has a rich tradition of story-telling which has involved its own versions of the canon, its own accounts of authorship and creativity, its own myths of motivation and accomplishment. And as Michael Jarrett argued at the same conference, we should be wary of creating a new musicology of record production that reproduces the problems and mistakes of the old musicology that ignored recording. Or as we would put it, the one thing this book does not want to achieve is a new academic orthodoxy.

---

[7] E. Clarke, *Ways of Listening: An Ecological Approach to the Perception of Musical Meaning* (Oxford: Oxford University Press, 2005).

[8] G. Lakoff and M. Johnson, *Metaphors We Live By* (Chicago: Chicago University Press, 1980).

PART I
Historical Approaches

Chapter 2

The Lacquer Disc for Immediate Playback: Professional Recording and Home Recording from the 1920s to the 1950s

George Brock-Nannestad

As the camera allows you to fix the first steps, the Memophone permits you always to re-hear the first attempts at speaking of your smallest one.[1]

Introduction

At a family event with speeches in the 1930s the head of the house switches on the wireless and opens the gramophone with the recording equipment, takes out a blank lacquer record from its sleeve, places it on the turntable and fixes it using a large nut with a left-hand thread. He takes a bottle of lubricating liquid and distributes some on the blank with an already shiny surface with a wad of cotton wool. He takes a cutting needle, which has a funny, scooplike shape, from a small packet and places it carefully in the hole of the cutterhead. He swings the threaded rod carrying the cutterhead across the record so that it locks to the centre spindle of the turntable. He takes a microphone, places it in its sprung holder in front of the next speaker and connects it to the wireless set (see Figure 2.1).[2]

Pinching the cutting needle between his fingers he asks the speaker to clear his throat, and he adjusts the level so that the vibrations of the cutting needle feel all right. He turns on the turntable and gives the signal 'go' while lowering the cutting needle on the lacquer surface, hoping that the speech does not last longer than 3½ minutes. However, finished or not, at the end of this time period the head of the house has to lift the cutterhead, replace it in its holder and stop the turntable. The cutterhead has been moved from the outside of the record to the inside by the threaded rod. He swings back the rod assembly and removes the threadlike swarf[3]

---

[1] Thorens brochure, *Memophone: Ihr Heimstudio*, (Ste. Croix, Switzerland: H. Thorens *c.*1939), trans. George Brock-Nannestad.

[2] The audio amplifier in the wireless that usually powered the loudspeaker provided the audio amplification that was needed to drive the cutterhead.

[3] The terms swarf (UK) and chips (US) are known from machine shops for the material you cut away.

Figure 2.1   Home recording machine in the family environment

from the centre of the lacquer, undoes the nut and removes the new record. It is wiped clean of the lubricant and replaced in the sleeve. The sleeve is duly marked and the information is repeated on the label of the record. Later that evening, the guests all listen to the speech again; the head of the house puts the lacquer record on the gramophone, he fits a trailing needle into the pickup and plays it as if it were one of the dance records.

In essence, this was what well-off people could do at home from about 1930. The less well-to-do perhaps paid a service to come and preserve an event, and another segment, the hobbymen, built their own equipment and even made their own blanks. Why were they doing it? A manufacturer of such equipment had this to say in 1939:

> Private music making give more pleasure when there is the possibility of re-listening to the pieces played. By means of the records made on the Memophone you will lighten your evenings and check and improve your playing.
>
> Persons involved in the theater or politics may check and improve their performance and diction by means of the Memophone.
>
> Memophone will prove invaluable to businessmen. Important confidential meetings are recorded without difficulty, verbal agreements fixed forever.
>
> In the interrogation and the recording of witness statements the Memophone is valuable, providing a safe, lasting recording of every utterance.
>
> Send friends and relatives in far away countries spoken greetings and information; there can be no nicer and more pleasant surprise![4]

In this way, 'preserving the moment', which is done without thinking today could be arranged 80 years ago on a regular basis, and a surprising number of those recordings still exist today and are playable when they are found. We have since grown used to having living images with our sound, but it is extremely doubtful if a digital audio file found on its own in 80 years' time from now will provide any useful information. The technological obsolescence has developed at an alarming rate.

The whole process of private recording was in stark contrast to the standard commercial production process for gramophone records that had essentially been in place since 1900. It was a multistage process, mostly under industrial conditions. When a record had been cut in the recording wax, this was shipped to an electroplating plant where a negative impression of the record was obtained in metal. Further electroplating work with several generations of intermediate metal plates finally produced a stamper, a tool to be used in a record press. The pressing plant had a whole row of presses all connected to supplies of steam and cold water. From a separate factory came the black record material, which was a mixture of fine stone dust and a shellac binder. When the press operator had made a record its edge was polished, it was put in a sleeve and carried to the shipping department of the record company. Large record companies had all of the manufacturing

---

[4]   Thorens brochure.

processes in-house, that is, wax preparation, electroplating, record material manufacture and record pressing, whereas smaller record companies might buy everything as commercial services. The road from recording to serviceable record was long and would normally take days, if not weeks.[5]

The Technological Pre-Requisites for Amateur Home Recording

Getting a useful record straight from a home recording session with the head of the house in full control as described above would not have functioned smoothly, however, unless a number of prerequisites were in place. They were: a suitable turntable mechanism, a cutter head, a cutting stylus and a suitable surface to cut into and to reproduce from by means of a gramophone needle. If uniformity of results was to be expected, all the items had to be manufactured by a supporting industry, which was very different from the record companies. And yet, some of the activity in the area was undertaken by pioneering amateurs, who even found ways to prepare their own recording blanks. Hence a further prerequisite is know-how; how to make the things work. We shall look at some of these prerequisites as they manifested themselves in the UK, in Germany and in the USA from about 1930 to 1950.

Already, from around 1900, the better kind of cylinder phonograph had a provision for recording on blank cylinders, but placing a bulky machine and recording horn in front of a speaker at a dinner was quite obtrusive – a microphone would be much less so. The sound from the cylinder was obviously recognizable, but not really life-like. Neither, though, was the sound emanating from a telephone, which was the first electrically generated sound most people experienced. By about 1926 the general public had become used to natural sounding voices from the wireless via loudspeakers. Gramophone records did not sound nasal any more, so it was only natural that preserving the moment had to involve fidelity to the original sound. With the fairly simple technology, and skipping some very costly and investment-heavy steps, a record was produced that while not as durable as a commercial record, was still competitive in sound quality on the machines available for playback at the time. The early discs for direct replay after recording were soft metal, such as zinc or aluminium, and machines for recording them were without any amplification, that is, reproduced acoustically like the cylinder phonograph. These were commercial products with a comparatively small market.[6]

---

[5]   George Brock-Nannestad, 'The Lacquer Disc for Immediate Playback: Professional Recording and Home Recording from the 1920s to the 1950s', presented at Art of Record Production, Second Annual Conference, Edinburgh, 8–10 September 2006.

[6]   J. Case, *Instantaneous Recordings*, in F. Hoffmann (ed.), *Encyclopedia of Recorded Sound*, vol. 1 (2nd edn, New York and London: Routledge 2005), pp. 519–20.

The professional record companies had very high quality standards, and they had refined the use of wax[7] compounds for the original recording medium. However, this wax was so soft that it was absolutely useless, except as the first step in a manufacturing process that aimed at making strong, durable grooves. So, for amateur use, it was essential to have recordable surfaces that were strong immediately after recording. Various types of 'instantaneous disc' cropped up, from soft aluminium discs that were embossed, via various forms of gelatine-based mixtures and lacquers on an aluminium or glass base to various mixtures of anorganic and inorganic compounds that frequently needed to be polymerized by heat or by the application of hardening liquids once they had been cut and before use.

There is no difference in principle between amateur instantaneous recording and professional recording, only the quality of the components is higher in the latter. The first professional use of the lacquer record was probably in the American film industry, where it turned out to be an expedient way of interacting with sound on the set, in quite a different way than sound was otherwise recorded optically on film for distribution. Discs had been used for synchronous reproduction with films 1927–33, in particular by Warner Brothers, but recording on film was gradually introduced. The problem was that instantaneous playback of a sound just recorded was desirable if for instance the same scene was to be re-shot from a different camera angle, because all the movements had to be synchronous to the recorded sound. Traditionally, this had been obtained by recording on wax and full record manufacture to a shellac pressing, which could be turned around in about 24 hours. However, this meant that everybody had to be called back on stage a day later. As Mr Best recounts in the spring of 1935:

> On location a few weeks ago in a down town Los Angeles theater we mounted the location truck alongside the film-recording truck in the alley, and playback records were made while one camera angle was being photographed and the soundtrack recorded. The disk was rushed inside and placed upon a turntable, and the other camera angles of the same scene were made to the playback, resulting in no delay whatsoever to the production setup. With the former method, if immediate playbacks had been required, we should have had to construct a soft wax recording set-up, with the bulky truck and the difficulties usually encountered in levelling the soft wax machine. The great advantage of the acetate record is that recordings can be made with the truck leaning at an angle; so long as the recording instrument is rigidly held in its mounting. If the sliver of acetate piles up, the recording stylus plows its way through without jumping or in any way affecting the recording. So, it is rather a haywire-looking device upon location, it works and saves a lot of time.[8]

---

[7]   Wax was the industry term for historical reasons, but for economy and consistent results a different compound was used: a wax-like, non-soluble soapy substance.

[8]   G.M. Best, 'Improvements in Playback Disk Recording', *Journal of Motion Picture Engineering*, vol. 25, no. 2 (1935): 115–16.

Surprisingly, the broadcast industry was quite late in introducing the lacquer disc in their production processes. So-called air-check recordings were well known from the early 1930s. These were recordings of performances taken from the transmitted signal and recorded remotely. They were made by independent recording operations that catered to performing artists who were appearing on a live radio show and wanted to have a permanent record. Later the lacquer disc made its way into broadcasting in the US,[9] and it became the norm to use 33⅓ rpm. For technical reasons,[10] vertical recording (hill-and-dale) was sometimes preferred. The British Broadcasting Corporation experimented with magnetic recording in the early 1930s and did not enter the disc-recording field until about 1935.[11]

The home recording machine was different from a normal gramophone in several respects. First of all, the motor had to be considerably stronger, because cutting swarf out of a lacquer surface required considerable torque, in particular at the outer edge. Secondly, even though the pickups of the time had such efficient magnetic circuits that they could in principle be used as cutter heads, it was easier to keep the circuits separate. This means that there had to be the usual tone arm with pickup device and a special carrier for the cutter head. The carrier had to transport the cutter head across the recording surface so that there was an even spacing between the groove turns. Three different types of construction were used: a strong tone-arm controlled from below the deck to move gradually across the turntable, a linear transport from the centre to the edge and driven by the turntable spindle, and a linear transport moving outside the surface of the turntable. The latter was the simplest to construct for home constructors. The drive for the transport was frequently taken from a pulley on top of the fixing nut for the lacquer disc (see Figure 2.2).

In Germany in particular there was a huge range of recording machines available. Some developments had taken office disc dictation machines as their starting point, and home recording with an adequate transfer of the cutting sound box[12] across the blank was already occurring acoustically from the mid 1920s.

---

[9]   M. Biel, 'The History of Instantaneous Recording and the Development of the Recording Studio Industry: Part One', handout at the Annual Conference of the Association for Recorded Sound Collections, Nashville, Tennessee, 1 May 1997; M. Biel, 'The History of Instantaneous Recording and the Development of the Recording Studio Industry: Part Two', handout at the Annual Conference of the Association for Recorded Sound Collections, Syracuse, New York, 22 May 1998; M. Biel, 'The Introduction of Instantaneous (direct) Disc Recording in America', handout at the Annual Conference of the International Association of Sound and Audiovisual Archives, Vienna, Austria, 21 September 1999.

[10]   Vertical recording permitted narrower tracks that enabled longer recordings on any one side.

[11]   *BBC Recording Training Manual* (London: British Broadcasting Corporation, 1950), pp. 49–83.

[12]   This was typically a soundbox for hill-and-dale as known from the Edison cylinders.

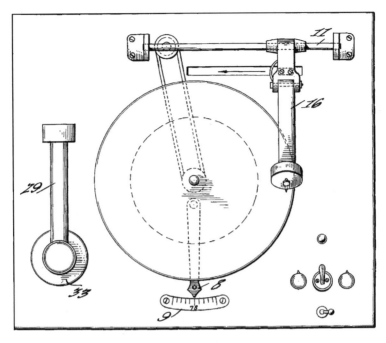

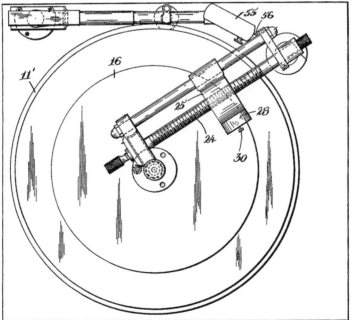

Figure 2.2   Two common types of recording machine

The Users of Amateur Home Recording Technology

The literature on amateur home recording reflects the fields of interest that it grew out of. In the UK, it was mainly the broadcast amateur who diversified from the building of radio sets to the building of recording machines. In Germany, the drive also came from the small-gauge or home movie amateurs, and the literature was published both from publishers catering for this hobby and for radio home constructors.[13] In the UK, the first handbook was a puny pamphlet published in 1944 by a publisher of practical instruction manuals in many diverse hobby fields and war technology, V. Bernards (Publishers) Ltd. It was by Donald W. Aldous and simply called 'Manual of Direct Disc Recording' (11.5 × 17 cm and 49 pages), including a very complete bibliography. He was a founding member of the semi-professional interest group, the British Sound Recording Association, in 1935 that included equipment, stylus and blank manufacturers as well as professional and amateur users.[14]

By 1932 in Germany there were already three books of about 100 pages each, with revised editions emerging during the 1930s as well as many articles in home constructor magazines and home movie magazines.[15] There seems to have been more extensive support for home recording in Germany than in the UK. Both countries were well supplied with professional recording services.

Technological Developments in Disc Recording For Immediate Playback

The professional recording machine for lacquers was not very different in principle from the recording lathe used for wax. Both were distinguished by a suction device that drew the tiny cut out thread of swarf directly from the cutting stylus and into a container. And both had a microscope fitted to observe the groove and in particular the width of cut while the cutting was taking place. Old hands at wax cutting might still use a small hand-held magnifier on a stick. Also, for some uses, the professional machines were adapted to be able to commence cutting at a small radius, proceeding outwards to the edge of the record. The professional recording machines used by the large recording companies were converted from acoustical recording, and they were hence much more unwieldy than modern (1930s)

---

[13] E. Schwandt, *Technik der Schallplatten-Heimaufnahme*, Funk-Bastler, vol. 36, no. 4 (1931): 561–5. W. Daudt, *Praktische Erfahrungen bei der Selbstaufnahme von Schallplatten*, Funktechnische Monatshefte 4 (1933): 177–81.

[14] G.A. Briggs (ed.), *Audio Biographies* (Idle, Bradford: Wharfedale Wireless Works, 1961).

[15] W. Frerk, *Selbstaufnahme von Schallplatten: Eine Anleitung für Phono- und Tonfilm-Amateure* (Berlin: Photokino-Verlag; 1st edn, 1932, 2nd edn 1935, 3rd edn 1939); H. Kluth, *Jeder sein eigener Schallplattenfabrikant* (Berlin: Weidmannsche Buchhandlung, 1932; 1st edn, January; 2nd edn, April); E. Nesper, *Nimm Schallplatten selber auf!* (Stuttgart: Franckh'sche Verlagshandlung, 1932).

recording machines dedicated to lacquer work. One development in particular was very innovative, that of Cecil E. Watts, who supplied the BBC with recording machines, also for outside broadcasting, from his company, Marguerite Sound Studios (M.S.S.). It was all a question of applying the strength of lightweight materials where it did the most good. In order to combat problems with lack of flatness of the recording blank, the M.S.S. turntable was very slightly concave so that the centre nut was able to pull the blank into good contact with the turntable surface.[16] Later the BBC experimented with their own constructions, and during World War II they imported American Presto equipment.

There were several types of lacquer discs, and some of them cannot properly be termed lacquer at all, because they were a solid material in circular sheet form that was amenable to cutting. Essentially it was a question of obtaining the mechanical conditions for good swarf separation just as in the everyday mechanical workshop practice of using a lathe. In a workshop you have several parameters available to obtain this, among which are the linear speed of the blank, the angle and depth of the cutting tool, and lubrication and cooling. All of these parameters are varied to obtain a good result in a given material; steel being different from, say, brass. In record cutting the linear speed is predetermined, and it falls to about a half from the outside to the inside of the disc. The depth is also a given; it is determined by the width of the groove, but the angle of cut and the materials are available as variable parameters. A good swarf separation gives a shiny surface to the cut, and that in turn means a relatively low noise.[17]

The humble cutting needle was hence at the heart of cutting, although it was the smallest component. It was a sharp cutting tool, and its dimensions decided the profile and surface quality of the groove. The downward force decided the depth of the groove (and thereby also the width), and this was adjusted by the operator. The cutting needle for lacquer records was made of steel, a tungsten alloy or sapphire. The latter was the work of Swiss lapidaries in particular, and they were mounted in an aluminium shank. While a metal cutting needle could survive cutting so deep that it hit the aluminium disc carrier, a sapphire needle would be destroyed. For this reason it was essential that it was lifted off the lacquer record if the feed mechanism was stopped, otherwise it would only cut deeper and deeper for each revolution. A metal cutting needle could be re-sharpened, and for this fixtures and abrasive tools were available.

For reproduction of the relatively soft lacquer material other needles were used, and in contrast to ordinary gramophone needles these were bent at an angle – so-called trailing needles. These were already available for commercial 'flexible' or 'unbreakable' records which had similar soft surfaces, such as the Goodson Record in the UK and the Phonycord in Germany. When an outside service made

---

[16]   A. Watts, *Cecil E. Watts: Pioneer of Direct Disc Recording* (privately published, 1972).

[17]   *PRESTO Instantaneous Sound Recording Equipment and Discs* (New York: Presto Recording Corporation, 1940).

a lacquer recording for a customer, a small supply of such needles was provided with the sleeve of the original recording.[18] The trailing needles gave a very much reduced treble in exchange for a longer life of the record. Obviously, the best pickups of the period used sapphire styli for reproduction and gave a much better reproduction and less wear.

The Types and Manufacture of Blank Discs

The materials used for home recording were: nitrocellulose lacquer, cellulose acetate lacquer, gelatine and spent X-ray film. In most cases the layer was coated onto a carrier: an aluminium sheet (steel or zinc was also used), a glass sheet or some kind of fibre board. The gelatine might be used as a solid, fairly thick sheet, or it could be cast on a carrier and the X-ray film was simply the cellulose di- or tri-acetate film base that could be cut on both sides, through the emulsion on one side. You had to choose your cutting needle by the material you were cutting in.

The manufacture of coated lacquer discs was a complex operation mostly taking place in factories. A few such manufacturing plants will be described.

In France a supplier of paints and varnishes for the automobile industry, Societé des Vernis Pyrolac in Créteil near Paris first developed a solid record material, then a lacquer coat for a fibrous support and finally an aluminium disc with a lacquer coating, sold under the trademark Pyral, which later became the name of the company. They became the main supplier of recording blanks to the French broadcasting authorities. The name is related to pyroxylin, a nitrocellulose compound. They took out patents on various coating processes in France, Germany, Great Britain, USA and Canada, but as the information on the actual manufacturing of blanks worldwide is scanty, it is not presently possible to see the full extent of manufacture under license.

In Great Britain there were a few competing firms. The most important supplier, with a contract with the BBC, was Marguerite Sound Studios which manufactured blanks as well as recording machines. The owner's widow Agnes Watts recounts how the aluminium sheets were dip-coated in a nitrocellulose solution and the solvent left to evaporate:

> In the early days these required a least four coats on both sides, and each had to be applied before the previous one had become too dry. Timing this at first was a hit or miss affair and many hours of labour and valuable material were wasted. Once the first side was sprayed, it had to dry sufficiently to be turned over to spray the reverse side – and yet not be allowed to become too firm when it was time to apply its next coat. As there were eight cellulose spraying operations to carry out with drying intervals between, Cecil generally stayed up

---

[18]   H.D. Linz, *Gramophone Needle Tins: History and Catalogue with Current Valuations* (Regenstauf: Battenberg, 2006), p. 206.

until midnight. Then he would set the alarm to wake him in time to put on the next layer and continue like this throughout the night until the operations were complete, allowing time for the final coat to dry, dismantle the booth and tidy up ready to open the studio at nine o'clock.[19]

A competing supplier manufactured gelatine-coated discs. This was the SIMPLAT sound recording disc manufactured by the V.G. Manufacturing Co., which used a glass disc with a thin specially prepared gelatine layer. The inventor, a Dutch chemist by the name of F.M. van Gelderen, used water glass (sodium silicate) to ensure adhesion between the gelatine and the glass base. Using Donald W. Aldous as a consultant, various accessories were developed, such as hardening liquids and a surface hardness tester to ensure that cutting would be successful. If the recording blank was too hard, it could be softened by 24 hours in a humid atmosphere.[20]

Recording blanks were expensive, and several articles in the specialized British magazines described how old coats could be stripped and new cutting surfaces deposited. For instance, it was described in 1941 how a solution of the enzyme pepsin could be used to remove gelatine from the expensive part of the lacquer record, the even and flat metal blank, and how to cook new gelatine and how to dip-coat the cleaned blank. When using an industrial metal lacquer it had to be dissolved in a thinner before coating a raw blank. As Donald Aldous wrote in a letter to the Editor of *Wireless World*:

> The air-drying process is unfortunately a lengthy one as it takes two or three weeks before the surface is absolutely 'tack-free' and hard enough for cutting, after which it can be 'stoved' for one hour at 120 to 125 deg. C., when a hard permanent surface is produced.[21]

In comparison it was simpler to deal with old nitro-cellulose coatings: they were partly dissolved by means of a solvent, which upon evaporation would leave a shiny and somewhat suitable surface.

In Germany there was a wide selection of commercially produced recording blanks to choose from. In the early 1930s there were still pure aluminium and zinc blanks available, but they were gradually replaced by three kinds of organic surfaces: several makes of solid gelatine disc (Pliaphan, Helios, Contiphon); one using a cellulose-based organic coat on an aluminium base (Metallophon); and one made in what was described in contemporary literature as a ceramic composition on a steel sheet that had to be hardened before reproduction (Draloston). However, the selection was much larger: several brands (for example,

---

[19] A. Watts, *Cecil E. Watts: Pioneer of Direct Disc Recording* (privately published, 1972), p. 23.

[20] D.W. Aldous, *The 'SIMPLAT' Sound Recording Disc and Supplement* (London: V.G. Manufacturing Co. c.1939).

[21] D.W. Aldous, *Wireless World*, vol. 47, no. 10 (October 1941), p. 270.

Tilophan) used a cardboard base as a carrier. At least one type (Phonoson) required a softening operation for the surface before cutting. In the late 1930s a further type was introduced, the Decelith, which had a transparent plastic carrier with two celluloid-based surfaces and appeared as a solid, stable disc 'useful in the tropics'. One problem was the shelf-life of blanks. In 1934 it was considered a large step ahead when Draloston was able to prolong the shelf life to six months by means of a virtually hermetic packing system.[22]

In the USA the lacquer disc was replacing metal by 1934. In fact the Presto Recording Corp. imported French Pyral lacquer records, and in 1938 Audio Devices, Inc., New York, became the exclusive US licensees of the patents and knowhow of the Societé des Vernis Pyrolac, manufacturing Pyral-type discs under the name Audiodisc until their in-house research took over.

Disc Recording for Immediate Playback after 1940

By 1940 the market for recording machines and supplies for them had grown immensely, as evidenced by catalogues from large mail-order houses, such as Sears Roebuck (Silvertone), Montgomery Ward (Airline) and Lafayette Radio Corporation (distributing the makes Wilcox-Gay, Presto, Rek-O-Kut and others). Lacquer discs of all qualities were widely available. When aluminium was needed for the war effort, glass replaced it as a base material for the better qualities. Aluminium had been very practical, but glass was actually better, because of its inherently greater smoothness.

Most of these recording surfaces were relatively noisy, the more primitive but durable types even noisier than commercial shellac records. This was in many cases 'good enough' for home recording, but it was the reason why for a long time they were not used for commercial recording in the manufacture of records for sale. In Germany, home recorders were advised against having their recordings made into pressings, because a licence fee would have to be paid on patents owned by Telefunken.

C.J. LeBel, who was the co-founder of Audio Devices, the maker of Audiodisc recording blanks and Audiopoints recording needles, wrote this about the industry's attempt to accommodate customers in 1940:

> Realizing that any type of coating (regardless of formula) can be softened and made quieter by addition of a higher percentage of plasticizers, a number of broadcasters have requested such a soft coating. This is not a move for better results. If the record is to be an audition or artist's record, exceptionally low initial noise level is of little importance compared to the rapid rise of scratch due to low durability. Some soft records have lasted for only four to eight playings. If the record is to be processed [made into a pressed record], the lower noise

---

[22]   Frerk, *Selbstaufnahme von Schallplatten.*

is completely submerged by processing, whereas the reduced high frequency response (inevitable in a softer coating) will serious injure the record quality. A soft and resilient coating may be seriously down in frequency response (both in the original and in a pressing) even at 5000 cps, which compare poorly with ordinary 75-cent black-label pressings, many of which are now produced with frequency response flat to 8000 or 10,000 cps.[23]

Towards the end of the 1930s, wax recording was used in the headquarters of the record companies as always, but in the big record companies lacquer records made of cellulose nitrate began to sneak in via the so-called 'indigenous recordings'; recordings of music from the colonies, from which shellac records were made for export back to those markets. The reason was one of logistics. A contemporary (1938) in-house report from EMI illustrated the transport problems (see Figure 2.3).

Smaller record companies took to the lacquer disc much quicker than the large concerns, because they did not have investments in the wax manufacturing and preparation equipment. As mentioned above, large record companies had all of the manufacturing processes in-house, that is, wax preparation, electroplating, record material manufacture and record pressing, whereas smaller record companies might buy everything as commercial services. It was hence a minor undertaking to convert to the use of lacquer records, and this permitted location recording at short notice to a much higher degree than the record companies that had to make recording expeditions. Except for a brief interlude of using recording discs made by flow-coating wax onto glass sheets, all record companies had converted to the use of lacquer in the course of the 1940s.

A lacquer record for processing purposes would not tolerate reproduction, just as for wax, the surface had to be 'virgin' for processing. However, it was very simple to run two recording machines with the same signal, one for the hopefully good take, the other for immediate reproduction and replay to ascertain the quality of the balance, the orchestration, and the soloist. If those were acceptable, the unplayed master disc was sent to complete processing into a pressed record.

In commercial use for the manufacture of vinyl records the lacquer disc went from strength to strength, improving in order to be able to render the much finer grooves used from 1948. The supporting industry that had enabled the use of wax as the mastering material had no problem in converting to lacquer, and all the processes were essentially the same. The lacquer disc is still used in vinyl record manufacture, although for a time a further improvement was available in the form of the Direct Metal Mastering process. In this process, the recording was cut directly into a metal surface, and it made two electrotyping processes superfluous.

In recent years the instantaneous disc that grew from either an amateur undertaking or a professional one-off activity has seen a revival in the form of the recording of dub-plates. This is a product that is required by turntablists, DJs

---

[23]   C.J. LeBel, 'Recent Improvements in Recording', *Electronics*, vol. 13 (September 1940): 80–81.

Relative weights & bulk of consigments of Cellulose Type Discs & Wax Blanks.

(for ten inch records).

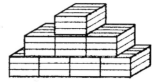

Cellulose type Recording Disc
Aluminium Core

72 weigh gross 97 lbs
Stowage space 3 cubic feet.

Wax type Solid Blank.
Fine shaved

80 weigh gross 860 lbs
Stowage space 35 cubic feet

Figure 2.3   Comparison of cellulose and wax logistics (1938 EMI. From an original in the EMI Archives)

specializing in beat matching and scratching. The raw material for this art form is two vinyl 33⅓ rpm records cross-faded and inter-edited on the fly on two turntables with suitable pickups. The gradual disappearance of suitable vinyl versions of the music needed has created a demand for instantaneous records that will perform in this environment. A lacquer disc is not suitable, because it is not durable enough, but several types of polymer sheet have been made available in 12" dimensions and which are suitable for cutting on modern equipment. These are both durable and suitably noise-free.

Conclusion

There is no doubt that a certain amount of audio fidelity was achievable by fairly simple means. It was definitely something that an amateur might undertake with results commensurate with commercial results, either using suitable components found from other manufacture or by means of fairly simple tools and raw materials. The successor in the field of amateur sound recording, tape recording (from around 1953), was already much more controlled by industry. It was not practicable for an amateur to manufacture recording tape and expect to have a result that could be measured against commercially produced tape. Most tape amateurs bought their tape stock and equipment, possibly making amplifiers and loudspeaker enclosures themselves. When the Compact Cassette came out (from about 1963), it was so amenable to mass production that the prices were in the range of most ordinary people, and the most democratic access to recorded sound yet had been created. Up to the mid 1980s the lifetime of a recording was essentially controlled by how you treated your storage system and how often you played the recording. Pickups and turntables could be converted to use 78 rpm, even when the manufacture of the records had stopped. When digital technology entered, this situation was completely changed. The lifetime was now entirely decided by the supporting industry and its continued support of a system and format. It was no longer something an amateur could undertake from scratch. The very flexibility that digital technology brought to sound manipulation and editing was also at the root of format obsolescence that has all but destroyed the modern recorded history of private individuals. Migration, rather than careful storage, is not something that a busy daily life is able to accommodate.

Chapter 3

The Sounds of Space: Studio as Instrument in the Era of High Fidelity

Susan Schmidt Horning

At the September 2000 Audio Engineering Society convention, the AES Historical Committee featured its first historical exhibit, aptly named 'When Vinyl Ruled'.[1] In a room in a distant wing of the Staples Centre, Los Angeles, far from the trade show exhibits of the latest audio technologies, visitors could see displays of vintage gear, photographs, advertisements, and a working control room set-up from the 1960s complete with an Ampex Model 300 3-track, half-inch tape recorder, a custom-built Universal Audio 12-input, 3-output vacuum tube recording console, designed by legendary engineer Bill Putnam, three McIntosh tube amplifiers, three Altec 604 speakers – even a classic 'Recording' light for effect. Most importantly, the organizers had procured direct analogue half-inch tape copies of original 3-track studio masters of several classical and popular recordings, including Elvis Presley's 'Are You Lonesome Tonight?', Peggy Lee's 'Old Devil Moon' and cuts from Henry Mancini's original score for the TV series 'Peter Gunn'. I had listened to those records many times before, but hearing the playback in mono, stereo and discrete three-channel sound was a transcendent listening experience. The music contained air, dynamics and an acoustic identity that imparted a sense of physical space. In contrast to later twentieth-century CDs, the recordings sounded three-dimensional, like artefacts of an earlier time, products of the 1960s Space Age in which they were made.

Later that afternoon, in an auditorium at the opposite end of the convention centre, a panel of producers and engineers discussed state of the art recording technology, focusing in particular on the merits of ProTools, then touted as 'the future' of recording. As an example of what could be done on a digital audio workstation (DAW), the session opened with Everclear's 'AM Radio', in its own way a tribute to the past. A postmodern pastiche of pre-recorded and original music and rapping, the cut opened with a 1950s or 1960s radio station identification jingle, followed by a transcribed programme announcement, then straight into the first few bars of Jean Knight's 1971 hit 'Mr Big Stuff' as it would sound over

---

[1]   *'When Vinyl Ruled': An Exhibit by the AES Historical Committee.* The event was sponsored by the AES Historical Committee (AESHC), chaired by Jay McKnight, and was organized by Irv Joel and Paul McManus. [Online]. Available at: www.aes.org/aeshc/docs/mtgschedules/109conv2000/109th-vinyl-report-1.html.

cheap AM radio speakers, then overlaid with a crescendo of sound culminating in a blasting rap riff. Loud and intense, brimming with sonic information and very much a product of the digital age, 'AM Radio' could not have sounded more removed from the music played at 'When Vinyl Ruled'. More striking than the technological or stylistic gulf that separated these two musical eras, the sound of the room so evident in the 1950s studio recordings was completely absent from the Everclear record.

That aural experience got me thinking about the disappearance of acoustical space in recorded music since the era of high fidelity, that period between roughly the mid 1940s and the mid 1960s when numerous technical achievements, notably the microgroove LP record, magnetic tape recording, improved microphones, and especially the introduction of stereophonic sound in the late 1950s, made records sound more vivid, more lifelike than those of the past. With the extended recordable frequency range covering almost the entire audible spectrum and the third dimension offered by 3-channel stereo, the long-standing goal of achieving a more 'authentic' re-creation of a live performance on record had finally become possible, making big rooms with fabulous natural acoustics highly desirable and an integral part of the sound of big band, small combo jazz, popular and classical recordings of the 1950s and early 1960s. While some felt the pinnacle of recording technique had been reached, emerging technologies, notably multitrack recording, expanded the possibilities of what could be achieved in the studio by clever engineering and creative overdubbing. By 1966, popular recording had rejected any notion of fidelity to live performances in favour of studio creations, or what one producer called 'the sound that never was'.[2]

During the 1970s, the era commemorated in 'AM Radio', the increasing dependence on the technologies of the control room to shape the sound of records led to the concept of studio-as-instrument, but a look at the history of recording during the 1940s and 50s reveals that this was not an entirely new concept. For a time in the mid twentieth century, engineers and producers struggled to attain optimal sound quality in rooms that in most cases were converted spaces not designed with recording in mind. The sound of the studio or concert hall became so integral to the final product that the studio as acoustical space became an instrument in its own right.

This chapter examines that critical juncture in record making when the dead studios of the acoustic era gave way to live rooms, lending the recorded music of the 1950s airy dynamics, space for invention and an audible sense of the recording room. After a brief history of early studios, the chapter explores how room acoustics became important in recording and what engineers had to do to exploit them effectively. With the introduction of multitrack recording in the 1960s, the need to maintain separation of individual tracks in order to better control each instrument in the final mix forced engineers to once again obliterate the sound of

---

[2]   J. Somer, 'Popular Recording: or, The Sound That Never Was', *HiFi/Stereo Review* 16 (May 1966): 54–8.

the room. The 'big hall sound' increasingly associated with an earlier era of big band music gave way to a different kind of big sound more dependent on artificial reverberation, multiple layers of instruments and numerous effects. The era of high fidelity ended with a return to dead acoustics and, ironically, the birth of the modern concept of 'studio-as-instrument'.

From Padded Walls to Big Halls: Recording Studio Acoustics to the 1940s

From the 1880s to the early 1920s, phonograph records were made with an acoustical recording machine. Musicians played and singers sang into a horn, the sound moved a diaphragm which in turn moved the needle to engrave sound into the record. Positioning instruments and vocalists around the horn in such a way as to capture the music posed the greatest challenge to the recordist, and the weak power of the recording machine rendered room tone inaudible. Studios were bare, utilitarian and functional, with the recording apparatus often separated by a wall or curtain from the studio proper. The science of acoustics, still in its infancy, had surprisingly little impact on recording practice in these early years. Some equipment manufacturers did employ scientific consultants, but firms were chiefly concerned with improving the devices of home reproduction rather than enhancing the design and construction of the studios in which recordings were made. By 1920, phonograph improvements made reverberation and echo audible but problematic because they tended to blur sustained notes and 'impart an effect more or less banjoish to the reproduced sounds'.[3] With the introduction of electrical recording in 1925, microphones replaced recording horns, instruments could be amplified and engineers gained more control over sound, bringing vastly better sounding records. But as control of room acoustics became even more important, recording and broadcasting studios employed sound absorbing wall coverings, rugs and drapes to eliminate reverberation. Typical of the studios in the 1930s was RCA-Victor's New York studios on East 24th Street, which appeared to one young NBC employee 'like a mortuary', with black velour drapes, padded walls and rugs on the floor.[4]

By the late 1930s, the electrical transcription (ET) business of pre-recorded radio programmes introduced listeners to better sounding records. ETs were 16-inch lacquer discs capable of reproducing a frequency range of up to 10,000 cycles (10kHz), 2,000 more than the highest quality commercial discs then on the market, and the success of the transcription business demonstrated the commercial viability of truer, more faithful musical reproduction, raising listeners' expectations and consequently, record company attention to improved sounding commercial

---

[3]   William Braid White, 'Aspects of Sound Recording: 1 – The Echo Difficulty', *Talking Machine World* (15 July 1920), p. 159.

[4]   D. Plunkett, interview with author, New York City, 9 February 1999.

records.[5] None of the major American record labels' company studios were large enough to accommodate orchestras or the big bands of the era. Consequently, each company regularly used alternate venues for their large ensemble recording during the 1940s and 50s. Columbia Records used the studios of World Broadcasting, and RCA Victor used Manhattan Centre, a former opera house, and Webster Hall, a dance hall once used for bohemian costume balls, society weddings and as a speakeasy during Prohibition.[6] Decca used the Pythian Temple, an elaborate Egyptian-themed structure built by the Knights of Pythias in 1926.[7] These large rooms had natural acoustics conducive to recording symphonies and big bands, but because they were not designed to be soundproof, engineers had to devise ways of minimizing the effects of external sound being picked up by the recording equipment. Cooing pigeons on windowsills caused problems at Manhattan Centre, rain hitting Webster Hall's roof could be enough to stop Victor sessions, and the rumble of the nearby Seventh Avenue subway line near Carnegie Hall forced engineers to either halt the session, or try to filter out the low tones by using high-pass filters.[8] When Columbia Records encountered similar problems at its 799 Seventh Avenue studio, engineers anchored the recording lathes in 500 lb. blocks of concrete to counteract the subway rumble.[9]

One site appears to have been ideal from the beginning: Liederkranz Hall on East 58th Street, the nineteenth century home of the Liederkranz Club Chorus, which was transformed during the 1920s into a recording and broadcasting studio used first by RCA Victor and later by Columbia Records.[10] Acoustically, Liederkranz earned a reputation as one of the finest recording spaces ever to exist

---

[5]   R. Sanjek and D. Sanjek, *Pennies from Heaven: The American Popular Music Business in the Twentieth Century* (New York: Da Capo Press, 1996), p. 144.

[6]   History of Manhattan Center, currently an active recording and entertainment venue. [Online]. Available at: www.mcstudios.com/about-mc-studios/mc-studio-history. php [accessed: 21 August 2009]; detailed history of Webster Hall in the report of the Landmarks Preservation Commission: [Online]. Available at: http://www.nyc.gov/html/ lpc/downloads/pdf/reports/websterhall.pdf [accessed: 21 August 2009].

[7]   Manny Albam, interview with author, New York City, 9 February 1999; Brooks Arthur, telephone interview with author, 30 April 1999; Meyer Berger, 'About New York', *New York Times* (20 January 1958); Christopher Gray, 'Recalling the Days of Knights and Elks', *New York Times* (24 August 2003).

[8]   Ray Hall, telephone interview with author, 21 March 1999. Engineers use different types of filters to intensify, attenuate, or equalize specific audio frequencies. High-pass filters transmit all frequencies above a certain cutoff frequency and attenuate all lower frequencies. Oliver Read, *The Recording and Reproduction of Sound* (2nd edn, Indianapolis, IN: Howard W. Sams, 1952), p. 370; Robert Emmett Dolan, *Music in Modern Media: Techniques in Tape, Disc and Film Recording, Motion Picture and Television Scoring and Electronic Music* (New York: G. Schirmer, 1967), p. 176.

[9]   William Savory, telephone interview with author, 21 October 1999.

[10]   Bernhard Behncke, 'Liederkranz Hall: The World's Best Recording Studio?'. [Online]. Available at: http://vjm.biz/new_page_3.htm [accessed: 9 September 2007].

in New York, and by all accounts became the most desirable recording room throughout the 1940s.[11] George Avakian, head of A&R for Columbia's Popular Albums and International departments in the 1940s, said Liederkranz Hall signified the new emphasis on the sound of the studio, not just the music being recorded. 'By the time the music business really started to get big in terms of sales', Avakian recalled, 'the sound on recordings became important'. With solid wood floors and walls, the L-shaped room had a natural sound that was 'quite terrific'. Victor used the hall in the late 1920s, but Avakian believed the early 78 rpm recordings of the Columbia pop artists of the late 1930s and 1940s 'established that hall as the industry's standard for sound'.[12] Others concurred: 'To have played there is to be spoiled forever as far as acoustical standards are concerned', recalled conductor Andre Kostelanetz. 'One mic picked up everything'. Kostelanetz conducted the Coca Cola radio programme from Liederkranz Hall for five years beginning in 1938, and claimed that his ear had grown so sensitive to the acoustical perfection of the room that after a while he could tell just 'by how the orchestra sounded on a given morning whether the floor had been swept the night before'.[13]

Acoustical perfection was not the only benefit of recording at Liederkranz Hall. Don Plunkett recalled that the spaciousness of the room and the reverberant quality of the wood had the effect of giving a record more presence and seemingly more volume. Greater volume had become particularly desirable as companies sought to make their popular records stand out on radio and when played on jukeboxes that tended to be located in noisy public places. A quiet record might go unnoticed, but a record *with presence* would grab the listener's attention and thus be more likely to sell. One of the first recordings to exemplify this effect, '"Joltin" Joe DiMaggio,' was recorded at Liederkranz Hall in 1941 by Les Brown and his Orchestra.[14] The record actually demonstrates both dead room and live room ambience since the lead vocalist sounds dry, as if she sang in a vocal booth, whereas the brass section, trombone solo, the drummer's rim shots mimicking the sound of a bat, and the male chorus shouting 'Joe, Joe DiMaggio, we want you on our side!' all have tremendous acoustic presence, revealing the spaciousness of the studio. Plunkett noted that in those days it was important to achieve volume without exceeding groove dimensions; the louder the record the greater the excursion of the cutting needle and that meant wider grooves and therefore less playing time. Consequently, a studio that could lend that quality of apparent loudness without diminishing recording time became extremely valued in the big band era, both in terms of the record's aesthetic quality and its commercial success.

---

[11]   John Hammond, with Irving Townsend, *On Record: An Autobiography* (New York: Summit Books, 1977), p. 217.

[12]   George Avakian, telephone interview with author, 10 December 1996.

[13]   Andre Kostelanetz, in collaboration with Gloria Hammond, *Echoes: Memoirs of Andre Kostelanetz* (New York: Harcourt Brace Jovanovich, 1981), p. 82.

[14]   Donald Plunkett, interview with author, New York city, 9 February 1999. '"Joltin" Joe DiMaggio' composed by Alan Courtney and Ben Homer, OKeh 6377.

Tuning the Room: Birth of the Studio as 'The Final Instrument That Is Recorded'

By 1947, the success of records made at Liederkranz Hall and the cumulative experience gathered in various recording studios, concert halls and music rooms demonstrated that acoustics had become an essential consideration in recording. As engineers discovered, however, many factors contributed to those acoustics, including the shape of the room and characteristics of the surfaces. Size alone was not enough to determine the reverberation time, and because styles of popular music were constantly changing, flexibility in acoustical treatment was now considered of the utmost importance in studio design. Acoustical treatment incorporated reflective surfaces as well as absorbent areas, movable panels, drapes, polycylindrical surfaces, all of which could be adjusted to obtain 'optimal acoustical results'.[15] It was as if the studio, like the musicians' instruments, could now be tuned to meet the needs of a given recording session. Indeed, one thing had become clear to acoustical consultants and recording professionals alike, that the studio itself had become 'the *final instrument* that is recorded'.[16]

When in the late 1940s CBS president William S. Paley made the fateful, and apparently highly unpopular, decision to transform Liederkranz Hall into television studios, Columbia engineers and recording directors canvassed Manhattan for a suitable replacement. They eventually found an ideal venue in an abandoned Greek Orthodox Church on East 30th Street. Built on solid rock, with three layers of inch-thick maple and pine flooring providing a solid wood sounding board, Columbia's 30th Street Studio would eventually earn a reputation as 'the "Stradivarius" of recording studios', thereby bestowing upon it the ultimate designation as a musical instrument.[17] That reputation came only after a good bit of acoustical tweaking by Columbia engineers, who faced the challenge of transforming a vast empty space with impressive but unruly reverberation into a functional recording studio in which that reverberation could be controlled without altering the structure. The biggest challenge engineers faced, according to William Savory, was the fact that the acoustics of the room, measuring 97 feet long, 55 feet wide and 50 feet from floor to ceiling, had to be 'brought into focus'.[18] Savory described the reverberation as very good for some things, but too long. 'As a result, if you were playing something staccato or rather rapid, it would tend to

---

[15]   G.M. Nixon, 'Recording Studio 3A', *Broadcast News*, 46 (September 1947), p. 33.

[16]   Lonsdale Green, Jr., and James Y. Dunbar, 'Recording Studio Acoustics', *Journal of the Acoustical Society of America* 19 (May 1947): 413. Emphasis in original.

[17]   Vincent J. Liebler, 'A Record Is Born!' *Columbia Records* (1959), p. 4.

[18]   The dimensions are from Liebler, 'A Record is Born!', p. 4. Columbia engineer Frank Laico estimated the ceiling at one hundred feet, which probably refers to the apex of the central arch. Frank Laico, telephone interview, 13 January 1999.

merge with everything else. A string of very distinct sixteenth notes would come back as a smear [because] you were *immersed* in reverberation.'[19]

To counteract this, engineers placed microphones as close to the source as possible to get more direct rather than reflected sound. But this close-miking in turn made it difficult for musicians to judge how loud they should play. Members of The New York Philharmonic, for example, were accustomed to playing with their own dynamics, developed over years of playing together. As Savory recalled, 'you sit them on this thing where they have microphones closer to them, they can't use those dynamics. They have to restrain themselves.' To counteract that, engineers tried flat baffles – upright partitions positioned in different areas of the room in order to break up or redirect sound waves. Eventually, Savory came up with his own design: eight-feet tall parabolic-shaped baffles placed on wheeled tripods so they could be easily repositioned. Savory often put the reflectors behind the musicians so they were unaware of their presence. This gave the recording engineers more control over the sound, and the musicians a better listening environment, but not all were pleased with what they heard. Some of the musicians, 'especially the brass men', Savory recalled, 'thought it was wonderful ... it's like having your music under a magnifying glass'. Placing the reflectors close to the musicians produced a more direct rather than reverberant sound; moving them back reduced the intimate presence. But some of the musicians thought it was strange, and one violinist told Savory, 'This is going to make me go home and practice a hell of a lot more. I can hear all my mistakes!'[20] Just as musicians began to adjust playing style after hearing themselves on record for the first time, technical fixes for acoustics caused musicians to change technique, another example of what musicologist and historian Mark Katz described as the 'feedback loop' between recording and musical performance.[21]

The decades-old challenge to engineers of positioning musicians in a recording studio, once a matter of crowding and jockeying for position around the acoustical horn, had taken on new proportions with the increased sensitivity of microphones, magnetic tape recording and the ambience of truly 'live' studios. The problems of controlling sound did not vanish; they simply changed, forcing engineers to contrive new solutions. Because of this, many producers were initially reluctant to use the 30th Street Studio until Columbia Masterworks vice-president Goddard Lieberson recorded the original Broadway cast album of *South Pacific* there in 1949, just as the musical opened to rave reviews and record-setting advance sales.[22] Lieberson had told the engineers he wanted to make a studio recording that

---

[19]   William Savory, telephone interview with author, 21 October 1999.

[20]   Savory interview, 21 October 1999.

[21]   Mark Katz, *Capturing Sound: How Technology Has Changed Music* (Berkeley: University of California Press, 2004).

[22]   Morris Hastings, album liner notes to Richard Rodgers and Oscar Hammerstein, *South Pacific*, Columbia Masterworks Lp 4180; Brooks Atkinson, 'At the Theatre', *The New York Times* (8 April 1949): 30.

sounded 'like a Broadway stage' and for that, the 30th Street studio proved ideal.[23] The engineers had succeeded in reining in the church's reverberation without muffling it, and the album became a blockbuster hit. The results impressed other artists and producers who soon began using the studio. Mitch Miller produced his first Columbia recording session there in February 1950 with singer Rosemary Clooney and continued to favour the 30th Street studio, which along with Liederkranz Hall he considered 'the best'.[24] Miller apparently loved using Savory's parabolic reflectors, especially with singer Johnnie Ray, who stood between two of the reflectors to bounce his voice, enhancing the natural reverberation and thus his vocal presence on a number of recordings, including his first big hit, 'Cry'.[25] Ray's exaggerated articulation, what one critic described as a 'hyphenated style of singing' that emulated doo-wop and early rock and roll vocalists, coupled with the use of studio techniques to enhance his voice, worked to create the singer's unique, identifiable sound.[26]

In the burgeoning popular music field of post-war America, having a unique sound that differentiated one from another artist was becoming almost as important as the choice of material. The use of a studio's natural acoustics and its manipulation by engineers had become essential in achieving that unique sound for major label recording artists and certain studios were considered better than others for some styles of music, so producers chose studios on that basis. As one engineer noted, 'when you're trying to record in popular music, you're not only trying to record certain instruments, but a certain feel, "cause that's what sells records"'.[27] Difficult to define, this 'feel' was something engineers became sensitive to; some could even determine 'who made what record, and where it was made' just by listening to it.[28] Studios, like artists, had acoustical characteristics that made them identifiable and to some extent, those characteristics became imprinted on the work of the artists who recorded in them.

[23] William Savory, interview with author, Falls Church, Virginia, 29 November 1997.

[24] Mitch Miller interview, 21 January 1999. For more on the 30th Street studio, see Ashley Kahn, *Kind of Blue* (New York: Da Capo Press, 2000), pp. 75–7; Charles L. Granata, *Sessions with Sinatra: Frank Sinatra and the Art of Recording* (Chicago: A Cappella Books, 1999), pp. 42–5.

[25] 'Men Behind the Microphones: Makers of Music for Millions,' *Newsweek* (8 September 1952): 56–9.

[26] Will Friedwald, CD liner notes to *Johnnie Ray: 16 Most Requested Songs*, Columbia/ Legacy Compact Disc, CK46095. I thank the late William Savory for sending me this recording and noting which selections utilized the parabolic reflectors.

[27] Clair Krepps, telephone interview with author, 23 March 1999.

[28] Tom Dowd, telephone interview with author, 21 March 1999.

Manufacturing the Sound of Space: Chambers, Plates and Slapping Tapes

Not every studio possessed naturally good acoustics, so engineers devised means of compensating for this, borrowing techniques from radio and motion pictures. Artificial echo had been used in broadcasting and film sound since the 1930s to create specific dramatic effects.[29] In attempting to achieve certain sound effects for radio programmes, engineers cobbled together unlikely combinations of devices. When guitarist Les Paul performed on radio programmes in the 1930s he witnessed two Chicago radio engineers serendipitously invent a makeshift echo effect while attempting to create the sound of thunder for a soap opera. By removing the needle from a phonograph pickup, inserting a long spring, then hitting the spring with a mallet, they created the crashing sound of thunder. When one of them inserted a pickup on the other end of the spring, thus creating a 'send' and a 'receive', Paul recalled, 'to their amazement, they had echo'.[30]

The terms echo and reverb have been used interchangeably, and technically are based on the same acoustical phenomena: the repetition of a sound as it bounces off a hard surface. But an echo is an audibly distinct repetition that rapidly diminishes, whereas reverberation is many repetitions of an audio signal so close together as to be indistinguishable, thus sounding like a gradual decay. Studies have shown that although each evokes a different sense of place and emotional response in the listener, both also conjure up the sense of physical space.[31] More conventional acoustic means of achieving echo and reverberation involved the redirecting of a signal through a chamber, with the signal then being picked up by a microphone and fed back to the control room. The delayed signal could then be combined with the natural voice or used alone. In the 1930s, NBC engineers experimented with pipes of various lengths to achieve different periods of delay, and other engineers experimented with electronic means of creating reverberation using a loop of magnetic steel tape.[32]

As producers and artists sought to achieve the reverberant quality of natural acoustics on their records, engineers devised ways to mimic the Big Hall sound, and vast physical space ceased to be a prerequisite. In 1937, eccentric bandleader Raymond Scott had achieved what one listener called 'a big auditorium sound' on

---

[29] 'How Echoes are Produced: NBC Engineers Perfect Artificial Sound Reflection', *Broadcast News*, 13 (December 1934): 26–7; E. Thompson, *The Soundscape of Modernity: Architectural Acoustics and the Culture of Listening in America, 1900–1933* (Cambridge, MA: MIT Press, 2002), pp. 281–4.

[30] Les Paul, interview with author, New York City, 19 January 1999.

[31] Peter Doyle, *Echo and Reverb: Fabricating Space in Popular Music Recording, 1900–1960* (Middletown, CT: Wesleyan University Press, 2005); Daniel J. Levitin, *This is Your Brain on Music: The Science of Human Obsession* (New York: Dutton, 2006).

[32] 'NBC's New Echo Chambers', *Electronics*, (July 1935), p. 227; Dr S.J. Begun and S.K. Wolf, 'On Synthetic Reverberation', in *Magnetic Tape Recording*, ed. Marvin Camras (New York: Van Nostrand Reinhold Company, 1985), pp. 413–14.

his records, simply by placing microphones in the hallway and men's room outside his record company's office, which also served as the label's recording studio.[33] The hard surface of ceramic tile provided the ideal level of reflectivity to produce the desired reverberation. Chicago engineer Bill Putnam used the same idea a decade later when recording The Harmonicats' version of 'Peg o' My Heart' at his Universal Recording studio in Chicago, but with a more exaggerated effect, making the harmonicas sound drenched in reverberation.[34] In New York, Columbia engineers at the 799 Seventh Avenue studio used the building's stairwell, a seven-story steel-and-concrete chamber that worked so well they never changed it. William Savory described Columbia's famous 'stairwell echo chamber' as the brainchild of chief engineer William Bachman: 'It started on the 7th floor with a microphone, and with a dual cone fifteen-inch loudspeaker on a landing one-half floor down the stairs. Below that, six and one-half floors of concrete and steel – *sensational!*'[35]

During the 1950s custom-built echo chambers became one of the more identifiable qualities of a studio. John Palladino was an engineer for Radio Recorders, where Capitol made most of its Hollywood recordings until it moved to its own studios on Melrose Avenue. Radio Recorders built an echo chamber on the roof of their building shortly after he started working there in 1943, at a time when, as he explained, 'nobody knew too much about how it should be shaped or anything. But you just worked with it a little bit and put the hardest plaster you could get on there and put a good mic and a good speaker – and that was it'.[36] Irv Joel recalled that the echo chamber at Capitol's New York studio had been built by an Italian contractor who, Joel reported, upon being told about the desired project said something like, 'Oh! I know what you want; you want one of them cockeyed rooms.'[37] The contractor, who apparently had experience in building echo chambers, brought in broken pieces of cinder blocks and other materials from his truck and situated them to form a ramp on the floor which he covered with concrete, then he built a new wall at an angle at the end of the space, covered all room surfaces with a skin coat of very fine cement. After everything had dried he shellacked the walls to make it even brighter sounding. The chamber performed so well that outside clients booked Capitol's New York studio specifically because they liked the sound of the echo chamber. By the time Capitol built its Tower Studios in Hollywood, the first major record label to custom-build its studios literally from the ground up,

---

[33]   Al Brackman recalled the incident in Irwin Chusid, 'Raymond Scott', liner notes to *The Music of Raymond Scott: Reckless Nights and Turkish Twilights*, Columbia CD 53028.

[34]   Robert Pruter, *Doowop: The Chicago Scene* (Urbana, IL: University of Illinois Press, 1996), pp. 16–17.

[35]   Savory interview, 29 November 1997.

[36]   John Palladino, telephone interview with author, 15 October 1999.

[37]   Irv Joel, email correspondence, 4 September 2001.

the decision was made to minimize studio reverberation and create four sublevel compatible reverberation chambers 'to provide optimal acoustical properties'.[38]

With the rise of independent studios, equipment manufacturers began to market controlled reverberation in affordable, compact devices. Exploiting the reputation of Liederkranz Hall, Fairchild Recording Equipment Corporation advertised its 'Reverbertron' as a means of achieving the kind of reverberation the legendary studio had been famous for 'in a compact, portable, attractive and rack mountable package 24½" high by 19" wide'.[39] Another firm, the Audio Instrument Company of New York, advertised an electronic echo chamber that occupied '2 instead of 10,000 cubic feet', and at $1,485 promised to 'pay for itself in 3 to 5 months'.[40] The *Elektromesstechnik* Company of Germany introduced its EMT 140 Reverberation Set, developed by Dr Walther Kühl in 1953. With a reverberation time adjustable between one and five seconds, the 'EMT plate' became the most popular source of reverberation and echo during the 1960s because of its portability, tunability and size. Although not easy to move, and tuning it required skill, EMT plates were the best option for studios with limited space, and provided more control over reverberation than busy stairwells, men's rooms and hallways. Bridging the gap between the past and the future of acoustical manipulation in recording, these devices promised affordability, portability, and controllability, key features that appealed to the many independent studios popping up in the 1960s.

Another popular means of achieving echo utilized two tape recorders and had a slightly surreal quality. Referred to as 'tape slap' or 'slapback', this form of echo operated on the same principle as the other methods, but in this case the time it took for the tape to travel between the record and playback heads introduced the split-second delay. Les Paul used tape-slap, and in Memphis, Tennessee, Sam Phillips used it to great effect recording the first Elvis Presley and Jerry Lee Lewis records, creating what came to be known as the 'Sun Sound'. But tape slap did not create the effect considered desirable on most major label pop and classical records; it produced a distinct echo rather than the reverberant quality of a concert hall, and it worked best on small bands or singers, not orchestras or big bands. When in 1956 Elvis Presley made his first RCA Victor recordings at the company's Nashville studio, according to Elvis biographer Peter Guralnick, the engineers there 'professed ignorance as to just how Sam Phillips had achieved' the slap-back echo that was so integral to Elvis's appeal.[41] Whether ignorance or simply refusal to try something new, their reaction was not surprising given the

---

[38]   J. Bayless, 'Innovations in Studio Design and Construction in the Capitol Tower Recording Studios', *Journal of the Audio Engineering Society* (April 1957): 75–6.

[39]   Fairchild Recording Equipment Corporation advertisement, 'Famous for Reverberation', *Journal of the Audio Engineering Society* 13 (Oct. 1965), p. A-234.

[40]   'Leading Recording Organizations Use Ai Electronic Echo Chambers' Audio Instrument Company advertisement, *Journal of the Audio Engineering Society* (July 1958).

[41]   Peter Guralnick, *Last Train to Memphis: The Rise of Elvis Presley* (Boston: Little, Brown and Company, 1994), p. 237.

established studio techniques of the major labels. Staff engineers had been refining the recording process for decades in an effort to improve sound quality. For them, suddenly being instructed to recreate the sound of low-budget recordings was incomprehensible. On the other hand, up and coming independents like Phillips and Lee Hazlewood, who created guitarist Duane Eddy's 'million dollar twang' by using a cast-iron grain storage tank as an echo chamber, were not trying to create the big hall sound.[42] They were open to experimentation and the recording techniques they devised became, to a great extent, the 'sound' of rock 'n' roll, a style that appealed to a new generation of listeners asserting their own identity and musical tastes. Born of necessity and limited technology, this new sound was as different from the production quality of big band and popular singers of the post-war era as the music itself, just as the performers were from their predecessors, and the listeners from their parents. The sound of rock and roll, emanating most often from lo-fi car and transistor radios, had more to do with energy and electronics than with fidelity or acoustical perfection.

Conclusion: The End of Space

With the introduction of multitrack recording in the mid 1960s, engineers in pop and rock recording sessions faced the challenge of capturing live performances while maintaining separation of instruments in order to have control in the final mix. They walled off instrumentalists from each other, and found it increasingly necessary to minimize room acoustics which they could now recreate if desired with the use of chambers, EMT plates or tape echo. In the 1970s, the dead studio that had fallen out of favour during the 1940s once again became desirable and the focal point of the studio-as-instrument had shifted from the studio to the control room, where electronic instruments – guitars, basses, keyboards, synthesizers – were being recorded by plugging directly into the mixing console. Classical recording sessions continued to take place in churches, ballrooms and concert halls, but even in these venues some engineers began to use close-miking to achieve clarity, thus minimizing the hall's natural resonance in favour of a more focused primary sound.[43]

This story of the changing uses of studio space over the first century of recorded sound could be understood as a consequence of changing technological possibilities and cultural tastes. During the early decades of sound recording when the equipment could neither capture nor reproduce room tone, engineers

---

[42]   Susan Schmidt Horning, 'Recording: The Search for the Sound', in Andre Millard (ed.), *The Electric Guitar: A History of an American Icon* (Baltimore: Johns Hopkins University Press, 2004).

[43]   Eric Salsman, 'Where Sound Sounds Best' (orig. pub. March 1961) in *High Fidelity's Silver Anniversary Treasury*, ed. Robert S. Clark (Great Barrington, MA: Wyeth Press, 1976), p. 301.

and manufacturers strove to bring the concert hall to the living room, a goal that only became achievable with improvements in the technologies of recording and reproduction. By 1947, acoustical engineers considered the studio an instrument in its own right, acoustically alterable to meet the needs of any type of recording session. As technology and engineering skill met economic opportunity and consumer demand in the post-WWII years, the sound of records reached a peak during the 1950s and 1960s. Stereophonic sound made big recording rooms both desirable and available, forcing engineers to find ways to control excessive reverberation and to devise artificial means of creating it where there was none. But no sooner was the sound of the room achievable than musical culture underwent a radical shift. During the 1960s, increasing experimentation with new electronic sounds that had little or no use for natural acoustics made the popular recording control room the site of the studio-as-instrument and many studios, particularly the small independent studios that flourished during this period, had become once again acoustically dead. Diminishing demand for large recording rooms along with the economic challenge of keeping up with state-of-the-art technology led many studios to close.[44] And as consumers adopted more portable listening devices, big home stereo speakers gave way to ear buds and PC speakers, resulting in a generation of listeners who have never heard the sound of the room.

Five years after my transcendent listening experience at the Audio Engineering Society Historical Committee's demonstration of original 3-track master recordings from the era 'when vinyl ruled', engineer Lesley Ann Jones sat in on a remastering session of some of those recordings originally released in the RCA Living Stereo series. 'You couldn't get a modern recording to sound like this', she marvelled; 'the spaciousness of the orchestra and the presence of the soloist, who was Heifetz, was really pretty extraordinary'. Asked why she thought this was no longer possible, Jones said, 'I just think that our tastes and how we record now and what we're looking for things to sound like have changed.'[45] In fact, as Jonathan Sterne observed, 'every age has its own perfect fidelity', and during the first decades of sound recording, 'the idea of "better" sound reproduction was itself a changing standard'.[46] Ever since then, the history of sound recording has been a series of changing standards as technological change leads to new sounds and new ways of producing, experiencing, and disseminating music. In the process, listeners' expectations have been shaped by many factors, but none more than the changing uses of the studio as an instrument.

---

[44]   Allison Stewart, 'Of Mikes and Men: Old Studios Fall Silent', *Washington Post*, 20 March 2005.

[45]   Lesley Ann Jones, telephone interview with author, 16 September 2005.

[46]   Jonathan Sterne, *The Audible Past: Cultural Origins of Sound Reproduction* (Durham, NC: Duke University Press, 2003), pp. 222–3.

Discography

Everclear. *Songs From an American Movie. Vol. One: Learning How to Smile.* (Capitol Records. 2000) CDP 7 2434-97061-2 5.

Glenn Gould. *A State of Wonder: The Complete Goldberg Variations 1955 and 1981.* (Sony/Legacy. 2002) CD: S3K 87703.

Henry Mancini. *Peter Gunn.* (RCA Victor Living Stereo. 1959) Vinyl LP: LSP-1956.

Jerry Murad's Harmonicats. *Greatest Hits.* (Columbia Records. 1960) Vinyl LP: PC 9511.

Johnnie Ray. *Johnnie Ray: 16 Most Requested Songs.* (Columbia/ Legacy. 1991) CD: CK46095.

Les Brown and His Orchestra. '"Joltin" Joe DiMaggio'. (OKeh Records. 1941) 78 rpm disc: 6377.

Les Brown and Vic Schoen Bands. *Stereophonic Suite for Two Bands.* (Kapp Records. 1959. Reissue: MCA Records. 1983) Cassette: MCAC-1548.

Les Paul. *The New Sound.* (Capitol Records. 1950) Ten-Inch EP: H226.

Raymond Scott. *The Music of Raymond Scott: Reckless Nights and Turkish Twilights.* (Columbia Records. 1992) CD: 53028.

Richard Rodgers and Oscar Hammerstein II. *South Pacific.* (Columbia Masterworks. 1949) Vinyl LP: OL 4180.

Sounds in Space: A Stereophonic Sound Demonstration Record. (RCA Victor Living Stereo. 1958) Vinyl LP: SP-33-13.

Chapter 4

No-Fi: Crafting a Language of Recorded Music in 1950s Pop

Albin Zak III

In the years following World War II, record sales surged. Columbia Records alone reported a sales increase of 850 per cent from 1945 to 1946, and all of the other large companies registered profit increases of at least 100 per cent in the same year.[1] Record buyers gained new influence as record men tallied and noted their purchases. Established labels and start-ups alike courted the consumer as never before, even as public tastes in pop music veered to the idiosyncratic. In the resulting commercial hubbub, ideas about acceptable musical sound and attitudes to records themselves evolved in surprising ways. In previous decades, real-time musical performance provided the standard frame of reference as technology and music began an uncertain partnership. Network radio broadcasts were mostly live and recordists did their best to accurately render live performances. But in the post-war clamour, this arrangement changed. Pop records went from documentary snapshots representing past events of remote provenance to aesthetic artefacts in their own right, their place and time forever here and now. They were absolved of representational responsibility; the natural sound world ceased to be their primary referent.

This heady liberation was accompanied by a problem recordists had not faced before. The notion of fidelity, faithful electronic representation of source sounds, which had served as sound recording's guiding principle, lost its authority, even as the term 'high fidelity' became a ubiquitous marketing slogan (one of those delicious paradoxes routinely, and usually unwittingly, served up by the music industry). Without the traditional signposts provided by real-world musical performances, recordists faced a virtual blank slate. They responded by crafting a language of record production – one record at a time – whose rhetoric relied not on fidelity but on situating a record in a universe of other records. This essay explores the early days of what has come to be an electromusical common tongue.

---

[1]   Joe Carlton, 'Columbia Profits Jumped 850 per cent in 1946; Industry Dough Swirls for Majors', *Billboard* (29 March, 1947), p. 16.

Hi-Fi

Through its first decades, sound recording developed as a progressive technological project guided by the sound of the natural world. Advances consistently aimed at ever more accurate renditions of sonic events. Music turned out to be the medium's driving commercial force and recordists strove to make records sound as life-like as possible, seeming to 'originate in the room instead of in the headphones', as a *Popular Mechanics* piece phrased it.[2] The 1920s saw a profound qualitative change when electrical recording began replacing the mechanical acoustic method. Microphones allowed recording devices to capture far more sonic detail and nuance, with greater dynamic and frequency ranges. The fact that some listeners continued to prefer the sound of acoustic recordings – *Gramophone* founder Compton Mackenzie, for one – spoke to the implicit aesthetic problem with a strictly progressive agenda. But the consensus was clear: electrical recording sounded more like the source and would become the industry standard; it was more *transparent*.

By the early 1950s, the idea of transparent representation had gained a popular handle: 'high fidelity'. The term had been around since the 1930s but now represented what *New York Times* critic Howard Taubman called 'the growing rage ... a big industry, a fad, a mania ... a way of life'.[3] The technologies supporting the craze were impressive, providing for home use such marvels as the 33⅓ rpm long-playing microgroove disc and magnetic tape machines. In 1951, *High Fidelity* magazine was launched. Introduced as 'a magazine for audiophiles', the periodical featured articles ranging from foundational topics, such as principles of acoustics and electronic design, to reviews of sound reproduction equipment and recordings.[4] In 1954, the flagship entertainment weekly, *Billboard*, began running a regular 'High Fidelity' column to report hi-fi related news. Record companies touted their products' high fidelity credibility with such proprietary phrases as '"New Orthophonc" High Fidelity sound' (RCA Victor) and 'Full Dimensional Sound' (Capitol). Columbia 'guaranteed high fidelity' for all its '360 Sound' recordings 'on a money-back basis'.[5] An Institute of High Fidelity Manufacturers was established in Chicago in 1955 with an initial aim of establishing '"standards of measurement" for sound reproduction products' stated 'in terms the public can readily recognize'. The goal, as defined by the Zenith Radio Corporation's chief engineer, J.E. Brow, was 'the completely faithful reproduction of every single sound wave that occurs in the original performance of the music'.[6]

---

[2]   'Adventures in Sound', *Popular Mechanics* (September, 1952), p. 216.

[3]   Howard Taubman, 'High Fidelity in American Life', *New York Times* (22 November, 1953), X39.

[4]   Charles Fowler, 'As the Editor Sees It', *High Fidelity* (Summer 1951), p. 8.

[5]   Columbia advertisement, *Billboard* (4 August, 1956), p. 25.

[6]   'Hi Fi Institute Sets UP Product Standards', 'Zenith Opens Display Room in Chicago', *Billboard* (17 April, 1954), p. 30.

High Fidelity's editors devoted most of the magazine's record reviews to classical music, whose canon predated electronic mediation. Classical performances were purely acoustic phenomena, unbeholden to microphones or amplifiers. The music had reached its perfect sounding form in a pre-electric era and, as such, gave the hi-fi project a fixed target for comparison. Recording equipment at a classical music session was assigned a role of neutral observer; any mediating influence on the musical sound was to be minimized, disguised, rendered somehow transparent. (The fact that the project was nevertheless shot through with subjectivity – 'a compound of acoustical science and sheer mysticism', as *New York Times* writer John Briggs put it – does not undermine the validity of the aspiration.)[7] A successful result was a record that 'recreate[ed] as perfectly as possible, for the individual listener in his home, the *illusion* of the live performance', in the words of *High Fidelity* editor, Charles Fowler.[8]

But sonic transparency was not the whole story. Fidelity meant not only distortion-free sound, well-balanced mixes, full frequency range, and nuanced dynamics – the concerns of recording engineers – but also a fair representation of the music's performance tradition. Conventions of instrumentation and performance practice, along with the characteristic sound of performances in typical venues, were the recording team's guiding criteria. Any apparent electronic wizardry struck a false note. Although it would be a simple matter, for example, to electronically amplify a low-register alto flute phrase to greater prominence than a sharply accented trumpet doubling, such a manipulation of normal acoustic behaviour rendered the result nonsensical according to the music's sounding tradition. (Leopold Stokowski got away with such stunts, but he was a rare breed. Willing to virtually recompose pieces using electronic means, he was a kindred spirit of today's remix specialist.) The high-fidelity project was devoted to honouring that tradition in all its aspects.

Although it was chiefly live performance traditions that fed the aspiration to high fidelity, studio contrived pop music, too, pursued what one *Billboard* reporter called 'the El Dorado of the record as well as the phonograph business'.[9] In 1953, for example, Capitol released an album called *Full Dimensional Sound: A Study in High Fidelity* whose aim was to 'demonstrate to audiophiles the full range and capabilities of sound reproducing systems'.[10] The disc intermingled pop and classical selections – Les Paul, Les Baxter and June Hutton alongside Tchaikovsky, Copland and Bloch – all presented (in the words of the accompanying booklet) with 'the strictest adherence to exacting technical specifications that is possible today',

---

[7]   John Briggs, 'A Look at Commercial High Fidelity', *New York Times* (22 November, 1953), X43.

[8]   Charles Fowler, 'Fidelity and Illusion', included in *Full Dimensional Sound* booklet.

[9]   Bob Rolontz, 'High Fidelity Record Firms' Magic Phrase', *Billboard* (27 March, 1954), p. 37.

[10]   'Capitol Hi-Fi album Release', *Billboard* (26 September, 1953), p. 21.

achieving 'fidelity which retains the music's original range, balance, and depth'.[11] The album offered a curious assortment of tracks, given that these repertories projected entirely different understandings of fidelity. The pop selections thus represented a distinct departure from the classically oriented hi-fi principle, for their primary performance context was the artifice-laden recording studio, where real-world acoustic moorings were lost to endemic electronic mediation. Post-swing pop styles evolved in a climate of relentless novelty fuelled by a structural change in the record business whereby the usual series of events leading to a record's production became reversed. 'In the old days', recalled veteran Tin Pan Alley songwriter, Johnny Green, 'the impetus for making a successful popular song came first from the composer and lyricist, through the publisher, and finally to the performer ... Nowadays, it's the performing artist who makes or breaks a song and who is the initiator of all activity, the funnel through which the song reaches the public.'[12] 'By the early 1950s', one old-line publisher lamented, publishers did not 'dare publish a song until some artist perhaps likes it, or the whim of an A&R "genius" decides it should be done with echo chambers, or a "cracking-your-knuckles" type of arrangement'.[13] In other words, pop music's creative home was now the recording studio.

Rather than faithfully representing existing musical practices, many of the most successful producers created hybrid mixtures of musical styles and instrumentation put together in studios for a single session, or even a single song. There was no precedent for such concoctions as Frankie Laine's 'Mule Train' (Mercury 1948) or Peggy Lee's 'Lover' (Decca 1952), the like of which fascinated record buyers. On 'Mule Train', a Mitch Miller production featuring a faux-country sensibility (actually written by a group of Hollywood songwriters during a car trip from Las Vegas to Los Angeles), listeners heard guitar and accordion accompanying the percussive emulation of hoof beats and shouts of 'Get along, mule! Get along!' followed by the crack of a whip-like sound, the vocal all the while bathed in a cavernous reverb suggesting the vastness of a Western landscape. 'Lover', a Gordon Jenkins arrangement, was a study in delirium: a frantically paced full orchestra cum Latin percussion section topped by Lee's agitated performance, which grew more so as the track progressed through a series of rising step-wise modulations. The song's lilting waltz meter was changed to a rushing 4/4 and the massed instrumental sounds echoed freely around Decca's large Pythian Temple recording space in a cacophonous haze. Fellow vocalist, Ella Mae Morse, 'thought [Lee] must be kidding' when she heard the frenetic version of the 1932 Rodgers and Hart song. 'I kept waiting for Mel Blanc to come in and start purring like a

---

[11]   Booklet included with the album *Full Dimensional Sound: A Study in High Fidelity*, Capitol SAL 9020 (1952).

[12]   'Songwriter Johnny Green Likens R&R to Tarragon', *Down Beat* (19 September, 1956), p. 44.

[13]   Abel Green, '"New" Music Biz Faces the Crossroads', *Variety* (6 January, 1954), p. 225.

cat or quacking like a duck', Morse wrote in a stinging *Down Beat* rebuke.[14] Lee claimed she got the idea for the arrangement from a film scene depicting rushing horses, which was appropriate given that the new way of record production more resembled movie making than hi-fi recording.

To be sure, professional recordists produced skilled sonic renderings, but increasingly these featured added reverb, echo, overdubbing, and timbral manipulation. Bill Putnam, for instance, was one of the great recording engineers of the era, yet in his productions of the Harmonicats' 'Peg O' My Heart' (Vitacoustic 1947) or Jane Turzy's 'Good Morning, Mr Echo' (Decca 1951) we hear sounds impossible to reproduce in contemporary live performances. Les Paul was among the most successful and innovative recordists of the time, but his records were feats of musical construction. Their relative clarity of sound simply served to highlight the fact that their only fidelity was to artifice. Patti Page's hugely successful 1950 recording of 'Tennessee Waltz' is a perfectly acceptable sonic rendering, but her overdubbed voice signals that the harmonizing we hear never actually took place.

In 1952, a rare *High Fidelity* article on pop records hit on a telling discovery. Holding several releases up to high-fidelity scrutiny, a group of discerning listeners found all but three deficient. The records – such major-label offerings as Nat Cole's 'Too Young' (Capitol), Guy Mitchell's 'My Truly, Truly Fair' (Columbia), Stan Kenton's 'Laura' (Capitol), and Perry Como's 'Cara Cara Bella Bella' (RCA Victor) – sounded 'falsely brilliant', 'lacking in depth', and 'sadly devoid in clarity of tone'.[15] Curiously, the only records deemed acceptable were Turzy's 'Good Morning, Mr Echo' (Decca), Les Paul's 'Josephine' (Capitol), and Les Paul and Mary Ford's 'How High the Moon' (Capitol), each of which featured such special effects as echo and overdubbing. The writer suggested several reasons for the pop records' inferior sound compared to classical recordings, but he offered no opinion about why the most gimmicky of the records passed muster. Listening now, it's clear that none of the records sounds appreciably 'better' than any of the others. The jury's preferences seem not to have been a matter strictly of audio criteria but of psychological attitude. In foregrounding their artifice, the Turzy and Paul records removed the subliminal distraction of comparing the recording to sound images stored in the listeners' mental databases, freeing them to take pleasure in the thing itself without worrying about how closely it aped something else.

Following the common contemporary practice of covering records that were a hit with the public, Mercury (Georgia Gibbs) and Capitol (Margaret Whiting) released their own versions of 'Good Morning, Mr Echo', both of which followed the original to chart success. Although each record has markedly different instrumentation and arrangement, all feature the same central gag: an electronic

---

[14]   Ella Mae Morse, 'Terrible Thing Is happening to Singers! Everybody Shouts', *Down Beat* (19 November, 1952), p. 2. Mel Blanc was the voice of such famous cartoon characters as Bugs Bunny, Daffy Duck, and Porky Pig.

[15]   Carl Eton, 'Tops ... for the Juke Box', *High Fidelity* (1:2, 1951), p. 62.

echo reflecting the song's subject. 'Good morning (morning, morning, morning) Mr Echo (echo, echo, echo)/How are you today (today, today, today)', sings each performer along with her electronic double. And echo was not the records' only special effect; overdubbing and added reverb also featured prominently. The success of all three was a sure sign that the marriage between musical arranging and electronic manipulation had been blessed by the public. And the cover producers' acknowledgment that an electronic gimmick was an essential element of the record's identity – more so than its instrumental arrangement – spoke to an evolving notion of fidelity referring not to the natural world, but to other records.

If 'Good Morning, Mr Echo' was a one-off stunt, more subtle electronic processing was becoming pervasive. Les Paul developed an extensive palette of echo effects that he used to create textural and rhythmic variety. Similarly, he used overdubbing not merely for its novelty impact, but to develop and shape sonic textures. Still, Paul's were among the most overt manipulations. Many recordings disguised the artifice employed to shape their sound. Columbia engineer Frank Laico tailored a specific combination of EQ and reverb for each of the singers he recorded (the likes of Frankie Laine, Johnnie Mathis and Tony Bennett), which served as a signature sound for that voice. He noted the settings and recalled them at successive sessions; in effect, the electronic tinkering was intrinsic to the recorded voice's identity.[16] Thus, high fidelity, as it applied to major label pop, had little to do with transparency. It meant, rather, successful representation of a creative concept. Clarity and balance were elements of the sonic appeal, but a record's ultimate aim was to thrill listeners with a distinct personality.

Lo-Fi

As high fidelity fascinated one segment of the record market, another trend brought to the popular soundscape an opposing aesthetic. Records that would have been appalling to any audiophile began at first to trickle and then to flood into the popular mainstream, released by the new breed of independent record men scattered across the United States. Made on shoestring budgets in all sorts of makeshift 'studios' – often employing amateur musicians, songwriters and arrangers – such discs were improbable sales contenders. It was incredible to industry veterans that these rough-hewn, lo-fi sounds proved such a hit with record buyers, particularly those at the younger end of the market. On such discs as Johnny Ace's 'My Song' (Duke), Don Howard's 'Oh Happy Day' (Essex), or the Five Satins' 'In the Still of the Nite' (Ember), there seemed to be no thought whatever given to the production standards that major labels considered key selling points. Moreover, the records' lack of polish often extended to the songs and musical performances as well. Yet the records sold briskly, flaws and all. Indeed, their apparent shortcomings seemed to add an intriguing patina unique to the world of recorded sound. Taken together,

---

[16]   David Simons, *Studio Stories* (San Francisco: Backbeat Books, 2004), pp. 29–30, 37.

such lo-fi productions would come to represent a new pop idiom – rock and roll – and as they accumulated they sent a clear message: for masses of record buyers fidelity was trumped by character.

Ace's disc was remarkably shoddy-sounding, even for an indie product – 'distinctly inferior' as a *Down Beat* reviewer summed it up.[17] The song, which is based on Ruth Brown's 'So Long', was written and recorded at Memphis radio station WDIA as a last-minute attempt to salvage an aborted Bobby Blue Bland session. It was, as co-writer Dave Mattis recalled, 'a fifteen-minute job'.[18] The sound is raw – a cramped frequency range, uneven mix, distortion, a general timbral crudeness – yet the record spent nine weeks at number one on the *Billboard* R&B chart in the summer of 1952. That same year Don Howard's 'Oh Happy Day' made a commercial stir on the pop chart, rising to number 4 in the course of a 15-week run, though it was reportedly recorded in the 17-year-old's family garage in Cleveland. According to *Billboard*, the record 'kicked off a shocked reaction in the business', which was struggling to grasp the public's aesthetic whims.[19] Describing the performance, a *Time* magazine reporter wrote, 'Donnie himself moos his happy tune with the hoarse lilt of a fogbound ferry whistle'.[20] Yet *Billboard* contended that 'the chanter's odd style produces a definite sound and where the record has been well exposed has resulted in definite sales'.[21] And that, in the end, was what mattered. 'Although most publishers and many record men were somewhat aghast and puzzled when they first heard the disk, they swallowed their astonishment and actively went after the tune and the record when they found out that the public liked it.'[22]

The Five Satins' 'In the Still of the Nite' was recorded in 1956 in the parish hall of St Bernadette's Church in East Haven, Connecticut and released on Standord and later Ember Records. Standord was owned by two New Haven teenagers, Marty Kugell and Tom Sokira, who, lacking any kind of recording studio, hauled their two-track tape machine to the church to make the recording. They had also used the VFW hall to record Five Satins' tracks. The result of their effort is a piece of sonic surrealism, a sound canvas configured such that through most of the track the only instrument heard distinctly is a deep snare on each back beat. The piano appears to be in an entirely different acoustic space from the voices, sharing their temporal frame but inhabiting a separate, parallel dimension of sound. The vocal balance highlights the middle voice of the harmony throughout, its persistent two-

---

[17]   'Rhythm and Blues', *Down Beat* (8 October, 1952), p. 11.

[18]   Quoted in J.M. Salem, *The Late Great Johnny Ace and the Transition from R&B to Rock 'n' Roll* (Urbana, IL: University of Illinois Press, 1999), pp. 42–3.

[19]   'This Week's Best Buys', *Billboard* (29 November, 1952), p. 34.

[20]   'Mystery Hit', *Time* (9 February, 1953), p. 49.

[21]   'This Week's Best Buys', p. 34.

[22]   'Few New Diskery Artists Able to Hit Big Time in '52', *Billboard* (3 January, 1953), p. 13.

note part just behind Fred Parris's lead vocal. The track's overall texture has a slight haze of distortion permeating the whole.

Although the roughness of many indie records was largely a matter of circumstance, their general sonic aura nevertheless lodged in the public consciousness without apology. Noises inadvertent or unwitting in their origins took on rhetorical status when identified with a successful record. The accumulation of coarse sounds in the hit parade thus had a similar cultural effect to the high-polish gimmicks of the majors: lo-fi, too, moved the public's conception of recorded music away from expectations of real-world analogy. Records not only delivered music, they exuded an aura. As such, the primitivist rock and roll discs were recast from inferior audio products to intriguing characters whose exuberant noise more than held its own in the mainstream pop market.

One record in particular – Elvis Presley's 'Don't Be Cruel' b/w 'Hound Dog' (RCA Victor) – stands out as a prime example. The record's two sides present in themselves a glimpse of the broadening range of record production styles. Each has a markedly different sound situating it on either end of the hi-fi/lo-fi spectrum. 'Don't Be Cruel' sounds as clean as any Columbia recording of Guy Mitchell or Frankie Laine. 'Hound Dog', by contrast, argues insistently for the legitimacy of lo-fi as an aesthetic prerogative. When he signed with RCA Victor in 1956, Presley began producing his own sessions, following the method he had learned from Sam Phillips during his time on Phillips' Sun label. For Phillips, the recording studio was a place for exploration and discovery, and the end result was achieved only when something extraordinary emanated from the studio's monitors. With his move from Sun to Victor, Presley went from a fairly low-tech production environment to a state-of-the-art operation where top-line engineers, first-rate equipment and carefully designed rooms were the norm. Yet it was still the *feel* of a record, not its fidelity to actual sound events, that remained his primary criterion.

'Hound Dog', written by Jerry Leiber and Mike Stoller, had been a hit a few years earlier for Willie Mae Thornton who delivers the song with an authority both musical and sexual. Presley's version – borrowed from the one he heard performed live in Las Vegas by Freddie Bell and the Bellboys – is altogether more innocent and frenetic. The words are distilled to a couple of verses repeated again and again. In place of the original's suggestive double-entendre, Presley's version seems to be directed quite literally at a feckless pooch. The instrumental responses to the voice, slyly understated on Thornton's recording, are reduced to noisy guitar fragments and a yammering set of snare triplets at the end of each verse. The harmony voices accompanying Scottie Moore's guitar solos wheeze away as the guitar careens on the verge of imminent breakdown ('ancient psychedelia', Moore later described it).[23] Most astonishing, however, is the record's overall sound, or, better, racket, which blasted from radios and jukeboxes for weeks as the record topped the pop, R&B and country charts. A nonplussed critic for *Melody Maker*

---

[23]   Quoted in P. Guralnick, *Last Train to Memphis: The Rise of Elvis Presley* (Boston: Little, Brown and Company, 1994), p. 298.

assured readers that his 'interest in Presley's "Hound Dog" does not lie simply in the fact that I don't like it. The point about the whole thing is that, by all and any standards, it is a thoroughly bad record.'[24] Yet the disc was the result of hard work. Far from a victim of the typical indie lo-fi circumstances, it defied its high-tech major-label setting to express a deliberate blast of lo-fi noise. It took 31 takes before Presley was satisfied. Through a painstaking process, he finally got what he was after: not simply a good performance cleanly recorded, but a record that, in its crude raucousness, fulfilled his artistic vision.

No-Fi

Although hi- and low-fi pop recordings of the 1950s represent vastly different production standards, both posed a similar problem: each in their own ways rendered the idea of fidelity irrelevant. The scuffed sounds of rough-and-ready indie productions were clearly distinct from their acoustic origins. Distorted by poor acoustics, inferior equipment and often unskilled engineering, such sounds required of listeners a suspension of disbelief, an acknowledgement that records were not necessarily windows on acoustic reality. But the high-polish sounds of post-swing major-label pop were fanciful distortions in their own right. In their ad hoc ensembles and novel arrangements they often presented timbral combinations without real-world counterpart, further tinted by electronic processing widely criticized as what the storied A&R man, John Hammond, called 'electronic fakery'.[25] These records' self-proclaimed high fidelity referred not to a transparent representation of the natural sound world, but a souped-up electromusical invention. In other words, they, too, begged listeners' credulous indulgence.

The criticism faced by such producers as Mitch Miller and Les Paul returned repeatedly to the idea that their projects undermined authentic music making. 'Tune and talent have frequently been secondary to accompaniments that snap, crackle or pop, [and] singers who gasp or shriek', complained New York Times jazz and pop critic John S. Wilson. He singled out Miller as 'one of those most responsible for the present interest in sounds per se'.[26] Metronome editor, Barry Ulanov, accused Miller of 'apply[ing] camouflage to the efforts of singers willing to lose their identity to the sound-effects man'.[27] Another Metronome reviewer found Les Paul's 'Carioca', a top-twenty hit, 'a great mechanical feat', but 'musically it's a good deal less'.[28] Paul's biggest hit, 'How High the Moon', with vocals by Mary Ford, was the country's number-one record for nine weeks in 1951. It brought this

---

[24]   Quoted in Laurie Henshaw, 'Rock-'N'-Roll Swamps '56 Music Scene', *Melody Maker* (15 December, 1956), p. 21.

[25]   'Natural Sound', *New Yorker* (17 July, 1954), p. 17.

[26]   John S. Wilson, 'Creative Jazz', *New York Times* (Apr 5, 1953), X9.

[27]   Barry Ulanov, 'Mitch the Goose Man', *Metronome* (July 1950), p. 34.

[28]   'Les Paul Mary Ford', *Metronome* (July 1952), p. 31.

from a *Down Beat* reviewer: 'All *Moon* needed was to have a Les Paul version of it to kill it for all time. He's now taken care of that detail in a sometimes-funny satire in which he mixes bop clichés, banal riffs, hillbilly twangings and the multiplied voice of Mary Ford. Not for tender ears.'[29]

By the end of the 1950s, Wilson reckoned that 'the bulk' of contemporary pop discs were 'propped up by some form of gimmick or engineering acrobatics', indeed that a singer 'may actually be nothing more than the product of a recording engineer's creative ingenuity'. The general reliance on what he called 'non-musical crutches' had led to an array of tricks:

> A small, flat voice can be souped up by emphasizing the low frequencies and piping the result through an echo chamber. A slight speeding up of the recording tape can bring a brighter, happier sound to a naturally drab singer or clean the weariness out of a tired voice. Wrong notes can be snipped out of the tape and replaced by notes taken from other parts of the tape.[30]

What perplexed and often angered critics was a growing split between age-old verities of musical practice and modern production methods that appeared to substitute beguiling sound for musical substance. The happenings at major labels were perhaps even more disturbing than rock and roll, which initially could be written off as a symptom of teenagers' irrational naivety. But the majors were purveyors of adult pop, home recently to the great swing bands and a repertory of classic pop standards. Now, their song material was judged lacklustre and their records wholly reliant on artifice. 'Miller's unique contribution to the trade is his ability to make pretty bad songs sound pretty good, by means of musical-*cum*-electronic hocus-pocus', wrote Robert Rice in a 1952 *New Yorker* piece.[31] And it was not only critics but also the fading star performers who found it all bewildering. In his autobiography, Bing Crosby summed up a familiar lament:

> Those who are now in charge of production at the various recording companies tell me that to awaken popular interest in a record they've got to produce a new 'sound': an unusual combination of instruments or voices which record buyers haven't heard before. If you can do this, they say, you've got a chance to turn out a hit record. It doesn't matter what the material is like or how good the song is or what it's all about, how it's done, or how it's performed. It's just whether it features an unusual sound which hasn't been heard before.[32]

[29] Jack Tracy, 'Les Paul', *Down Beat* (20 April, 1951), p. 15.

[30] John S. Wilson, 'How No-Talent Singers Get "Talent"', *New York Times* (21 June, 1959), SM16.

[31] Robert Rice, 'Profiles: The Fractured Oboist', *New Yorker* (6 June, 1953), p. 46.

[32] B. Crosby and P. Martin, *Call Me Lucky: Bing Crosby's Own Story* (New York: Da Capo Press, 1953), pp. 142–3.

Rock and roll records confronted the music industry with a challenge. Their amateur cast made no sense to established pros. 'People like me and Crosby were confused', recalled Paul in 1977, 'because everything we had learned was just thrown out the window. The music world had taken a different shape and I didn't know what to do about it.'[33] But in the bigger picture, the tension between hi- and low- fi recordings was just the fractious interaction of competing elements in a single system based on a common creative principle: the recording studio was a place for making musical artefacts without specific referent; the electronic medium was no longer tasked primarily with representing existing musical culture but inventing a new one. Once the representation project was abandoned, pop recordists of all stripes engaged in developing a new musical language written not only in the traditional musical syntax of pitches and rhythms, but also in the sound of performers engaged in specific performances. Dialects differed, as did aesthetic stances and rhetorical styles. But pop records shared a fundamental conception of the music-technology interface. Moreover, they shared the same mainstream pop market tracked by *Billboard*'s radio, retail and jukebox charts. Their common mode of production – sonic inscription – and dissemination defined a universe encompassing both indie and major label records and incorporating their differences (including audience demographic) in an overarching pop language.

The mid 1950s flap over R&B covers by major labels pointed up the common threads running through the pop market, as well the tensions inherent therein. Although it was a longstanding practice in the record industry to release multiple versions of hit songs on competing labels, it was usually the case that the records used different arrangements. The cover issue became heated, however, when some major label versions of R&B tunes were recorded with arrangements nearly identical to the originals. In 1949, Supreme Records took the matter to court in an unsuccessful lawsuit against Decca over Evelyn Knight's cover of Paula Watson's 'A Little Bird Told Me'. A few years later, as R&B records crossed over to the pop market with increasing frequency, the practice was widespread enough to spur an indignant ban on such records by New York radio station WINS (Alan Freed's employer) and an angry letter from LaVern Baker to her congressman Charles Diggs, Jr. It was not the cover principle itself she objected to, Baker wrote, but the 'arrogance in thefting my music note for note'.[34] WINS programme director Bob Smith, too, distinguished between what he called 'copy' records – those that imitated 'often note for note the arrangement and stylistic phrasing of the singer' – and legitimate covers, which were considered 'an integral part of the disk business and … regarded as completely ethical by all'.[35] The station's stand asserted a principle that as yet had no legal standing: a record's entire contents – not only its

---

[33]   Quoted in M.A. Shaughnessy, *Les Paul: An American Original* (New York: William Morrow, 1993), p. 224.

[34]   'LaVern Baker Seeks Bill to Halt Arrangement "Thefts"', *Billboard* (5 March, 1955), p. 13.

[35]   'WINS Issues Ban on Copy Records', *Billboard* (27 August, 1955), p. 21.

song but also its performance, arrangement and sound – were equivalent to any other form of intellectual property.

Aside from a unilateral move like the WINS ban, however, nothing came of the various complaints because arrangements and recordings were not subject to copyright statute, and attempts to address the so-called interpretation issue had languished in Congress for years without resolution. But aside from the legal and ethical ramifications, the 'copy' records illustrate vividly the move from sheet music to records as the primary unit of musical commerce and musical use. Cover records had traditionally been remakes of songs; copy records were remakes of records. Whereas companies had routinely sold hit songs in various versions, they were increasingly aware that not only a record's song but also many of its specific sonic elements were key to its appeal. Atlantic engineer Tom Dowd, for example, recalls that when Mercury decided to record Georgia Gibbs's cover of Baker's 'Tweedle Dee', the producers not only used the same arrangement but also tried (unsuccessfully) to hire him to duplicate the sound.[36] And one of the issues brought out in the *Supreme v. Decca* suit was that the only evidence before the court was sonic. Watson's recording was based on a head arrangement, not a proper lead sheet, which forced the judge to rely exclusively on an auditory comparison of the records. For audiences, record firms, publishers, and even courts of law, pop's fundamental musical lexicon was expanding beyond the elements of lead sheets – the elements historically understood as textual by the writers of copyright laws – to include every sound that made an impression on the market.

By the late 1950s, *Billboard* editor Paul Ackerman, who had followed developments closely, reckoned that rock and roll had become 'so firmly integrated with the pop medium that backings on even so-called quality songs are scored with distinctive rock and roll figures', a practice that had become 'so common as to go completely unnoticed'.[37] Conversely, rock and roll mined the classic Tin Pan Alley repertory with such records as the Platters' 'My Prayer' (Mercury), the Dominoes' 'Stardust' (Liberty), and the Flamingos' 'I Only Have Eyes for You' (End). A record such as Buddy Holly's 'True Love Ways' (Coral), adorned one of rock and roll's original voices with the trappings of old-style pop: strings, understated rhythms and polished sounds. This mixing and matching of elements across genres spoke to the new mindset of record producers. Although none would have put it so academically, they conceived of records as texts; and they created their new works mindful of a burgeoning field of other texts similarly composed. That is, they made records *as* records, not high-fidelity renderings but distinctive rhetorical flourishes in a new language of musical sound.

---

[36]   C. Gillett, *Making Tracks: The Story of Atlantic Records* (London: Souvenir Press, 1988), p. 109.

[37]   Paul Ackerman, 'Diversified Sphere of American Music at Peak Influence', *Billboard* (29 April, 1957), p. 21.

Discography

Ace, Johnny. 'My Song'. Duke 102 (1952).

Baker, LaVern. 'Tweedle Dee'. Atlantic 1047 (1954).

Cole, Nat. 'Too Young'. Capitol 1449 (1951).

Como, Perry. 'Cara Cara Bella Bella'. RCA Victor 20-4203 (1951).

Dominoes. 'Star Dust'. Liberty 55071 (1957).

Five Satins. 'In the Still of the Nite (I'll Remember)'. Ember 1005 (1956).

Flamingos. 'I Only Have Eyes for You'. End 1046 (1959).

Full Dimensional Sound: A Study in High Fidelity. Capitol 9020 (1953).

Gibbs, Georgia. 'Good Morning, Mr Echo'. Mercury 5662 (1951).

Gibbs, Georgia. 'Tweedle Dee'. Mercury 70517 (1954).

Harmonicats. 'Peg O' My Heart'. Vitacoustic 1 (1947).

Holly, Buddy. 'True Love Ways', on *The Buddy Holly Story, Volume 2*. Coral 57326 (1960.)

Howard, Don. 'Oh, Happy Day'. Essex 311 (1952).

Kenton, Stan. 'Laura'. Capitol 1704 (1951).

Knight, Evelyn. 'A Little Bird Told Me'. Decca 24514 (1948).

Laine, Frankie. 'Mule Train'. Mercury 5345 (1949).

Lee, Peggy. 'Lover'. Decca 28215 (1952).

Mitchell, Guy. 'My Truly, Truly Fair'. Columbia 39415 (1951).

Page, Patti. 'The Tennessee Waltz'. Mercury 5534 (1950).

Paul, Les. 'Josephine'. Capitol 1592 (1951).

Paul, Les. 'Carioca'. Capitol 2080 (1952).

Paul, Les, and Mary Ford. 'How High the Moon'. Capitol 1451 (1951).

Platters. 'My Prayer' b/w 'Heaven on Earth'. Mercury 70893 (1956).

Presley, Elvis. 'Don't Be Cruel' b/w 'Hound Dog'. RCA Victor 47–6604 (1956).

Thornton, Willie Mae (Big Mama). 'Hound Dog'. Peacock 1612 (1953).

Turzy, Jane. 'Good Morning, Mr Echo'. Decca 27622 (1951).

Watson, Paula. 'A Little Bird Told Me'. Supreme 1507 (1948).

Whiting, Margaret. 'Good Morning, Mr Echo'. Capitol 1702 (1951).

Chapter 5

The US vs the UK Sound: Meaning in Music Production in the 1970s

Simon Zagorski-Thomas

Introduction

This chapter is based on a slightly contentious notion: that there is an identifiable and definable difference between the sound of 1970s recorded popular music from the United States and that from the United Kingdom. Malcolm Addey, the British Abbey Road engineer who moved to New York in the 1960s, is sceptical:

> To compare the sounds from the hundreds of studios in the many culturally different regions, created by many hundreds more recording engineers in such a vast country as the USA with only a half dozen major studios in London, operated by no more than perhaps a couple of dozen engineers in tiny UK, is, in my opinion, impossible.[1]

On the other hand, many record producers, musicians and sound engineers who were also professionally active during this period have suggested that there was a difference. Peter Frampton, interviewed in *Beat International* in 1973, said:

> I thought, well, if I can't do it at Olympic [in London] let's go there [Electric Lady Studios, New York] because at least I know the place ... When I came back I mixed about six tracks at Olympic. It bridges the gap between the American and the British sound.[2]

Malcolm Toft, the designer of Trident mixing consoles, said in 2009:

> I think there is definitely a distinction. I travelled a lot, in the early '70s in particular, because Trident became very popular in America, and I think there is a distinctly different way that the English and the Americans did things ... I don't think our Brit acoustic designers thought the same way as maybe the

---

[1]   Malcolm Addey, personal email communication with the author, 12 February 2010.

[2]   Peter Frampton interviewed by an uncredited writer in the May 1973 edition of *Beat International*. [Online]. Available at: www.rocksbackpages.com/article.html?ArticleID=4559 [accessed: 12 February 2010].

Americans did ... Our rooms sounded different, the way we designed things was definitely different. I think it was the approach that the engineers had.

There's definitely a British sound and an American sound ... So there was a difference, I think, from both sides of the Atlantic, to do with music, to do with the producers, to do with the engineers, to do with the studios.[3]

In a series of emails on the Audio Engineering Society's History Committee (AESHC) mailing list between 7 and 12 August 2005 and 11 and 15 February 2010 it becomes clear that the 'sound' of record production can be interpreted very widely, relating to engineering practice, room types and sizes, musical styles, technology, electronics, mastering and pressing practice. Despite that, these email exchanges also reveal that there *was* some kind of perceived or real difference experienced by these professionals.[4] Richard Hess, a systems designer for ABC-TV in New York in the 1970s, points out that not only did Neve differentiate its audio consoles through Britishness but also that, even today, Mackie proclaims 'Perkins "British Style" EQ on each channel!' as part of the marketing for its ONYX-I series desks.[5]

Pip Williams, a British guitarist, arranger and producer, describes the UK/US differences as follows:

US productions were brighter and had a more controlled bass end in the 60s and 70s – the brightness was especially true of dance records. Bands like the Turtles and the Four Seasons didn't have the boomy notes in the bass end that recordings by the Hollies and so on had. Listen to Spirit, Buffalo Springfield and [Crosby, Stills and Nash's album] *Déjà Vu*.[6]

As part of my research for this project, I have listened to a large number of recordings from this period[7] and have developed a (personal and subjective) list of the features that I think characterize the differences between the sound of UK

---

[3]　Interview with Malcolm Toft by Marsha Vdovin on the Universal Audio Webzine. [Online]. Available at: www.uaudio.com/webzine/2009/november/doctors.html [accessed 14 February 2010].

[4]　Email postings from Brian Roth, Bob DeGraw, Ben Torre, Klaus Blasquiz, Tom Fine, C. Butler, John Woodgate, Richard Hess and Robert Auld on the AESHC mailing list 7–12 August 2005, and from Bob Olhsson, John Woodgate, Robert Auld, Tom Fine and Richard Hess on the AESHC mailing list 11–15 February 2010.

[5]　[Online]. Available at: www.mackie.com/products/onyxiseries/ [accessed: 14 February 2010].

[6]　Pip Williams' interview with the author, July 2005.

[7]　Many of them were listened to from original vinyl pressings but the majority are in remastered digital formats (CD, MP3 and AAC). The selections were made from US and UK album charts of the time, further refined by selecting albums and tracks where I could find information about the studios and recording personnel involved. These subjective

and US production during this period. This is supported and contextualized by the main body of my research which includes discussions and interviews with producers and engineers, a study of studio specifications, product manuals and brochures, photos, films and videos of sessions and spectrographic analyses of tracks. Before I describe these features though, I should list some caveats and reservations that I think are also pertinent.

A crucial point which is evident from Malcolm Addey's quote above, and which has been raised by many of my interviewees, is that individual practice and creativity is a more important factor than broad tendencies. My hypothesis is that certain social, economic and technical factors have influenced production practice in the two regions in different ways but individual practitioners' reactions to those factors will vary enormously. A theoretical construct that Mikhail Bakhtin[8] developed for literary theory and which Ingrid Monson[9] developed in relation to musical practice, involves the identification of centrifugal and centripetal forces in social and creative practice. Centripetal forces are the forces of 'centralization, unification, authoritativeness (hegemony) and standardization' and centrifugal forces include 'decentralization, disunity, and competition among multiple social voices'.[10] In this instance I would argue that, for any individual practitioner, there are centripetal forces stemming from the training, technical, economic, social and even architectural infrastructure of the time that are sufficiently powerful in relation to the centrifugal forces of their personalities to constitute a recognizable and definable British Sound that stands in opposition to that of the United States of America.

I would also say that these differences developed slowly during the 1960s, probably becoming fully formed in the last couple of years of the decade, though there may well have been a different set of differences that were operating in earlier decades. The particular factors of the late 1960s developed in relation to the global changes in recording practice that were happening at the time. I would also say that the differences I will describe below became less marked as the next decade progressed although, having said that, there is still a discernible difference between British punk and disco music in the late 1970s and their counterparts in the United States. I will discuss the possible reasons for this later in the chapter.

Having stipulated these provisos to avoid an absolutist stance, the overall hypothesis of this chapter is that the following features distinguish UK from US record production in the 1970s:

---

listening tests involved tracks from around 200 albums covering the period from 1970 to 1979.

[8] Mikhail Bakhtin, *The Dialogic Imagination: Four Essays*, ed. M. Holquist, trans. C.Emerson and M. Holquist (Austin and London: University of Texas Press 1981).

[9] Ingrid Monson, *Saying Something: Jazz Improvisation and Interaction* (Chicago, IL: University of Chicago Press, 1996).

[10] Ibid., p. 99.

- There's a clearer differentiation between lead voice and backing in US production. This, like all these features, is a tendency rather than a rule but US mix engineers seem to favour this aesthetic approach.
- There is less 'natural', full frequency range ambience in US productions.
- The sound of close microphone placement is more prevalent either through more frequent use or through its more prominent position in mixes in US production.
- The use of acoustic treatment to reduce ambience and isolation rooms to allow greater separation is more prevalent in the USA during this period.
- Drum tuning and damping in the US created drum sounds that were generally more short and tight with less resonance than drum sounds in the UK.
- The sounds of the available recording technology in the two countries were still quite strongly differentiated at this point.

The tendency in US production is for cleaner and more defined sounds that are less like the sound of live concerts and more technologically mediated. One suggested explanation of this is that the US concept of high fidelity in consumer audio technology was more pervasive and more clearly defined and that this influenced the practice of sound engineers. As Keir Keightley[11] has noted, high fidelity audio involved artificially enhanced high and low frequency extremes rather than actual faithful reproduction. These features of brightness and a more controlled bass are precisely the characteristics of the US sound that Pip Williams identified as characteristic of US production.

Most references in the press from the time relate to 'The British Invasion' as a musical phenomenon rather than a different approach to mediation through record production. This chapter will be looking for issues relating to recording practice and aesthetics rather than composition and performance practice. The second British Invasion of late 1960s, early 1970s rock[12] related to rock music almost uniquely but how do these ideas about mediation relate to other music forms and styles? Are there consistent differences?

The chapter proceeds by investigating what the terms UK and US sound might mean, followed by an examination of some spectrographic examples. I will then discuss differences in the techniques and practices of recording professionals in the two countries, differences between studios and the differing available technologies and product types. This will be followed by a more speculative discussion about cultural and aesthetic differences and some further conclusions.

---

[11]   Kier Keightley, '"Turn It down!" She Shrieked: Gender, Domestic Space, and High Fidelity, 1948–59', *Popular Music*, vol. 15, no. 2 (1996): 149–77.

[12]   See for example Ken Barnes' 1975 *Rolling Stone Magazine* review of the Yes *Relayer* album or Mitchell Cohen's March 1976 interview with Queen in *Phonograph Record*: [Online]. Available at: www.rocksbackpages.com/article.html?ArticleID=6852 and www.rocksbackpages.com/article.html?ArticleID=6881 [accessed 14 February 2010].

Defining the UK and US Sounds

In the quote above, Malcolm Toft differentiates between the musical content of the records and the forms of mediation that were applied in the recording process and suggests that there are British characteristics in both spheres. The focus of this chapter, however, is on the mediation rather than on song writing or performance differences that might have existed between Britain and the United States. In order to clarify the definitions of these differences in mediation on the two sides of the Atlantic I will draw upon the terminology of the systems approach to creativity developed by Csikszentmihalyi[13] and applied to record production by McIntyre elsewhere in this book. Csikszentmihalyi analyses creative practice as 'a system composed of three elements: a culture that contains symbolic rules, a person who brings novelty into the domain, and a field of experts who recognize and validate the innovation'.[14] Thus, I would argue, the cultural domains and social fields in the UK and the US provide national infrastructures and centripetal forces within which the various individuals develop their own creative practice through the centrifugal forces of their personal experience. Before progressing to a more detailed analysis I will therefore lay out a broad outline of these cultural domains and social fields.

The cultural domains in the two countries consist of the physical infrastructure with its inherent influences and restrictions and the system of symbolic rules relating to recording practice as they are embodied in the norms of professional practice and training. I will address the very specific questions of studio architecture, the availability and uptake of various forms of technology and the norms of microphone selection and placement, the use of isolation techniques and approaches to signal processing, in later sections but initially I want to examine some of the broader socio-economic factors that differentiate these cultural domains.

Since the beginning of the 1960s the percentage of households owning various forms of entertainment-based consumer durables was both higher in the USA than the UK and grew more quickly.[15] This continued into the 1970s although the gap became gradually less marked. This would suggest that the types of playback experience available to consumers of recorded popular music were different in the two countries and that listeners in the US, with generally higher specification audio systems in the 1960s, would have developed the more pervasive and clearly defined notion of high fidelity that was mentioned earlier. Taylor[16] and Keightley[17]

---

[13]   Mihaly Csikszentmihalyi, *Creativity: Flow and the Psychology of Discovery and Invention* (New York: Harper Collins, 1997).

[14]   Ibid., p. 6.

[15]   Sue Bowden and Adner Offer, 'Household Appliances and the Use of Time: The United States and Britain since the 1920s'. *Economic History Review*, New Series, vol. 47, no. 4 (1994): 725–48.

[16]   Timothy Taylor, *Strange Sounds: Music, Technology and Culture* (New York: Routledge, 2001).

[17]   Keightley, *Turn It Down*.

have both discussed the notion of modernity as expressed through audio technology as an important strand in the development of post-war cultural identity in the United States. I will explore this further in the discussion of the social field of value judgements that follows but the differing levels of prosperity in the two countries at this time is also reflected in the spread of both audio production and reproduction technology.

Another factor that served to maintain the differences between the spread of technologies in the two countries were the trade tariffs and currency restrictions that added artificial costs to the free flow of equipment. This was gradually reduced by the various rounds of the General Agreement on Trade and Tariffs (GATT) and these reductions culminated in 1979 with the end of the Tokyo round of GATT negotiations.[18]

When discussing the social field of Csikszentmihalyi's approach, we can once again differentiate between the value judgements of subject specific experts in the various spheres of professional practice and broader streams of cultural values in the two societies.

In the US popular music forms were more central to the norms of cultural power. The residue of the British class system maintained an infrastructure of cultural values that was much more resistant to the relative novelty of recorded popular music and more firmly entrenched in the classical concert hall. The ruling classes and media gatekeepers in the UK were thus slower to engage with popular culture than in the US and I would suggest this is because each country's national identity was built on very different foundations. Britain's was rooted in its imperial past whereas America's was growing out of its recent and continuing economic expansion. This provided a British social field of values in relation to musical excellence grounded firmly in the classical traditions of the past. Hence the particularly British phenomenon of progressive rock with its adoption of complex and extended musical form, greater reliance on instrumental sections and virtuosity and its general aspiration towards creating a new form of art music. Even the seemingly anti-classical forms of blues rock typified by artists such as Led Zeppelin and Eric Clapton were based on extended displays of instrumental virtuosity and attempts to characterize their work as serious art music such as those lampooned in the film *Spinal Tap* (1984). In the US, on the other hand, popular music and musical theatre and the more commercially oriented values that can be associated with them were more widely embraced by the ruling classes and media gatekeepers. So whilst I'm not suggesting that Bob Dylan or the Grateful Dead were any more accepted or appreciated by American mainstream cultural values than Genesis or Led Zeppelin were in the UK, I would suggest that the broader cultural aesthetic of the recorded popular song with a strongly foregrounded vocal performance was more firmly entrenched as valid artistic activity in the US than

---

[18]   William A. Lovett, Alfred E. Eckes and Richard L. Brinkman, *U.S. Trade Policy: History, Theory, and the WTO* (Armonk, NY: M.E. Sharpe, 2004).

in the UK and that this is reflected in both professional recording practice and consumer preference.

It's also interesting to note that Edward Hall's[19] theory of proxemics characterizes differences between the English and American, somewhat stereotypically and anachronistically it must be said, in terms of their social propensity for differing levels of proximity. He suggests that Americans of this period generally socialize in closer proximity than the English.[20] If it's true that British culture in the 1960s and 1970s favoured less intimate and personal forms of communication then it would be expected that this would be reflected in the staging of recorded vocal music, especially in relation to the levels of perceived proximity and intimacy in the recordings of singer songwriters. This is borne out to a large extent by the structured listening I have engaged in.

Spectrographic Examples

As examples of my proposed characteristics I will first examine two segments of The Who track 'Behind Blue Eyes' which were recorded and mixed in 1971. The first was recorded in New York and was produced by Kit Lambert and the second, the released version, was recorded at Olympic Studios in London and was produced by Glynn Johns. Obviously this is only one example but I think it demonstrates a point that can be heard fairly consistently elsewhere in recordings of the time. For me the American recording has more separation whilst the British recording is fatter but less well defined. Whilst the drums aren't quieter they have more ambience in the British recording and thus don't seem so close. This seems to be confirmed by spectrogram analysis in Figures 5.1 and 5.2.

The vertical axis is pitch, the horizontal axis is time and the darkness of the graph depicts the strength of the signal. Thus, in the American example (the lower image in Figure 5.1), the snare drum hits have more high frequency energy than the British version and the energy bursts are shorter and sharper. There are photographs of the New York recording sessions that show tissue taped to the top heads of the snare drum and tom toms to reduce the resonance and microphones placed around 15 centimetres (6 inches) from the drum heads.[21] In the UK example (the upper image in Figure 5.1) the snare drums have a less intense attack transient but they last longer. The British recording also has a wider and stronger range of frequencies in the bass end. Both of these features are consistent with greater ambience in the recording and the British example's more even amplitude,

---

[19]   Edward Hall, *The Hidden Dimension* (Garden City, NY: Anchor Books, 1966).

[20]   Ibid., pp. 119–23 and 138–43.

[21]   [Online]. Available at: www.thewho.net/whotabs/gear/drums/drumsborrowed.html [accessed 14 February 2010].

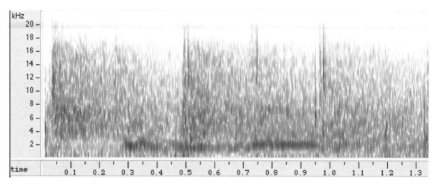

UK Recording of Behind Blue Eyes

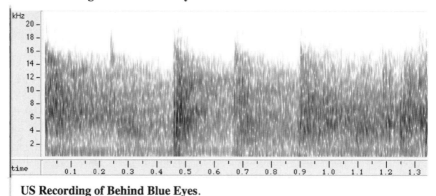

US Recording of Behind Blue Eyes.

Figure 5.1   Spectrograms of UK and US recordings of 'Behind Blue Eyes' by
               The Who (1971)

especially in the lower frequency range would account for its 'fatness':[22] The US
example may have higher peaks but the UK sound seems to have a higher average
amplitude which means those lower frequencies are perceived as louder even if
the individual peaks are lower than the American ones.

My second pair of examples comes from the Rolling Stones' *Sticky Fingers*
album, which was recorded from 1970 to 1971. The images on the right of Figure
5.2 were recorded at Muscle Shoals studio in Alabama and the images on the left of
Figure 5.2 were recorded at Olympic Studios in London. The same things apply to
these examples as far as ambience is concerned but they also illustrate the related
concept of separation. The American recordings have a much greater separation
of the instruments whilst the instruments in the British recordings merge together
more. Separation is much harder to see in a spectrogram but the areas of acoustic

---

[22]   I have not found any photographs of the drum microphone placement for the
Olympic Studios sessions for the *Who's Next* album but photos of UK sessions in the first
few years of the 1970s generally show fewer microphones on drum kits.

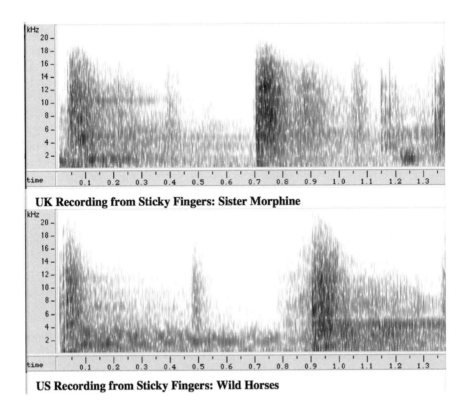

UK Recording from Sticky Fingers: Sister Morphine

US Recording from Sticky Fingers: Wild Horses

Figure 5.2   Spectrograms of UK and US recordings of tracks from *Sticky Fingers* by The Rolling Stones (1970–1971)

energy in the American recordings are more clearly defined than the UK ones. This makes the British recordings more live sounding but less clear than the more artificially distinct recordings of the American tracks.

Differences in Practice

The overall impression I have received from my research is that recording practice in the UK differed from recording practice in the USA by being more institutional and conservative and less explicitly commercially motivated and entrepreneurial. This manifested itself through a more formal approach to apprenticeships in Britain and more strictly enforced time limitations and commercially focused management systems in the US. Thus, for example, Malcolm Addey notes that when he worked for EMI at Abbey Road in London artists were not billed for studio time and producers set the session schedule.[23] Pip Williams also remembers that studio time in the UK was cheaper than in the US in the early 1970s and that American studios charged extra for non-basic equipment.[24]

Edward Kealy[25] defined three stages in the development of sound engineering practice: the craft/union mode, the entrepreneurial mode and the art mode. Kealy was referring primarily to the North American recording industry and I think it's important to establish the differences that existed during this period and earlier between the US and the UK. The entrepreneurial mode associated with smaller independent studios developed more quickly and more extensively in America than Britain where the craft/union mode associated with the large institutional studios held sway for longer. Alongside the question of the physical number of each type of studio there is also issue of their impact on the wider perception and definition of profession excellence. Robert Auld points out that it is recordings' commercial success that encourages practitioners to 'make records that sound similar'.[26] In the UK the craft/union mode models that were in place at EMI, Decca and Pye enjoyed great commercial success in the 1960s whilst in the US the smaller entrepreneurial studios lead the market. In fact the larger companies in the US developed business models in the 1960s that often involved them placing their artists in smaller, independent studios to get a particular sound.[27]

Kealy also discusses the art mode of production as emerging in the mid 1960s but the oft cited pairing of the Beach Boys' *Pet Sounds* (1966) and The Beatles' *Sgt. Pepper's Lonely Hearts Club Band* (1967) display both similarities and differences in UK and US approaches to this art mode. The similarities relate to Kealy's broad definition of the mode: defining 'the craft of sound mixing as a means of artistic expression'.[28] Kealy suggests this development 'makes sound mixing an extension of the musician-composer's art' and so the way in which the UK and US social fields judge particular forms or aspects of creative musical practice are also reflected in the way that creative practice was developed in record

---

[23] 'An Oral History' by Malcolm Addey (recorded 17 November 2008). [Online]. Available at: http://oralstudiohistory.com/audio/osh_maddey_part2.mp3 [accessed: 29 June 2010].

[24] Pip Williams' interview with the author, July 2005.

[25] Edward Kealy, 'From Craft to Art: The Case of Sound Mixers and Popular Music', reproduced in Simon Frith and Andrew Goodwyn (eds), *On Record: Rock, Pop and the Written Word* (London: Routledge, 1990).

[26] Email posting by Robert Auld on the Audio Engineering Society's History Committee Mailing List, 12 February 2010.

[27] See for example Bowman, R., *Soulsville USA: The Story of Stax Records* (New York City: Schirmer Books, 1997): 88–106, who describes Atlantic Records sending their own artists to the Stax Records studio as well as licensing Stax product.

[28] Kealy, 'From Craft to Art', p. 178. This should also, in my opinion, refer to the creative capture, editing and manipulation of recorded performances as well as mixing techniques.

production. I would argue that British forms of innovation in recording practice thus centred more on emulating experimental and art music whilst American innovation focused more on novel forms of clarity and separation.[29] These are obviously broad generalizations for which counter examples can always be found but it should be borne in mind that I am proposing these as centripetal forces within the cultural domains and social fields of the two countries and not as all-embracing national characteristics.

Bob Olhsson, an engineer at Motown's recording studio in Los Angeles, notes that:

> For sure there were some pretty big differences [in recording practice] but a lot of it had to do with the U.S. moving sooner to more tracks but a bit later into letting go of live ensemble recording. English consoles had lots more eq. available and English engineers used more than most of their American counterparts. An exception was Motown where I worked.[30]

I will discuss differences in the technology later but one key way in which I am suggesting that recording practice differed is in the use of multiple microphones. Several engineers have pointed out that while practices differed between companies there were also larger scale differences. John Woodgate, for example, comments that:

> Microphone techniques varied in UK – EMI (Blumlein pairs) and Decca (spaced mics), for example ... [but] ... I think it's true that multiple close micing simply wasn't thought appropriate by many in UK.[31]

Robert Auld, whilst strongly asserting his belief that artistic, commercial and company 'in house' practice was more important than national differences, makes the same point by implication, that is, that the British companies were more conservative in their adoption of multiple microphone techniques than the American ones:

> I think it would be much more valid to talk about the differences in recording practices and sound between individual record companies, especially large companies with history going back many years. For example, there was

---

[29]   For example the adoption of tape loops from the San Francisco minimalists by The Beatles on 'Tomorrow Never Knows' (1966) and Pink Floyd on 'Money' (1973) as opposed to the extreme close microphone placement, drum damping and exaggerated high fidelity of Steely Dan's 'Reelin' In The Years' (1972).

[30]   Email posting by Bob Olhsson on the Audio Engineering Society's History Committee Mailing List, 12 February 2010.

[31]   Email posting by John Woodgate on the Audio Engineering Society's History Committee Mailing List, 8 August 2005.

certainly a kind of rivalry between EMI and Decca in the UK, just as there was between RCA and Columbia in the U.S. ... Decca came up with their famous 'Decca tree' method, which employed three Neumann M50 mics in a spaced array, augmented (especially later) by spot mics on various instruments. EMI, meanwhile, started with mid side stereo mics, and later went to spaced arrays, sometimes augmented with helper mics on the string sections. EMI also did not use as many spot mics as Decca (with some exceptions). In the U.S., RCA started recording orchestras in stereo with very simple spaced arrays of 2 to 4 microphones, and then added helper mics, similar to EMI–until the late 1960s, when they went over to multi-mic arrays of 15 or more mics. Columbia tended to use more mics than RCA during the early 1960s (conservative multi-miking), then also went very heavily into multi-miking – their recording of Carmina Burana in 1973 with the Cleveland Orchestra used over 30 microphones![32]

In relation to close microphone placement and the avoidance of room ambience in US recordings, anecdotal and photographic evidence can be used to support the claim that close microphone placement was less common in the UK in the early 1970s.[33] Geoff Emerick describes the problems he faced as late as 1967:

For example, on Ringo's drum sound, I wanted to move the mic closer to the bass drum. Well, we weren't allowed. I was caught putting the mic about three inches from the bass drum, and I was reprimanded. I said, 'Look, this is the bass drum sound we've got, and we don't want to touch it'. And so I was sent a letter, from one of the guys in the office down the corridor, giving permission – only on Beatles sessions – to put the microphone three inches from the drum. They were worried, you see, about the air pressure, that it would damage the mic.[34]

While, from a US perspective, Tom Fine recalls that:

Back in the 70s, in the LP era, one feature of the larger-room British studios was a punchy and deep drum sound ... Now compare that to the dry and constricted drum sound out of almost any U.S. studio in that early 70s period ... To my ears, there was a different philosophy about how to record and produce drums during

---

[32]   Email posting by Robert Auld on the Audio Engineering Society's History Committee Mailing List, 12 February 2010.

[33]   See, for example, the extensive library at www.gettyimages.co.uk provided several hundred images from recording studios in the 1970s and books such as J. Cogan and W. Clark (eds), *Temples of Sound: Inside the Great Recording Studios* (San Francisco: Chronicle Books, 2003), and D. Simons, *Studio Stories* (San Francisco: Backbeat Books, 2004).

[34]   Interview by Maureen Droney with Geoff Emmerick, *Mix Online*, 1 October 2002. [Online]. Available at: http://mixonline.com/recording/interviews/audio_geoff_emerick [accessed: 12 July 2010].

that period. The US moved back to more 'room-sounding' drums by the 80s, I remember what a big deal it was when the Power Station started churning out hits and one of the distinct features was the huge drum sound from a big, live room. That was very different from where things had been, typical process was put the drums in a dead iso booth, put mics right up on them and pan them wide so each drum is disjointed from the others. There are exceptions to any trend I've described here, so I would again caution against simplistic stereotypes.[35]

Pip Williams made a similar point about American engineers being more concerned with close microphone placement, more separation and minimizing the sound of room ambience, citing his experience of recording with UK band Bloodstone at Village Recorders in 1973 which included looking in on the Steely Dan sessions in another studio in the complex.[36] However, there was not unanimity amongst my interviewees on this subject. Ted Fletcher noted:

> In the early 70s there was a significant difference between UK and US techniques … In the US the influence of the movie soundstage was still very prevalent; engineers had been taught to make the best out of recording the ensemble rather than separating performers whereas in the UK, there was a sudden shift to as much separation as possible. I spent some time at the Record Plant in Los Angeles recording Joe Walsh, and it seemed odd to me at the time that they were all together in the studio with the minimum of separation, but the room sounded good, and the engineer and producer made use of the ambience.
>
> Back in the UK we were all getting bigger and better screens made!
>
> I think the US rooms were very much better acoustically than those in the UK … the American rooms had the advantage of years of film work. Certainly my experience was that bands in the US recorded using the room to advantage, but in the UK (at Olympic and Decca particularly) the room was huge but the mic positioning was close and the room size was irrelevant.
>
> I don't agree that close miking was more widespread in the US … but that may be just a personal thing; I grew up with Joe Meek and mics stuffed as close as possible![37]

My final point in relation to recording practice is about mixing practice. Ted Fletcher and others, particularly those involved with mixing console design have asserted that British engineers in the late 1960s and early 1970s used equalization and compression on individual channels more extensively than their American counterparts and that this was reflected in console design. At first glance this would seem to be at odds with the notion that has also been expressed by interviewees

---

[35] Email posting by Tom Fine on the Audio Engineering Society's History Committee Mailing List, 13 February 2010.

[36] Pip Williams' interview with the author, July 2005.

[37] Ted Fletcher email correspondence, 1 July 2010.

that British mixes of the period are referred to with terms such as power, warmth and 'fatness' whilst American mixes are described as 'tight' and 'clear'. Perhaps this apparent contradiction can be resolved by suggesting that in general, and decreasingly as the decade progressed, recording in the USA utilized smaller or more acoustically treated rooms, isolation and microphone placement to achieve clarity and that in the UK the larger recording spaces and signal processing resulted in a warmer, fatter sound.

I would also refer back to my previous argument about a broader difference between the two cultural domains and social fields that related to the aesthetics of the recorded popular song and Hall's[38] theory of proxemics. Robert Auld and John Woodgate's comments above attest to the more firmly entrenched traditionalism of British classical sound engineers and producers, holding on to the 'best seat in the concert hall' aesthetic of recording. I would argue that this aesthetic reflects these broader social values and can also be seen to have filtered down into the practice of popular music producers and engineers. Thus Rolling Stones mixes have vocals further in the background than Eagles mixes, Cat Stevens' voice is more embedded in the instrumental tracks than James Taylor and the vocals in Steeleye Span recordings are more evenly balanced with the accompaniment than Simon and Garfunkel. Of course examples are only evidence and not proof but any hypothesis such as this can only hope to be persuasive rather than provable.

Studio Size and Design

Malcolm Addey, despite his earlier assertions about the impossibility of defining an American sound to compare against a British one, has also said:

> American records were our standard ... by which everything was judged and it is not easy to get. For one thing we were working ... with very different acoustics in the studios here [USA] from ... our big rooms [UK]. There wasn't that compact, condensed sound that you can get from a studio like this [being interviewed in Avatar Studios NYC]. You can't get that sound in Studio 2 [Abbey Road]. Even if you screen it off, the room is still going to be there. No matter what you do. And most of the big records coming out of the States were done in closets! That's the sound. That intense, tight sound which we could not get in England in lots of ways.[39]

This quote encapsulates the one difference that jumps out quickly both from interviews and from a study of photos and websites: that the studios used for popular music production in the UK tended to have larger recording spaces with

---

[38]   Hall, *Hidden Dimension*.

[39]   'An Oral History' by Malcolm Addey (recorded 17 November 2008). http://oralstudiohistory.com/audio/osh_maddey_part4.mp3 [accessed: 29 June 2010].

THE US VS THE UK SOUND

higher ceilings. Table 5.1 shows some examples of studio size in the two countries but doesn't include ceiling heights or available isolation rooms.

Table 5.1   Comparison of recording studio sizes in the UK and US

UK	
Olympic Studios	Studio 1: 186m², Studio 2: 106m²
Trident Studios	75 m²
EMI Abbey Road Studio 2	190 m²
Air Studios	180 m²
Decca Tollington Park Studio	153 m²
Island Basing Street Studio (Sarm)	117 m²
USA	
Muscle Shoals Studios, Alabama	Studio A: 42 m², Studio B: 18 m²
Sunset Sound Recorders, Los Angeles	Studio 1: 78 m², Studio 2: 80 m²
Village Recorders, Los Angeles	Studio A: 42 m², Studio B: 25 m², Studio D: 56 m²
Wally Heiders Studio, San Francisco	Studio A: 80 m², Studio D: 57 m²
Electric Lady Studios, New York	Studio A: 132 m², Studio B: 36 m², Studio C: 48 m²
Criteria Studios, Miami	Studio A: 180 m², Studio B: 120 m²
Capitol Studios, Los Angeles	Studio A: 150 m², Studio B: 100 m²
Westlake Studios, Los Angeles	Studio A: 110 m², Studio B: 46 m², Studio C: 93 m², Studio D: 104 m²
Gold Star Studios, Los Angeles	Approx. 50 m²
Sigma Sound Studios, Philadelphia	78 m²

Of course, there were smaller studios in Britain, like Trident, and larger studios in America, like Columbia's 30th Street studio in New York and Criteria Studios in Miami. According to Malcolm Addey and other engineers/producers,[40] the larger studios in the US seem to have been used more for orchestral and musical theatre recordings though. These smaller recording spaces combined with more extensive use of close microphone placement in the US would certainly account for the less ambient recordings with greater separation that I'm suggesting are characteristic of the American sound. I would also contest that studio architecture in the US was

---

[40] See for example http://oralstudiohistory.com/audio/osh_maddey_part3.mp3 [accessed: 12 July 2010].

quicker to move towards less ambient acoustics and the use of separate isolation rooms.[41] At the start of the 1970s the American company Westlake started a trend for deadened acoustics in the design of studio performance spaces. The idea was to make the spaces neutral so that recordings made at a Westlake studio could be added to at any other Westlake studio in the world. Tom Fine said:

> In my opinion, by far the worst trend that caught hold in the USA was the 'dead room' / 'fix it in the mix' syndrome that gripped the business from the late 60s until the 80s. This was partly a crutch for lousy engineers in small rooms with lousy mics to use electronics processing to try and recreate a viable music environment, but it became de rigour with some sound-design firms (partly driven by real estate costs in some large cities) ... As I understand it, the British stuck with larger and liver rooms and smaller mixing consoles (hence no way to put 20 mics on a drum set, etc) longer into the 70s, and the results show.[42]

Also a survey of available plans and photographs of studios during the 1970s does seem to indicate that refurbishments and redevelopments that built more isolation rooms into previously large recording spaces were happening earlier and more extensively in the US. The use of portable screening to aid separation in recording seems fairly ubiquitous on both sides of the Atlantic.

Availability of Technology

There are two factors that affect this question. The first is whether the designers and manufacturers of studio equipment in Britain and Europe were creating very different sounding products than their counterparts in America and the second relates to whether there was a free flow of these products in both directions across the Atlantic. Malcolm Toft pointed out:

> There were probably more English desk manufacturers in those days than there were American. I seem to remember in the early 70s there were in America API, ... Quad-8, Spectra Sonics ... But we had far more. We had Raindirk ... Cadac ... Trident ... Neve, Sound Techniques, Soundcraft, Amek, Allen and Heath ... I suppose our consoles found their way over there. There weren't many American consoles that came across to the UK, in those days. I can only recall actually a few ... API consoles, in London, and that was it. All the consoles were British made.
> So the technology was very much British led, and of course Neve became such a big player. Then Solid State Logic, all British companies. So we tended,

---

[41]   As opposed to movable booths and screening that had been common on both sides of the Atlantic since the 1950s.

[42]   Email posting by Tom Fine on the Audio Engineering Society's History Committee Mailing List, 7 August 2005.

for many, many years, to dominate the console market. So there was this British sound, I think, because we had a British way of doing things. A European way of approaching circuit design … and it had an English slant to it. So I think just by sheer numbers … we did create a British sound.[43]

Some interviewees suggested that the use of solid state electronics might have spread more quickly in America than in Britain but it's difficult to find any consistent patterns. Whilst America was generally quicker off the mark with solid state technology, Rupert Neve in the UK was designing solid state EQ and consoles for studios in London from 1964 onwards. Integrated Circuits that were developed in the early and mid 1970s probably did propagate more quickly in the US than in the UK but again it's hard to discern any consistent patterns. It does seem, however, that the differences in EQ circuit standardization in the US and Europe may have made a noticeable difference to the sound of American-built consoles. In a personal interview, Pip Williams told me that he noticed that American-built desks such as API and Quad-8 that started to appear in some British studios from 1973 onwards had a 'less choked' sound than the early Rupert Neve desks.[44]

Ted Fletcher notes:

Trident and Helios developed a different type of circuitry that gave seemingly huge flexibility at individual frequencies, but proved to sound 'hard' … but good for some rock productions … UK engineers based their choice of recording desks very much on the sound of the EQ at that time. The rock studios went for Trident and Helios while MOR and general studios preferred Soundcraft, Neve and sometimes mine![45]

A survey of the available EQ on desks in the early 1970s does seem to indicate that British manufacturers tended to provide greater flexibility and control.[46]

Bob Olhsson remembers:

When I visited EMI's London Studios in 1968 there was a great deal of talk about people wanting that 'American sound'. When we compared notes, our conclusion was that most of the differences were who was in front of the mikes

---

[43] Interview with Malcolm Toft by Marsha Vdovin on the Universal Audio Webzine. [Online]. Available at: www.uaudio.com/webzine/2009/november/doctors.html [accessed 14 February 2010].

[44] Pip Williams' interview with the author, July 2005.

[45] Ted Fletcher: personal communication 1 July 2010 (Fletcher was designing Alice mixing consoles in the 1970s).

[46] This survey involved examining manuals and photographs of various models of desk by MCI, API, Quad-8, ADM and Sphere from the US and Neve, Trident, Helios and Sound Techniques from the UK.

and the very different recording consoles. EMI had just installed consoles with a compressor on every track and I could brag about our new 16 track machines.[47]

Overall, it does seem that at the start of the 1970s the dissemination of technology proceeded at different rates in the two countries but that this process evened out in the second half of the decade. Thus the use of noise gates started earlier in the US but the use of compression on individual audio channels was more widespread in the UK. The new multitrack formats spread more quickly in the US than in the UK and studios in the two countries tended to have more locally sourced microphone stocks at the start of the decade. This meant that European condenser microphones such as AKG and Neumann were more common in the UK and that makes such as Shure, Electrovoice and RCA were more frequently found in US studios. As I have mentioned previously, the trade tariffs and currency restrictions that were progressively reduced during the 1960s and 1970s restricted the free movement of products across the Atlantic. I also mentioned the differences in relative affluence in the two countries and this would have affected both the development of new products and studios' ability to buy in these technologies from outside. Despite that there were exceptions: London Decca's Threshold Studio built for the Moody Blues in 1973 had an American API desk and Advision had a Quad-8 desk. The penetration of British desks into the US market was greater but Norbert Putnam notes:

> When David Briggs and I started Quadrafonic Studios in Nashville [in 1975] …
> We wanted a Trident A-Range, because we loved that British sound, but back then they cost around $175,000 which was a lot of money; the MCI only cost about $25,000.[48]

Conclusions

I will start by reiterating that the attributes I am proposing are general tendencies relating to the differing cultural domains and social fields existing in the two countries prior to and during this period. I am not suggesting that these characteristics negate individual creativity but that they inform it and I am also not suggesting that these are innate national features but that they are transient and socially constructed. I will also reiterate that these differences relate most strongly to the last couple of years in the 1960s and the first half of the 1970s and that they became progressively less marked throughout the decade.

---

[47]   Email posting by Bob Olhsson on the Audio Engineering Society's History Committee Mailing List, 14 February 2010.

[48]   Interview with Norbert Putnam, part of the original Muscle Shoals rhythm section and Nashville producer: [Online]. Available at: www.soundonsound.com/sos/sep03/articles/putnam.htm [accessed: 29 June 2010].

The attributes that I proposed in the introduction to this chapter can be seen to flow from a series of propositions that have emerged from my research. Firstly, that there are certain characteristics associated with the production technology in each country which were restricted (as opposed to prevented) from moving across the Atlantic for economic reasons. Secondly, that the training and habitus for sound engineers was different in each country and that this can be seen in the norms of microphone usage, acoustic treatment, isolation and mixing practice. Thirdly, that the faster development of the entrepreneurial model of independent studios and the economies of scale in the US market (allowing studios to specialize more in particular musical styles) meant that American popular music was generally recorded in smaller studios and this impacted on the sound of these recordings. Fourthly, that the freer movement of technology and labour as the decade progressed progressively weakened these effects.[49]

The fifth proposition is more subjective and tentative: that social and cultural forces in Britain tied the identity of musical excellence more exclusively to the values of the classical tradition, the sound of the unmediated concert hall and perhaps also to instrumental music. In the United States these social and cultural forces associated the more mediated sound of high fidelity more closely with modernity and thus success and the connection of this more polished sound with commercial products did not carry the same negative connotations as it did in the UK.

---

[49] A further complication is that the expansion of Japan as an independent third supplier of music technology in both the UK and US markets in the late 1970s and throughout the 1980s further eroded the differences.

Discography

The Beach Boys. 1966. *Pet Sounds.* Capitol Records. Vinyl LP: STK 74 147.

The Beatles. 1966. 'Tomorrow Never Knows' on *Revolver.* Parlophone Records. Vinyl LP: PMC 7009.

The Beatles. 1967. *Sgt. Pepper's Lonely Hearts Club Band.* Parlophone Records. Vinyl LP: PMC 7027.

Pink Floyd. 1973. 'Money' on *Dark Side of the Moon.* Harvest Records. Vinyl LP: SHVL 804.

The Rolling Stones. 1971. *Sticky Fingers.* Rolling Stones Records. Vinyl LP: CUN 59100.

Steely Dan. 1972. 'Reelin In The Years' on *Can't Buy A* Thrill. Probe Records. Vinyl LP: SPB 1062.

The Who. 2008 (original release 1971). *Who's Next Deluxe Edition.* Universal International. 2 × CD: UICY-93750.

Film

Reiner, Rob (dir). 1984. *Spinal Tap* (video recording). Embassy Pictures.

Chapter 6

The End of the World as We Know It: The Changing Role of the Studio in the Age of the Internet[1]

Paul Théberge

In June of 2007, Sony BMG, with little warning or ceremony, announced that it would be closing its flagship Manhattan recording facility known as Sony Music Studios: located on West 54th Street, Sony Music Studios was a massive, multi-studio recording, mastering and sound stage complex that had been used for over a decade in numerous commercial music recordings and television broadcasts (many episodes of the *MTV Unplugged* series were shot there, for example). One engineer, more than a little dismayed by the news, remarked in an online forum: 'the world is coming to an end'. On the surface, the closure of Sony Music Studios was just the latest in an ongoing history of such closures: the studio had fallen victim to changes in record industry fortunes, on the one hand, and the voracious New York real estate market, on the other. The Hit Factory had suffered a similar fate just a few years earlier (the building that housed the studio is now a condominium complex) as did numerous other studios in New York, such as Columbia's famous 30th St Studio, decades earlier.

The reason behind slating Sony Music Studios for the wrecking ball was, however, also more specific than this: Sony Music of Japan and BMG in Germany had a few years earlier managed to bypass most of the antitrust legislation in Europe that had prevented earlier merger attempts, by companies such as EMI and Warner, and formed a new corporate entity – Sony BMG Music Entertainment – thus increasing its overall market share of the music business and reducing the former Big Five record companies to the Big Four. Interestingly, one of the arguments that Sony and BMG had put forward to the European Union was that the Internet was having such a devastating effect on the industry that merging operations was the only way they could ensure their survival: while the bigger-is-better logic of such a proposition might appear specious, especially as a response to recent technological change, it seems that it was persuasive enough for the

[1] This chapter is an expanded version of a paper first given at the Fourth Annual Art of Record Production Conference 2008, at the University of Massachusetts, Lowell, 14–16 November 2008.

European Union to allow the merger – a decision that was roundly criticized by just about everyone in the music industry outside Sony BMG.

After the merger, the company engaged in a series of layoffs and reorganization exercises aimed at rationalizing day-to-day operations and eliminating duplication. In this context, it was perhaps only a matter of time before Sony Music Studios would be sold off: it had been rumoured that the facility had been rather poorly managed for years and, as one of the last unionized operations in the industry, profitability was difficult to maintain in the competitive New York studio environment. For the short sighted within the new corporation, the property was certainly worth more as real estate than any amount of financial gain, organization efficiency or corporate prestige that the studio might have garnered. Ironically, it was only a little more than a year later that internal bickering within the Sony BMG enterprise brought the joint corporation to the brink of dissolution; but this came far too late to save the studio.[2]

The relationship of these various phenomena – from the rise of the Internet as the primary distribution medium for recorded music, to the organizational challenges faced by the music industry, to the closure of recording studios – is a complex one and certainly not as linear and causal as record industry executives would have us believe. And as far as recording studios are concerned, even the scale of the problem is difficult to ascertain: the general feeling among many producers and engineers is that studios everywhere are closing but the evidence to support this feeling is largely anecdotal.

One of the things that motivated the study found in the following pages is a desire to add a little more precision to our understanding of just what might be going on in the world of recording studios at the beginning of the twenty-first century. Indeed, the main aim of this study has been to discover whether the recording studio is in fact threatened with extinction or whether we are perhaps witnessing another stage in its evolution, a reconfiguration of the studio as a technology, a means of production and a form of musical practice.

There is no easy way to find reliable data on studios, their overall number, and their relative size and profitability, let alone changes in this type of data over time.[3] And this latter point is important, I think, because the recent changes in the studio need to be put into some kind of historical continuum: a continuum that is based,

---

[2] By August of 2008, it was announced that Sony had agreed to acquire Bertelsmann's fifty per cent share in the joint Sony BMG venture, thus bringing the four-year-old merger to an end. The acquisition was completed on 1 October 2008, leaving Sony Music Entertainment as the sole owner of the record enterprise.

[3] As regards the data used in this study, I have tried to combine and cross check information gathered from a number of different sources, ranging from statistical figures gathered in census data and other government surveys, music industry directories, and web sites. I cannot vouch for the accuracy of any individual set of data – each was gathered through different methods and for different purposes – but each does present its own specific insights as well as its own limitations.

however, on a recognition that what constitutes a 'recording studio' – in terms of a specific configuration of spaces, equipment, techniques and human resources – has changed radically over the years. So whether there is data to support the idea that it is indeed 'the end of the world' for the recording studio may depend, ultimately, on one's understanding of what a studio is in the first place.

What is a Recording Studio?

The first thing that should be noted about the example of Sony Music Studios, cited above, is that it represented a very old studio model: it was one of the last of the large, unionized, multi-purpose recording facilities owned and operated by a major record company. There is a considerable amount of nostalgia attached to this kind of studio, with its large, purpose-built recording rooms and professional staff: these 'temples of sound', as they have been called, serve as a model of what a recording studio should be in historical accounts by Granata, and Cogan and Clark,[4] for example; nevertheless, Sony Music Studios was an anomaly within the present day industry context.

By and large, company-owned facilities became increasingly irrelevant within the record industry beginning as early as the 1950s: according to Peterson and Berger's classic argument made in the early 1970s,[5] the rise of new styles of popular music from the 1950s onward had created a condition of 'turbulence' within the marketplace for recorded music and this encouraged record companies to rely less on centralized, in-house production and more on outside, entrepreneurial producers. Compared with the big record company studios, many of the recording studios associated with the new forms of popular music were small, makeshift affairs, owned and operated by independent producers and engineers.

And it is from this point on that I would argue we have to understand the recording studio as something of a cottage industry: the studio is structurally independent from the record industry, it is dominated by single, stand-alone facilities,[6] and recording studios are, for the most part, owned by individuals and small groups of individuals as limited partnerships. This is not to say that recording studios cannot be large and very expensive to operate: in major centres such as New York, it is

---

[4] Of course, it is precisely a kind of nostalgia – an acknowledgement that these company-owned studios are a thing of the past – that motivates these authors' accounts: Charles L. Granata, *Sessions with Sinatra: Frank Sinatra and the Art of Record Production* (Chicago: A Cappella Books, 1999); Jim Cogan and William Clark (eds), *Temples of Sound: Inside the Great Recording Studios* (San Francisco: Chronicle Books, 2003).

[5] Richard A. Peterson and David G. Berger, 'Cycles in Symbol Production: The Case of Popular Music', *American Sociological Review*, vol. 40, no. 2 (April 1975): 158–73.

[6] Only a handful of music recording studios have been able to maintain multiple facilities in different geographical locations or marketplaces, although this is somewhat more common in post-production sound for film sound.

not uncommon to find million-dollar facilities that house multiple studios, post-production facilities and editing rooms. However, these facilities remain essentially independent, operating on the periphery of the industries they serve.

Two things were paramount in Peterson and Berger's[7] account: increased turbulence in the marketplace and the rise of new, relatively inexpensive and easy to use technologies of music production, specifically, the spread of magnetic tape recording during the post-war period. While the introduction of magnetic tape was a significant moment in the history of sound recording, Peterson and Berger did not consider the extent to which technological change was quickly becoming a factor in everyday life in music production and consumption during the second half of the twentieth century and, hence, a partly independent contributor to turbulence in the marketplace.

These conditions of change continued to create pressures within the record industry and gave rise, in the late 1960s and early 1970s, to the widespread use of analogue multitrack recording in popular music production: while the history of this phenomenon is often reduced to simple accounts of the development of the multitrack tape recorder, I have argued elsewhere that we need to understand the evolution of the early multitrack studio as dependent on the development of a number of different techniques and technologies, including the increasing use of close-miking techniques, the reliance on 'dead' acoustic spaces, and the adoption of large format mixing consoles.[8] As a result of these changes, the physical configuration of studio architecture also changed: the recording room (today often referred to as the 'live' or 'tracking' room) gave way, in size and importance, to the control room where much of the equipment and activity associated with recording, processing and mixing was located.

Ultimately, it was the 24-track analogue studio of the 1970s and early 1980s, which established itself as something of a norm – both in practical and iconic terms – within popular music production during this period, that largely displaced the earlier, corporate mode of studio recording; it continues to be the primary model that many think of when they use the expression '*the* studio'; and, in terms of technology, it continues to be the explicit model upon which many software-based recording systems are designed. Furthermore, it is the multitrack studio that became the basis for many of our contemporary notions of the 'art of record production': the analogue multitrack studio, and the recording practices associated with it, gave rise to the notion of the engineer as 'artist', and it is the evolution of

---

[7]   Peterson and Berger, 'Cycles in Symbol Production'.

[8]   The story of the multitrack tape recorder, which usually begins with an account of the early recording experiments of guitarist Les Paul, is a familiar one and need not be rehearsed in detail here. I have discussed some of these developments in an article entitled, 'The Network Studio: Historical and Technological Paths to a New Ideal in Music Making', *Social Studies of Science*, vol. 34, no. 5 (2004): 759–81.

the multitrack model that underscores many accounts of rock recording aesthetics.[9] The association of multitrack studios with the sound of much classic rock has, in the digital age, resulted in its own form of nostalgia for 'vintage' analogue gear. Ironically, the 1970s is also the period during which the first, tentative challenge to the very idea of a 'professional' recording studio was made: the rise of consumer multitrack equipment produced by Tascam and other manufacturers made the notion of a 'home studio' possible, on the one hand, and gave rise to an alternative aesthetic ('lo-fi', with its own characteristic medium of distribution, the audio cassette), on the other.

It is important to recognize, if only in very general terms, the importance of not only changing economic contexts, technologies, and studio configurations during this period but also changing concepts and practices in sound recording: in this regard, multitrack recording concepts and practices differed from those associated with earlier forms of record production in fundamental ways. Emily Thompson has argued that during the early days of the twentieth century, both engineers and consumers, working across a variety of electronic media, adopted a more scientific understanding of sound that was based less on the idea of sound as an acoustic event than sound as an electrical signal.[10] This emphasis had a significant impact on how sound was understood, used and experienced and, I would argue, something similar occurred again in second half of the twentieth century: by thinking of music less as a performed event and more as a set of individual 'tracks', engineers and producers were able to develop a more procedural and compositional approach to the recording process – an approach that placed mixing at the forefront of engineering skill and artistry.

But if Albin Zak's 'poetics' of rock is based on the idea of maintaining some kind of balance between performance, recording and composition,[11] that balance shifts even more decisively towards the idea of composition with the introduction of digital technologies during the 1980s. With the advent of MIDI sequencers, synthesizers, drum machines and sampling in the early 1980s, and inexpensive digital recording technology by the early 1990s, the 24-track analogue studio began to be squeezed out between the large studio complexes, on the one hand, and the smaller, low end digital studios, on the other, thus increasing the gap between large and small studios in the decades to come. In practical and aesthetic terms, it is interesting to compare Zak's account of rock production with Timothy Warner's study of the pop production practices of Trevor Horn, published only

---

[9]   See, for example, Edward R. Kealy's classic article, 'From Craft to Art: The Case of Sound Mixers and Popular Music', *Sociology of Work and Occupations*, vol. 6, no. 1 (1979): 3–29. For a more recent example of rock recording aesthetics see Albin J. Zak, *The Poetics of Rock: Cutting Tracks, Making Records* (Berkeley: University of California Press, 2001), especially from chapter 5 onward.

[10]   Emily Thompson, *The Soundscape of Modernity: Architectural Acoustics and the Culture of Listening in America, 1900–1933* (Cambridge, MA: MIT Press, 2002), pp. 235–93.

[11]   Zak, *Poetics of Rock*, pp. 54–7.

two years later: Warner's study assumes a completely different configuration of the recording studio, with its reliance on drum machines and sequencers, and an increasingly important role for the producer/engineer.[12]

Toward the end of this period, the term 'project studio' began to appear in professional magazines as a way of referring to this new type of small-scale recording facility. The so-called 'project studio' – essentially a home studio that takes in commercial work and often consisting of little more than a well-equipped control room and perhaps a small booth for recording single instruments or vocals – came to full fruition at roughly the same time as the spread of personal computing and the rise of the Internet as a means of music distribution: based on increasingly powerful home computers and software-based recording tools, the project studio can be considered as yet another model of what a professional recording studio can be.

But while software tools emulate, in digital form, all the characteristics of the multitrack studio – from recording, to processing, to mixing – they also engender a new set of concepts and processes: the contemporary DAW (Digital Audio Workstation) is a visually oriented, random-access form of technology that allows engineers to record not only 'tracks', in the traditional sense, but to operate at the sub-track level, freely editing, processing and moving bits of digital audio data around in ways that would be impossible in a linear, analogue system. If early engineers were encouraged to think of sound events as electronic 'signals' that could be analysed and manipulated, and multitrack technologies turn performances into 'tracks' to be processed and mixed, then working with DAWs encourages one to think of music and sounds as individual 'segments' or 'regions' (the terminology varies from one software platform to another but the concepts are the same) that can be used as individual building blocks for music composition. As a means of composition, DAWs challenge engineers and musicians alike to integrate their performance and music-making activities with the micro-possibilities of digital recording, thereby reorienting, again, fundamental notions of acoustics and music.[13] The added emphasis on routines related to cutting, pasting, looping, micro-timing, pitch correction and on-board signal processing place an increased emphasis on the computer itself as the primary tool of contemporary sound recording, thus further altering the relationship of digital audio production to earlier, spatial and technical configurations of the recording studio.

In the industrial context of the early twenty-first century, the disruptions in the music marketplace caused by downloading and file sharing via the Internet make Peterson and Berger's idea of 'turbulence'[14] seem rather quaint:

---

[12] Timothy Warner, *Pop Music: Technology and Creativity: Trevor Horn and the Digital Revolution* (Aldershot: Ashgate, 2003).

[13] A provocative account of how working in a DAW environment can affect even traditional music-making in the recording studio can be found in Eliot Bates, 'Mixing for *Parlak* and Bowing for a *Büyük Ses*: The Aesthetics of Arranged Traditional Music in Turkey', *Ethnomusicology*, vol. 54, no. 1 (2010): 81–105.

[14] Peterson and Berger, 'Cycles in Symbol Production'.

'tumultuous' might be a more accurate term. And, from a technological point of view, the recent proliferation of software based tools for recording, editing, and mixing audio with personal computers is at least as precipitous as the advent of magnetic recording during the post-war period. Indeed, computer and software developers have spread the tools of production more widely than any previous technology, including the cassette-based Portastudios of the 1970s, MIDI during the 1980s, or modular multitracks of the 1990s: in typical fashion, Apple bundles its consumer-oriented multitrack recording software programme, 'GarageBand', free of charge with the sale of its computers, thus promoting multitrack recording as a form of common practice. More importantly, hardware/software developers, such as Steinberg (developers of Cubase and Nuendo) and Digidesign (ProTools), increasingly design consumer and professional versions of their audio products with similar feature sets: the sheer power of these technologies has largely fulfilled the dream of a professional quality home recording that earlier technologies, in varying degrees, only promised; in this sense, the distinction between what can be considered a 'professional' or 'commercial' project studio and simply a 'personal' or 'home' studio has become increasingly difficult to make.

Turbulence, new technologies and economies of scale are certainly not the only factors that challenge older models of the recording studio. But while there has been a clear tendency toward smaller and smaller recording facilities, larger studio complexes found in major cities have in fact sought to embody many of the characteristics of the various models described here: typically, larger facilities consist of multiple studios, some with spacious 'live' rooms and large format mixing consoles for the purpose of acoustic recording, and other, smaller, project-sized rooms and editing suites for recordings with more modest demands. The sequence of events outlined above is not, in this sense, a history of 'progress' in studio design: one studio configuration does not simply supplant the other, but rather, each phase in the development of the studio represents different moments in the accumulation of various concepts, practices and sensibilities related to audio production, each of which can coexist to some degree (although, aesthetic, technical and economic conditions may lead to some studio configurations becoming dominant at any given time). It is the assumption of this coexistence that underscores the second half of this essay.

Is it Really 'the End of the World'?

To return to the idea that recording studios are quickly disappearing at the beginning of the twenty-first century, it is important to recognize that recent studio closures are far from a uniquely New York phenomenon: for example, a 2006 issue of the *San Fernando Valley Business Journal* outlined a number of conversions of former commercial studios and post-production facilities to private status in the San Fernando and North Hollywood areas, as well as several out and out closures, buyouts, and bankruptcies.[15] Stories like these have helped fuel the general feeling among many producers and engineers that the recording studio is an endangered species.

Despite the apparent widespread character of these events, however, it might come as a surprise that the number of commercial studios appears to have actually grown in recent years although, as discussed above, their size and configuration has no doubt changed significantly. According to census data collected in the US over the past decade, the number of commercial studios grew to almost 1500 in the year 2002: that number represented an increase of approximately 18 per cent over the previous period (ending in 1997); the number of people involved in sound recording also grew although at a somewhat lower rate (about 12 per cent). What is more striking is that the gross income for recording studios rose during the same five-year period by about 28.5 per cent, and the amount paid to studio employees on payroll rose by as much as 47.5 per cent.[16] This data would seem to suggest that recording studios were not only alive and well at the turn of the twenty-first century – at precisely the moment when the record industry was beginning to feel the first effects of Internet file sharing – but that they were also relatively profitable as well.

More recent census figures suggest that this trend has continued but at growth rates that are more uneven than during the previous period: the number of recording studios in the US had risen to almost 1700 by the end of 2007 (an increase of over 13 per cent) but the increase in the number of individuals employed by studios slowed considerably (amounting to an increase of only a little over 3 per cent). Surprisingly, overall revenues were again up more than 28 per cent over the previous period, while payroll increased by a somewhat more modest 22 per cent.

How one is to interpret these figures is not entirely clear: it would be nice to think that many studios are indeed doing quite well and that engineers and other studio employees make more money than ever before. But I suspect that a more likely explanation is that with the proliferation of ever smaller studios – among them, so-called 'project studios' described above – an increasing amount of the money generated goes to studio proprietors (who are often, in the case of smaller studios, also the house producer and engineer) and less to payroll for support staff and contract engineers.

It should also be noted that about one third of the total number of studios surveyed are located in New York and in California; however, those two states account for almost 60 per cent of total studio revenue. This leaves over 1000 studios spread out all over the US competing for only 40 per cent of the marketplace and this may make them even more vulnerable than studios in the larger metropolitan areas.[17]

---

[15]   M.R. Madler, 'Recording Studios Growing Silent: Closures Hit Industry', *San Fernando Valley Business Journal* (23 October 2006).

[16]   US Census Bureau, *Economic Census 2002: NAICS 51224, Sound Recording Industries: 2002* (Washington: US Department of Commerce, November 2004).

[17]   Secondary areas of recording studio concentration include Tennessee and Florida, traditional homes to Country (Nashville) and Latin (Miami) music production, respectively;

Some of these interpretations are borne out in Canada, where industry data allows one to paint a more detailed picture of changes in the size and configuration of studios over time.[18] As in the US, the number of commercial studios is unevenly distributed, with the highest concentration in Ontario, followed by Québec and British Columbia. In 1983, at the end of the heyday of the analogue multitrack studio, over 40 per cent of studios tended to be large and well equipped: during this period, it was relatively easy to judge the size of studios by track count, number of rooms, the presence of large-format Neve consoles and the like; for my purposes, 24-, 32-, and 48-track studios constituted the 'large' category, 16-track the 'mid-size', and 4- and 8-track the 'small' category. Overall, the number of large, commercial studios remained relatively stable throughout the 1980s and even rose to as high as 55 per cent in British Columbia, which I attribute to its growing importance as a centre of film production, Canada's so-called 'Hollywood North'. During the 1980s, the number of mid-size studios varied somewhat, ranging from 20 to 30 per cent of the total, and small studios, some 20 per cent overall.

The picture becomes complicated by the 1990s, and even more so after the turn of the century, as digital technology comes to the fore: during this period, track count becomes a very unreliable indicator of the size and professional character of most facilities. For example, in 2007 (the last year for which comparable data exists) virtually every studio seemed to offer some form of ProTools compatibility and it was not uncommon for some studios to claim track counts from 192 to 256 tracks – all of which could be had for as little as $35 an hour at some facilities: clearly, the upper theoretical limits of virtual track capacity is no way to judge the size or character of a studio. But other indicators, such as the presence of SSL vs Mackie mixing consoles, or vintage EQ, microphone preamps and other kinds of specialized equipment, when taken together do suggest significantly different levels of investment and can be used for the purposes of comparison.

What became clear in the Canadian context is that while there is a continuous increase in the total number of studios claiming commercial status (as much as a 20 per cent increase during the decade between 1997 and 2007), there is a precipitous drop in the number of large studios during the same period. During the early 1990s the number of large studios had already begun to drop, to about 24 per cent of the total, while mid-size studios – what one might now refer to as 'project studios' – reached a figure of about 28 per cent, and small studios rose to about 25 per cent of the total: thus, there would appear to have been an almost even distribution of studios across all types and sizes at the beginning of the 1990s. During the decade between 1997 and 2007, however, large studios experienced

---

when these areas are taken into account, the remaining portion of revenue spread out over the rest of the continental US is indeed small.

[18]   The data cited here was gleaned from a series of industry directories that have been published irregularly over the past several decades: *Music Directory Canada* (Toronto: CM Books); several editions of the directory, spanning the period between 1983 and 2007, were consulted.

an even sharper decline, falling to as low as perhaps 10 per cent of the total, while mid-size and small studios rose to a combined total of almost 75 per cent.[19]

The decline in the overall importance of large recording studio facilities and the rise of smaller operations is complemented and, in some cases reinforced, I think, by the changing role of the studio during the past two to three decades. During the 1980s, many larger studios were able to maintain themselves by branching out into a wider range of services, in particular, video editing and post-production audio. As post-production services became more specialized, however, competition in this field became more pronounced; meanwhile, project studios, small commercial studios, and home studios (which do not even figure into the survey data) became more numerous and took over much of the music recording and mixing that was once the mainstay of the larger studios.

With the rise of the Internet as a medium of both commerce and communication, the role of the recording studio is changing once again. For example, the distribution and sharing of the music recording process – where much of the initial tracking and overdubbing is done in smaller studios (and, in a many instances, home studios) and only taken to more professional facilities later for processing and mixing – had already become prevalent during the 1990s; in the age of the Internet, where it has become commonplace to send digital files across the globe, this process is extended and many studios find themselves participating in recording projects involving three or more independent studios based in remote locations. Some studios, such as Net Post Production (netpostproduction.com) in Montréal, for example, even advertise themselves as exclusively Internet-based operations, managing their services primarily via high speed file transfer over the Internet; Net Post Production studios include various Foley and music recording facilities for in-house use but the assumption is that all client services are essentially conducted at a distance.

While this level of long-distance collaboration might be more common in the world of film and video post-production, one might want to ask how the 'art of record production' changes in circumstances where a similar degree of long-distance collaboration now occurs in the production of music: how can any one individual put his or her characteristic sonic stamp on a project that only passes through their hands for a brief period of time? Despite such concerns, producers, engineers and even session musicians are increasingly looking for ways to offer their services online. Web sites such as eSession[20] have been proposed as management-style forums for putting recording artists together with various professionals, from songwriters to producers. Based on earlier technologies such as the 'Rocket Network', eSession also offers ways for its clients to collaborate

---

[19] Figures do not add up to 100 per cent because of the difficulty in assessing the size and character of some of the studios based on the information provided.

[20] The online eSession service ceased operations in early 2012, shortly before publication of this volume, and the esession.com website is no longer functional; however, similar services are offered at other sites, such as StudioPros, (studiopros.com).

over the Internet in real time. But perhaps the most unique part of eSession is the way in which it attempts to maintain a kind of exclusivity, providing guarantees that the clients it represents have a certain minimum number of album credits on their resumes.[21] It is not clear whether Internet-based collaboration of this kind will lead artists to seek out well-known producers, engineers and session musicians with whom, prior to the Internet, they may have had only limited access, in this way, further reinforcing the concentration of knowledge and expertise in particular geographical centres, or whether it will offer new opportunities to previously unknown producers and musicians.

This collaborative dimension, at the studio level, is also characteristic of a new and potentially broad-based kind of music making that is coming into being on the Internet: the prevalence of PC-based music production has already given rise to a variety of remix sites where musicians share files, compete and discuss each other's mixes. Well-known artists (Nine Inch Nails, Radiohead, Barenaked Ladies, and Sarah McLaughlin, among them) have posted multitrack stems on websites inviting remixers to use the raw tracks, as they will. The artist's mix becomes just one version of the music and the 'art of record production' is shared with the consumer. In such a context, online collaboration invites us to think of the studio and the Internet as an integrated network of technologies and relationships, where fragments of music flow through a series of multivalent exchanges only coming to completion when, and if, the participants decide to bring the process to an end.

This notion of the studio as a set of social relationships is, of course, not new: we've always known the studio as a place where musicians, producers and engineers come together to create music in a process that is at once social and technological. And in this regard, some of the research I've conducted suggests that there is another part of the studio spectrum – a part that still defines itself in brick and mortar terms – where some small and mid-sized studios align themselves with larger, musician-oriented facilities that include rehearsal space and even instrument instruction, thus embedding themselves within the local communities that they most immediately serve and guaranteeing themselves a degree of financial stability.

Another aspect of the social relationships within the studio that has changed over the years is the system of apprenticeship that has been the traditional mode of entry into the business of engineering and producing records. During the peak of the analogue multitrack studio, every facility had a number of part-time apprentices – 'tape-ops' – whose jobs ranged from the mundane (coiling microphone cables at the end of a session) to the technically skilled (aligning the tape machines). With the arrival of digital recording during the 1990s these jobs virtually disappeared and, to a large degree, formal education programmes in universities and polytechnics have filled the gap left by the lack of apprenticeship placements.

---

[21]   For an account of the Rocket Network and its role in promoting the idea of online collaboration see Théberge, 'The Network Studio'.

Today, for those who cannot afford the cost of college tuition, some engineers in small and mid-sized studios are now opening their doors to interns for a fee, thus generating income during periods when the studio would otherwise be unused. This reversal of the traditional apprenticeship model is even supported by a structured instructional curriculum and a web-based placement service, such as that offered by The Recording Connection, (recordingconnection.com), that helps place students in local studios and offers engineers ready-made pedagogical materials.

Given the mobility inherent in digital technologies, some mid-sized studios also now advertise themselves as offering location recording services. This too may be an increasingly important area of expansion for recording studios that previously did not engage in such activities: indeed, from artist websites, to MySpace, to YouTube and a host of other sites, live performance videos have become a common way for bands to promote their live shows; in this, and a variety of other ways, the Internet has become, ironically, a significant supporter of live performance.

For recording studios, this activity might include everything from doing postproduction work on low budget videos, to major projects such as those undertaken by artists like Tori Amos who, in the fall of 2007, offered a series of live recordings of her 2007 North American tour on iTunes: more than simply a live album featuring the best performances of the tour, the release was billed as an 'exclusive live bootleg series' and included no fewer than 26 albums of material (mostly variations on the same, or similar set lists), one for each of Amos's tour stops in the US and Canada. Elsewhere, I have discussed some of the ways in which the Internet has become integrated with live concerts and touring, serving not only as vehicle of promotion but also as a means of fostering identification, employing temporal means (anticipation and prolongation) as a way of intensifying the relationship of fans to live events.[22] In completely sidestepping the potential risk of producing CDs for such a project, Amos was able to offer digital downloads to her fans that both highlighted and extended their particular experience of the concert performance as an otherwise singular event, taking place at a specific location in time and space. From the standpoint of the recording studio, the job of recording, editing, mixing and preparing 26 shows as separate releases was no doubt enough work to keep several engineers busy in their studios for a considerable period of time.

Conclusion

I want to emphasize that in thinking about the history of the recording studio, we need to pay attention to the varying industrial and technological changes that

---

[22]   Paul Théberge, 'Everyday Fandom: Fan Clubs, Blogging, and the Quotidian Rhythms of the Internet', *Canadian Journal of Communication*, vol. 30, no. 4 (2005): 485–502.

have given rise, over the course of several decades, to a number of different studio configurations – the diverse 'worlds' of the recording studio as we have known them. Furthermore, I would argue that this diversity should not be understood as simply a succession of changes in the nature of the studio and its technologies over time, but rather, as a contemporary fact: in many ways, we are now confronted with as diverse a range of options as at any time in the history of the recording studio. However, the distribution of those options has changed radically during the past decade and, as I have demonstrated above, while the overall number of recording studios may actually be expanding, the status of the large, high-end studio is in question.

This, no doubt, has come as something of a surprise to many in the recording industry. Since the late 1990s, many engineers and producers working at the forefront of the industry occupied themselves with the idea that we were on the cusp of a new era in sound recording: for many among them, breaking out of the constraints of the stereo, 16-bit CD format into a world of surround sound and high-resolution audio was inevitable. In many ways, events such as the 31st International Audio Engineering Society Conference, held in London, UK, in 2007, which was dedicated to the idea of promoting high-resolution audio, from recording to playback, represented the apogee of the notion of audio as electronic signal over sound as acoustic event, described by Emily Thompson as the dominant scientific understanding of sound in the modern age.[23]

However, it is clear that the consumer market during this same period was headed in the opposite direction: the sheer convenience of the MP3 file (itself a product of that same scientific notion of sound as signal) as a storage, distribution and playback format appears to outweigh its inferior sound quality; and with headphones (or ear buds) as the primary delivery system for mobile music listening, the move towards surround mixing in popular music appears to have been put on indefinite hold. So, in the new industrial context of shrinking profits, the imminent demise of the CD as a commodity form, and the triumph of the MP3 file and the Internet as the primary format and medium of music distribution, the demise of many large-scale recording facilities, at a purely economic level, was not surprising at all: as a kind of institutional corollary to the record industry, a recording facility like Sony Music Studios had come to be regarded as an appendage that had lost its *raison d'être*.

But as I have attempted to argue here, there is also something in the logic of the development of the studio and its practices that has contributed to the current plight of the high-end studio: with the increasing emphasis on the use of studio tools as a means of music composition, the status of sound as an acoustic event, to which, in many ways, the architecture of the larger studios still lent itself, has become largely irrelevant. This is not to say that recording sounds, as such, is no longer an important activity in the studio, but rather, as the micro-manipulation of digital audio has become more and more the primary focus of contemporary

---

[23]   Thompson, *Soundscape of Modernity*.

recording practice, it has become increasingly difficult to justify the expense of maintaining large-scale facilities for the purpose of obtaining what is, essentially, only the starting point for a much more lengthy and engaged set of compositional practices.

The rise of the Internet and what has been called, in more general terms, 'digital culture', has posed both challenges and opportunities to contemporary musicians, engineers and producers; indeed, the widespread dissemination of software-based tools for music recording challenge the very idea of who can lay claim to those roles in contemporary culture. In this context, it would appear that some models of studio recording, perhaps especially those associated with the large-scale recording studio of the past, may have only a limited role to play in contemporary music production. But, whether it is out of simple economic necessity, a sense of strategic advantage, or the logic of studio practices themselves, the recent trend towards the adoption of smaller, more flexible and mobile recording facilities, all potentially interconnected via the Internet, may well be the best model of 'the studio' that we presently have for confronting the new economic and cultural realities of music-making at the beginning of the twenty-first century. And in this sense, we may not be witnessing 'the end of the world' for the recording studio, but a new beginning.

Interlude 1
Comments and Commentaries by Industry Professionals and Producers

Phil Harding

Pop music production is often overlooked in the world of academia and is often seen as somewhat irrelevant compared to more 'serious' music such as rock, dance, classical and jazz. How often do you see or hear of 'Abba' being discussed or used as an example for good music production or pop performance by academics? In my view this needs to be reconsidered for more serious discussion at academic conferences such as ARP and during lectures at universities and colleges worldwide.

Pop music production has changed enormously since the 1970s and 1980s. The technology that has been developed since those days means that anyone can make a high-quality recording at home and release it to the public via the Internet in a very short space of time. On the other hand the analogue technologies and techniques of record making from the 1970s are still with us, and inform much of the processes used today. As such, it is important for anyone wishing to enter the game in the twenty-first century to possess the contextual background of the industry as it once was as well as the current possibilities. However, over and above this is the need to understand the skills, attributes and the *being* of the music producer.

Not many people in the music industry would go along with this, but in my view, music is a 'service' industry. And if there is an area or genre of music production where one can almost definitely say that this *service industry* view is true, it is in pop music production – more so now than ever. Quite possibly it has existed since the 1960s, but maybe in the artistically indulgent 1970s, it disappeared for a while when budgets for even pop albums were at their highest ever. Nevertheless, from the 1980s through to the present time, the modern pop producer has largely been a service agent to record companies, artists and managers (albeit a creative agent).

Producing a pop record has, for some time, been like painting a picture, and many pop producers view their work as constructing a large and complex, layered canvas where it is not uncommon for there to be well over a hundred audio tracks to deal with in a mix. The brush strokes applied by the musicians and the producer are never really finished or complete until the producer says so and decides that the painting has reached the original vision that was seen by the producer (and hopefully the artist) at the time of the first instrument being recorded for the piece. More often than not these days, the producer is not one individual, but a production team consisting of anything from 2–4 members. That team will generally consist of one or more musicians, with at least one that is a keyboard player and programmer, able to navigate the current music sequencer packages such as Pro-Tools, Logic or Cubase. There will need to be an engineer, capable of not only being able to operate and edit those same music sequencers, but also with a good knowledge of recording techniques, microphones and most importantly, mixing talent and the ability to 'excite' the room (the artist and other production team members) with a good working balance and ultimately a final mix balance that completes 'the picture' that everyone has been working towards. Finally, there will need to be a 'team leader' – an entrepreneur with good organizational skills, good administration skills, excellent communication skills and, most importantly of all, the ability to make the projects run smoothly from start to finish. That includes taking the pressure applied by the client (generally the record label or artist manager) away from the creative members of the team, so that they can concentrate on the music only (that is, this person needs to be an excellent diplomat).

Increasingly, pop production is done remotely, with producers and musicians not in the same room and working via the Internet, swapping files and ideas via email and large file download sites such as YouSendIt.com. Generally, the producer will begin by sending out files of a basic backing track, with guide vocals, to a set of session musicians – keyboardist, guitarist, bass player, drummer, and so on. Then all of those musicians will need to have their own 'home studio' set-up, where they can perform and record, in their own time, the required overdubs that the producer has asked for, plus any other ideas they wish to present to the producer for consideration.

It is of course entirely possible that one person can attain all of these skills and abilities and be able to produce a superb and successful record, but these individuals are quite rare in the twenty-first century. I don't believe that one person should seek to master all of these skills and abilities – much better to excel at one or two and leave the other jobs to partners or team members. Often a good producer manager can take the role of the 'diplomat' described above. So there it is – the rather strange analogy that pop production is akin to painting by numbers and the person in charge is the producer (or production team).

Bob Olhsson

In my opinion Albin Zak (Chapter 4 this volume) concentrates too much on journalistic notions of high fidelity and ignores some of the logistical and practical changes affecting music and production at the time. The movement of popular music away from the swing era was inevitable with the decline of the venues where it was played and part of the musical movement that Zak describes relates to the economic necessity for smaller bands. Gene Lees, the

Canadian music critic and lyricist, made the excellent point that amusement park dance pavilions had been the bread and butter venues for big bands. The parks in the US went away when the public transit systems that had built them were absorbed and scrapped by the oil companies, bus and tire manufacturers right after WWII. Far fewer venues meant much greater travel times and expenses that most bands simply couldn't afford. It also meant an end to the music being exposed to young people.

The change in technology style probably had far more to do with the expiration of patents in the late '40s that independent labels couldn't afford and the rise of playing records on the radio as the stations began devoting most of their attention to television. Tom Dowd told me this and it makes perfect sense. (The use of echo greatly enhanced one's apparent volume on AM radio.) The introduction of magnetic tape recording meant one was no longer tied to the constraints of the disk lathe and the need for wax masters. Overdubbing had been reasonably common beginning in the acoustic era but was considered a crutch that one never discussed in public.

Steve Savage

As a practitioner who has also become immersed in the academics of record production there is little doubt where I stand in regard to the value of the larger project in evidence here. At the same time, much of my work as an academician has been to counter certain academic characterizations of the record-making process as the enemy of music.

My modest contribution here is to note a development in the San Francisco Bay Area that might serve as a kind of addendum to the Paul Théberge piece: 'The End of the World as We Know It: The Changing Role of the Studio in the Age of the Internet' (Chapter 6 this volume). Théberge correctly points out that 'as the micro-manipulation of digital audio has become more and more the primary focus of contemporary recording practice, it has become increasingly difficult to justify the expense of maintaining large-scale facilities for the purpose of obtaining what is, essentially, only the starting point for a much more lengthy and engaged set of compositional practices'. We have witnessed the closing of several large-scale facilities here, but we have recently seen the opening of two new such facilities.

While the success of these ventures is still very much in question it is of interest to note an element that may be key to their survival. At the heart of the above quote from Théberge is the issue of expense. Significant budgets for music production are required to support high-end studios. While these have certainly dried up for traditional audio projects, where they have seen explosive growth is in the production of music for video games. Music budgets for some big video game titles can approach $500,000. The Bay Area is a centre for video game production and most of the companies have their own recording facilities

– often the equivalent of many project studios housed together. Though the bulk of the production will be handled in-house – along the lines Théberge outlines as the new models for audio production – budgets now allow for the recording of orchestral and other complex recording elements at large-scale studio facilities. Audio recording for video games has become a significant factor in the capability for high-end studios to survive here the Bay Area.

As Théberge suggests, the tidy theory of techno-evolution doesn't hold up: television didn't replace radio, the Kindle and the iPad are not going to replace books, and the project studio is not going to replace the large-scale studio. On the other hand, from the synthesizer to the sampler to the DAW there are fundamentally new ways of producing recorded music. The project studio and the Internet are dramatically changing the studio business. While the new paradigms of production are working in favour of the smaller studio/Internet model, they are not completely marginalizing the high-end studio. For the time being at least, large-scale studios still serve some of the rapidly evolving needs of music production.

Paul D. Miller

Simon Zagorski-Thomas: *What use do you think the academic study of record production serves?*

History, for most of the last several centuries, has been about looking at how life has been documented. We all know that. But the way we recall the past is radically changed with digital media technology. Writing history, more than it ever has before, becomes a kind of editing process.

Simon Zagorski-Thomas: *There's a general focus in the chapters in this section on 'historical' examples from 1900 to the 1980s. Do you think that we're 'too close' to contemporary music to study it effectively and usefully?*

Marshall Mcluhan wrote about 'simultaneity' and 'synchronicity' in his 'Global Village' book. But the way we listen to and experience media these days is more immersive and non-linear than he could have ever imagined. Music is a shock absorber for this kind of process: it's not just *in* the rear view mirror: it *is* the rear view mirror! So no, I think contemporary music needs more study than ever.

Jerry Boys

Simon Zagorski-Thomas: *Do you think it's useful for people at universities to be studying the history and musicology of record production as well as how to do it?*

I wouldn't say it should be the major part of a course but it is interesting and important for younger people to know a bit about the history of music: about what came before and how it all came to where we are today. My generation are starting to leave this mortal coil and if it's not written down and recorded now, there won't be people with first-hand experience of all these things, like The Beatles, to tap into. I think music is always born from its history and the great innovators all know about that history, Even The Beatles' influences were Chuck Berry and rock and roll and all those sorts of things and without that they wouldn't have happened. I think it's important – but what do students think?

I've always been interested in how people did it before me. And I was lucky, when I first started at Abbey Road, there were still people there who started in the era of direct to disc and I remember having conversations with them about how the process had moved on to where it was as that time.

Obviously if you're not deeply involved in wanting to know in an academic musicologist sort of way, you want to learn it in an easier to assimilate way I guess. Even modern dance music has a history – it came out of various things. And it doesn't do them any harm to know these things. I think it's one of those things that, at the time when you're young, you think well I'm not that interested but later on you remember some of it – one day you're sitting in a studio and think – 'Oh I remember. That's what they meant' – and it starts you off down another road. Maybe students wouldn't want to spend too much time on it but I think they should be aware about the history of the technology of recording. In my limited experience, when I've come to colleges to give talks, everyone wants to ask about how they did it in the past.

Richard James Burgess

Simon Zagorski-Thomas: *How can understanding the history of production help us to develop its future?*

To understand the history of production is to expand the methodologies available to producers and to trace paths from the past that may lead into the future. There are now more than one hundred years of production techniques and practices that can be utilized. The producer's role and production techniques have largely been limited and driven by the technologies of the time. Moreover, the extensive range of studio technologies available today have developed out of the producer's desire to be liberated from the limitations of contemporary electronic and acoustic equipment and knowledge. As in any area of science, combining old methodologies with fresh understandings and capabilities can produce exciting new results. An example is the massively increased flexibility when recording an ensemble in the studio, which was the only way recordings could be made at the start of the twentieth century. Nowadays, musicians playing together can communicate and perform better thanks to advances in acoustic treatments, isolation techniques, personal headphone monitor systems and improved visual contact via advanced studio design and/or closed circuit TV systems. Superior microphones, preamps, equalizers, compressors and so on, and an appreciation of how the best of the old equipment can be used, produce a better sonic result. Instruments and vocals can be recorded almost noiselessly and losslessly to unlimited tracks with near limitless capability for non-destructive rearrangement and the repair of mistakes, as well as maximal flexibility for optimization in mix mode. Understanding production history enables us to choose the most advantageous musical, technical, creative, business, administrative and interpersonal methods for the project at hand.

PART II
Theoretical Approaches

Chapter 7
Beyond a Musicology of Production

Allan Moore

The production of recordings is a field of study in its own right. The practice of making recordings is understood, and repeatedly addressed;[1] the quality of production decisions is also addressed in various ways[2] and technological developments thereby considered. The aesthetics of production have a very obvious voice, in that productions are valued (or not) by virtue of the fact of being heard, but they seem to have no evaluative voice, other than through discussion of the normative practices associated with particular genres,[3] practices which are frequently taken for granted[4] and can be (but are not necessarily) based on technological limitations. None of these areas of study would qualify as musicology, however, for musicology addresses musical decisions which have been, or can be, made, and the consequences of such decisions within one or another frame of reference. A musicology of production, then, would need to address the musical consequences of production decisions, or the consequences attendant on the shifting relationship between production decisions and the decisions of musicians about their performative practice. Production decisions are made principally by producers (who may also be the musicians involved in a production), and secondarily by engineers who are responsible for the decisions which mediate what musicians do to what listeners hear. It is with the (musical) results of these decisions that a musicology of production would be concerned.

In this chapter I make use of a methodology formed from the confluence of a number of theoretical positions. The first two relate to the spatial conditions of the stereo field and the players within it. First, the soundbox, which is a heuristic model of the way sound source location works in recordings.[5] The soundbox acts

---

[1] See, for example, William Moylan, *Understanding and Crafting the Mix* (2nd edn, Burlington: Focal Press, 2007).

[2] See, for example, Francis Rumsey, 'Spatial Quality Evaluation for Reproduced Sound: Terminology, Meaning, and a Scene-Based Paradigm', *Journal of the Audio Engineering Society*, vol. 50, no. 9 (2002): 651–66.

[3] See, for example, David Gibson, *The Art of Mixing* (2nd edn, Boston: Course Technology, 2005).

[4] See, for example, Maureen Droney, *Mix Masters: Platinum Engineers Reveal Their Secrets for Success* (Berklee: Berklee Press, 2003).

[5] Allan F. Moore, *Rock: The Primary Text: Developing a Musicology of Rock* (2nd edn, Aldershot: Ashgate, 2002), 120–26; Allan F. Moore and Ruth Dockwray, 'The

as a virtual spatial enclosure for consideration of the location of sound-sources. Location within the soundbox is metaphorically described at any single moment in three-dimensional space: laterality of the stereo image; perceived proximity to a listener; perceived pitch-height of sound-sources. Second, the personic environment, which differentiates the persona evidenced in a recording from the musically coded environment in which that persona is virtually located.[6] This environment is normally articulated through three factors: location of sound-sources within the soundbox; harmonic vocabulary; form and narrative. The persona is normally activated through lyrics and their articulation, a topic that includes aspects of melodic contour. Third, through a reformulation of proxemics,[7] to refer to recorded presences, relations among the listener, persona and personic environment can be theorized. Proxemics describes the distances (social, public, personal, intimate) between individuals-in-interaction, a factor not only of audible distance but (on recordings) of the degree of congruence between a persona and the personic environment. A fourth construct is Philip Tagg's anaphone, which forms part of his semiotic apparatus.[8] Anaphones are musical events, at the level of the phoneme or larger, which act semiotically to iconize aural, visual, and kinetic events in everyday experience. Despite the value of this particular concept, I make little use of semiotics per se, the foundation of this methodology resting on theories of ecological perception (particularly as developed and utilized by Eric Clarke)[9] and embodied cognition (especially concepts of image schemata and conceptual blending.[10]

Establishment of the Virtual Performance Space in Rock', *Twentieth-Century Music*, vol. 5, no. 2 (2009): 63–85; Ruth Dockwray and Allan F. Moore, 'Configuring the Sound-Box, 1965–72', *Popular Music*, vol. 29, no. 2 (2010): 181–97.

[6]   Allan F. Moore, 'The Persona/Environment Relation in Recorded Song', *Music Theory Online*, vol. 11, no. 4 (October 2005).

[7]   Edward T. Hall, *The Hidden Dimension* (London: Bodley Head, 1969), pp. 110–19.

[8]   Philip Tagg, *Introductory Notes to the Semiotics of Music*. [Online]. Available at: http://www.tagg.org/xpdfs/semiotug.pdf, n.d. [accessed: 17 May 2008].

[9]   I argue in Allan F. Moore, 'Interpretation: So What?', in Derek B. Scott (ed.), *Popular Musicology Research Companion* (Aldershot: Ashgate, 2009), pp. 411–25, that with relation to interpretation more generally, a reformulation of iconicity and indexicality by way of ecological perception (see Eric F. Clarke, *Ways of Listening* (New York: Oxford University Press, 2005) has greater explanatory power than that offered by a rigorous semiotics.

[10]   George Lakoff, *Women, Fire, and Dangerous Things* (Chicago: Chicago University Press, 1987); Mark Johnson, *The Body in the Mind* (Chicago: Chicago University Press, 1987); Gilles Fauconnier and Mark Turner, *The Way We Think: Conceptual Blending and the Mind's Hidden Complexities* (New York: Basic Books, 2002), p. 18. This methodology is more fully explored and utilized in Allan F. Moore, '"Where Is Here?": An Issue of Deictic Projection in Recorded Song', *Journal of the Royal Musical Association* vol. 135, no. 1 (2010): 145–82; Allan F. Moore, 'One Way of Feeling: Contextualizing a Hermeneutics of Spatialization', in Stan Hawkins (ed.), *Festschrift for Derek Scott* (Farnham: Ashgate,

I start with a quote from Andy Wallace, who says the following of his studio practice: 'I try to provide things so that upon repeated listening there will be some new things to find that are cool ... something that will continue to augment whatever I'm trying to get out of the mix on further and further subterranean levels.'[11] Wallace clearly envisions listeners who will not only want to differentiate between passive hearing and active listening, but who will want to undertake repeated listening, which implies a similar degree of concentration and attention that one might want to devote to a carefully plotted novel. This 'whatever I'm trying to get out' is, of course, always beyond precise verbalization, but to avoid the attempt is to render our evaluations worthless. To try to put Wallace's practice into words, I take initially two brief examples from the Biffy Clyro album *Puzzle*. Prior to the appearance of the vocals, the opening track ('Living Is A Problem Because Everything Dies') presents the listener with a number of features to keep her/him off balance. First we hear strings, failing to settle on any particular pitch. Then we hear a guitar, with an undifferentiated series of fast low Gs. It is almost impossible not to group these in listening, probably in groups of four, but then the forceful string-based chord (actually just massed Gs) continually upsets any grouping we may have mentally imposed. At 48" a brief interruption seems to have no consequence, and then at 1'25" isolated choral notes appear with a totally different sense of reverberation. All these features combine to create a sense of disorientation, or perhaps meaninglessness, a sense which is increased on the entry of the voice, as the opening line 'Come on baby do you think it's good to feel' is broken after 'you', a strange place for a gap. In this way, we are prepared to conform to the protagonist's despair, encapsulated as it is in the repeated line 'Everywhere I look someone dies, wonder when it's my turn'. Later in the album, on the track 'Love Has A Diameter', ringing guitar dyads are sustained into the chordal backing for the track. This transformation leads to the chorus's power chords, particularly those of the second chorus which, counter-intuitively, crescendo leading up to the beginning of each line of the chorus, and again to the word 'whoaaa'. The function here seems to be simply to increase momentum, and thus strengthen the climax at around 2'25". This may mark a starting point for an investigation, but for communicative value, I would argue that whatever sense we do make, it needs to be on the basis of a range of available information, rather than solely occupying a space in our own mental lives. And I would go further, and argue that the major context for production decisions is the other musical decisions which go into the making of a track. Thus, I believe we should already be moving beyond 'a musicology of production'. While production details are vital, they do not stand outside other musical decisions, a position which can be demonstrated

---

2012), and Allan F. Moore, Patricia Schmidt and Ruth Dockwray, 'A Hermeneutics of Spatialization for Recorded Song', *Twentieth-Century Music*, 6 (2009): 83–114.

[11] Quoted in Albin J. III Zak, *The Poetics of Rock: Cutting Tracks, Making Records* (Berkeley: California University Press, 2001), 156.

by consideration of the Ben Folds Five track 'Don't Change Your Plans For Me', on which Wallace was the mix engineer.

After the rather explosive opening, phatic[12] in function, the opening chord sequence is in A mixolydian[13] with regular harmonic motion, harmonizing four-note downward sequences all of which contain C#. The phrase cadences with a modulatory plagal cadence in C, halving the harmonic motion, and harmonizing a three-note upward sequence exchanging the C# for a C – in terms of harmony and melody, a change of almost maximal degree (see Example 7.1). The expressive nature of the change is as yet unclear; with hindsight it suggests that the song will not follow the course of so many songs (that of simply exploring a given instant) but will explore some notion of change of situation. It is this which renders synoptic views of the song only partial. One review, for example, suggests that the track ' … is an amazing self contradiction in that the song's main character is in love with a woman whom he credits with saving him, but he is unwilling to "move to L.A." to be with her …'.[14] But this 'contradiction' takes place in time – it is an alteration of position on the protagonist's part – and an explanation can be offered for this change. Its truth is clarified by the way that, after a repeat of the opening sequence, the first four chords are again isolated and repeated (separating them off from the cadence) before all six chords round off the verse. A second verse ensues, with a fuller texture; we now hear the full band, the resonance of a medium-sized (perhaps sparsely furnished living-)room, and an increase in piano arpeggiations, which fill out the space which the first verse had left, through its homophonic chordal articulation. The plot at this point has simply introduced a protagonist who, having newly arrived in an unfurnished apartment to be shared with his lover, and clearly devoted to her having encountered her when 'there was nothing left', nonetheless turns and leaves the building, carrying his suitcase, despite the fact that he declares this action 'makes no sense'. Ah, but perhaps it does.

The chorus, which begins from the song's title, declares his inability to move to 'LA' (presumably the location of this apartment), and his determination to follow his heart 'back east' to where the 'leaves are falling'. Harmonically, this chorus offers a variant on the verse but its alterations are significant: alterations to the second and fourth chords move us from A mixolydian to C ionian. As if to acknowledge this 'victory' of the latter, the melody line eschews both C#s and (but for one passing instance) C naturals. So, perhaps this is the change which we could have foreseen? What else is notable at this point? Well, three things at least. Firstly,

---

[12]   That is, its function is simply to maintain the openness of the channel of communication.

[13]   The particular sequence is quite rare: I am aware of only two other songs using it, the Jam's 'Absolute Beginners' and Level 42's 'Something About You', although it has a very close relative in the 'doo-wop progression', which shares all but the third of the four chords. However, I can make no sense of any possible intertextual reference here.

[14]   Anon1:   www.amazon.com/gp/product/B00000IMYT/002-9794229-0633631?v= glance&n=5174 [accessed: 9 June 2009].

Example 7.1   Ben Folds Five: verse vs chorus schematized

the pace of the track has slowed – the 'new' chords (D and C) now last twice as long as those retained. Secondly, the stylistic reference of the material has changed – less power pop than ecclesiastical voice-leading, by which I mean that the root of the chord no longer appears unproblematically in the bass of the texture (as it does with the vast majority of pop music); the bass parallels the melodic movement, far more redolent of J.S. Bach than of Elton John, say (see, again, Example 7.1). And then, thirdly, there is the ambience. Instead of a busy texture – lots of piano figurations – which we might identify with a normal urban location, the space expands. It adds a ghostly touch of echo and the merest hint of a tolling bell, it loses all the trivial foreground movement, and even adds long, held organ chords far in the distance. From an everyday urban space we have moved to a large, empty, cavernous space, private but imposing, the sort of space in which one's voice is immediately hushed (with wonder?), or in which one would pass on information of much more gravity, indicated by both the held organ chords and the ominous bell. And that is exactly what the music signals here – rather than the protagonist's busy monologue, he is addressing his (probably absent) lover in tones of utmost seriousness – he is not going to move in with her, after all, despite the fact that she's 'saved him'. As another review offers, the song 'is an affectingly frank farewell to a relationship that he realizes can never even get started'.[15] But why not?

The music gets going again – the gradual return of the kit to literally illustrate the falling of the leaves (as the drumstick falls onto the head of the drum) is but one of a number of beautiful, subtle touches, and this chorus is followed by a long bridge section. No lyrics here – the music has to do all the work itself, but a reading of this segment is crucial. It begins with a series of wordless, quasi-polyphonic vocal embellishments, reminiscent for naïve listeners of baroque churches, perhaps. These give way after more piano figuration to a repeated flugelhorn phrase, over lush strings, before we re-enter the world of the verse. It

---

[15]   Anon2: www.furia.com/page.cgi?type=twas&id=twas0231 [accessed: 9 June 2009].

is these two details – the vocal passage and the flugel phrase – which are key, as I hear it, to why the protagonist chooses not to move in with his lover.

The stylistic references of this section are clearly not incidental: '"Don't Change Your Plans" pays homage to Burt Bacharach with a muted horn section, inspired by the group's role as representative of the younger generation on the Bacharach TV tribute last year. But the song wears its period clothing to reinforce the mood of emotional numbness, with hearty strokes of dated lyricism like the way Folds croons "The leaves are falling back east".'[16] And for another listener, 'A flugelhorn solo evokes Burt Bacharach's Sixties pop romances, but we're no longer in that particular Kansas, where undying love routinely transforms ordinary life into a wonderland.'[17] Bacharach is certainly the understood reference, then, at least as far as the strings and flugelhorn go. And there is little doubt that this was intentional, as Ben Folds himself writes:

> I was writing a much slower song, and it was the chorus. The instrumental part with the flugelhorn was probably the only thing that we were really excited about when we left North Carolina. We'd been playing that together and it sounded finished and tight. There was a lot of editing going on in that song. It took a lot of turns and was a real evolution. There's a total Burt Bacharach rip-off section in it, flugelhorns and the whole thing. I would admit it. It was just a tip of the hat to him.[18]

But all this says nothing about the voices, and it also leaves unmentioned something rather particular about that flugel register, and the way the notes are phrased.

To my ears, both the vocal embellishments and the flugel phrase act as what Philip Tagg calls a genre synecdoche[19] for 1960s Los Angeles. This works by recalling the sound of particular musicians associated with LA, namely Herb Alpert's horn, and the vocal interplay of various voices. The most obvious references are to Howard Kaylan and Mark Volman, aka Flo and Eddie (as on a Turtles track like the chorus of 'Happy Together'), or the voices of the Association (such as the chorus to 'The Time It Is Today' (1968), or the opening of 'Requiem for the Masses' (1967)). And yet that interplay is muted, in comparison to these 1960s voices. The flugel phrase in 'Don't Change Your Plans' is repeated six times, each time exactly – it could as well have been sampled. Although the tone signifies 1960s LA (and specifically Herb Alpert), to my ears, this repetition is stylistically false. Alpert would not have played like that, he would have inflected

[16] Anon3: www.villagevoice.com/music/9918,weisbard,5320,22.html. [accessed: 9 June 2009].

[17] Anon4: www.rollingstone.com/artists/benfolds/albums/album/178578/rid/6212863/?rnd=1140538083125&has-player=true&version=6.0.12.857 [accessed: 9 June 2009].

[18] Anon5: http://www.benfoldsfive.com/thesongs.html [accessed: 9 June 2009].

[19] Philip Tagg, Introductory Notes to the Semiotics of Music. [Online]. Available at: www.tagg.org/xpdfs/semiotug.pdf, 23. [accessed: 9 June 2009].

the articulation subtly (the break in the track 'This Guy's In Love' illustrates this). As I have argued elsewhere,[20] it is not sufficient to note differences which seem to carry significance, it is necessary to try to articulate that significance. What can be made of this observable difference? It suggests to me that the reason the protagonist cannot leave his beloved east is that, in his mind (the lack of lyrics here mark an introspective moment), LA (in what he perceives as its lack of action, its repetitiveness) offers insufficient variety, or something along those lines.

Now, whether this was in the mind of Ben Folds as he conceived the song (it appears unlikely to have been, from what he has written about it), or of Andy Wallace as he searched for that little something which would 'continue to augment' the feeling he was creating, as he set the reverb levels for the chorus, or listened to the tone of the trumpet, is immaterial. What is material, though, is that this interpretation makes sense of something left unsaid in the lyrics, and in its communication, is therefore left open to other listeners to negotiate with, as they wish. I am not declaring what 'the song means' nor even less 'what Ben Folds meant', but I am proposing a plausible interpretation that can be discovered within the sounds, noting that an interpretation is an act of choice (a choice I have inevitably made to hear it this way, however unintentionally), using cues provided by the music.

But I think it is insufficient simply to offer a reading without exploring some aspects of its validity. The research which underpins this chapter (and which I explored at the opening) was largely funded by a recent research council grant,[21] in which we attempted to develop a theoretical underpinning for the aesthetic reach of intimations of space in recordings – crucial to the above understanding of 'Don't Change Your Plans' is the change of ambience from room to cavernous space, matched as it is by density of musical texture. Without an (implicit) recognition of this the seriousness of the protagonist's tone in the chorus would be missed. At the root of this underpinning is the interpretive aesthetic offered by Paul Ricoeur, who argues that the interpretation of a text can, indeed must, engage with neither authorial intention nor the life experiences of its original addressees: 'What is indeed to be understood … is the meaning of the text itself, conceived in a dynamic way as the direction of thought opened up by the text … the disclosure of a possible way of doing things, which is the genuine referential power of the text ….'[22] While the project's theoretical position is somewhat eclectic, it is based on a realist, embodied aesthetic, as evidenced in my discussion of 'Don't Change

---

[20]   A.F. Moore, 'The Act You've Known for All These Years: A Re-Encounter with *Sgt. Pepper*', in Olivier Julien (ed.), *Sgt. Pepper and the Beatles: It Was Forty Years Ago Today* (Aldershot: Ashgate, 2008), pp. 139–45, at 142–4.

[21]   The meanings of spatialization, funded by the UK Arts and Humanities Research Council, University of Surrey, 2008–2009, undertaken with my colleagues Patricia Schmidt and Ruth Dockwray.

[22]   Paul Ricoeur, *Interpretation Theory: Discourse and the Surplus of Meaning* (Forth Worth: Texas Christian University Press, 1976), p. 92.

Your Plans'. The discussion of Annie Lennox's 1992 track 'Walking on Broken Glass', which follows, is based on that theoretical position.

Example 7.2 outlines the two-bar groove which is so definitional of the track. Note first the timbre of the opening keyboard. It has a hard-edged, crisp quality, which is intensified by its being doubled at the octave (and with a prominent harmonic a further octave higher). It seems unproblematic to describe the crispness of this timbre as a sonic anaphone, reminiscent of the crispness of the sound of shattering glass. It is not an exact reproduction of the sound, of course, but is a musically coherent representation of that sound's key quality. The force of this representation can be gauged by imagining the same notes and rhythms, but the sound of a trumpet, perhaps, a clarinet or a bassoon. The trumpet would embody the hardness of attack; the clarinet would completely fail in this regard; the bassoon would be too deep in pitch. The actual sound chosen is possibly the best representation one could get from a sound-source with a precise pitch (unlike the actual sound of shattering glass). Note secondly the string portion of the groove. Because the attack is so precise across this timbre, I suspect it is a synthesizer patch rather than actual strings, but the difference is not material to my argument – I shall continue to identify them simply as 'strings'. The most obvious feature of these two lines, those of the keyboard and the strings, is the nature of their interlocking. After an opening in which they threaten to work across each other (both the strings' first two rests are masked by the keyboard line), they coincide on no less than four successive offbeats. The precision of this coinciding, while easy to achieve through quantizing, is nonetheless striking because it avoids the obvious downbeats. It is as if the two dare not get out of alignment until the end of the second bar. Even if one has not experienced the sensation, it is easy to creatively imagine walking across a floor, reaching broken glass, treading very carefully so as not to injure oneself, and then reaching the other side and walking normally again; and if one is at all familiar with the exaggerated steps of tiptoeing Toms and Jerrys, then the imagination requires little creativity.[23] That process seems to

Example 7.2   Annie Lennox: 'Walking on Broken Glass', bars 1–4

---

[23]   My thanks to Simon Zagorski-Thomas for this acute observation. I suspect cross-domain mapping accounts also for the presence of such features in cartoon music of all sorts.

me to be rendered into music by these two bars: what is represented needs to be contextualized, as this is by the song's title, which Lennox announces immediately after we have heard these four bars, but once this is done, the potential link in the listener's mind is made. On two counts, then we have a potential experience from everyday life (the sound of breaking glass, and the experience of walking across it) rendered into music.

Having made such associations, accounts normally leave it at that, and move on. But I think we should not be so hasty. What is it that permits us to make such analogies? We take them for granted in respect of language – that is, after all, primarily what language is for, as a communicative medium. Music, however, is not universally recognized as such a medium, and so we need some additional evidence to enable us to make such a link. Such evidence, it seems, is found within embodied cognition, and specifically in the concept of cross-domain mapping. 'Cross-domain mapping is a process through which we structure our understanding of one domain (which is typically unfamiliar or abstract) in terms of another (which is most often familiar and concrete.'[24] Zbikowski illustrates the concept by suggesting we understand electrical conductance through a hydraulic model – we talk of electricity flowing, for example. In this case, I argue that two specific aspects of the music at this point (the timbre of the keyboard and the delicate avoidance of downbeats in both sound-sources) are telling us how to cognize particular features of our interaction with breaking/broken glass. Such an understanding would seem to me to lie behind all attributions of extra-musical meaning to specifically musical processes, and this is an awareness worth having. A great deal more could be said even about this tiny moment of one particular track, but I restrict myself to just one further comment. At the end of bar 3 of Example 7.2, the two instrumental strands offer alternative harmonic realizations of the underlying I–IV–V process. The keyboard inserts a potential I (giving I–IV–I–V), while the strings are more fussy, perhaps a further illustration of the care one must take walking across such a terrain: their ornamentation gives us a fussier succession: I–IV–I–IV–I–V. the result of these two separate realizations is that on the second half of the third and fourth beats of bar 3, the two strands disagree – we twice have an F against an E, and the fact that neither ever gives way (the two simultaneities are, of course, dissonant, even if the second has a lower level of dissonance) intensifies both the carefulness and the hardness already referred to.

As I noted above, at 8" Annie Lennox's voice enters the track with the title. She repeats the first two words, and then on 'broken', a second Annie can be heard in the distance, and slightly to the right, doubling the line an octave higher (thereby conforming to a pattern already set by the keyboard). At the end of the verse, just as she heads into the repeated refrain (at 54"), a second Annie offers a simplistic contrapuntal ornamentation of the main melody. This device, of vocal self-accompaniment, is so pervasive that it is barely worth mentioning; a

---

[24] Lawrence Zbikowski, *Conceptualizing Music: Cognitive Structure, Theory, and Analysis* (Oxford University Press, 2002), p. 13.

somewhat later track, 'A Thousand Beautiful Things' (2003) is something of a *tour de force* in this respect, particularly from the bridge at 1'45". The ecological perspective which lies at the root of an embodied understanding, however, calls attention to such self-accompaniment: such a thing cannot be experienced in either a natural, or a constructed, environment, outside the presence of such media. And yet, almost as soon as Les Paul began experimenting with double-tracking in the early 1950s, such a presence has become accepted. Explanations have, of course, been offered, particularly in relation to Bakhtinian double-voicing (deconstructing the idea that an individual's subjectivity is embedded in her/his physical voice), but they do not address why their very presence passes uncommented.

Cognitive theory offers a near-relative to cross-domain mapping in conceptual blending, a 'basic mental operation' which Fauconnier and Turner describe as 'an invisible, unconscious activity involved in every aspect of human life'.[25] Conceptual blending takes place when two or more 'input' mental spaces[26] are compressed into a single output 'blended' space, while 'the structure that inputs seem to share is captured in a generic space'.[27] A subordinate category is that of the mirror network, an 'integration network in which all spaces – input, generic, and blended – share an organizing frame'.[28] I am indebted to Fauconnier and Turner for an example which clarifies this.[29] They report an article from the New York Times, noting that the Egyptian miler Hicham el-Guerrouj had broken the world mile record. An illustration showed el-Guerrouj, together with the fastest runners from each of the previous five decades, illustrating the distance behind el-Guerrouj that each would have been had they raced together. To introduce two terms I shall employ below, the illustration is *realist* in that it is possible to experience the sight of runners on a race-track, but does not represent *reality* in that these particular runners could not have appeared together, not least because of their very different ages. The illustration prompts a reader to construct a blended space which takes in many aspects of six individual races (the individual times, the presence of a finishing line, and so on) but does not carry across other features (the actual location of those race-tracks, the identities of the races' other runners, for instance): although the blend 'is immediately intelligible and persuasive', Fauconnier and Turner describe its construction as 'remarkably complicated'.[30] It seems that the unreal realism which we find in Annie Lennox's self-accompaniment is an example of just such a blend. In this sense, the reason we find it unremarkable (although it cannot be experienced without the aid of recorded media) is that we make such blends so

---

[25]   Gilles Fauconnier and Mark Turner, *The Way We Think: Conceptual Blending and the Mind's Hidden Complexities* (New York: Basic Books, 2002), p. 18.

[26]   'Mental spaces are small conceptual packets constructed as we think and talk, for purposes of local understanding and action'. Fauconnier and Turner, *Way We Think*, p. 40.

[27]   Ibid., p. 47.

[28]   Ibid., p. 122.

[29]   Ibid., pp. 123ff.

[30]   Ibid., p. 124.

very frequently in our everyday lives. A more extreme example of the same kind of thing is Jimi Hendrix's 'Purple Haze'. In this track, Hendrix's voice is not central within the mix, but is far off to the right. His guitar, however, appears in the centre of the mix. In comparison to any number of other recordings then the presence created by Hendrix' persona is huge and conceivably dismembered. However, I believe we construct a blended space, our understanding of the recording we actually hear, from a minimum of two input spaces, one of which has Hendrix' voice, in the far right of the soundbox, and the second of which has his guitar, in the centre of the soundbox. Thus we readily create two 'Hendrixes', as we create two or more 'Lennoxes', as we create six race-tracks, and superimpose them in their respective blended spaces.

At 17" into the Lennox track, a drum kit enters. Kick and snare drums are situated in the centre of the stereo field, behind Lennox's voice, with hi-hat and tambourine (elements which largely share a frequency range) at opposite extremes. The offbeat, however, is marked simultaneously by the snare and by a handclap slightly to her right. At 42" we have the entry of a guitar, but now slightly to her left. At 1'38", three cymbal crashes to the extreme right illustrate the sung phrase 'windows smash' (another example of a Taggian sonic anaphone – in such carefully produced work as this, it seems very difficult to avoid these illustrative anaphones), but the first of these subtly echoes on the left. During the bridge section (from 1'58"), a subtle piano arpeggio figuration which is situated to the left gives way to a string arpeggiation which climaxes to the right; the piano repeats but this time is answered by a repeated two-note guitar figuration to the right (*c.*2'10"), and then an electronic perturbation, pulsing at the rate of a semiquaver, moves around the stereo space from side to side, from 2'12". This is simply a description of some of the textural events which can be heard in the track, behind Annie Lennox's central voice. It can be seen (and heard) that there is a concern to match what is happening on one side of the stereo space with something happening on the other side; and this is by no means unusual, as I have noted elsewhere.[31] So what is the import of what is taking place here?

One of the key components of the theoretical position I alluded to above is the notion of the image schema. Mark Johnson's discussion gives a very clear identity to them: 'in order for us to have meaningful, connected experiences that we can comprehend and reason about, there must be a pattern and order to our actions, perceptions, and conceptions. A schema is a recurrent pattern, shape, and regularity in, or of, these ongoing ordering activities. These patterns emerge as meaningful structures for us chiefly at the level of our bodily movements through space, our manipulation of objects, and our perceptual interactions. It is important to recognize the dynamic character of image schemata. I conceive of them as

---

[31] Ruth Dockwray and Allan F. Moore, 'Configuring the Sound-Box, 1965–72', *Popular Music*, vol. 29, no. 2 (2010): 181–97. I chose to write about this track purely because of the opening groove – such details of balancing are ubiquitous.

structures for organizing our experience and comprehension.'[32] This track, as so many others, exemplifies the schema Johnson calls BALANCE. In introducing this, Johnson observes the (standard) metaphorical extension of this schema from the experience we have of bodily balance towards our understanding of such things as 'balanced personalities, balanced views, balanced systems, balanced equations, the balance of power, the balance of justice, and so on'.[33] Our bodily experience of balance comes first, and organizes these subsequent experiences as metaphorically related to this physical balance. It will be noted that the series of balances I have observed above, between left and right, are not symmetries: Johnson is clear symmetry is only a limiting case of balance operating in the visual domain.[34] Perhaps the key idea is that what happens on either side of an axis does not provide equality but equivalence. It is a norm, then, for sound-sources to be balanced in the stereo field, either side of a central axis which is normally occupied by the lead voice, the persona. The question is, why should this be? Johnson encourages us to start from the body. Eric Clarke's work on ecological perception (the other foundational component of our theoretical position) similarly suggests beginning from the observation of the organism in the environment. When hearing a new sound in the environment, we turn our heads toward it, so that the sound-waves set in motion by the sound-source reach both ears simultaneously. Achieving this orientation, we are able to identify the source of the sound (which is to be understood as an environmental invariant, in ecological terms) and thus to determine what action to take. The seeking of balance is thus endemic to our acting as aural beings; rather than have to determine why it should be that we prefer the soundbox to be balanced, it would require determining how we would cope were the soundbox not to be balanced. Indeed, as I have argued elsewhere,[35] we are struck by the strangeness of an orientation which does not operate this way: such an orientation is the marked term of the pair and requires addressing.[36]

So much for these small portions of the song. One thing remains, and for this I return to the opening groove, which so aptly encapsulates the experience Lennox refers to by way of the track's title. Having heard the track, we realize that those elements which remain firmly in place, both in terms of stereo and in terms of their distance from the listener, are Lennox's voice and persona, and the groove which represents the placing of the protagonist's feet on broken glass. Neither has moved from its central position. Or, rather, they have moved but in one dimension only, that of time. And, again, this is what we would expect of our own actions if we

---

[32]   Mark Johnson, *The Body in the Mind: The Bodily Basis of Meaning, Imagination and Reason* (Chicago: Chicago University Press, 1987), p. 29.

[33]   Ibid., p. 87. His discussion of BALANCE can be found on pp. 73–98.

[34]   Ibid., pp. 81–2.

[35]   Ruth Dockwray and Allan F. Moore, 'The Establishment of the Virtual Performance Space in Rock', *Twentieth-Century Music*, vol. 5, no. 2 (2009): 63–85.

[36]   When a hi-hat is panned hard left, for example, this is held to reflect something of the physical layout of a drum kit.

were walking, carefully, on broken glass. No sudden shifts of direction or speed, everything careful, considered and poised.

In promoting a methodology founded on aspects of ecological perception and embodied cognition, and incorporating discussion of the soundbox, of the personic environment, of proxemics and anaphones, this paper has asserted both the existential necessity of interpretation of a cultural artefact, and the necessity of the communication of that interpretation, assertions which I argue elsewhere.[37] Although I have used analysis as the investigative mode through which I make such an interpretation here, and have therefore been at pains to elaborate specific musical details, the positivistic assumption that the significance of musical details lies most importantly in their relation to other musical details is not substantiated here. I have not sought to explore their significance to other experiential domains through semiotics for I believe a stronger explanatory methodology can be found in bodily experience and in ecological perception.[38] And, while production details are compulsory in leading to interpretations of the tracks I have discussed here, they are so only in conjunction with the results of the other musical decisions which were made in their realization. We are, of course, interpretive animals – if we don't interpret[39] our environment we die. This, I believe, is why understanding the activity of using music is so vital, and why we cannot afford a musicology of production any more than we can afford a separately located musicology of the voice, a musicology of timbre or harmony, or a verbology (or whatever). Our interpretive apparatus has to be all-inclusive. As Paul Ricoeur says, in interpreting we 'coincide with ... the disclosure of a possible way of looking at things'.[40]

Discography

Herb Alpert, *The Very Best Of Herb Alpert* (A&M, 1991). 397 165–2.
The Association, *The Association's Greatest Hits* (Warner Bros., 1968). WS 1733.
Biffy Clyro, *Puzzle* (14th floor, 2007). 82564 699763-3.
Ben Folds Five, *The Unauthorized Biography Of Reinhold Messner* (Sony, 1999). BK 69808.
Jimi Hendrix, 'Are You Experienced' (Track, 1967). 612 001.
The Jam, 'Absolute Beginners' (Polydor 1981) POSP 350.
Annie Lennox, *The Annie Lennox Collection* (Sony, 2009). 88697368052.
Level 42, 'Something About You' (Polydor 1985) DJP175.
Turtles, 'Happy Together' on *The Very Best Of The Turtles* (Music Club, 1991). SPEC 85024.

---

[37] 'The Act You've Known for All These Years.'

[38] As I argue in 'Interpretation: So What?'

[39] By 'interpret', I include those pre- and sub-conscious uses we make of *image schemata*, *mental spaces* and *ecological perception*.

[40] Ricoeur, *Interpretation Theory*, p. 92.

Chapter 8

'I'm Not Hearing What You're Hearing': The Conflict and Connection of Headphone Mixes and Multiple Audioscapes

Alan Williams

R. Murray Schafer proposed the term 'soundscape' to encompass and account for the complete aural experience within an environment. In analysing the presence of various sounds and sound sources, he made a distinction between sounds emanating from a 'natural source', and those that were reproduced apart from their original source, as is the case with sound recordings. Schafer labels this sonic experience as 'schizophonia', the separation of sound from sound source, created and replicated at different points in time.[1] Recording practice extends the concept of schizophonia into the experience of the mediated present. In order to make this distinction more clear, I wish to modify Shafer's term to reflect the mediation inherent in the recording process. I posit the term 'audioscape' to address the phenomenon of simultaneous multiple aural experiences that result from the use of microphones, loudspeakers, and their cousin, headphones.

Traditional recording studio environments initiate and exacerbate the audioscape schizophonia. The architecture of the studio is divided into the control room where technicians reside and in which exists one audioscape through the loudspeakers, and the performance space inhabited by the musicians where a separate soundscape is formed.[2] As musicians are separated by baffles and isolation booths, a singular soundscape of the performance space no longer exists, replaced instead by multiple isolated soundscapes. When a musician dons a pair of headphones, the soundscape of the performance space is substituted for an audioscape more akin to that of the control room. Headphones allow musicians to bridge these physical divisions, but in the case of multiple headphone mixes, each isolated audioscape appears autonomous to the musician who inhabits it.

This chapter is part of a larger ethnographic study of recording studio practice. Much of my argument is based upon several years of fieldwork, documenting

---

[1]   Murray R. Schafer, *Soundscape: Our Environment and the Tuning of the World* (New York: Alfred A. Knopf, 1977).

[2]   For more on the control room/performance space divide, see Alan Williams, 'Divide and Conquer: Power, Role Formation and Conflict in Recording Studio Architecture', in *Journal of the Art of Record Production*, vol. 1, no. 1 (2007).

observations and participating in recording sessions in a number of roles –
musician, engineer and producer. In many instances, I sat in on sessions as an
observer, making rough diagrams of the studio layout, transcribing moments of
conversational exchange, following the various methodologies employed during
a session, and noting incidents of conflict. Sometimes tensions were expressed
directly as verbal argument, though more often disagreements were communicated
indirectly through body language, sub-par musical performance, or the *refusal* to
communicate verbally. In other situations, I adopted the role of musician, engineer
or producer. Such participant-observation methodologies can yield fascinating
research data, as experience and practice allow the researcher the opportunity to
analyse one's own thought processes as a means to formulate and test a theoretical
postulate. Later in the chapter, I will examine an incident involving myself as a
session musician that illustrates one form of conflict resulting from headphone use.[3]

The Dislocated Sound: Headphones and the Musician/Instrument Divide

> "When you're in the [open] air, you're not just hearing the music, you're also
> hearing like … some sort of mystical overtones that are flying through the air …
> Headphones put this box on your head." – Peter[4]

Headphones often become the locus of a musician's discomfort in the studio,
and the first instance of dissatisfaction concerns the sound of their instrument as
mediated by technology and technician, compared to the sound of their instrument
in the room, a tale of two audioscapes.

Vocalists appear to suffer the most from the dislocation of sound that headphones
engender. Because sound is produced in their bodies, resonating in the chest cavity
and sinuses, a singer's audioscape is both heard and felt. As with many musical
instruments, certain areas of the frequency spectrum emanate from various parts
of the body – lower frequencies in the chest, middle frequencies in the upper
palette, upper frequencies in the front of the mouth. The full picture cannot be
apprehended without some space for the various frequencies to combine.

The sound of the voice in the room is vital to the singer's ability to control
the parameters of their sound – pitch and amplitude. Headphones interrupt
this constant interaction, often emphasizing the lower frequencies because the

---

[3]   During these sessions, taking field notes was impossible. Instead, I kept "headnotes"
that I wrote in a journal after coming home from the session. Dialogue presented in
full quotation marks (") is taken directly from field notes written during the session in
progress. Dialogue presented in single quotation marks (') is a paraphrase or re-creation
of conversation recalled after the session. Additionally, I have supplemented this research
with interviews, some of which I quote in the body of the chapter, using pseudonyms in
attribution in order to protect their professional careers.

[4]   Author interview, conducted September 2004.

headphone speakers are coupled with the skull further resonating the fundamental at the expense of overtone perception, mystical or not. The timbre of the voice as it exists in the headphone audioscape is greatly modified by the accuracy and placement of the microphone, and any subsequent processing applied in the control room. Equalization can alter the frequency spectrum of the sound. The amplitude of the signal may be electronically modulated by using dynamics signal processing such as compression and limiting.

One might consider that the electronic mediation is responsible for the disbelief with which the recording novice vocalist responds to the sound of the recorded voice – 'That's not how my voice sounds.' While this reaction is partially symptomatic of Schafer's 'schizophonia', the disembodied voice of the recording, it is also a response related to the isolation of one component of the vocalist's sound from another. Vocalists' conception of their sound, their vocal self, is a product of bone conduction coupled with room resonance. Because a microphone does not capture the internal vibrations caused by the act of singing, it only replicates part of the equation. Therefore, to the ears of the vocalist, recorded playback produces the sound of someone else – 'That's not my voice.' But the singer's colleagues in the studio have no trouble identifying the source of the recorded voice because, like a microphone, they have not experienced the bone conduction of the voice – 'What do you mean? It sounds just like you.' Headphones complicate matters because they substitute the sound of the singer's own voice as interpreted by the microphone for the familiar sound of their voice resonating in the room, upsetting the balance between direct conduction and reflected sonic energy. Rather than a case of exchanging one audioscape for another, headphones present vocalists with the simultaneous experience of the divided self.

The inability of a singer to reconcile the disparity between the mediated and unmediated audioscape can lead to performance problems. It is not unusual for singers to sing slightly below pitch when using headphones. A commonly employed solution involves removing one headphone speaker from the ear, so that the vocalist can attenuate their sound based on the familiar interaction with voice and room reflected sound, while simultaneously monitoring the mediated audioscape (and thus all other sound as well) through the headphone speaker still in place on the opposite ear.[5] Musicians who work this way with headphones exert a degree of agency, rejecting an either/or choice of audioscape for a combination of unmediated and mediated, creating a third audioscape which can be further modified by adjusting the proximity of headphone speaker to the ear.

A few professional singers I know attempt to correct the vocal problems associated with headphone use by establishing a comfort level with the simultaneous experience of mediated and unmediated audioscapes through repeated practice. They have set up a microphone, mixer and headphone system in their domestic

---

[5]   John Lennon, finding the unused speaker awkwardly placed behind or in front of his ear, requested a headphone set with a single ear piece for this reason. Mark Lewisohn, *The Beatles Recording Sessions* (New York: Harmony Books, 1988), p. 147.

music-making spaces and rarely practice vocalizing *without* wearing headphones. In time, mediated dissociation becomes naturalized, and their conception of the sonic self is more in accordance with the audioscape they experience when singing under headphones in recording studio conditions.[6]

Other instrumentalists experience similar dislocation, though perhaps to a lesser degree. A distinction can be observed between those instruments whose sound is produced acoustically and those whose sound is mediated by electronic amplification. In the latter instance, the musician's experience of their sound is *always* dislocated, and it is these musicians who are most at ease wearing headphones. The degree of dislocation present in the normal use of an amplified instrument is simply extended by headphone use.

This is not to say that these musicians are not subject to a measure of discomfort at this extended dislocation. Many electric guitarists are frustrated with the lack of amplitude their instrument is afforded relative to the other instruments in their headphone mix, or with the level of overall volume the headphones can generate before distortion. Electric bassists often find that the headphones themselves are incapable of reproducing the lower frequency spectrum that their instruments produce. In such situations, these instrumentalists are more than willing to accept a further physical dislocation from their amplified sound in exchange for their presence in the control room during recording, where the studio monitors can more capably replicate the full frequency spectrum and volume that they are accustomed to in live performance.

The presence of the performer in the control room challenges the recording space/control room divide. This breach is significant in two ways: (1) the presence of musicians in the control room is often at the instigation of the technicians who recognize how the sonic limitations of headphones will constrict musical performance, and (2) the control room audioscape is often modified to accommodate the musician's auditory preferences, that is, the guitar is louder in the control room mix than it would be if the musician remained in the recording room.

Some musicians find headphones provide welcome protection from the sounds made by other instruments. This is most often the case with musicians performing in the same room with the drum kit. The headphones help reduce the amplitude of the sometimes painful volume level of the drums in the open acoustic environment. Even some drummers welcome the dislocation from their instrument that the headphones supply. Many times a producer will ask the drummer to hit the drums with an amount of force that renders a desired sonic character, which can be contained by the mediation of microphone, pre-amp, and dynamics processor in the control room. However, the drummer may find such sounds cross the threshold of comfort. Headphones act as a buffer against this sonic assault on the ears while simultaneously providing a measure of the producer's conception of the instrument's role in the overall audioscape.

---

[6]   This situation has become more commonplace on the concert stage as a number of professional musicians have adopted in-ear headphone monitoring during live performance.

The Bridge as Barrier: Headphones and the Musician/Musician Divide

Though headphones bridge the divide created by physical isolation, they also place musicians in conflict as each struggles to reconcile the disparity between their own idealized audioscapes, and the realities of the mediated headphone audioscape. This situation is most difficult when the number of headphone mixes is limited, forcing musicians to share the same less-than-ideal audioscape, where requests for adjustments in balances must be negotiated between musicians.

In these situations, musicians come up against the limitations of the recording technology particular to the studio they are working in. Seasoned professionals will have a difficult time accepting a choice of limited, shared mixes, when experience in other facilities has given them their own personal mix. The number of available headphone mixes becomes a status marker reflecting the professional standing of the studio among competing facilities.

Another ramification of headphone use concerns verbal communication between musicians. Headphones do provide an avenue of communication, but only for those with verbal access to closely proximate microphones. Engineers and producers have access to these communication channels, as do vocalists. Acoustic instrumentalists can participate in studio dialogue by leaning towards, and speaking into their instrument microphone. But for those most dislocated from their instruments, microphones may not be as accessible. Sometimes a 'talk forward' microphone will be set up in the recording room for the express purpose of establishing a channel of communication for and with these individuals. These microphones can assist in communication with the control room, as long as music is not being made. The relative loudness of music making as compared to the single, spoken voice renders their attempts at communication inaudible over the sound of the ensemble in the control room audioscape, as well as those of the headphone mixes. Many engineers forego the use of a talk forward mic because it requires extra time and work to set it up, and once in operation, will demand constant attention as the engineer must remember to turn the mic off during recording. If the engineer fails to un-mute the mic between takes, or if there is no talk forward at all, the net result is that two individuals standing four feet apart cannot communicate with one another as long as they are wearing headphones. It is not unusual to see a pantomime of gestures indicating that a neighbouring musician should remove their headphones so that a conversation may take place.

Competing Audioscapes: Headphones and the Musician/Music Divide

Just as the limitations imposed by shared headphone mixes can adversely impact the musician's performance, the experience of the control room audioscape during playback may conflict with the experience of the headphone audioscape during performance. What sounds good – prominent, clear, *important* – in the headphones may be buried, murky, irrelevant, through the control room speakers.

A customized audioscape created to better enable the individual's performance can result in a myopic perception of the value of the individual's contributions relative to the whole. Control room playback reasserts the technician's dominance, in effect demonstrating the inconsequentiality of the musician's personal audioscape. This sense of insignificance can permeate every minute of the musician's studio experience, causing a pronounced un-ease and dread of recording sessions, where nothing ever sounds or feels 'right'.

Headphone audioscapes that have been tailored to the musician's specification create illusions that are quickly shattered once the 'real' audioscapes are auditioned. Once convinced of the illusion of their perceptions, these musicians are always standing on shaky ground, every idea second-guessed, every judgement in doubt. Those musicians who become accustomed to competing audioscapes arrive at *détente* only by accepting the subordinate position of their own audioscapes to the only audioscape that counts, the producer's. This acceptance gives approval to the studio hierarchy that governs every effort during the recording process.

"How Can You Hear With Those Things On Your Head?": An Example of Mediated Confusion

I sit down at the B3 facing the wall, while the engineer sets up a few microphones for Trina's voice and banjo. Though my back is to Trina, I am sitting only a few feet away, and can hear her clearly. I can barely hear the Leslie speaker rising up from the basement, through the floor of the studio, and so I rely on my imagination to provide the sound of my musical contribution. While the microphones are being set up, Trina begins to play the song. With the organ essentially inaudible in the room, I play along with Trina while I work out my parts, voice leading, sustained suspensions, etc.

We run through the song twice this way. Trina asks if I'd like to go through it again, or if there's a specific section I'd like to work on. Without making eye contact, I say, "Sure. No particular section, let's just run it again." I am focused on making smooth transitions between chords, sustaining notes wherever possible, while giving enough room to slowly work my way up the keyboard as the song builds. Occasionally, I will quickly repeat a phrase, or try alternative voicings while Trina continues with the song. I assume that she is unaware of the musical puzzles I am working out on my part.

"Are you sure there aren't any chords you need, or any section you'd like to work on?" says Trina, with a trace of irritation creeping into her voice. "No, I'm fine. Just thinking about possible chord voicings." "Are you sure you've got the right chords?" "Yeah, (does she think I'm an idiot?) all set." "Well, let's run it again." The transition into the bridge presents a few options that I haven't decided on. I cycle through that moment several times working out the possibilities while

Trina continues singing. Though she is well into the last verse by this point, it's easy for me to tune her out and mentally replay the bridge transition while I work out the finer nuances of the part.

I'm still doing this when we finish the song, though I'm beginning to settle on one approach that seems to work the best. The engineer has quietly entered the control room and sits patiently at the board. This time when Trina speaks, the exasperation is palpable. "Let me give you the chords to the bridge." "I've got 'em." "Are you sure?" "Yeah, pretty sure (what is up with the fixation on the bridge chords?)." "It goes to A, then F# *major*." "I *know*." "Well let's just try that section again." "Ok …".

We start the bridge and as we move from the first chord to the second, I try out one last voice leading alternative. This time Trina stops singing. "It's F# *major*." I turn around to confront her (that tone of voice isn't called for). It's then that I discover that she is wearing headphones. While my back was turned, the engineer set her up with a headphone mix, and not wanting to disturb the flow of our practice, has quietly placed a set beside me on the bench.

"Can you hear the organ in your phones?" "Yeah." "This whole time?" "For the last few run-throughs." "Oh my God. I had no idea you could hear what I was doing. I was just trying out stuff." As the situation becomes clear to Trina, she lets out a sigh of relief. "Oh, good. I was wondering what your problem was." "Yeah, I noticed." As we both laugh, the engineer asks if we're ready to roll. "Sure, absolutely." The engineer turns to cue up the tape, and I laugh to myself again as I mentally relive the last fifteen minutes. We play the song through, and when we get to the bridge, I swear I hear the trace of a smile in Trina's voice as I finally play the right chords without incident.

In this case, the discrepancy between auditory worlds brought about by one person wearing headphones while the other hears only what is in the room led to an atmosphere of musicians in conflict. The absence of headphones allowed me to assume that my mental musical wanderings were private, that the replays of brief passages in my head while I worked out an organ part were contained in a separate realm from that of the musician I could hear in close physical proximity. Oblivious to the fact that every sound I made was injected directly into another musician's world, I was free to focus my attention on the sounds actually being made in my presence or on the audioscape constructed in my mind. While Trina attempted to make music despite my often illogical accompaniment, her headphones forced an unintended juxtaposition of the 'real' – the sound in her headphones, with the 'imagined' – the sound in my head.

The hermetically sealed auditory experience under headphones made it less easy for Trina to entertain her own 'imagined' audioscapes, precluding the possibility that I was simply working out ideas. The headphones presented a singular experience, presumably shared by all. And that experience strongly implied that I had no idea what I was doing. With each successive run-through, Trina grew increasingly anxious about my abilities. And yet, not wanting to directly confront me, she instead simply proposed more attempts to play the song.

With my back to her, I assumed that each request to play the song was for her benefit, not for my own. Each run-through was a bonus chance to try out alternatives. The only clue that something was amiss was in the increasingly aggressive tone of voice in our brief conversational exchanges. I was unable to determine the cause of her frustration, but since I was feeling secure with my approach and understanding of the music, I attributed this to a frustration with *her* performance, or possibly with an impatience at having to wait for the engineer to finish setting up. Of course, since my back was turned to him as well, I was unaware that he had long completed his tasks, and was patiently waiting for us to finish rehearsing.

Within the established recording procedure, the placement of headphones is part of a sequence of steps towards committing performance to tape. First, there is equipment set up. While this takes place, musicians often loosely rehearse the music they plan to record. As the technical set up phase nears its end, headphones are donned and musicians continue to rehearse, though in a more focused and direct manner. Wearing headphones signifies that the count-down has begun, that soon the tape will roll, and intended performances will be given.

In this session, Trina had proceeded to phase two – the count-down to record, while I was still in phase one – the un-timed warm up. When Trina was singing the second line of the bridge while I continued to replay the transitional bars into the first line, we were not only in two different places in musical time, we were also in two different phases of process time. The realization of the cause of our conflict – the headphone/lack of headphone discrepancy, necessitated that I fast forward to the final phases of the pre-record countdown.

This same moment for Trina required her to rewind and erase the previous 15 minutes. She not only had to wait for me to catch up, and even take a few steps backward to meet me half way, she had to erase any memory of her negative perceptions of my musical worth. This was an impossible task, for while the general problem was cleared up, identified as a misconception, the memory of the experience of the problem remained. Now as we began an actual recording, she experienced multiple audioscapes, real and imagined. When we approached the bridge, she heard both our concurrent music making, and her sound memory of prior attempts at this same point in the song. While I was no longer a deficient musical partner, I had created an unintended performance that continued to exist and resonate for Trina, the combination of anxiety, irony and relief producing a smile as she sang.

The sound of this smile may or may not be perceptible to the listening audience. But should its presence be detected, the cause of this performance moment will be unknown. The presence of an unintended musical moment will remain in the recording like the ripples on the water's surface, long after the stone has sunk to the bottom; the recording preserving the moment as if frozen in ice.

Controlling Practice

Issues of control surround every phase of the recording process, though most are concerned with capturing and manipulating performance. The necessity of headphone use places demands upon all the participants of a recording project, and is most responsible for shaping the various practices employed in capturing a recorded performance. For musicians, headphones demand the surrender of control over their audioscape. For them, a good headphone mix can facilitate a good experience and inspire a good performance. For technicians, a good headphone mix does nothing to change the sound produced in front of the microphone; headphones are a distraction, they take away time and focus and yield no apparent value in the sounds they are attempting to record. And yet, it is the technician's drive to control every sonic component of an ensemble performance that erected the barriers that headphones must now bridge.

The amount of time spent addressing headphone mixes varies greatly from project to project, and from engineer to engineer. Nashville producer Billy Sherrill complained that headphones interrupted the recording process, in his view wasting time by catering to individual needs that don't 'matter':

> In the 60s, earphones suddenly came in like the plague – the first 30 minutes of a session were now taken up by guys asking the engineer to turn them up and turn the drums down. One day, I just blew up and told everyone to take the damned 'phones off. I said, "Trust me, if it sounds good to me, that's all that matters."[7]

None of the producers I spoke with were as blunt as Mr Sherrill, but at many sessions, I witnessed engineers and producers express a mild irritation at the constant request for adjustments to headphone mixes. In many instances, the requests were met with a gently voiced 'Sure, how's that?' over the talkback mic, followed by a less congenial comment once the talkback mic was turned off. Such disingenuous behaviour reflects the degree to which headphone mixes present the potential for volatile eruptions on the part of over-taxed engineers or isolated and manipulated musicians. Engineers who adopt a subservient posture while attending to a musician's headphone needs appear to value the musicians and the difficult conditions that musicians are working in. Voicing concern can placate the musician, even if the engineer does little to actually meet those needs.

---

[7]   Billy Sherrill, quoted in Dan Daley, "Producer Billy Sherrill: Brilliant Career of a Nashville Legend", in *Mix*, vol. 26, no. 8 (July 2002): 68.

"Is It In My Head?": Perception in Doubt

Headphone mix dialectics involve a process of reinforcing or destabilizing the musician's perception of their headphone-supplied audioscape, the validity of which is always in question. For many musicians, the exchange of the unmediated audioscape for the mediated audioscape leaves them permanently disoriented. It is not uncommon to hear a musician request that their instrument be turned up in their mix, only to request the opposite change a minute later – 'I don't know, maybe it was fine before.'

These doubts are not always unfounded. On some occasions I witnessed an engineer move his hands to a send control knob, but not actually make any change. This gesture, only partially observable from the control, was an outright act of deception. The engineer would then ask, 'How's that?' The now hopelessly confused musician would most often reply, 'Yes, that's better', further reinforcing the idea in the engineer's mind that the musician had no idea what they wanted, each request essentially an attempt to control the technician by demanding irrational adjustments. The musician, already disoriented, must now not only consider the question, 'What am I hearing?' but also, 'Am I hearing what I'm being *told* that I'm hearing?' It is no wonder that many musicians become increasingly paranoid and uncomfortable each time they place the headphones over their ears.

Misleading a musician is abhorrent; ignoring them all together is something worse. When a technician lies to a musician, they are at least acknowledging that the musician is part of the process, and that their needs should be addressed, even if it is merely to placate them. More dire circumstances occur when the musician is altogether devalued, their requests falling on deaf ears.

During one particularly memorable session I was involved in as a musician, the singer made several comments early on in the process that there was something wrong with her headphones. At first, the engineer addressed her concern by monitoring in the control room the same signal being sent to her headphones. Judging what he heard to be acceptable, he turned up her microphone in the mix, and moved on to other matters. After several more repeated requests, the singer gave up. After recording several takes, the engineer eventually came into the recording room to set up for an overdub, and happened to pick up the singer's headphones to check in with the control room. Only then did he discover that the phones themselves were malfunctioning, only working intermittently, and then, out of phase. The singer had performed the entire time without being able to clearly hear *anything* – not herself, nor the other musicians. The engineer apologized profusely and found a working set for her to use.

The engineer in question is actually a very kind and considerate man. He had not deliberately set out to put the singer in such a position, but given the list of tasks he had to complete, he had assumed that the singer was being overly particular, as so many before her had been, and knowing from experience that he could never completely satisfy her, he made a cursory attempt to placate her, and moved on. The control over another musician was his to exercise, hers to challenge. If the singer had been in a more elevated position in the hierarchy, a superstar, someone with more experience, or someone financing the session, perhaps she would have insisted on correcting her problem. But alas, this was not the case, and the power inherent in headphone mixes contributed to an atmosphere of anxiety that never completely dissipated, even after correcting the problem.

Power to the People: Personal Headphone Monitoring

Personal headphone monitoring systems alleviate a great deal of tension on both sides of the technician/musician divide. From the engineering side of the glass, initial set up time is minimized – all incoming signals are bussed to 8 or 16 different channels; it is up to the musician to combine and balance these signals at their discretion. Once engineers have completed this routing matrix, they need not worry about headphones again.

Musicians in this scenario exert a newfound agency over their headphone audioscape. The disorientation borne of mediated audioscapes is still present, but is considerably minimized as musicians quietly test their perceptions without disrupting the proceedings. A direct correlation exists between turning a knob or moving a fader and the resulting change in the sonic landscape. In time, musicians begin to trust their own ears. By removing the cause of much tension between musician and engineer, personal headphone monitoring systems enable musicians to trust the engineer. Personal systems also negate the source of conflict between musicians previously forced to share a common, and compromised, audioscape. All are happier in their own little worlds.

It can be argued, however, that removing a primary cause of dialogue, even if such exchanges are problematic, leads to further isolation between all the participants. The reduction of communication across the performance space/ control room physical divide further reinforces the technician/musician social divide. Perhaps less obviously, the ability to control the appearance of other musicians in each personal audioscape minimizes the need to address each musician individually. Rather than negotiate a collective approach to performance, each musician can individually shape and control the overall picture. Instead of asking the guitar player not to hit the downbeat on the verse with so much force, other musicians can simply take the guitar player down, or out, of their mix, in effect removing the presence of the offending player.

Other problems may arise as musicians exercise their headphone monitor-enabled technical control over their own domain. The ability to turn knobs and punch buttons can distract musicians from their primary function of delivering performance. Given the opportunity to mould their headphone audioscapes, many musicians embark on a quest to actualize their idealized audioscape, an endeavour which not only takes away time and focus from their performance duties, but may introduce additional levels of discomfort and frustration as they attempt to reconcile the difference between their idealized audioscape and the one they are able to construct with the personal monitoring system. And just as with the shared headphone mix, potential problems exist from under-mixing important, though unrecognized as such, musical elements. If someone creates a drum-light audioscape, that musician may deliver a performance that is rhythmically out of sync with the rest of the ensemble; if the bass is too quiet, a vocalist having lost a pitch reference may have intonation issues.

The number of discrete audioscapes present during initial recording postpones the conflicts that arise when faced with the problem of accepting a single, meta-audioscape during the mixing stage. Personal headphone systems create an illusory experience of music making, one that exists only 'in the head' of the musician. The preserved or operative audioscape still lies in the hands, ears, and minds of the control room technicians.

Barrier as Bridge: Headphone Connection

Although headphones dissociate musicians from their environment, and many musicians find this disconnect problematic, such dissociation can have the opposite effect. A few musicians I spoke with indicated that headphones provide a hyper-realism that actually brings them closer to their instrument. When close proximity microphones register a level of detail often unnoticed by the performing musician – minute differentiations in finger, pick, or bow manipulation on strings, for example – these musicians respond by further refining their articulations. Other musicians respond to the brilliance of tone, or a quality of 'presence', a heightened perception supplied by electronic mediation. The distance of the ear from sound source itself imparts a measure of dislocation of their instrument from the sonic experience. Some musicians *prefer* the sound of their instrument as mediated by microphone and headphone:

> "I feel like I'm a better musician when I'm wearing headphones. I'm able to hear detail in a way that I miss without them. I can correct subtle flaws. But I think headphones keep me focused, more at the top of my game because if I'm off, the sound is immediately in my head. It's a really positive pressure." – Jackie[8]

When the microphone and headphone revealed previously hidden flaws, this musician grew to appreciate the degree that such hyper-focused monitoring enabled her to correct these issues – making her "a better musician". Other musicians have become somewhat addicted to the mediated audioscape, choosing to practise their instrument in front of a microphone, their ears enclosed under headphones. For them, their 'sound', their musical identity, is only realized via electronic mediation. They have permanently substituted one audioscape for a mediated other.

---

[8]   Correspondence with author, January 2002.

Headphones do not simply provide a connection between musicians and their instruments, they link each musician to the other. In a manner similar to the hyper-realism that connects musician to instrument, so too can headphones bring musicians closer together than unmediated verbal communication and visual cues allow:

> "You're sort of mentally in another dimension through headphones ... You're throwing your ideas out and everyone is responding just in that moment ... It's just like the best thing in the world. It's just an amazing place to be ... Something can change just in a split second. You're processing someone else's ideas, and it's just being thrown around in your head that quickly ... With the headphones on, there's this other connection. You're almost inside this other person's brain in a way." – Tony[9]

Far from an alienated distancing, for this musician, headphone use erodes the singular identifiers of self, melding individual consciousness into a collective one – "inside the other person's brain". This pinnacle of musical experience – "the best thing in the world" – is what draws this musician, a freelance session player, back to the studio time after time. Though he has often made his living as a touring performer, recording sessions have the most potential for a kind of intimate collaboration that can result in a near-ecstatic freedom from self. These examples indicate that for musicians willing to accept headphones as more than just a 'necessary evil', recording practices that at first appear to inhibit performance, may instead provide, perhaps even prescribe, entirely new avenues for the exploration of musical growth and creativity.

Conclusion

The mediated experience of making music in front of microphones and under headphones places musicians outside the sonic landscape of the immediate physical environment. But microphones and headphones also create alternative audioscapes for performers, malleable alternatives to a static, singular experience. Recording studio participants exercise a great measure of agency in shaping and controlling their auditory experience. Of course, just who is allowed to exert this control is a more complicated matter. For much of the twentieth century, that power lay in the domain of the technician. As recording studio practice incorporated headphone use beginning in the 1960s, the engineer's ability to construct the monitoring signal that is sent to musicians in the performance space via headphones reinforced a hierarchy that placed musicians in a subservient position to those who inhabit the control room. Musicians are only allowed to hear what the technicians let them hear. Likewise, the sounds captured and preserved by microphones and

---

[9]   Author interview, conducted December 2000.

recording devices were largely determined in accordance with the technician's idealized audioscape. Musicians were forever at the mercy of technicians who shaped, assessed and approved the definitive audioscape preserved by the recording. Intrusions upon performance practices by obtrusive microphone stands, constricting cables or precarious microphone placement further reduced musicians to the role of 'guinea pigs' in the technicians' sonic experiments.

Over time, technology evolved to better serve the music, and musicians gained a larger measure of control over their studio environment and experience of the recording process. As musicians became familiar with the tools of the trade and the practices that ensue from their usage, they were better able to describe their internal ideal audioscapes and to articulate their demands towards achieving the ideal. After repeated experience with recorded playback, musicians begin to hear through an engineer's ears and, by learning the technological language of the engineer, they begin to re-shape the ideal.

Personal headphone mixes not only reclaim a musician's agency over the technician, but also over their fellow musicians. No longer must everyone in the recording room agree upon a shared audioscape. Instead, personal headphone systems enable the triumph of the individual over the collective whole. The fact that this technological change greatly improves the musician's experience of the recording process is inarguable; whether these mediated/isolated performances lead to a better result is far more questionable. From my initial research, it would appear that technologically imposed division inherently sets up oppositional binaries between recording studio participants. The performance space/control room divide pits musician against technician, and isolation places musicians in conflict with one another, whether physically imposed by baffles and booths, or psychologically imposed in the form of multiple headphone mix audioscapes.

And yet, even as these same technologies are employed in the service of the individual, they represent a collective attempt to create and capture a shared idealized performance. For every instance of clashing ideals caused by multiple mediated perceptions, there are other examples of a collectively experienced and heightened performance that can only be made possible by technology. Every tool may have multiple possible uses, and as many scholars have pointed out, these uses are socially constructed. The social construction of studio practices is evidenced in the ever-shifting roles and experiences of each participant, and while conflicts inevitably arise, my observations indicate that most musicians and technicians operate under the principle of generosity and mutually shared values and goals. The division of space and the mediation of performance sound introduce conflict into the recording process. But most recording participants exert considerable energy towards overcoming or correcting these impediments. Far from a fascistic exercise of power, most technicians make serious efforts to understand the musicians' dilemma, and to accommodate them wherever possible, and musicians demonstrate considerable patience and flexibility as technicians attempt to reconcile the technological demands of the recording process with the delicate atmosphere that surrounds the creative act. The desire for mutual satisfaction is strong, but it is the often unrecognized sources of studio irritation that make the recording process so difficult and unfulfilling for so many participants. For every instance of a collectively experienced and heightened performance that can only be made possible by technology, there are other examples of clashing ideals caused by multiple mediated perceptions. Even when technological practices are employed in the service of the individual, they represent a collective attempt to create and capture a shared idealized performance. Headphones introduce both the potential for expanding tension and conflict, and the possibility of extended intimacy, and are often the locus for the experience of dissatisfaction or the ecstatic collaboration that can result during the recording process.

Chapter 9

The Self-Effacing Producer: Absence Summons Presence

Michael Jarrett

The line sounds like it comes from *Tommy*. It doesn't. Speaking to his followers, John the Baptist says of Jesus: 'He must increase, but I must decrease' (John 3:30). His declaration could function as a motto for record producers, at least until the success of Phil Spector made conspicuous production – the visible producer – a possible, though seldom-exercised, pop-music option. To summon music with presence – music that 'animates the body of the signifier and transforms it into a meaningful expression' – the producer effaces himself.[1] Otherwise, he'll become the artist. Or more precisely, using techniques at his disposal, the self-effacing producer inhibits the emergence of 'the producer' as an animated body – a self or subjectivity who breathes life into sound. The withdrawal of the producer perpetuates what Jacques Derrida famously labelled a 'metaphysics of presence': the emergence of subjectivity in the guise of 'musician'. The self-effacing (or invisible) producer's job, therefore, is not a simple matter of capturing music. What we hear as music is not merely determined by which sounds get recorded and which ones don't. Rather, producers have to work hard to enable and to record sounds that, when listeners hear them, convey the impression of having escaped (better, of not needing to escape) the clutches of production and the constraints of recording technologies. A 'metaphysics of presence', founded on Romantic notions of musicianship, requires no (audible) production.

Producers tend to describe their roles in language more practical than theoretical, even as they proceed from a conceptual understanding of their place in the record-making process. To illustrate and to document, I've assembled an ethnography, featuring a number of producers explaining what they do and how they work. I conducted all of the interviews (most during the mid '90s). For purposes of identification, I've paired producers with representative or notable work: designations for a music track to accompany talking heads. The ethnography is dominated by jazz and country producers. Most of them are self-effacing. They believe the producer who serves best is the least audible or intrusive or noticeable. His vision, his musical personality, is latent – not manifest. All of the producers in this ethnography have well-formed – often well-rehearsed – beliefs, less about

---

[1]   Derrida, quoted in Jonathan Sterne, *The Audible Past: Cultural Origins of Sound Reproduction* (Durham: Duke University Press, 2003), p. 77.

aesthetics, the way music should sound, than about ethics, the proper use of the recording medium. What emerges out of their declarations and descriptions is a coherent ideology of production.

Blake Mevis [George Strait, *Strait from the Heart*]

The theory that I hold most is that a producer should help artists get their music on tape and, really, stay out of the colouring process as much as possible. It's the artist's music that has to be on tape – not the producer's.

Every artist that you do should sound different. If you can accomplish that, then I think, hopefully, you're doing the job of being invisible, yet you're making sure that quality music is there. You know it's impossible to totally stay out of the process because you're in it. If a producer's music starts sounding alike, and he's got five different artists, then he's being too intrusive.

Jerry Wexler [Willie Nelson, *Phases and Stages*]

A documentarian is somebody who goes out, hears or sees a performance, and takes that into the studio, and replicates it. That would be a Leonard Chess, right? He saw Muddy Waters at a bar, and that's what he did. John Hammond was the same kind of producer that I believe myself to be.

What does it mean 'to serve the project'?

Serving the project has to do with whatever the modality is. It can be country, soul, R&B, jazz. It means trying to perceive the essence of the artist and, then, providing him with the most comfortable and fruitful setting to elicit what that essence may be. That has to do with, not only attitude in the control room and the talkback, it has to do with, once you've established the parameters, letting the musicians and the singer, if there is one, bring out the best in themselves. What you do is try to find the studio, the players, the arranger, and the time, the venue that will be most comfortable for them. And if they're interested in your view of their material, to see whatever they may have self-written and try to agree with them, reach an agreement on which will be the most appropriate for a particular session. If they don't have material, then part of my job is to bring them a smorgasbord of songs for them to select from.

In the case of Willie Nelson, you recorded him when his 'essence' was shifting.

I wish I could give you Willie's answers because they'd be better than mine. He says, 'Jerry Wexler listens to my songs and, then, devises the best way to frame them in the studio. And also, after the song is done, to do the best with it – with the mixing and the equalization, the engineering and so on.'

Tony Brown [Wynonna Judd, *Wynonna*]

I was groomed by [Jimmy] Bowen's theory of producing, which is, basically, it's the artist's record. You're there to help the artist. Occasionally, the artist looks to the producer for lots of help. But I find that most of the artists I am drawn to – like [George] Strait, or Vince [Gill], or in the past Lyle [Lovett] or Steve Earle – know what they want, and you sort of become invisible.

Tom Dowd [Derek and the Dominoes, *Layla And Other Assorted Love Songs*]

The most important function that anybody who tries to contribute or encourage jazz artists and jazz performances is not to paint the picture but, rather, capture it. It's like being a sports photographer, instead of a portrait painter. The artist is the impressionist, the artist is the creator, and you are just a damn witness. The minute you start getting in their face with 'why don't you do this or that', it's not a good marriage to my way of thinking.[2]

James Stroud [Clint Black, *Killin' Time*]

There are things you have to do with certain artists to set them up for the creative process. Some artists write their own material, for instance, and have a handle on their direction before you go in and make the record. All you have to do is keep them in between the ditches. You don't want them to crash and burn with something they shouldn't be doing. But there are other situations where you have an artist that may not be a writer. He or she needs to focus on the direction of the music, the type of lyrics, the emotion of the songs. You need to be more involved with song selection and focus on lyric and musical direction. You have to be able to determine when to be a little more forceful with what you need to do with ideas. And you also have to be able to back out, and let the artist follow through with what you start.

---

2 Michael Jarrett, 'Cutting Sides: Jazz Record Producers and Improvisation', in Daniel Fischlin and Ajay Heble (eds), *The Other Side of Nowhere: Jazz, Improvisation, and Communities in Dialogue* (Middletown, CT: Wesleyan UP, 2004), pp. 324–5.

Paul Worley [The Dixie Chicks, *Wide Open Spaces*]

A producer should try to maximize the creativity and the point of view and the musical vision of the artist that they're working with. So in my view the role of the producer is of a facilitator and a translator, someone who communicates the artist's musical vision and direction to the engineers and the musicians and ultimately to the record company involved and tries to give any specific project its own identity.

Blake Chancey [The Dixie Chicks, *Fly*]

Ten years from now, nobody's going to care whether I produced it. They're going to look down and see, 'Oh, there's Darrell Dodd's album, or there's Mary Chapin Carpenter's album, or there's a Dixie Chicks album. I love that record!' So it's my job today to make sure that these artists, where they are today, put that music down on tape the best that they can. Wherever they are in their lives or wherever they're wanting to go, I have to help guide them: help put that down, get the right musicians, get the right engineers, and pull that off.

Tony Brown [*Lyle Lovett*]

The two things that good producers have is the ability to cast the right people, as far as musicians and engineers, not only for their musicianship but in the case of personalities, where they don't conflict with the artist. The other thing is the psychology of how to make those musicians perform for the artist.

Helen Keane [Bill Evans, *Symbiosis*]

Director is the correct term for what most good producers do. A producer in the theater and in films is usually the person who has the money, who raises the finances. In the record business, the producer, when you see that producer credit, if it's the kind of producer I am, it should say director. I'm involved in all aspects of production.

Give me an example of those different aspects.

There's a totally unknown singer called Giacomo Gates, who came to me, was recommended to me, and asked me to produce a master for him. Which I did. This meant going over the material, rehearsing with him, choosing the material, hiring the musicians, choosing the musicians, getting the studio, getting the engineer. By the way, the master's just been sold to DMP, I'm quite happy to say. So that is my role as a producer.

I don't know another woman in jazz who does what you do.

Well, I am virtually alone. That is true. I came to it through Bill Evans. I actually had produced other records, but I hadn't been given credit. I was given consultant credit or something like that, but never full producer credit. With Bill, I was so much a part of his life as his manager, it was just a natural step to have me produce the records.

Blake Mevis [Keith Whitley, *Don't Close Your Eyes*]

The only difference between the movies and, say, a record is that a movie star doesn't have to go out and duplicate his performance again once he's on film. And the musician does. You have to know that you have an artist that is capable of going out in front of an audience and reproducing something similar to what's on tape.

Hal Willner [Various, *Amarcord Nino Rota*]

Joel Dorn taught me to create a framework. You'll get the best performance from artists, if you make them feel a certain way. Sometimes that's even making them uncomfortable, putting them in with people they normally wouldn't be with. You've got to get that performance.

It was really exciting for me to witness and work with Robert Altman on *Shortcuts* because that's the way he works film. His scripts and what he wants provide such a strong foundation that he can let you loosen it: [he works with] people that he trusts. If he hires you, he knows who he is hiring. He knows what you do, and then he lets you loose within that framework. That's why an actor, appreciating that, will give 200 percent.

Tony Brown [Vince Gill, *The Key*]

Vince wanted to do something really country, and I wanted him to do something really country, too. We'd always put a few country tunes on every album, like 'When I Call Your Name' and 'No Future in the Past'. But we wanted to cut something classic. That's why we sort of strayed from using the normal session players and got [pianist] Pig Robbins and Randy Scruggs. We used the same band on every session; we scheduled sessions around those particular musicians.

The only preproduction we did was talking amongst ourselves about how we wanted it to sound.

Like when we cut 'If You Ever Have Forever in Mind', we talked about doing a song that sounded like Ray Charles' *Modern Sounds in Country Music*. I had Bergen [White] listen to 'Born to Lose' and copy that little string bend when he did the chart. When we got ready to cut the track, we talked about it sounding like that stuff. Before we rolled the tape, I looked at Pig, and I said, 'Pig, give me a famous intro' – just joking.

And then, when he played, I was going, 'God, this sounds incredible! It sounds famous'. As soon as he did the intro – you could see it in the room – the rest of the band all clicked back into retro-time. They became Ray Charles' band. A lot of magic moments happened during that album. Plus, when Vince sings in the headphones – some singers don't really sing their songs like they're performing them – but he does. It's inspiring.

A lot of times you'll cut a track, and you'll almost get it. Something will happen, and you'll bring everybody in and say, 'Hey, there's a good sketch here. Listen to the intro. Do that again'. Start telling everybody, 'You did this on the second verse. Do it on the first verse instead of the second'. You start telling them what to do.

But occasionally, you'll just say something like what I said to Pig. They kick it off, and every guitar fill, all the solos, are live. You keep going, 'This thing is going to fall apart any minute. This is not going to be a take.' And then, it is a take. It sounds incredible.

You say, 'Let's do it a couple more times – see if we can beat it.' And you do it two more times. They know that you liked what you heard because, you know, I'm in there screaming. They play it two more times. It sounds really good, but then you go back and listen to the very first time they did it, and it's better than the next two times. They're such great musicians. They actually had something, that little, whatever that thing is. You know what it is when you hear it.

Hal Willner [*Lost in the Stars: The Music of Kurt Weill*]

When I started out, active producers didn't just stick to one kind of music. As a kid, I saw names on records, like John Hammond and Tom Wilson, Joel [Dorn] and all those. Take Tom Wilson. His name was on records by Sun Ra, Cecil Taylor, also Simon and Garfunkel, Dylan, Mothers of Invention, Velvet Underground. And Joel would be on records by Rahsaan [Roland Kirk] and Yusef [Lateef] and the Allman Brothers, Bette Midler. I sort of thought producers were supervisors, responsible for how the record was, which went all the way from taking over and being hands-on to, if need be, leaving it alone. Knowing what the record was supposed to be – what you're going after – and then making sure it's realized. That determines how much hands-on or hands-off it will be ...

At that time many, many producers couldn't even play an F on the piano. Of course, that's changed. Most of the guys now are glorified engineers or glorified something else. They're more in charge, it seems to me, in general these days.

Buddy Killen ['I Believe I'm Gonna Make It!' *The Best of Joe Tex*]

I made a lot of mistakes businesswise, because I was not a businessman. They weren't devastating things, just little decision-making processes that you go through. But I had a feel for the song. I had a feel for the music. I had a feel for if someone was good or not. When you're a publisher or a producer, the most important thing that you can have is an ear for the song. You must recognize a good song …

Search around for the best songs you can get. If your experience doesn't tell you which way to go with a song, and if you have the right song, then that's where you'll fail. I feel that my experience that grew through the years helped me recognize, not only a star or a person who was capable of being a star, but also the song that fit him, the song that would work for him. I argued many times with singers. I'd say, 'I want you to do this song.' They'd say, 'I don't like it. I'm not going to do it.' I'd say, 'Well, why don't you at least try it?' Many times they'd argue, 'Well, I'll sing it, but I'm not going to sing it good.' I'd say, 'Well, you can't sing good anyway.' Kidding with them. But I would force them to do a song, and it turns out to be the biggest song of their career.

Jack Clement [Jerry Lee Lewis: *18 Original Sun Greatest Hits*]

Sam Phillips was in Nashville at a music convention. It was in October. Jerry Lee came in. He'd been to Sun before, and I'd made a little tape with him. Played it for Sam. Sam liked it and everything. And I was right on the verge of calling Jerry. I had his phone number right on the tape.

Before I got around to it, he came back with his cousin, J.W. Brown, who later became his father-in-law. Well, his bass player. So anyway, they came in, and I said, 'I've been meaning to call you.'

When he first came there, he was singing me George Jones songs and stuff. I asked him if he knew any rock 'n' roll.

'No, not really, but I can learn some'.

I said, 'You need to go work up some rock 'n' roll, 'cause country just ain't happening right now.' Now I read where he said that I told him that rock 'n' roll is dead, but that's total bullshit. Why would I say something like that?

The fact is, the people in Nashville were really worried. There was a pall over the Grand Ole Opry and all that stuff. Anyway he came back, and he'd written a song called 'End of the Road'.

I said, 'Okay, that's rockin' enough.' And he had a version of 'You're the Only Star in My Blue Heaven' where he changed it from a waltz to 'You're the only bomp, bomp, bomp'. And I loved that. So I told him, 'Come back Thursday. I'll have a couple of guys in there, and we'll cut some tapes.'

We went into the studio, and the heat went out that day. I had this little electric heater back in the control room. It kept tripping the circuit breaker on everything, and the board would go out. It was kind of chilly in there. But we cut that first record, which turned out to be 'Crazy Arms'.

Did you suggest that tune?

I did. We'd cut 'End of the Road' to start. No, I think we started with 'You're the Only Star in My Blue Heaven'. I just loved that one. It was really good. And then we did 'End of the Road' and maybe something else. Then, toward the end of the thing, I said, 'Do you know "Crazy Arms?"'

He said, 'I know a little of it.'

I said, 'Let's cut it.' So we did. He sort of made up some of the words, but at that time 'Crazy Arms' had been a hit for six months or more. It had been a big hit with the Andrews Sisters – pop. Well, Ray Price to start with and, then, a big pop hit with the Andrews Sisters. Everybody knew the song, but we put it out anyway. And it still sold 150,000 or something. It was a good first record. And it only had two instruments on it: piano and drums.

The bass player was in the bathroom at the time. He comes in on the end. Old Billy Lee Riley was playing bass. He's in the bathroom, and he just thought we were screwing around. He opened the door, walked out there and the song was about to end. He put that little bad chord on the end of it. And it's still there. But there wasn't any guitar on it. It was nothing but piano and drums.

But it has a sound to it. I had put thumb tacks on the piano hammers. Well, that wasn't new. It was a spinet piano, and I got to miking it down underneath, rather than on top. So you didn't really hear that ping very much, but it gave it a sound. That was the sound we used on 'Whole Lotta Shakin' Goin' On' and 'Great Balls of Fire'.

At RCA they had an old upright piano with thumbtacks on it just for that purpose. A lot of studios might have one around. I had to put them in and, sometimes, take them out. They don't help the hammers. I didn't invent that process. What I did is mike it differently. It made it sound almost like a grand piano. On 'Whole Lotta Shakin' Goin' On', you can't hear the ping. You get a definite ping with those thumb tacks, but it didn't record that way. So it was a neat sound.

Sam came in the studio on the following Monday. I said, 'I've got something I want to play you.' So we went back into the control room, and I put on 'Crazy Arms'. Before it ever got to the singing, Sam reaches over, stops the machine, and says, 'Now, I can sell that.' And then he started playing it again. Of course when he got to the voice, he loved it.

We made a lacquer, an acetate disc, right there in the control room, and Sam took it down to Dewey Phillips that night. In the meantime, we sent the tape off to Chicago to have it mastered. We had records by Thursday. But on Monday, Dewey put that thing on, and the phone lines lit up. It was kind of instant. We had records in some of the stores probably by [the next] Monday evening. Now you think that wasn't fun?

Creed Taylor [Stan Getz and João Gilberto]

I had a 45 copy of 'Going Out of My Head' by Little Anthony and the Imperials. I gave it to Wes [Montgomery] one night at the old Half Note down on Hudson Street. He took it home and listened to it, and he nearly flipped out. I had to talk to him. 'It's not the treatment. We're not talking about the treatment, and the fact that it's done by a doo-wop' – or whatever the idiom was called at that time – 'has nothing to do with it. This song's got great changes. It's a well structured composition. Give [arranger] Oliver Nelson a shot at putting this thing together, something you can play on.' That's how that came about.

He was all for it?

Once he got into the studio and started playing, he was beaming from ear to ear. Then that just carried forward to the A&M stuff that happened after Verve. There was no pressure on me. I thought we had the chance with good distribution to make Wes Montgomery popular. Period. I certainly couldn't care less what anybody else thought about it. My business is to make an appealing framework, a setting for the artist and not to say hands-off because he's jazz and that's pure art. Wes couldn't play anything that wasn't appealing anyway. He had to be put into orchestral contexts in order to get the programmer directors' attention at radio, to get him out to people who could not fathom the quartet context.

Orin Keepnews [Thelonious Monk, *Brilliant Corners*]

I've always held that the first time somebody goes into the studio, he's the concept. You're presenting somebody who hasn't been presented before, so it's a nice idea to get in as many different aspects of his artistry as you possibly can. I do, however, think it is reasonably necessary – not always but frequently so – that there be some connective thread, some reason why separate performances are together on the same disc. For the most part, there needs to be a concept. The exceptions to this come about when the artist is enjoying some period of vast popularity, and it becomes possible to just issue the next album by so-and-so: sound the horn and attract crowds of people.

Bob Ferguson [Dolly Parton, *The RCA Years 1967–1986*]

Some artists didn't need much help choosing their material. Dolly [Parton] is like that. Porter [Wagoner] brought her to RCA, and I was producing Porter so I became her producer and their producer. Porter himself would be well prepared for a session when he came: he and the band, when we did use his road band. That's another thing. Some of the artists didn't have that, and a producer would hire the musicians and help formulate the persona that the artist was going to present. But they would get out on the bus – Porter and Dolly – and they would have rehearsed a lot and discussed a lot of things as they traveled during those road dates. So my job with them was to find out what they needed – what role to fill with them.

Dolly wrote good songs. It was just a matter of listening to how she did them and approving the takes, encouraging her and being something of a confidant. Porter has a strong personality, and Dolly would sometimes mention things to me, privately, that she had aspirations to achieve. My role was to urge her to continue her writing, to do some things. As a producer, I didn't have to worry about the songs, the material, or the instrumentation that was brought in. I worried about how we were going to mix songs to make them special.

You know those tape machines with voice-activated, automatic recording controls? I had an idea once of trying to produce a record where the voice would come out when the artist was singing, when they were loud and up close to the mic, and it would knock down the sound of the music. As soon as the artist quit singing, that automatic volume would raise the music's level back up and grab the instruments.

I talked to our engineers at RCA, who were the best, and explained this idea. I got a call one day from Al Pachucci.

'Hey, what are you doing? Come down to the studio.'

I went down, and he said, 'I think I've figured out how we can do what you've been talking about.' It was a production technique whereby we had the same effect on the voice – in this case Dolly's voice – as on the lead instruments. But the rhythm, we wanted to keep that steady. We didn't want the piano, bass and drums going up and down. So they weren't fed through this system. It gave us some very effective sounds.

You remember 'Jolene'? It's probably the best example of that technique. We just got in the studio alone, when Dolly and Porter were on the road one time, and remixed it that way. It was a knockout. I was delighted with it, and I think the public was too. The meter doesn't move ten dBs all the way through the song. When she's singing, that automatically pushes down the lead instruments, and when she quits, it pops them right back up so they're right in there with her but out of the way. It's a tricky technique. You couldn't use it on everything. If you tried to do that when you had a string section or anything, it sounded terrible. But it sounded good on 'Jolene', and I believe we used it on 'Muleskinner Blues'. It's compression, that sort of thing.

Don Cook [The Mavericks, *What A Crying Shame*]

My philosophy is try to work with somebody who you like already and figure out a way to make them sound the best they can with the material that shows them at their best advantage – whether it be theirs or somebody else's. As I sometimes tell people that I work with, sometimes putting the chisel and the hammer down is a more substantial act of production than hitting the statue with the chisel in a place where it doesn't hit.

John Snyder [The Derek Trucks Band]

I have always thought the major role of the producer would be the first audience. An audience is some group of people who reacts in a kind of a pure way. You go there, you are sitting, and you are waiting. Whatever happens is going to affect you in one way or the other. You know yourself, when you go to hear music, you can feel satisfied, or you can feel excited, or you can feel sleepy, or you can feel pissed off, or whatever. The music is going to have an effect on you – even if it is 'ho-hum'. That's an effect. Then the question is, 'Why?' The audience listener may not have to answer that question, may not give a shit. I don't know why this went wrong; it just wasn't right. The producer has to not only have that initial feeling – a very open sort of receptiveness. In the midst of all this political mayhem and chaos in a recording studio, it's not easy. After you hear it and feel it, you have got to be able to express it and, then, even take it further: How do we now change it? How do we make it better? Or that was perfect. Identifying first takes that are right is an acquired ability. I am with producers a lot who are not that experienced. They hear something great, and they think they can get it greater. One of the things you have to learn is when it is right you leave it alone.

Allen Reynolds [Crystal Gayle, *We Must Believe In Magic*]

With a lot of the most successful records I've been involved with, the vocal went down largely the day that it was recorded. Maybe you do a few fixes. But that was true of 'Don't It Make My Brown Eyes Blue'. It was true of 'Where Have You Been?' with Kathy Mattea. It was true of a great many Garth Brooks records.

I tell the artist, before we go to work, 'Don't be in there trying to give me a tracking vocal. I want the vocal. I want you out there flying like everybody else is.' If you can get that moment, it's a discernible difference. It's the thing that's most precious.

That vocal on 'Don't It Make My Brown Eyes Blue' happened the first time we rolled tape. We had run it through maybe two or three times, and the first time we ran tape, we got that record. The only thing I did was add strings later. The only other thing I did was give Crystal time enough to come back and try to re-sing it and see if she could improve it, 'cause she thought she could. Ultimately, we left it alone. Those are the moments that you pray for. And once you've got that moment, you've got to work at messing it up. If you're going to mess it up, you've got to really try. From then on, you can add something and take it off. Add something, and if it works, you keep it. In other words, you can putz around with it, but getting that moment of inspiration is the thing. Once you've got that, you've got a record. You can do many things to it to enhance it and, then, flesh it out. But you can never put that spark in there if it isn't there to start there. And if it is there, you can hardly mess it up. At least that's what I think.

Again, to look at 'Don't It Make My Brown Eyes Blue', that identity lick on the acoustic keyboard? That was the gift of Pig Robbins, Hargus Robbins. When he threw that in, early on, it was like everything gelled. All of a sudden, it just began to fall into place – everything. The drummer was doing this wonderful, real simple work with the brushes. The other keyboard player, Charles Cochran, who later wrote the strings, was playing the Wurlitzer. And if you listen to the record, the Wurlitzer is really playing the horn parts. But I couldn't have planned that lick or conjured it up. That took Pig. When that happened it was like magic. It was like sparks. Everything happened fast after that. That often is the way it is, if you're working with good material to start with.

Esmond Edwards [Eric Dolphy, *Outward Bound*]

With Prestige, primarily we worked on a limited budget. Things were, more or less, done in the studio, no rehearsal as a rule. It was a matter of getting compatible musicians together and, to some extent, giving them a direction in advance. A lot of times things were kind of ad hoc. You get four or five guys in the studio and, 'What are we going to do now?' Bob Weinstock was my mentor because, prior to working for him, I had no experience. I used to go to sessions as a photographer, initially, and watch how he would function. You know like with guys scratching their heads, and you say, 'Okay, let's try such and such a tune. Let's try standard. Let's do a blues.' Blues were kind of a stock in trade. 'Let's do', what Bob would call, 'a funky ballad.' That's the way things more or less went down.

Ken Nelson [Hank Thompson, *Live at the Golden Nugget*]

Buck [Owens] was always well rehearsed. Certain artists, I knew when they walked in the studio with material that it was good for them. Like Merle Haggard, there was no reason for me to sit down and listen to what he was going to bring in. His manager Fuzzy Owen, who was a musician himself, he would work with Merle. They'd come in the studio. They knew what the hell they were doing. Other artists, I would have to suggest songs. They would bring me songs, and I'd say, 'Yes' or 'No', 'I didn't like it', or 'It's not for you' – whatever the case may have been.

Sid Feller [Ray Charles, *Modern Sounds in Country and Western Music*]

I lived in New York at the time. Ray Charles was in California. He called me and said that he was thinking of making a country album. No title was mentioned at that time, but he asked me to gather together the best country-western hits of the last 10 or 15 years. This happened in 1961, a few months before the sessions.

I made calls to all the big country publishers, mostly in Nashville but some of them were in New York. They sent me about 200 or more of their best material on tape as well as sheet music with the lyrics. I weeded through and found 40 of them that seemed great for Ray Charles. I edited all those little tapes they sent me and put it all on one reel. I sent it and copies of the music to him. From that 40, he picked 12 and that became *Modern Sounds in Country and Western Music*. But he picked them himself.

Then he arranged to have Marty Paich make the arrangements out there. So I had no involvement with picking the arranger or with setting up the routines. On that particular session I had no involvement until I came to California and supervised the recording in the studio. Then, I brought the tapes back to New York. He picked the tunes out of the ones that I found for him, and he picked the arranger, and he laid out all the routines.

There was no editing. When we said, 'That's it', that was the end of it. I brought home a master tape. At that time we didn't have mixing. The balances were made right in the studio at the time we made the recording, and that was my job to do. Ray was in the studio singing and playing the piano. He called the shots in there, and I called the shots in the booth.

Tom Dowd [Ornette Coleman, *The Shape of Jazz to Come*]

He'd be there before the date was to start, and he'd say, 'I want to play this for you, or this is what we are trying to do today.' Or he and Don Cherry would be standing there practicing how to make expressions together because the two instruments, the pocket trumpet and the plastic sax, were so dynamically different that you couldn't notate or anything like that. You'd have to play it and say I want it to go like 'WOOOW!'

'Oh you mean like WOOOW?' That's how the dialogue would be established. There are some things you can't write, and you hear.

When it's not the way you want it, you say, 'I didn't mean that. I meant this, or can you do it this way?' That's dialogue. That's something you'd just try and understand. Now, you might listen to their endeavor and say, 'Hey, it's better when you do it the other way.'

They might look at you and say, 'You mean like this?'

You'd say, 'Yeah'.

'Oh, okay. We'll try it'.

You might save time or have something that's tighter or more concerted if you made those kinds of suggestions. When we recorded, we knew what songs we were getting into, and it was just a matter of getting that quick sensation, that rush when something went by that you'd say, 'Damn, if only so-and-so had been more … let's try one more.'

Somebody would look and say, 'Why?'

'Well, man, maybe we can get a better one.' You don't want to say, 'So-and-so screwed up.' You don't do anything as obnoxious as that. You just say, 'Maybe when we get to this part or that part, we should try and do things, and it will be better.'

If somebody said, 'What do you mean?' You'd say, 'Come in and listen to it.' You'd play it, and then let them say, 'Hey you shouldn't have gone on that chord, or you played the wrong *bomp doo doont*.' You take the curse off. But you're also gaining their respect by letting them know you are sensitive that something went wrong.

Esmond Edwards [Ramsey Lewis, *The In Crowd*]

Each artist was different. Eric Dolphy, a case in point. You didn't need to do much with Eric except tell him that he had a session on a certain date. A person like Eric, you accept him for what he does. He played a certain way. He was very serious about his music. I think, to a large extent, it may have been improper in some situations to impose restrictions or philosophies on what he was doing. Some artists are so unique in their abilities that they just do what they do. If you want to record them, you record them. You take them as they are. If not, you leave them alone.

Tompall Glaser [Waylon Jennings, *Honky Tonk Heroes*]

If a producer gets too involved in someone else's work, he winds up overproducing it, and it ruins the soul in it. What really works the best, as far as getting the artist out, is to suck them dry, get every piece of input they've got and, then, enhance it, make sure the music's right. Maybe they don't have the ability to get the music right. That's what Owen Bradley always used to say, 'If you get the music right, let the singer sing the song.' I think that's probably the best. But then there are other types of music to do. If a singer wants to get a certain type of a situation, and he doesn't know how to get it and you do, then you kind of take over the reins and lead him down the road a way until he gets the feel of it. And watch the musicians that they don't shuck him or you, either one. They get pretty slick in that studio. They'll use the same licks over and over again. You think you're getting the original 'cause you didn't see them when they did it just yesterday.

Craig Street [Chris Whitley, *Dirt Floor*]

I like to get live performances essentially as the foundation. So in other words, if I go in with a group of musicians, I prefer to get everybody in the room playing a basic track. Now maybe in the end, I only use a portion of that. Maybe in the end, I just use the bass and the drums, and I go back and overdub everything else. But I like to start from the idea of 'here's a great song. Let's let everybody play this in the room.' I like when things bleed on each other. I don't like perfect ...

Probably part of why I don't really like recording studios. I prefer more non-traditional spaces. The spaces I tend to work in are more like barns or old warehouses or people's homes. They feel more conducive to making music. And then, at that point, maybe what I'll do is like a typical track. We'll get a basic track, and everybody in the room just has a great feeling about it. It feels good. Everybody loves it. And maybe, if it's a multitrack thing, maybe I'll go through and do fixes.

But that doesn't stop me, for example, from building tracks. With Shelby [Lynne], even though everybody was in the room at the same time, we essentially were looking at building tracks. The drummer and the bass player were the same person. I had a string-instrument player, I'll call him, because the guy plays more than just guitar. I had a keyboard player. So typically, what we would do is, depending on the energy of the song, we would track with either drums or bass. If we tracked with bass, we would usually make up a little loop that we could use as a point of reference for time, rather than say use a click track. A loop is just much more fun. You sit there and make up a goofy little loop, and it keeps everybody happy. It gives some point of reference for tempo. Then we would come back in and overdub drums, or we would do drums and, then, do the rest. Maybe we would do just part of a drum kit and, then, come back in and do the bass and, then, do the rest of the drum kit.

So it's about process, about building up what you can in a studio. There's a wide range to what it can be. I think mostly, I look for people that are really collaborative and really open to things. A lot of the preproduction, for me, is spent finding out what people like and what they don't like. It's not really about going over the songs. It's more about sitting down with somebody and talking.

Creed Taylor [Jim Hall, *Concierto*]

Don Sebesky and I talked a great deal before we went in to do it. I made suggestions about how to format a very simple and almost no-arranged kind of context, but where each player would come in, and then there would be that kind of interplay, for instance, between Chet [Baker] and Jim [Hall]. Then Paul [Desmond] would do that kind of contrapuntal stuff that he was so famous for. There was never a problem with Sebesky, because he was an absolute, polished professional. If I asked him to take out four bars of Letter 'A', take out that figure and, then, change anything, he'd do it immediately.

There were a lot of very simple changes that you don't hear in the bumps of that record. (It was just [a matter of] making more space than he had actually provided for when we went in.) I am not explaining it very well, but that's such a classical recording. For instance, once a solo begins, with those particular artists, nobody, including myself, made any suggestion as to whether or not a solo should be extended or whether it should be shortened. Those guys – Chet, Jim, Paul, and everybody – had such a magnificent sense of form.

Ken Nelson [The Louvin Brothers, *Tragic Songs of Life*]

It was my job to see that everything was under control and listen to the sound. Microphone placement at that time was a lot different than it is today when everybody's got a microphone.

It used to irritate me, all the musicians began wearing earphones. To me that destroyed the feel of the record. Each guy was listening to himself. He wasn't listening to the overall picture. I did a couple of things, overdubbing after the record was done. After we cut it, naturally I would have to go into the recording booth with the engineer and get the equalizations correct. But that was the most I ever did. I know today they record the instrumental track first and, then, the singer comes in and records. Again, that destroys the feeling of the record. The artist can't possibly get the feeling of live music around him. That's my opinion. I must be wrong, though, because they're selling millions.

Blake Chancey [Montgomery Gentry, *You Do Your Thing*]

Usually, when I hear a song, a person playing their song acoustically for me, just singing it, I hear the record already in my head. I hear a lot of the instruments or where I think something's going to go. I can actually hear a record being made in my head, sometimes, before I make it. I don't know if that happens to other producers or not.

Conclusion

Production is implied by the manufacturing and marketing of recorded music, but even more than in the film industry, the apparatus organizing recorded music coalesced around its key performers – musicians and singers. They were the cynosures of commerce. Marketing strategies were built solely around stars. Indeed, noticing that recorded music is configured – not around producers, record labels, genres, or regions and scenes – but around performers, risks calling attention to the obvious. Music's 'star system' simply feels inevitable, natural. And, hence, it is ideological.

At first, the film industry marketed movies around neither actors and actresses nor directors. Like automobiles, movie brands bore the names of production companies: for example, Edison, Biograph, Pathé Frères. By 1910, however, articles about personalities had begun to appear in trade journals,[3] and in short order stars became the primary means of selling movies. With D.W. Griffith's *Birth of a Nation* (1915), the public came to understand 'direction' as a (theoretical) site of control in the creation of films, even though it took 40 more years for French theorists to argue systematically that certain directors merited the status of *auteur*.[4] No self-respecting media theorist has made an analogous case for record producers: namely, that the best of the bunch managed to slip corporate restraints. Evidence found in the above interviews suggests that such a claim would be unsustainable. The producer who markets himself as a star – an *auteur* – remains an anomaly: Phil Spector, notwithstanding.

Not that producers did not (or could not) think out of the box. On the contrary, their job has been, precisely, to design and construct boxes that sound like full realizations of the performers' designs. For much of the past century, however, producers could control artists and repertoire, but the recording medium – wax and, later, lacquer – severely limited their ability to shape the sound of the record. The wide-spread adoption of magnetic tape in the mid 1950s demarcated a line between A&R and production.

To get production, in the fullest sense, control over the recording process needs to extend to the post-production phase of recording. (What would movies look like if, for over half-a-century, editing was impossible and the duration of films was restricted to three or four minutes?) Tape was the first medium to afford this level of control. Put more abstractly, the designation 'musician' is possible – it makes sense – only within an episteme (or paradigm) that allows someone to claim authorship of a performance heard as musical. The designation 'record producer' was made possible – which is to say, imaginable – only when someone – and

---

[3]   David A. Cook, *A History of Narrative Film* (4th edn, New York: W.W. Norton, 2004), p. 36.

[4]   Robert B. Ray, 'The Automatic Auteur; or, A Certain Tendency in Film Criticism', in Jeremy Braddock and Stephen Hock (eds), *Directed by Allen Smithee* (Minneapolis: University of Minnesota Press, 2001), p. 55.

not necessarily someone considered musically astute or musically literate – could claim authorship of a recording. 'I made "Hoochie Coochie Man" in 1954', we can imagine Leonard Chess declaring: He didn't write the song. Willie Dixon did. And Chess didn't sing the song. That was Muddy Waters. He didn't engineer the song. Jack Weiner? But his assertion makes sense because it derives from an emergent discourse formation that supports record production.

Before the advent of magnetic tape, technologies for recording and reproducing sound worked to the distinct advantage of record companies, not musicians. (An artist could hardly say, 'Hey, I think you're cheating me! I'm going to take my wax masters and shop them to other record labels.') Entertainment companies, in the guise of their designates, A&R men, managed musical production primarily by controlling preproduction. Tasked with choosing who and what to record, they functioned as agents of 'artificial selection', in the Darwinian sense of that term. However invisible – inaudible and self-effacing – the manifestations of their control may have been, in seeking to ensure the survival and profitability of corporate interests by serving musicians or various 'projects', A&R men profoundly shaped popular music by, what Simon Zagorski-Thomas calls, 'culturally appropriate staging for the musical content'.[5]

Developing the film-making analogy helps to clarify the role of A&R in manufacturing records. Early record men most resembled movie producers, not movie directors: Thomas Ince, Irving Thalberg, or Carlo Ponti; not Erich von Stroheim, John Ford, or Michelangelo Antonioni. Ultimately, their control derived from the power to grant or deny access to capital and the means of production. 'I invented Louis Armstrong', said Ralph Peer in a 1959 interview with Lillian Borgeson. He stated the claim matter-of-factly. To him, it didn't sound the least bit audacious or preposterous. 'I used to go frequently to Chicago for Okeh [Records] on sales trips', he explained.

> [Lil Hardin] came to me and said 'Louis has an offer to come to New York – Henderson's Orchestra – could you give us recording work there?'
>
> Later the girl came to see me again and said Louis wanted to go back to Chicago, so I created an Armstrong Orchestra for them so that they could get some work ... [W]e sent a recording unit out there ... Louis Armstrong and His Hot Five ... I got the best musicians you could get 'cause I liked Louis Armstrong. Of course, they were all from Oliver's band. The funny thing was, I wasn't even present when those records were made. I ok'd the musicians, all of whom I knew, and as long as Louis and the girl were there, I knew it would go alright.[6]

5 Simon Zagorski-Thomas, 'The Musicology of Record Production', *Twentieth-Century Music*, vol. 4, no. 2 (2008): 191.

6 Quoted in William Howland Kenney, *Recorded Music in American Life: The Phonograph and Popular Memory, 1890–1945* (New York: Oxford University Press, 1999), p. 123.

When we consider that Armstrong's Hot Five and his Hot Seven were bands created specifically for the recording studio, Peer's identification of A&R with production makes sense. To Peer, the producer's absence or presence in the studio was an insignificant determinant in creating the sound of a recording.

Magnetic tape converted every recording studio, at least theoretically, into a potential record company: Sam Phillips at Sun, Norman Granz at Verve, Ahmet Ertegun at Atlantic, Jim Stewart and Estelle Axton at Stax, Berry Gordy at Motown, and Phil Spector at Philles – to name only a few obvious examples. By making editing and, eventually, multitracking and a variety of effects practical (and, soon, *de rigueur*), tape placed record-making on par with film-making. (Pierre Schaeffer discusses this matter at some length in *Traité des Objets Musicaux*, his foundational text on *musique concrete*.[7]) Sounds could now be handled and manipulated, composited and collaged, just as readily as images. Record producers had become the music-industry analogue of Hollywood film directors. Which has now been the case for 60 years – half the history of commercial recording.

But here's a problem – demonstrated. Search for film director Erich von Stroheim at amazon.com. Results will yield *Greed* and *Foolish Wives*, but also *Sunset Boulevard* and *Grand Illusion*. In other words, the list includes the titles of films directed by von Stroheim, as well as films directed by others – Billy Wilder and Jean Renoir – but starring von Stroheim. Type in Edmund Goulding ('never a candidate for *auteurist* canonization').[8] *Grand Hotel* appears and a number of additional titles (32 when I searched). Now, enter 'Chet Atkins', 'Brian Eno', or 'Timbaland'. By default, the search engine generates lists of recordings that include these names – but only as performers: *Chester and Lester* but not *Elvis Presley*; *Another Green World*, not U2's *Unforgettable Fire*; *Welcome to Our World*, not Missy Elliott's *Under Construction*. A search for Phil Spector retrieves titles by the Ronettes, Darlene Love, Bob E. Soxx and the Blue Jeans, and Ike and Tina Turner, while albums produced for George Harrison, Leonard Cohen, and the Ramones do not appear. Type in 'John Hammond'. Work by the famed producer's son appears; nothing by the father. Advanced music searches include no 'search by producer' category. How to account for this disparity between film directors and record producers? How do we explain the relative invisibility of record producers?

Two answers come to mind. First, a rethink of the music industry's star system – the basis of all its marketing – would require something akin to a cultural paradigm shift, an alteration of ideology so massive as to be unimaginable. Perhaps Theodor Adorno had a point. An emphasis on star performers paints the music industry as distributing the endlessly varied expressions of a talented multitude. Identifying the men behind the glass – even including 'producer' as a search-engine category – nudges the star-making machine ever so slightly in the wrong direction: toward reality. It risks evoking the music industry as a tightly controlled (rationalized)

[7]   Pierre Schaeffer, *Traité des Objets Musicaux: Essai Interdisciplines* (Paris: Éditions de Seuil, 1966).

[8]   Ray, 'Automatic Auteur', p. 57.

process, organized as an oligopoly, mass-producing superficially varied products overseen by a relatively small group of gatekeepers. Second answer: no political unconscious determined that searching by 'producer' should be avoided because it might, just might, lay bare the ideological underpinnings of the music industry. More likely, web designers and programmers determined that not enough people would use 'producer search' to make the feature cost effective. Probably they were right. If self-effacement is the ethical norm for record production, then assembling the *oeuvre* of a producer would be, generally, a pointless exercise. Which makes this explanation a variant of the first one. The question: 'Who makes recorded music?' is not asked, and it presumes the comforting notion of authorship – agency. The more profound question: 'How is recorded music actually made?' allows that the creation of art in an age of mechanical or electronic reproduction might differ radically from what we're accustomed to. The labour of self-effacing producers – 'stoking the star-maker machinery behind the popular song' – substantially precludes it from occurring, ensuring invisibility.

Chapter 10

Rethinking Creativity: Record Production and the Systems Model

Phillip McIntyre

The Romantic ideal, typified by the conventional view of the quasi-neurotic artist, sees creative activity as primarily self-expressive and supposedly independent from any perceptible constraint.[1] As Peter Wicke has argued, this view has legitimized the individualism that is at the heart of the artist's world; a world perpetuated in many of the myths that surround the recording studio. The Dionysian tales of artists working under the inspiration of whatever muse is popular at the time are legendary. These perspectives, however, have:

> bound art to personality, individuality and lifestyle, but at the same time made it possible to see in art the liberation of man by reminding him of his own inner potential. Being creative meant removing the barriers which imprison man from within, meant self-realization and freedom ... Behind the criticism of commerce, which was seen as the opposite of creativity and communication, lay the Romantic appeal to the autonomy of the artist, an ideal of honesty, upright behaviour and directness.[2]

These understandings of artistic activity, and the field of creativity in which it is subsumed, appear to be cemented into place in the music industry. They are so strongly held that to challenge them risks ridicule at worst and disbelief at best. In short these ideas are now common sense. They are reflected in the way artists are sold to audiences, the way audiences think about what happens when records are made and they make regular appearances in articles and conversations about the studio and its practices. However, as Margaret Boden asserts in her book *The Creative Mind: Myths and Mechanisms*, these ideas, 'are believed by many to be literally true. But they are rarely critically examined. They are not theories, so much as *myths*: imaginative constructions, whose function is to ... endorse the practices of the community that celebrates them.'[3]

---

[1]   Keith Sawyer, *Explaining Creativity: The Science of Human Innovation* (Oxford, 2006).

[2]   Peter Wicke, *Rock Music: Culture, Aesthetics and Sociology*, trans. R. Fogg (Cambridge, 1990), pp. 98–9.

[3]   Margaret Boden, *The Creative Mind: Myths and Mechanisms* (London, 2004), p. 14.

But Keith Negus and Michael Pickering have argued that a 'critical interrogation of creativity should be central to any understanding of musical production'.[4] With Albin Zak recently declaring that 'record production is a mode of creative expression [and] turning musical utterance into electrical current requires, by the project's very nature, an intervening aesthetic sensibility which may, in turn, impinge on the final result'[5] one can also argue that, given the array of aesthetic sensibilities engaged in the making of a single recording, the creative activity of the recording studio is very much a collective one. Wicke goes on to say:

> music as the individual expression of an outstanding artistic personality is de facto impossible. [Popular music has become] a collective means of expression, to which the individual musician can only contribute in a collective activity with others, with technicians, producers and, of course, with other musicians.[6]

If this is the case how then do we explain what happens creatively in the studio if we can't rely on the tenets of romanticism?

Background to Creative Activity

Faced with mounting evidence researchers, relying on rational and empirical studies, have quickly dismissed the romantic ideal.[7] From this research literature a number of definitions of creativity can be readily discerned. Amalgamating these definitions into one it can be seen that creativity is:

> an activity whereby products, processes and ideas are generated from antecedent conditions by the agency of someone, whose knowledge to do so comes from somewhere and the resultant novel variation is seen as a valued addition to the store of human knowledge.[8]

There have been numerous attempts in the research to explain this phenomenon by focusing solely on the individual and simply investigating biological and cognitive

---

[4]   Keith Negus and Michael Pickering in David Hesmondhalgh and Keith Negus (eds), *Popular Music Studies* (London, 2002), p. 147.

[5]   Albin Zak, 'Editorial', *Journal of the Art of Record Production*, vol. 1, no. 2 (2007): 1.

[6]   Wicke, *Rock Music*, pp. 15–16.

[7]   For example see Robert Sternberg (ed.), *The Handbook of Creativity* (Cambridge, 1999) and Sawyer, *Explaining Creativity*, 2006.

[8]   Phillip McIntyre, 'Paul McCartney and the Creation of Yesterday: The Systems Model in Operation', *Popular Music*, vol. 25, no. 2 (2006): 202.

factors.[9] However, this overemphasis on psychological reductionism[10] has resulted in the opposite perspective, that is, sociocultural reductionism. This perspective has, at its extremes, presented the antithesis[11] to the individually focused ideas that were typical of the author/genius model. However, this antithesis also results in unsatisfactory explanations where 'the individual becomes a mere epiphenomenon without any causal significance whatsoever'.[12] Slowly, it appears a synthesis in the research has recognized that a confluence of factors, which includes social, cultural and psychological ones, needs to be in place for creativity to occur. While there have been a number of confluence models suggested[13] the most apt of these may be the systems model of creativity.[14] According to the systems approach creativity comes about through the ongoing operation of 'a system composed of three elements: a culture that contains symbolic rules, a person who brings novelty into the domain, and a field of experts who recognize and validate the innovation' (see Figure 10.1).[15]

This systems model suggests that for creativity to occur a body of knowledge or an accessible set of symbol systems must be existent. An individual acquires this knowledge by being immersed in it via learning and experience in order for them to then make suitable changes within it. This body of knowledge is called a *domain*. If uniqueness is an attribute of creativity a judgement also needs to be made about whether a new idea, product or process is in fact unique. However, no judgement ever occurs in a vacuum. Therefore those who hold the body of knowledge, and understand it to differing degrees, are also important contributors to the system as they are able to make those necessary judgements. This social group is called a *field*. The *individual*'s task is to make changes in the domain and present these to the field for verification of its originality. Furthermore, Pierre Bourdieu[16] has argued that the field in which cultural production occurs, an idea similar in scope to Csikszentmihalyi's use of the same term, can be described as

---

[9]   Sternberg, *Handbook of Creativity*.

[10]   Dean Keith Simonton, 'Creative Cultures, Nations and Civilizations: Strategies and Results', in Paul Paulus and Bernard Nijstad (eds), *Group Creativity: Innovation Through Collaboration* (Oxford, 2003), p. 304.

[11]   Roland Barthes, 'The Death of the Author', in S. Heath (ed. and trans.), *Image, Music, Text* (New York, 1977), pp. 142–53.

[12]   Simonton, 'Creative Cultures, Nations and Civilisations'.

[13]   Sternberg, *Handbook of Creativity*, pp. 10–12.

[14]   Mihaly Csikszentmihalyi, 'Society, Culture and Person: A Systems View of Creativity', in Robert Sternberg (ed.), *The Nature of Creativity: Contemporary Psychological Perspectives* (New York, 1988), pp. 325–39; Mihaly Csikszentmihalyi, 'Implications of a Systems Perspective for the Study of Creativity', in Sternberg, *Handbook of Creativity*, pp. 313–35.

[15]   Mihaly Csikszentmihalyi, *Creativity: Flow and the Psychology of Discovery and Invention* (New York, 1997), p. 6.

[16]   Pierre Bourdieu, *Field of Cultural Production*, ed. Randall Johnson (New York, 1993), and Pierre Bourdieu, *The Rules of Art: Genesis and Structure of the Literary Field* (Cambridge, 1996).

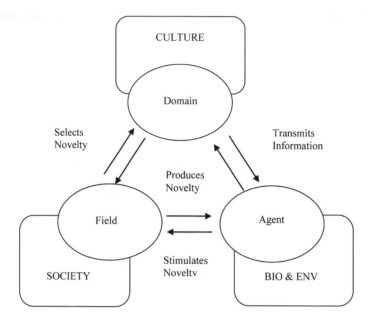

Figure 10.1   Csikszentmihalyi's system model of creativity

an arena of social contestation. Each of the active agents in the field, including the individual themselves, acquire what Pierre Bourdieu calls a *habitus*. Based on the premise that agency and structure are intimately entwined, acquiring a habitus can be seen as the development of:

> a 'feel for the game', a 'practical sense' (*sens practique*) that inclines agents to act and react in specific situations in a manner that is not always calculated and that is not simply a question of conscious obedience to rules. Rather it is a set of dispositions which generates practices and perceptions.[17]

This depiction of an agent's decision-making has some similarities to Donald Schon's argument that a practitioner's skills become 'internalized in our tacit knowing' and suggests that 'we are often unaware of having learned to do these things; we simply find ourselves doing them'.[18] Tony Bastick calls this process intuition.

---

[17]   Randall Johnson, 'Editor's Introduction', in Bourdieu, *Field of Cultural Production*, p. 5.

[18]   Donald Schon, *The Reflective Practitioner: How Professionals Think in Action* (New York, 1983), p. 52.

While intuition is seen conventionally as a vaguely mystical or metaphysical process, in his book *Intuition: How We Think and Act*, Bastick is precise in his definition of it as the 'nonlinear processing of global multi-categorized information'.[19] This latter process is how and where ideas are generated. Ideas seemingly pop out of nowhere but from this perspective are based on what has been input and processed. Richard Burgess, songwriter and record producer, also reinforces these ideas in his book *The Art of Record Production*. Burgess argues that:

> a great deal of the job is to do with instinct … when I started to write and produce, I realised that having to learn and play all those hits had instilled in me an instinct for what works and what doesn't. I didn't have to think about how to construct a hit. I just knew.[20]

Antoine Hennion also argues that a producer's intuitive capacity:

> can exercise itself spontaneously and in a non-cerebral fashion. He [sic] can forget the criteria he has interiorized and allow himself to give into his feelings, to react to what he perceives as purely physical sensations.[21]

The Productive Agents in the Studio

Producers have developed an 'important role as a cultural intermediary'[22] in the studio where their decisions contribute significantly to the final creative product. In terms of decision-making in the studio they draw on their domain and field knowledge right throughout the recording process and are generally responsible for the completion of the recording project. It is clear, however, that despite the variety of approaches they take producers are often placed inside a highly collaborative process:

> In the music industry, record producers are the invisible part of the creative team, and most listeners don't know what the producer does. The best analogy is that the record producer is like a feature film's director … While the recording engineer is responsible for getting things on tape (like the cinematographer) the producer must articulate a vision for what the end product should sound like. The musicians are somewhat like the actors, reading from a script (the written music) and the producer guides them through the reading. Even when the artist has written the song, the artist relies on the producer to present the song

---

[19]   Tony Bastick, *Intuition: How We Think and Act* (Chichester, 1982), p. 215.

[20]   Richard Burgess, *The Art of Record Production* (London, 1997) p. 177.

[21]   Antoine Hennion, 'The Production of Success: An Antimusicology of the Pop Song', in Simon Frith and Andrew Goodwin (eds), *On Record* (New York, 1990), p. 201.

[22]   Roy Shuker, *Understanding Popular Music* (London, 2001), p. 105.

properly, to run the recording session, and to help the artist be objective about
the quality of his [sic] own performances.[23]

As well as drawing on their domain knowledge to decide on song quality and
the quality of performances producers also monitor tuning and timing. Their
responsibilities include not only these musical parameters but also involve
technical and administrative ones. They have to ensure, usually through their
engineer, that all the equipment to be used is indeed ready and usable. They work
closely with other members of the field through booking the studios, hiring an
engineer if necessary, hiring musicians, hiring equipment and filing contracts. In
essence they oversee the whole production through all stages of pre-production,
production and post-production. Most importantly they set the mood of the
working environment. Dave Faulkner, formerly of the Hoodoo Gurus and their
principal songwriter, commented about Charles Fisher, his long-time producer:

> The best thing about Charles is what you'd call his bed-side manner. He's really
> easy-going. He's always got a wry comment to make. When you can have a
> laugh and relax it brings out, you know, the better qualities. It's when you're
> stressing out and someone's, you know, hammering you about something it
> tends to make you clam up and not be creative.[24]

Producers therefore need to be able to work well with all the members of the
field. Their arsenal of skills include degrees of tact and diplomacy so that they can
establish a firm rapport with all the people involved, maintain some empathy with
the performers and help to interpret and realize the creative vision of the project.
In this case the producer is hired not only to contribute to the creative process but
also in many ways to assure success on a financial as well as a musical level.

The engineer on the other hand, presuming of course that the producer is not
also the engineer as is increasingly the case, decides other aspects of the production.
Howard Becker contends that 'each kind of person who participates in the making
of art works, then has a specific bundle of tasks to do',[25] but the allocation of tasks
is arbitrary, though nonetheless traditional. Roy Shuker suggests that, 'initially
designated as "technicians", sound mixers have converted a craft into an art, with
consequent higher status and reward'.[26]

Despite its assumption of the constructed distinction between art and craft,
Shuker's description underlines the fact that 'the appearance of autonomy of the
individual artist is superficial'.[27] Each person working on the record has a set
of creative concerns that are tied to their own reputation 'for their own success

---

[23]   Daniel Levitin, 'John Fogerty Interview', *Audio Magazine* (January, 1998).

[24]   Dave Faulkner, personal interview (1997).

[25]   Howard Becker, *Art Worlds* (Los Angeles, 1982), p. 11.

[26]   Shuker, *Understanding Popular Music*, p. 53.

[27]   Becker, *Art Worlds*, p. 16.

depends in part on impressing those who hire them with their competence'.[28] In the case of the engineer, as they act as liaison between the producer and the machinery being used, they make creative decisions based fundamentally on what their own aesthetic will tolerate.

In essence the engineer's primary task is to capture sound just as a cameraperson on a film set captures light. The engineer needs to ensure that everything is recorded at the appropriate levels with, dependent on the project, no distortion or break-up and that the signal to noise ratio is appropriate. Like the producer they also have to interpret the language used in the studio. When the producer or a musician asks to make the bass sound fatter, deliver punchy brass or put some depth on the vocals, they will need to be able to translate these obtuse requests into technical action that is congruent with their own domain knowledge and field expertise. Therefore they need to be familiar with all the equipment from microphone types through to the software programmes being used. If things go wrong they're expected to be able to fix them. Once everything is working optimally engineers are expected to work efficiently:

> It all depends on who's engineering and Rob Taylor is really good to work with. We got my vocals down in two days and we were really happy with that. Nick took in seven different snares to get the sound he wanted on each track. Now they've [Scott Chapman and Glenn Dorman] gone in with Rob Taylor and the three of them are gonna start arguing about [the mix] for a few days.[29]

With the engineer in place, as well as the musicians, songwriters, performers, managers and A&R people, each of whom deserves a similar account, it can be seen that each of these productive agents contribute their various expertise and reputations to this art world in microcosm; in doing so they move the work through recognizable stages.

The Stages of Creative Activity

Each stage of record production has a set of decisions affecting the eventual creative output to be made within it. In working from Graeme Wallas's formulation[30] that creativity involves four stages; preparation, incubation, inspiration and verification, Tony Bastick saw that the first three could be subsumed inside the notion of intuition, leaving just two stages to creativity; intuition and then verification. However, as Csikszentmihalyi argues, adding a fifth stage of elaboration, while the staged view of the process may be misleading, 'it does offer a relatively

---

28   Ibid., p. 25.

29   Kate White, personal interview (1995).

30   In Albert Rothenberg and Carl Hausmann (eds), *The Creativity Question* (Durham, NC: Duke University Press, 1976), pp. 69–73.

valid and simple way to organise the complexities involved ... It is essential to remember ... that the five stages in reality are not exclusive but typically overlap and recur several times before the process is completed.'[31] This staged approach to the creative process parallels to some extent the characteristic stages of recording which normally includes pre-production, production and post-production.

Pre-Production

Most pre-production requires in-depth planning and preparation in organizational, equipment and budgetary terms. This is the stage typically used to identify the specific resources needed, to find suitable studios, and importantly to begin writing, revising, rearranging and rehearsing songs. Mark Tinson, producer of country artist Steve Gibson and rock band Freak Shop, describes his own *modus operandi*:

> When I work with say Steve Gibson, writing his stuff, he comes up generally with the idea for a chorus or a verse and a chorus. I just whip them into shape ... Writing with the Freak Shop is pretty much the same thing. The lyrics are taken care of by Steve Mclennan. He usually has a melodic idea. I'll usually come up with some sort of riff and then we'll just work it together between the two of us.[32]

Rick Brewster, one of the songwriters from the Angels, also asserts that preparatory input was essential for the success of their records:

> They [producers Vanda and Young] were very influential in the early days around the first couple of albums particularly. Although they didn't produce *Face to Face* or *No Exit*, I think we called them executive producers. What that meant was we didn't put down a song without running it by them, both in the writing stage and in the recording. As always happens when you play somebody you respect a song and you ask them for their comments you take them seriously and the song changes usually as a result.[33]

Not only must a producer be prepared to rework songs but they must also ensure that items pertinent to the field, such as permits and clearances are obtained, insurance requirements and other necessary legal details are attended to. Session musicians need to be booked, extra equipment or instruments that are needed have to be sorted out, programming time needs to be scheduled and transport and accommodation organized if necessary. Pre-production, therefore, also crucially involves working out the proposed budget. This budgetary function highlights the fact that without some form of financial patronage most creative work in a modern

---

[31] Csikszentmihalyi, *Creativity*, p. 83.
[32] Mark Tinson, personal interview (1997).
[33] Rick Brewster, personal interview (1997).

studio will not happen. The producer, if they're wise, will negotiate before the recording process begins with either the record company who is primarily acting as a venture capitalist or the artist who may be financing the project through other means, an outright payment, a salary plus bonus royalties, or a royalty – usually referred to as points.

Production

The next stage, that is production, includes the actuality of recording all the material for the project. Just as Wallas's stage of illumination is often mistaken for creativity itself, production is the stage of recording most people see as the beginning and end of the process. However, if pre-production has been sound, the production stage may often proceed on the basis of ensuring all of the necessary items of work are completed adequately and accounted for properly. This stage conventionally includes tracking and overdubbing and can typically involve a number of people, songwriters, performing musicians, the engineer and the producer all giving their creative input. For some songwriters these inputs can be seen as examples of constraint to their creativity, especially if they have an ontological base in Romanticism, rather than a set of contributing variables in the mediation of the creative system:

> You get into a studio situation and you've got guitar players wanting to go, 'Okay, where's the solo fit into this? Okay, I've got this part I want to put into the bridge and I've got this', and it just becomes to me the most frustrating part of wanting to do music.[34]

However, as Jon Fitzgerald asserts in his study of session musicians in the studio, recording is 'a highly collaborative process, requiring substantial skills and creative contributions'[35] from both session musicians and songwriters in order to realize a song. One musician in Fitzgerald's study observed that 'creative ideas are an essential attribute for a session musician'.[36]

Post-Production

Despite the necessary compromise and consensus involved in making a record the post-production stage is most often the phase where the project comes together as a complete piece. It is the stage where mixing, editing and mastering occurs. Mixing is the blending of various sounds into a cohesive combination that satisfies various

---

[34] Brien McVernon, personal interview (1994).

[35] Jon Fitzgerald, 'Down Into the Fire: A Case Study of a Popular Music Recording Session', *Perfect Beat: The Pacific Journal of Research into Contemporary Music and Popular Culture*, vol. 5, no. 3 (1996): 72.

[36] Ibid.

musical, sonic, technical, commercial and personal criteria. It involves, amongst many other things, volume balancing, creating relationships in three dimensional sonic space through the judicious use of panning and use of effects such as delay and reverb, equalizing various components of the mix to have them sit comfortably within the audio spectrum and the use of certain dynamics processors and noise reduction units, whether these are rack mounted or plug ins. While the mix is critically important to the finished product Stanley Alten argues that this needs to be kept in perspective as, 'a good mix cannot salvage a bad recording, but a poor mix can ruin a good one'.[37]

As a mix engineer is dependent on the work of the recording engineer, mixing, in its pragmatic application, is often the result of a number of creative minds at work despite the tensions involved. As an example John Fogerty, the producer, songwriter and arranger for Creedence Clearwater Revival commented:

> It's like that with every single band in the world, especially when they're young. They have no concept of what a producer does – they just know they played this part, their little drum part, or their rhythm part or whatever. They go into the control room, and the rhythm guitar player hollers, 'I can't hear my part.' So of course the guy defers to him and turns up the rhythm guitar. Then the bass guy comes in and screams, 'I can't hear my part', and he turns up the bass part. And the background singer comes in, 'I can't hear my part.' Shit you can't have everybody louder than everybody else; you're not making a record when you do that.[38]

The bass player for the same group, Stu Cook, commented in response that:

> it's not a question of should my instrument be louder, it's more a question of where it's fitting in the mix. If it's the bass it should be rich and warm and fill that bottom. One could say it's not loud enough, but the real point is, it doesn't sound right in the blend … It doesn't have to drown out the guitar or tambourine. A well mixed record should take this stuff into consideration. You deal with that in the mix if you haven't recorded it exactly right.[39]

While most producers will attempt to work without the artist being at the mix session they will inevitably seek verification of their work either from the artist, the record company or both once they are satisfied that the new work can be readily placed alongside other quality products within the domain. The studio practice of doing a 'vocal up' mix, in addition to the mix the band is usually satisfied with, resulted historically from A&R continually requesting these

---

[37]   Stanley Alten, *Audio in Media* (Belmont, 2002), p. 421.

[38]   John Fogerty quoted in Craig Werner, *Up around the Bend: The Oral History of Creedence Clearwater Revival* (New York, 1998), p. 96.

[39]   Stu Cook quoted in Craig Werner, ibid., p. 86.

types of mixes for radio. Editing, on the other hand, is the practice whereby any unwanted material can be deleted, mistakes fixed and ideas rearranged. This now more commonly occurs at mastering. Mastering is the stage of post-production where the overall final product is adjusted in terms of dynamics processing, levelling, equalization and noise reduction so that it is intelligible, in audio terms, across all playback systems.[40] It is here that track identifiers are also inserted and song order is finalized:

> The trick of it is to listen to the final mixes and to manipulate them so they are basically easy to listen to, if you like, so you don't have to adjust your system, you can just put 'em on, good and loud and everything's clear, there's plenty of top end and bottom end and good stereo spectrum happening.[41]

Bob Katz argues that 'mastering is the last creative step in the audio production process, the bridge between mixing and replication'.[42] While an audience may not realize that mastering is critical to the reception of the final product, negotiating with the reputation and creative sensibilities of a mastering engineer may afford a producer, songwriter or performer the limit of their potential to effect any further creative changes before the recording is manufactured.

Sometimes, however, it's the limitations of the process, be it in pre- or post-production, that suggest particular creative possibilities. Mick Glossop, for example, in discussing Phil Collins' drum sound on 'In the Air Tonight' argues that the lack of cymbals became 'a massive sonic creative effect being made possible only by a restriction of choice'.[43] Similarly, George Martin argues that the limitations he, Geoff Emerick and the Beatles faced in recording the *Sgt Pepper's Lonely Hearts Club Band* album 'actually acted as a stimulant to creativity':[44]

> What 4-track imposed on us was, firstly, you had to think ahead as to what you were going to do. Secondly, you had to get things right at the time; you couldn't just say, 'OK, let's leave that because we can fix it in the mix.' All those kinds of decisions, that kind of discipline, imposes constraints on you, but it also makes you focus much more, makes you think.[45]

---

[40] Phillip McIntyre and Bryan Paton, 'The Mastering Process and the Systems Model of Creativity' in *Perfect Beat: The Pacific Journal of Research into Contemporary Music and Popular Culture*, vol. 8, no. 4 (2007): 64–81.

[41] Don Bartley, personal interview (1997).

[42] Bob Katz, *Mastering Audio: The Art and the Science* (Oxford, 2002), p. 11.

[43] Mick Glossop quoted in Howard Massey, *Behind the Glass: Top Record Producers Tell How They Craft the Hits* (San Francisco, 2000), p. 235.

[44] Massey, *Behind the Glass*, p. 90.

[45] George Martin quoted in Massey, *Behind the Glass*, p. 79.

Conclusion

In several ways these facts put lie to the notion of creative freedom, of the sort typified by Romanticism, being the most beneficial mode of operating within a creative framework. As such, the discipline and structures that exist around the recording process for the individual producer, engineer, songwriter or performer can be seen not simply as constrainers but are in many ways also critical enablers of the process. This is to say they are factors that *allow* creative activity to occur. As Janet Wolff has argued:

> all action, including creative or innovative action, arises in the complex conjunction of numerous determinants and conditions. Any concept of 'creativity' which denies this is metaphysical, and cannot be sustained.[46]

For studio producers those determinants not only include the social expectations of the field they work in and the cultural parameters of the domain they're familiar with but, subsumed inside these, are also the imperatives of the other studio professionals they work with, the technological limitations of the studio itself, the performance capabilities of the musicians and the level of financial patronage at their disposal. This is not to say that the various agents in the field of record production are predetermined in their creative action. Instead they are predisposed to choose, as both Bourdieu[47] and Toynbee[48] argue, from a set of possible options presented to them. It can be argued in conclusion, therefore, that 'practical activity and creativity are in a mutual relation of interdependence'[49] with the structures, the domain and field of record making, that these record makers exist in.

With these ideas in mind one can ask the following question. If one is dealing with what is demonstrably a collective enterprise where agents make decisions within a structured environment, why do many of us who work in recording studios insist on thinking that creativity is still best described using primarily romantic terminology? The answer may be that to dismantle these deeply held romantic views would not only remove some of the shibboleths used to endorse studio practices but the level of ontological insecurity generated by their removal may indeed be too great for some who have spent their whole lives in thrall to those myths.

---

[46]   Janet Wolff, *The Social Production of Art* (London, 1981), p. 9.

[47]   Pierre Bourdieu, *The Rules of Art: Genesis and Structure of the Literary Field* (Cambridge, 1996).

[48]   Jason Toynbee, *Making Popular Music: Musicians, Creativity and Institutions* (London, 2000).

[49]   Wolff, *Social Production of Art*, p. 9.

Interviews

Don Bartley (mastering engineer), personal interview, 2 September 1997.
Rick Brewster (songwriter/guitarist), personal interview, 5 November 1997.
Dave Faulkner (singer/songwriter/guitarist), personal interview, 16 December 1997.
Brien McVernon (songwriter/musician), personal interview, 3 July 1997.
Mark Tinson (producer/engineer), personal interview, 2 December 1997.
Kate White (bass player), personal interview, 17 October 1995.

Chapter 11

Considering Space in Recorded Music

William Moylan

Background

The spatial qualities inherent to music recordings primarily function at two levels of the structure; one LaRue calls the 'large dimension' and the other at a 'middle dimension'.[1] Each level has distinct and unique spatial qualities. These qualities contribute greatly to shaping recorded music at these two primary structural dimensions. It is most common to have spatial elements or relationships of spatial qualities exist or function at these two primary levels, with spatial qualities also existing at lower structural levels; evaluating these levels brings a focus on materials from the subtlest of activity in microanalysis, to middle-analysis (of middle dimension materials and activity), and macro-analysis (at the highest structural level).[2]

The two levels of middle and large dimension serve as meaningful references for the study of spatial relationships in recorded music, as they dominate the listeners' conception of the music recording[3] and are the materials directly crafted in production practice. These levels can be defined as (1) the overall sound of the recording/music and (2) the qualities and relationships of the individual sound sources or groups of sound sources contained in the recording/music.[4]

The spatial elements of these two dimensions are outlined in Table 11.1.

Spatial Qualities of the Overall Sound

The spatial qualities of the level of the overall sound are (1) the characteristics of the perceived performance environment and (2) the dimensions of the sound stage.

---

[1] Jan LaRue, *Guidelines for Style Analysis* (2nd edn, Detroit, 1996), pp. 5–8.

[2] John D. White, *Comprehensive Musical Analysis* (Oxford, 1994), pp. 21–2.

[3] William Moylan, *The Art of Recording: The Creative Resources of Music Production and Audio* (New York, 1992), pp. 55–61, 239.

[4] William Moylan, *Understanding and Crafting the Mix: The Art of Recording* (2nd edn, Boston, 2007), pp. 233–9.

Table 11.1   The spatial qualities of music recordings in the two primary
structural levels

Overall sound
Sound stage dimensions
Perceived performance environment
Individual sound sources
Distance location
Image size (width)
Lateral location
Environment characteristics

The perceived performance environment (PPE) is the overall space where the 'performance' that is the music 'recording' is heard as taking place. It is the environment of the sound stage. This environment binds all sound sources and their separate environments into a single performance area, with its own global environmental characteristics.[5]

The characteristics of the perceived performance environment are (1) any frequency alterations to the overall sound of the recording (incorporating bass ratio), (2) how those alterations unfold over time, (3) reverb time and density, (4) pre-delay and the spacing of reflections in the early time field,[6] (5) ratio of direct to reverberant sound, and (6) unfolding dynamic relationships between the direct sound and reflections/reverberation.[7] These aspects of the PPE are created by any environmental characteristics applied to the overall programme, and/or the environmental characteristics of important, prominent or unique sound sources within the recording.

This brings the PPE to establish a context for the music: an overall space within which the listener 'hears' or 'conceives' the piece of music as existing (see Figure 11.1).

The sound stage is the singular area occupied by all of the sound sources of the music, as an aggregate or group. It has an apparent physical size of width and depth that are defined at the level of the individual sound source: (1) the dimension of width is defined by the furthest right and the furthest left sound (lateral localization) and (2) the dimension of depth is defined by the most distant sound source and the closest sound source. The size of the sound stage can be

---

[5]   Ibid., p. 54.

[6]   Alexander Case, *Sound FX: Unlocking the Creative Potential of Recording Studio Effects* (Boston, 2007), pp. 264–9.

[7]   Jens Blauert, *Spatial Hearing: The Psychophysics of Human Sound Localization* (Cambridge, MA, 1983), pp. 278–82.

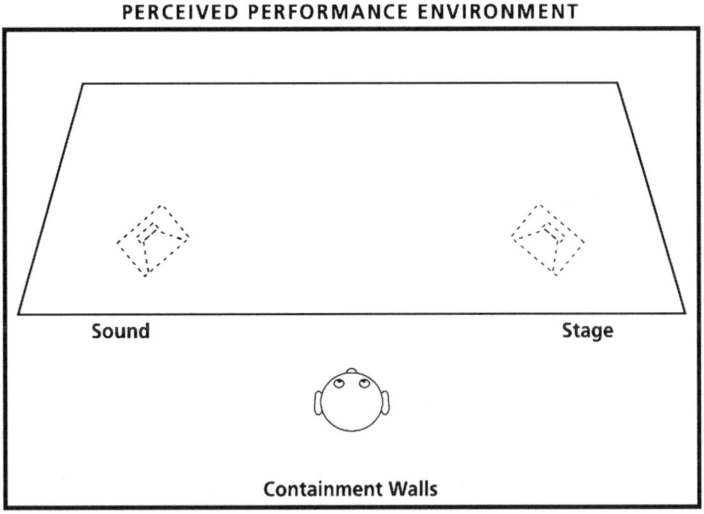

PERCEIVED PERFORMANCE ENVIRONMENT

Figure 11.1   Spatial dimensions of the overall sound

fluid, with potential to change size (bringing the listener to different relationships to the music); the sound stage also has the potential to establish and maintain a stable context for the music, as a fixed area within which all of the musical activity is perceived as taking place (see Figure 11.2).

Phil Ramone shares:

> The most effective mixes take full advantage of psychoacoustics, which is why I mix in two dimensions: in stereo and in depth. Creating a good layer from front to back and left to right offers depth and allows the instruments to breathe, which amplifies their tonal qualities. It also brings clarity to the mix.[8]

Spatial Qualities of Individual Sound Sources or Groups of Sound Sources

Individual sound sources in music recordings are located on the sound stage at a specific distance from the listener (distance location), and at a specific location in the stereo field (lateral location). Further, the lateral image will have a width that can vary from a very narrowly defined point in space up to a size that can occupy the entire potential 90-degree span of the stereo sound stage. A point source image occupies a narrow, precise point on the sound stage; a spread image occupies an area between two boundaries, its size can vary greatly. Any group of sound sources can have the same qualities, and be placed as a section within the ensemble on

---

[8]   Phil Ramone and Charles L. Granata, *Making Records: The Scenes Behind the Music* (New York, 2007), p. 187.

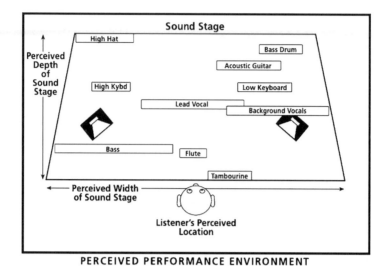

Figure 11.2   Individual sound sources placed on a sound stage

the sound stage. In surround sound, spread images can completely immerse the listener or occupy any sized area.

Sounds or groups of sound sources are often placed in their own environments. The qualities of environments fuse with the sound quality of their sound sources to create an overall timbre, and also provide the illusion of placement in a unique physical space. These created environments may be realistic or have sound qualities that defy our natural physics, described as 'the appearance of a reality that could not actually exist – a pseudo-reality, created in synthetic space' by Moorefield.[9]

Environments can impart a quality of depth, or a front-to-back area to a sound though this is not actual distance location – which fixes the 'front edge' of the sound on the sound stage, by the amount of low-energy detail present in the sound source's timbre.[10] The characteristics of environmental cues can be calculated as time, amplitude and frequency anomalies of the reflections of the direct sound in the captured or created environment.[11]

Sound sources are not placed at unique elevations in two channel or surround recordings, as elevation angles cannot be reproduced by loudspeakers located on

[9]   Virgil Moorefield, *The Producer as Composer: Shaping the Sounds of Popular Music* (Cambridge, MA, 2005), p. xv.

[10]   Blauert, *Spatial Hearing*, pp. 118, 123.

[11]   William Moylan, 'The Aural Analysis of the Spatial Relationships of Sound Sources as Found in Two-Channel Common Practice', 81st Convention of the Audio Engineering Society, Los Angeles, 1986, pp. 9–10.

the same median plane.[12] Some conceptualization of perceived elevation related to pitch/frequency level does exist on a limited basis, but has minimal actual influence on perceived elevation of sounds and differs between individuals.[13] Allan Moore's soundbox representing 'virtual textural space'[14] utilizes vertical placement as one of its four dimensions, where 'the frequency of sound determines its placement on the vertical plane, with higher frequencies perceived to be placed in the upper zone of the soundbox and lower frequencies occupying the lower section'.[15] Gibson presents a similar concept aligning pitch/frequency with elevation.[16] It is important to note this is not an element of the actual spatial locations and relationships of sounds, but rather a conceptualization of vertical placement of pitch (representing register), much aligned with the concepts of 'pitch density' and 'timbral balance;'[17] this element is therefore not incorporated into this exploration of spatial dimensions in recorded music.

Some Fundamental Analysis Questions and the Origins of a Methodology

This presents a start for evaluating impacts of space on music, its expression, and its materials. This basic outline of analysis questions, and this rudimentary premise for the initiation of a methodology to understand the content, construction and function of spatial materials are offered to supplement and incorporate the work of other scholars and to provide some point of reference as we move forward in exploring these elements.

Some Fundamental Analysis Questions

The fundamental questions for evaluating the impact of spatial characteristics on music (music recordings) are broad, encompassing the grandest and the subtlest detail. This approach requires an understanding that spatial qualities can be characterized by (1) the qualities of their states or characteristics – as unchanging attributes and dimensions – and by (2) any activity of changing states within any

---

[12]   John Borwick, *Loudspeaker and Headphone Handbook* (3rd edn, Oxford, 2001), pp. 11–15; David Moulton, *Total Recording: The Complete Guide to Audio Production and Engineering* (Sherman Oaks, CA, 2000), p. 120.

[13]   Brian Moore, *An Introduction to the Psychology of Hearing* (5th edn, Oxford, 2004), pp. 250–51.

[14]   Allan F. Moore, *Rock: The Primary Text: Developing a Musicology of Rock* (2nd edn, Aldershot, 2001), p. 121.

[15]   Ruth Dockwray and Allan F. Moore, 'Configuring the Sound-Box 1965–1972', *Popular Music*, 29 (2010), 181–97.

[16]   David Gibson, *The Art of Mixing* (2nd edn, Boston, 2005).

[17]   Moylan, *Understanding and Crafting the Mix*, pp. 225–9.

of the spatial dimensions, as exhibited by either individual sources, groups of sources, or by the overall texture.

This approach is also concerned with how spatial qualities can serve to create a context for the piece of music or for musical materials, and how they can provide enhancement of musical materials or ideas. It can also be extended to the possibility that spatial qualities have the potential to be or to generate musical materials in and of themselves.[18] It is important to remember that the term 'spatial qualities' refers to all of those outlined in Table 11.1, and that any of those qualities may be more active or more significant at any point in time, and at any structural level (small dimension, middle dimension, or large dimension).

Table 11.2 is a rudimentary outline to begin exploration.

Table 11.2   Some fundamental questions towards evaluating the spatial qualities of recorded music

---

In the following table 'it' is the activity or state(s) of distance, stereo or surround location, environmental characteristics, perceived performance environment, and/or sound stage dimensions.

- In what way does 'it' impact the musical material?
- In what way does 'it' enhance (contribute to) the musical message, musical meaning, or the delivery of the musical material?

Does 'it' ...
 – Represent substantive material or ornamental embellishment?
 – Shape the musical idea(s)?
 – Impart character to musical materials?
 – Impact the music directly?
 – Shape the musical experience of the listener?

- Is the activity or state(s) of any individual spatial quality a musical idea in itself?
- In what way does 'it' impact the musical material?
- In what way does 'it' enhance (contribute to) the musical message, musical meaning, or the delivery of the musical material?

Does 'it' ...
 – Represent substantive material or ornamental embellishment?
 – Shape the musical idea(s)?
 – Impart character to musical materials?
 – Impact the music directly?
 – Shape the musical experience of the listener?

---

[18]   James Tenney, *Meta – Hodos and META Meta – Hodos* (Oakland, CA, 1986), p. 89.

Origins of a Methodology for the Evaluation of Space in Music Recordings

A basic theoretical framework is proposed as the origin of a methodology for the evaluation of space in music recordings. This methodology will incorporate three basic activities: collection of information on the spatial elements, evaluating the content and characteristics of that data, and arriving at conclusions of the states and activities of the spatial elements and their impacts.[19]

Timelines will assist in collecting and analysing data. A one-page large dimension timeline can document the major structural divisions of the piece and their length; data on overall sound dimensions can be added to this in the following stages. A longer middle-dimension timeline with enough space to clearly show changes of distance locations and/or phantom image locations, and that displays entrances and exits of sound sources, will be of great assistance.

Collection   Information on all of the spatial elements (distance, stereo or surround location, environmental characteristics, perceived performance environment and sound stage dimensions) are collected, as they exist at the middle and large dimensions; activity in the small dimension presents itself as subtle detail within the middle dimension.

The soundbox[20] can be used to notate sources for distance and lateral placement. The following sound stage diagram for a two-channel stereo recording can also be used for these purposes (see Figure 11.3).

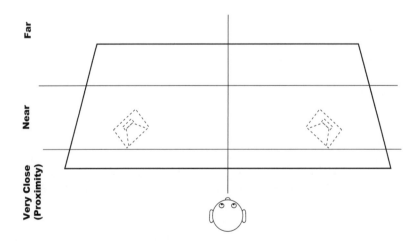

Figure 11.3   Stereo sound stage with distance designations

---

[19]   William Moylan, *An Analytical System for Electronic Music* (Ann Arbor, MI: University Microfilms, 1983), pp. 191–4, 206–26.

[20]   Moore, *Rock*, p. 121.

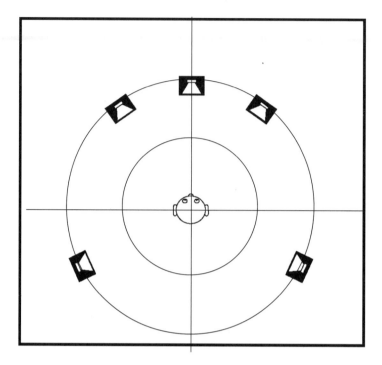

Figure 11.4   Surround sound stage with distance circles

For surround sound recordings the following diagram can be used. It will also document distance of sound sources from the listener location as well as lateral angle and phantom image sizes and locations (see Figure 11.4).

These diagrams present data in sections of time of stable activity. When sources change locations or sizes, or sources exit or enter the texture multiple diagrams or X-Y graphs are used. An alternative to sound stage or soundbox diagrams is to plot the spatial dimension against a timeline such as the following example (see Figure 11.5):

Spectral and time characteristics and dimensions of environments of individual or groups of sound sources, and of the perceived performance environment are documented. These are most often stable throughout the piece of music, but changes at major structural sections can occur.[21]

Evaluation   The 'evaluation' step examines data collected to determine the characteristics and usage of the spatial dimensions. Table 11.3 forms a rudimentary framework for initial evaluation, knowing each piece of music will be unique in some way and thus will need a flexible set of criteria for evaluation:

---

[21]   Moylan, *Understanding and Crafting the Mix*, pp. 176–223.

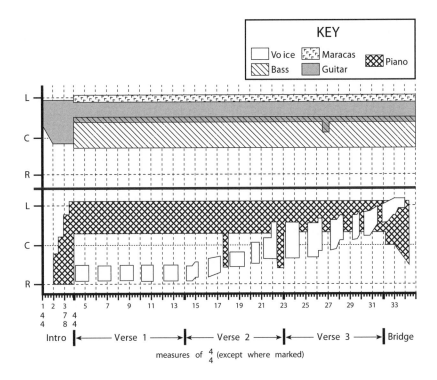

Figure 11.5 'A Day in the Life' from *Sgt. Pepper's Lonely Hearts Club Band*, stereo sound location graph, measures 1–34

Table 11.3 A rudimentary framework for evaluation of spatial dimension characteristics

- Number of states of an element (distance location or image sizes and locations)
- Number and types of different characteristics (individual environments and PPE)
- Rate and degree of changes of any element (especially image locations)
- Amount of activity in each element (that is, how often do sound stage dimensions change)
- Boundaries of ranges/states (that is, furthest left and right; nearest and furthest; longest and shortest decay times; etc.)
- Patterns of changes, speed of changes, rhythms of changes
- Patterns of characteristics and states (that is, similarities of certain environmental characteristics; certain image sizes; certain depth of sound stage location groupings)
- Identification of preferred or predominant types or characteristics
- Identification of characteristic use of elements
- Identification of unique use of spatial elements

Conclusions   Conclusions result from a study of the characteristics and usage of the spatial dimensions from *Evaluation*, to identify how they function and contribute to the shape, motion and message of the music. The uniqueness of materials, of usage and functions of spatial dimensions will become evident and understood here. Pertinent conclusions may take the form of some, all or none from the following Table 11.4:

Table 11.4   Potential topics for conclusions on the functions and usage of spatial dimensions

• Does the song establish a typical use of spatial dimensions (and coupling with musical materials) conforming to normative practices, or does it deviate from the norm?
• Has a unique language and stylistic usage of elements been established?
• Do spatial elements create a context appropriate to the musical conception and message of the song (overall dimensions)?
• Do spatial elements create relationships and characters appropriate for the musical materials they present and appropriate for the relative significance/importance of the materials to the texture/music (individual sound sources)?
• How do the individual spatial dimensions contribute to or create motion or movement in the song?
• How do the individual spatial dimensions contribute to or create shape and structure in the song?
• What spatial dimensions are used structurally as musical ideas and which are ornamental, embellishing the musical material?
• Where do extremes of states or activity occur structurally?
• Where do changes of the sound stage or perceived performance environment occur structurally?
• What unique structural design elements exist?

Exploring the Roles of Space in Music: At the Level of Individual Sound Sources

This section examines some of the roles of space in music at the level of the individual sound source, or small groups of sound sources. This structural level is also where musical materials (melodies, harmonies, rhythms, and so on) exist in their most complete and immediate forms.

The qualities of spatial elements in the music, and their impacts are explored through several different recordings and versions of The Beatles' 'While My Guitar Gently Weeps'.

Distance Location

Distance is the space between the listener and the music, the sound stage, and/or to an individual sound source. In creating or capturing a music recording, sounds are situated at a distance to the listener.

This amount of distance can play a significant role in shaping musical impacts and sound characteristics. Its impacts can be manifest in the listener's connection to the music and the musical material, the immediacy of the musical message, and a sense of context for the sound stage and the musical texture. Most important in terms of distance is the placement of the lead vocal; it establishes a position of the phonographic narrative, 'as the aural index of the artist's persona and represented emotions'.[22]

Some important observations are:

Table 11.5   Potential impacts of distance location

---

1. Level of intimacy with the source:

Very near to listener?

Heard from afar?

2. Degree of connection of the listener with the music and its message:

Strong connection?

Some detachment?

In Each: to what degree?

In these ways the physical presence of the voice and instruments, coupled with their musical materials may be transformed. The listener is brought into a physical relationship to the music; they can be drawn into becoming part of the 'story' (music) or observing the 'story' (music) from some distance. Either way, the relationship imparts an impact on the musical experience (see Figures 11.6 and 11.7).

For the *LOVE* version of 'While My Guitar Gently Weeps', the distance locations of the George Harrison lead vocal and guitar pull the listener into an intimate relationship to the musical material and the message of the music. There is a sense of closeness and a strong connection in these parts and, though a bit less so, the solo cello line during the material through the first verse. These are dramatically different from the more detached string parts of the chorus. In the chorus the sound stage changes in width and depth, although the distance locations

---

[22]   Serge Lacasse, 'Persona, emotions and technology: the phonographic staging of the popular music voice', Proceedings of the 2005 Art of Record Production Conference.

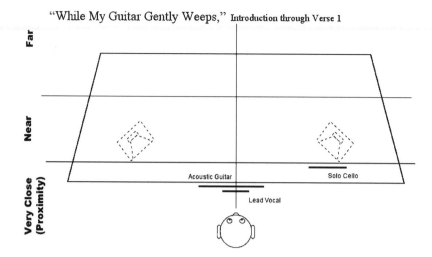

Figure 11.6   Sound source locations, beginning through verse 1 of 'While My Guitar Gently Weeps,' *LOVE* version

and relationships of guitar and vocals do not change markedly. Careful attention will reveal subtle changes to the image size and the environmental characteristics of Harrison's vocal, note: this is not a change of distance location – it is a change of the sound quality of the vocal's environment coupled with a broadening of the phantom image.

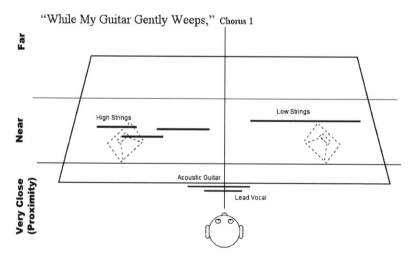

Figure 11.7   Sound source locations, first chorus of 'While My Guitar Gently Weeps,' *LOVE* version

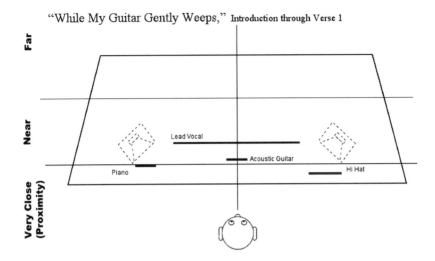

Figure 11.8   Sound source locations, beginning through verse 1 of 'While My Guitar Gently Weeps,' *White Album* version

The original *White Album* version of 'While My Guitar Gently Weeps' contains striking differences in the character and placement of the lead vocal and the acoustic guitar (see Figure 11.8).

There is a substantial difference in the distance location of Harrison's acoustic guitar and his lead vocal in comparison to those locations we observed in *LOVE*. They are no longer very close to the listener, within the listener's personal space.[23] They are now further away, and more detached from the listener. The listener is now observing the story from an appreciable distance, instead of being intimately connected with Harrison the storyteller.

Do these different distance qualities bring each version to be communicating something different? Or do they bring each song to communicate the same message differently? Perhaps both are possible when proposed from different perspectives.

It is clear the poignant, meditative, and sombre version of 'While My Guitar Gently Weeps' from *LOVE* is profoundly different musically from the 'raucous, electric' version on the *White Album*.[24]

The question remains: just how do the dimensions of distance location and sound source size and location bring the listener to a different relationship to – and understanding of – the music and its message? And how do these factors shape music's substance?

[23]   Moylan, *Understanding and Crafting the Mix*, pp. 190–91.

[24]   Mark Hertsgaard, *A Day in the Life: The Music and Artistry of the Beatles* (New York, 1995), pp. 252–3.

The answers will be found in an examination of the complete song, with its overall spatial characteristics and the spatial dimensions of the individual sources as they present, shape and/or propel the musical materials and the song's expression and message.

Lateral Imaging to Enhance Music

The placement of sources along the width of the sound stage brings lateral imaging. Sounds are provided with locations and size.

In both of the above versions of 'While My Guitar Gently Weeps' the lead vocal is mixed to the centre of the sound stage, but the *White Album* vocal image is considerably wider. In this way it remains prominent although it is at a greater distance than the *LOVE* version; notice, it is also at a lower loudness level. Zak describes the 'multifaceted nature of prominence perception' noting 'a sound's stereo placement can affect its prominence' and that prominence 'encompasses all of the other parameters of the mix' that allows for this perception.[25]

Consider these as well: Does the width of the lead vocal in each version contribute in other ways? Does this image width in the White Album version that brings the vocal more prominence also bring it more significance?

Important general observations regarding image size and location begins with identifying:

• Where are the sound sources on the sound stage?
• Where are the musical materials on the sound stage?
• What size are the sound sources?
• What size are the musical materials?

This leads to pertinent observations of image size, using the following Table 11.6 for a beginning.

Table 11.6   Image size concerns

• Amount of physical presence in the mix (space occupied on the sound stage).

• Prominence that is not related to loudness.

• Is the size of the image proportional to the musical importance of the sound source?

• Does the size of the source establish a context or reference for other sources?

---

[25]   Albin Zak, *The Poetics of Rock: Cutting Tracks, Making Records* (Berkeley, CA, 2001), pp. 156–7.

Table 11.7   Image location concerns

• Is the sound source in a location that separates it from others?
• Does the location of the source provide a level of prominence that is not related to loudness?
• Does the location of the source establish a context or reference for other sources?
• Does the image occupy a location with other sources? If so:
Are they presenting similar materials?
Do they have similar sound qualities?
Do they have similar musical functions?

Table 11.7 brings fundamental questions regarding location of sources. These two tables explore potential ways imaging can enhance, extend the character, or provide ornamentation to musical ideas. The impacts are potentially profound, and these tables are only a starting point for exploration and inquiry. Lateral and distance location can be used for blending or fusing sounds (and their musical ideas) with similar treatments, and various degrees of dissimilar treatments can bring various degrees of contrast, distinctiveness, prominence, and so on.

Allan Moore offers: 'the most important features of the use of this space [horizontal location, provided by the stereo image] are the types and degrees of density filling it (whether thin strands or blocks), and the presence in this space of "holes", that is potential areas left unused'.[26] The 'taxonomy of mixes' he and Ruth Dockwray are devising holds significant promise to help us recognize and understand more deeply certain 'common practices' that have developed in constructing mixes.[27]

Lateral Imaging as Musical Idea

Image location can be extended to be a primary musical idea in itself. Recordings have incorporated 'rhythms of locations' into musical fabrics. In these instances, rhythms are created by the locations of sounds on the sound stage; patterns of locations are presented to the listener, and the repetitions and alterations of these patterns can create musical interest just as the patterns of changing pitches, timbres or harmonies.

Drum solos are common places for rhythms of locations, functioning in parallel with the specific drum and cymbals of the passage; for instance in The Beatles' 'The End' (*Abbey Road*, 1969) the tom drum rhythms are underscored by their separate far-left and far-right locations, providing a rhythm of location to the drum

---

[26]   Moore, *Rock*, p. 121.
[27]   Dockwray and Moore, 'Configuring the Sound-Box 1965–1972'.

solo's rhythms of time and timbre. In practice this can also appear by repeating the same sound (or different sounds from the same source) and establishing a pattern of soundings from different, specific locations. This is found in the presentations of the 'cash register' sounds of the surround version of 'Money' by Pink Floyd (*Dark Side of the Moon*, 2003).

Imaging can be used to 'enhance the meaning of a song' by contributing to the delivery and depth of message. Katz discusses the opening of 'Strawberry Fields Forever' (*Magical Mystery Tour*, 1967) where sounds are placed in unlikely positions relative to the listener and exhibit impossible image sizes to create a 'fantastic disposition of sound that persuades us that "nothing is real"'.[28]

Providing a sound with motion or some level of movement is also found, and can function as a musical gesture in itself or can be used to enhance a musical idea. In 'Here Comes the Sun' (*Abbey Road*, 1969) a Moog glissando moves from left to centre at the end of the song's introduction; the motion of the sound complements and parallels its change of pitch and becomes an integral part of the musical gesture. Figure 11.6 presents the opening verses of 'A Day in the Life' (*Sgt. Pepper's Lonely Hearts Club Band*, 1967) where the lead vocal is given a subtle ornamentation of motion. Over the course of this lengthy section, it very gently moves from the right side of the sound stage to the left, with image width varying slightly along the way.

Unique Environments for Any or Every Sound Source

Music recordings can, and often do, place individual sound sources (or smaller groups of sources) in their own, unique environment or 'performance space'. These create alterations to the timbre, or sound quality of sound sources, as well as provide the sound sources (and their musical materials) with additional spatial dimensions.[29]

Environments have sound qualities that fuse with the timbre of the instrument/voice to create a new sound. This new timbre may be subtly different from the source without the environment, or substantially transformed.[30]

The perceived geometry or the 'illusion of physical dimensions' of sound source environments contributes to the sound quality and adds spatial characteristics. This allows environments the potential to generate reflections (time elements) and sound quality (frequency elements) for the sound source and to use the environment's sound to (1) provide colour (timbre) alterations to the instrument or voice (this is considered under 'echo' and 'ambience' by Zak[31] and

---

[28]   Mark Katz, *Capturing Sound: How Technology Has Changed Music* (Berkeley, CA, 2004), pp. 42–3.

[29]   Kurt Blaukopf, 'Space in Electronic Music', *Music and Technology* (New York, 1971), p. 170.

[30]   Moylan, *Understanding and Crafting the Mix*, pp. 195–201.

[31]   Zak, *Poetics of Rock*, pp. 70–85.

under 'presence' by Everett[32]) or to (2) extend size of the sound source image, as occurred to Harrison's vocal in the LOVE version of 'While My Guitar Gently Weeps' above.

Table 11.8 provides some preliminary considerations for evaluating how music is transformed or enhanced by environments.

Table 11.8   Environment sound qualities and dimensions

• Does the environment complement the sound source? The musical material?
• Does the environment enhance the sound source? The musical material?
• What is the size of environment relative to real-world physical size of instrument?
• What is the size of environment related to the type of musical material and its significance?
• Does the environment broaden the sound source image?
• Does the environment deepen the sound source image?
• Does the environment provide the source(s) with other distinguishing qualities?
• Does the environment provide the source or musical material with increased prominence in the musical texture? Significance?

Exploring Spatial Qualities of the Overall Sound

The overall texture has a number of dimensions; among these are the spatial aspects of the perceived performance environment (PPE) and the sound stage. These dimensions will (1) provide a context for the music, and (2) establish a point of reference against which activities and states of individual sources are measured and understood.

Perceived Performance Environment

The perceived performance environment (PPE) is the space where the song exists. Its size is the geometry and dimensions of the 'performance space' of the song, and is conceived as a combination of cues from all sources and any applied characteristics. It is static, or unchanging in its dimensions, although its dimensions may gradually show themselves as the song unfolds. This concept can shape the music in meaningful ways. To understand how, we can begin by considering:

---

[32]   Walter Everett, *The Foundations of Rock: From Blue Suede Shoes to Suite Judy Blue Eyes* (Oxford, 2009), pp. 339–46.

- How is the concept of the song reflected in the size of the song's 'overall space'?
- Is the song bigger than its space? Compatible with? Smaller than?
- Is the song enhanced by its perceived performance environment? In what way?

With the PPE establishing a context for the music as an overall space within which the listener 'hears' the piece of music as existing: we (1) consider the character of this environment and how it complements or shapes the music and (2) consider the state of this environment as static and unchanging, or if it changes we consider when and how.

In usage, the PPE can exist in many states. The following are most common, and others certainly exist.

Common and typical of classical and jazz recordings, the qualities of the PPE are static, and do not change. Recordings intended to capture or replicate a 'live' listening experience will have all of the characteristics of the PPE apparent from beginning to end.

In recordings with more manipulated productions the dimensions of the PPE might unfold, being gradually presented to the listener over time; still, one single environment exists and does not change. The Beatles' 'Here Comes the Sun' is one such recording, where instruments and voices are gradually introduced during the course of the song, and provide the listener with a sense of an expanding and contracting PPE. A single performance space is evident, but the listener is provided with only portions of the environment until the full instrumentation and breadth of the work arrives after two minutes have passed.

Some songs have more than one PPE. This is not common, but this does occur. It may take the form of juxtaposing two or more PPEs as the piece changes from section to section, with striking changes of character. The Beatles' 'A Day in the Life' transports the listener from one PPE to another by way of an orchestral bridge (1:45 to 2:15); Lennon's first section (0:00 to 1:45) has an overall environment that is substantially different from McCartney's section (at 2:15). The listener is then brought to a third PPE at 2:50, then at 3:18 abruptly returning to the first PPE.

Sound Stage

It is common to have sources change in distance location and/or horizontal location to the listener, and/or change image width, and still exist within the same overall environment (PPE). This often occurs between major sections, with verses having one set of relationships and choruses another. This is a typical example of the sound stage being used structurally in delivering the message and expression of a song: placing the listener at different perspectives to the musical materials and performers between major sections, while maintaining a consistent point of reference within the single PPE.

As we learned above, the boundaries of the sound stage (left-right width, front-rear distance) are fluid, and have the potential to change as the work unfolds. Returning to the two versions of 'While My Guitar Gently Weeps', we recognize that a change in the width and depth of the sound stage occurred in the *LOVE* version as the introduction, verse one and first chorus unfolded. The White Album version used the sound stage differently: the sound stage boundaries were established at the very beginning, and created a context within which all of the entering instruments and voices were placed and established their locations.

In considering the sound stage and its relationship to the musical materials, Table 11.9 serves as a point of departure for pertinent evaluations and conclusions:

Table 11.9   Considerations of the sound stage

Where are the [instruments, lead vocal, etc., and their musical parts, etc.]?
What size are the [instruments, lead vocal, etc., and their musical parts, etc.]?
How far from the listener are the [instruments, lead vocal, etc., and their musical parts, etc.]?
Where are the boundaries of the sound stage:
Its front edge?
Its rear wall?
Its furthest left sound source and its furthest right sound source?
Where is the listener located in relationship to the front edge of the sound stage?

Surround Sound's Sound Stage and Perceived Performance Environment

Surround sound brings a number of important potential states that can be very different from stereo recordings.

While all but one of the spatial dimensions discussed above remain conceptually unchanged, how they relate to the listener – and to the listener's location – can be markedly different. The medium can surround the listener with the music. This provides potential for a very different experience, with greater flexibility and potentially greater emphasis on the music's spatial qualities.

The overall spatial elements of the perceived performance environment and the sound stage remain. The PPE has the same dimensions and functions in surround as in stereo recordings. The sound stage in surround has the potential of new dimensions from stereo. The differences relate to the potential size of the sound stage, potential size of the sound sources, and the listener's relationship to the sound stage and its sound sources.

The spatial dimensions at the individual sound source level remain unchanged for distance location and lateral location and image size, with the differences that sound sources have the potential to be placed anywhere around the listener and have the potential for much greater size. Environments of individual sources (or groups of sources) have the potential to exist in a very different and unique manner in surround: the fusion of the direct sound with the reverberant sound that always occurs in stereo (and in our real-world experiences) may be altered in surround to place the two entities in different locations,[33] providing a very different – and potentially surreal – experience.

The following tables outline the important variables and dimensions of surround sound's sound stage and phantom image characteristics (Table 11.10), the unique potential locations of ambiance (Table 11.11), and the listener's potential locations and relationships to the sound stage (Table 11.12):

Table 11.10   Variables and dimensions of the sound stage and phantom images in surround sound

---

Size of sound stage

Same as the stereo sound stage

Wider than stereo, extending the sides

Multiple Sound Stages in Front and in Back

Complete Circle, with sounds covering 360°

Location of sound stage

In front of the listener

Behind the listener

Wrapping to/around the sides of the listener

Encircling the listener

Placement of sources

Similar to stereo

Instruments at sides

Instruments in back

Moving sources

Potential for sound sources to move slightly, through 360° around listener

---

[33] Tomlinson Holman, *Surround Sound: Up and Running* (2nd edn, Boston, 2008), p. 135.

Table 11.11   The potential locations for the placement of ambiance in surround sound recordings

---

Related to sound sources

    Fused with the sound source timbre and location

    Placed in different locations from the sound source

    Placed behind the listener

Related to perceived performance environment

    Room sound surrounding listener

    Stereo sound stage with surround channels used for ambiance

---

Table 11.12   The listener's potential locations and relationships to the sound stage in surround sound recordings

---

As observer

    Very close to the front edge of the sound stage

    Some detachment from front of sound stage

    Considerable detachment from the sound stage

    Sound stage or sources behind the listener

Enveloped within the recording

    Seated within the ensemble and inside the sound stage, immersed in the music and performance

    Surrounded by the music and ambiance (with some detachment – from very little to quite considerable – from the ensemble)

Distance in Surround

In surround sound, the listener's relationship to the sound stage continues to establish a relationship to the music and its communications (expressions/ emotions and meanings). The listener is placed at some distance from the concepts: perhaps intimately close (being very near the vocal's persona or other sound sources of significance), perhaps at a considerable distance. The relationship of the reverberant energy to the listener, and the use of the rear channels can bring the listener to be observing the performance (recording) within an environment they are experiencing but not necessarily occupying, within an environment they occupy, or even by being seated within the ensemble and its sound stage (especially when instruments are located behind the listener and the rear sides).

Potential distance location of the listener relative to the sound stage extends from largely detached from the sound stage, to very close to the front of the sound stage. These are the same as stereo recordings. Strikingly different in surround is the possibility to place the listener within the sound stage, which will provide a very different presentation of the music to the listener. Phil Ramone shares his approach to mixing a surround sound recording of Elton John's Radio City Music Hall concert in June of 2004:

> The beauty of mixing ... in 5.1 surround sound is that it allows us to purposefully design the mix to make the listener feel as though they're sitting in a certain spot in the venue. I think it's cool to bring the listener onto the stage, giving them the sense that he or she is standing right next to Elton [John] and his piano. There's something about that close proximity that allows for a lot of detail to be heard – detail that you would never hear if you were watching the concert in a big arena.[34]

Location in Surround

Location in surround continues to include the size and lateral location of images, with the concepts discussed above. Obviously, the size of the sound stage can be extended considerably in surround, as lateral boundaries can extend to surround the listener, and the size of images can exist at any size up to 360° around the listener (though difficult in production practice, conceptually this is possible). How the size of the images and locations of the images interrelate with the associated size and locations of the musical materials presented above factor equally in surround.

The separation of sound sources (and their musical materials) and their host environments is possible, and is potentially important. The location and size of ambiance/environment sound can substantially transform the significance, prominence, character and/or sound qualities of sound sources and their musical ideas. This must be factored into an examination of how spatial properties enhance, transform or present music. Figure 11.9 depicts the surround lateral locations of the Lowry organ, tamboura and John Lennon's vocal from 'Lucy in the Sky With Diamonds' (*Yellow Submarine*, 1999); the placement of the vocal's ambiance away from the direct sound image is represented by the density of dots.

Surround Sound Stage in Practice

Significant changes in the sound stage occur throughout the surround sound version of 'While My Guitar Gently Weeps' from *LOVE*. The acoustic guitar of the introduction slightly changes to its position and width to arrive at its location in the front-centre anchored sound stage of Figure 11.10. The mix then evolves

---

[34]   Ramone and Granata, *Making Records*, p. 254.

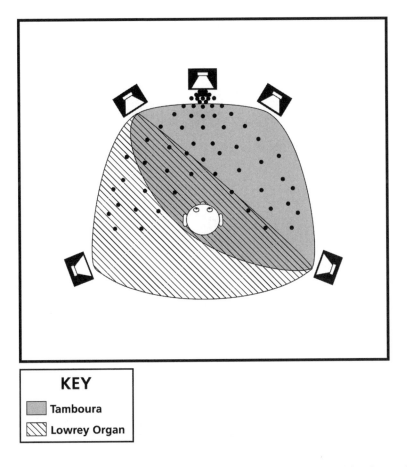

KEY

▨ Tamboura

▨ Lowrey Organ

Figure 11.9   Surround image placements from 'Lucy in the Sky with Diamonds' (*Yellow Submarine*, 1999)

taking all various entering sources through changes of width and locations in an ever-expanding sound stage to arrive at Figure 11.11's much wider sound stage.

The dimensions of the sound stage evolve as the music progresses, with the listener gradually becoming more and more immersed in the music of the song, as they are further and further enveloped by the sound stage and the sound sources/musical materials; still, the sound stage does not fully envelop or immerse the listener with instruments or voices from the rear, and a certain degree of observation (and detachment) is maintained. Differences in distance locations and lateral locations and image sizes are also evident and significant.

Listening to this surround version on an accurate surround sound system will provide an experience substantially different from the stereo version discussed

"While My Guitar Gently Weeps" Intro thru Verse 1, meas. 1-24.

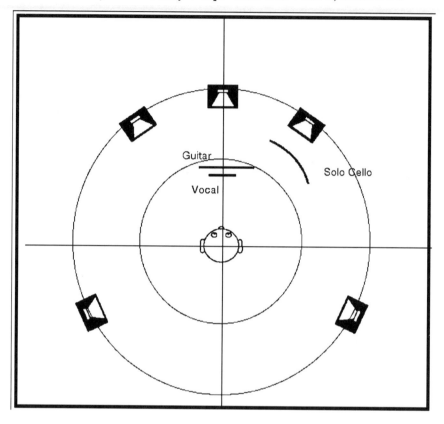

Figure 11.10 Surround sound mix of 'While My Guitar Gently Weeps' from
          LOVE, measures 1–24

above. The musical parts are spaced further apart in the surround mix, and given
more room and less competition – and in some ways less connection to one another.

Consider: How are these spatial differences between the stereo and surround
mixes significant musically? Do these changes in spatial quality communicate
something different (change the concept of the song or its meaning or its substance)?
Do these changes in spatial quality bring the materials and their presentations to
merely communicate the same substance differently (change the quality of the
material as ornamentation, but not alter its substance)?

"While My Guitar Gently Weeps" Chorus 2, meas. 57-72.

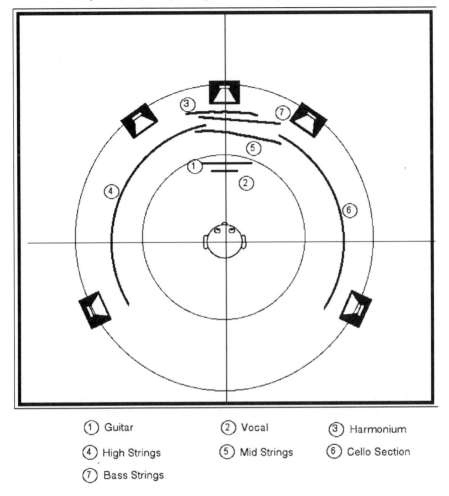

① Guitar	② Vocal	③ Harmonium
④ High Strings	⑤ Mid Strings	⑥ Cello Section
⑦ Bass Strings		

Figure 11.11   Surround sound mix of 'While My Guitar Gently Weeps' from *LOVE*, measures 57–72

In Closing

This represents the beginning of a search for a greater understanding, and not intended to offer an overview of practice, or a theory of principles. It seeks to offer a framework and to start a context for inquiry and for discovery of how space functions in recorded music.

Spatial qualities of recordings are potentially striking, and their sonic significance is undeniable. These spatial qualities can become an integral part of the composition or add important characteristics of many types. They can:

- Transform musical materials and relationships.
- Provide added dimensions to instruments and voices.
- Enhance the overall musicality of the recording.
- Give added meaning and character to a song's musical parts.
- Contribute to a convincing presentation of the song.
- Enliven and enhance the delivery of the message or the emotive expression the song/music is communicating.
- Bring substantive musical material to the song.
- Provide a context or point of reference for the recording/music.

The underlying questions remain: how do we define the activities and states of spatial qualities as musical materials (concepts) or as ornamental embellishments within the musical texture? How do we calculate their impact on the music, their functions and significance?

Discography

Beatles, The, 'Strawberry Fields Forever', *Magical Mystery Tour*. (EMI Records Ltd, 1967, digitally remastered 1987). CDPCTC 255.

Beatles, The, 'A Day in the Life', *Sgt. Pepper's Lonely Hearts Club Band*. (EMI Records Ltd, 1967, digitally remastered 1987). CDP 7 46442 2.

Beatles, The, 'While My Guitar Gently Weeps', *The Beatles* (the *White Album*). (EMI Records Ltd, 1968, digitally remastered 1987). C1-46443.

Beatles, The, 'Here Comes the Sun', *Abbey Road*. (EMI Records Ltd, 1969, digitally remastered 1987). CDP 7 46446 2.

Beatles, The, 'The End', *Abbey Road*. (EMI Records Ltd, 1969, digitally remastered 1987). CDP 7 46446 2.

Beatles, The, 'Lucy in the Sky With Diamonds', *Yellow Submarine*. (Subafilms Ltd., 1999). (DVD) CDP 7 46445 2.

Beatles, The, 'While My Guitar Gently Weeps', *LOVE*. (Capitol, 2006). (CD) 0946 3 81732 2 9.

Beatles, The, 'While My Guitar Gently Weeps', *LOVE*. (Capitol, 2006). (DVD-A) 0946 3 81732 2 9.

Pink Floyd, 'Money', *Dark Side of the Moon*. (Capitol, 2003). (SACD) CDP 7243 5 82136 21.

Interlude 2
Comments and Commentaries by Industry Professionals and Producers

Mike Howlett

In Chapter 9, Michael Jarrett proposes the concept of the 'self-effacing producer', and supports this with a rich 'ethnography' of interviews with a range of jazz and country music producers and engineers. Certainly, this proposition rings true to this producer – one part of the producer's art is to immerse in the artist's world and gain insight and understanding of the best approach to take to create conditions where the artist will deliver a 'true' performance. However, producers have many different approaches to the art, and, while the aim to be 'transparent' is evident in many of the statements Jarrett has collected, it is one of a number of factors that define the role. To attain a wider understanding, I posit the role of the record producer as a *nexus* between the creative inspiration of the artist, the technology of the recording studio, and the commercial aspirations of the record company.

The term 'nexus' is used here according to the *Shorter Oxford English Dictionary* (1983) definition: a bond or link; a means of connection; and, as a causal noun, *the necessary connection between cause and effect*. The record producer acts as a means of connection between the artist, the technology and the commercial interest. However, the connection is not a wholly transparent one – the personality and skills of the producer will shape and tone the outcome, as a colour transparency affects the light passing through it. Whether by directing the timbres and textural qualities of the recording through engineering processes; by structuring and arranging these qualities through musical direction; or simply by inspiring, enthusing and facilitating, the producer is engaged to direct the process and shapes the outcome by his or her presence. It can be argued that a producer is not necessary in this process, but the act of recording is not a passive *fait accompli*. Choices are made at many stages in the process: what studio to record in, which engineer, which microphone and where to place it? All of these decisions affect the character of the outcome. Critical to the outcome is the selection of performance. From the backing track to instrumental solos and embellishments, to particular lines of the vocal, each detail requires a process of *critical evaluation*. Whenever this function of critical arbiter is performed the role of the producer is inherent.

As well as linking the musical idea and the recording technology, a producer must address the expectations of the record company – the third factor in this process. The record company underwrites the enterprise and, more significantly, delivers the outcome to market.

The role of the producer is, therefore, to be the interface between these three sets of interests: the artist, including the song as creative object and its performance; the engineer, as agent of technological mediation in the realization of the creative object as sonic artefact; and the business, usually the record company, as financial facilitator, encompassing contractual arrangements and the extent to which marketing and promotional concerns impinge on function. Record companies place financial constraints that are a major influence on the choice of studio and other budgetary considerations, such as travel, accommodation and time. There is also a clear and explicit expectation that the producer will present an outcome that will satisfy commercial aspirations, and this constitutes a form of pressure that affects some of the creative decisions a producer makes.

Put at its simplest, the producer's task is to produce *a satisfactory outcome*. The definition of a satisfactory outcome varies considerably according to the aims and aspirations of all the involved parties. These aims can be simply to achieve a commercially viable result, or, at the other end of the spectrum, an artistically satisfactory finished article. The ideal outcome will satisfy both aspirations: commercial *and* critical success. The ways these outcomes are achieved vary widely from producer to producer. For this reason a consideration of the role as nexus is the most universally satisfactory approach.

From observations drawn from interviews with other producers, and my own experience, the various roles a producer undertakes can be listed as follows:

- arranger / interpreter / visualizer
- engineer
- creative director / performance director
- logistical facilitator / project manager
- psychologist / counsellor / priest
- mediator – between the objectives and aspirations of the record company and the artist

Of course, some or all of these roles may be undertaken in any given production – each production has a unique set of circumstances.

Each of the roles I have listed can be seen to fulfil some aspect of the nexus' requirements. One role, the project manager, is probably the most universal, and the one that defines the difference when, for example, an engineer becomes the producer. To be appointed producer of a recording means all the decisions about process – where to record, what to record and in which order, whether a given performance is right, and when the project is completed – are your responsibility. It may be more relevant to the purpose of role definition to consider the specific roles at various stages of a production.

Robin Millar

First let me say I am pleased that record production is to be valued and studied in this way. As there are no barriers to entry or exams to pass, the quality and level of expertise among producers has varied hugely. I would ideally prefer the soubriquet the *art and science of record production* as I feel that both sides are inextricably linked and each is vital.

I would, perhaps, mention that, studying your chapter headings, there does not seem to be a part of the book dealing with the psychology of record production – the human relationships which make or break performance, cooperation and harmony.

Richard James Burgess

Simon Zagorski-Thomas: *What use do you think the academic study of record production serves?*

Relative to other fields of artistic endeavour, such as the visual arts, the academic study of record production is a young discipline. The ability to record and then disseminate music through space and time has, by virtue of a recording's intrinsic objectivity, forever altered the manner in which we can examine and re-examine the subtleties of diverse music. Before recording was possible, descriptive analysis and notation systems, with their inherent limitations and subjectivity, did not allow for later verification of insights into a particular performance and the intent of the performers and composers. The objectivity of an audio recording has endowed us with an invaluable body of primary source material ripe for academic study. Although early recordings could initially only capture a performance event, continuous and rapid development of recording technologies and techniques over the past hundred years or so has transformed the way we compose, arrange and orchestrate music. Recordings have also changed the business of music because, unlike live performances, they allow for passive income streams for performers and have expanded those, which began with sheet music publishing, for composers. Record producer is a term that couldn't have existed before Edison's invention of the phonograph and its meaning has broadened to encompass many possible roles such as patron, composer, arranger, orchestrator, engineer, performer, director, administrator and more. The academic study of record production helps us to understand, document and promulgate all these various functions, processes and their effects. By quantifying processes and how they are entwined with effects we can identify best practice methodologies and more easily recognize breakthrough innovations and trends, which can inform and educate producers, artists, musicians, legislators and the music industry itself.

Maureen Droney

Simon Zagorski-Thomas: *What use do you think the academic study of record production serves?*

I think it serves a very important purpose. Record production is an art as well as a craft and people devote their lives to it because it satisfies an innate desire to communicate and create. To be a good producer requires many different skills. It has always been difficult to define the title of 'record producer'. As we all know, there are songwriter/producers, arranger/producers, engineer/producers, vibe/producers, musician/producers, and so on, and so on. All of these elements come into play as one attempts to capture or create a great performance. Producing is an ineffable art – very difficult to pin down. Of course, the bottom line is that the record producer is the person in charge of getting the recording made – whatever that takes is what he or she needs to do. But the levels of creativity and communication, musicality, life experience, work style, and all sorts of other abilities required makes for a rich subject indeed and one well worth studying. A great record producer communicates on a rarified level. That skill alone is worth examining as it is translates to all sorts of fields.

Bob Olhsson

Alan Williams, in Chapter 8, suggests that individual mixes can solve the headphone problem. I would propose that, in order to play with proper phrasing, dynamics and pitch, musicians all need to be relating to the same musical balance. While individual mixes can make for a smoother session they can also make for worse performances and the need for a lot more manipulation in the final mix.

PART III
Case Studies

Chapter 12

Simulating the Ideal Performance: Suvi Raj Grubb and Classical Music Production[1]

Andrew Blake

'Who is that black man over there?' asked, predictably enough, the Austrian conductor Herbert von Karajan, during a rehearsal for an early 1960s recording session.[2] In assessing the career of the 'black man' in question, Suvi Raj Grubb (who became producer Walter Legge's assistant at EMI in 1960, and arguably EMI's most important classical music producer in the 20 years after Legge's resignation from the company in 1964), this preliminary exploration will discuss his importance to the evolution of the common values of classical music as encoded in commercial stereo recordings; but Karajan's question still invites a nuanced answer, and the chapter will also necessarily, if very tentatively, begin to map race/ethnicity and empire onto the sonic values expressed by classical music, which is still among the most important registers of musical whiteness.

The Production of 'Classical Music': The Producer as the Empowered Listener

Classical music departments of major labels have historically tended to use company employees as producers (though recently, typically of capitalism's tendency to outsource risk, the freelance classical producer has become a routine professional figure). The permanent company employee doesn't usually have the freelancer's contractual driver of sales points, which encourages the producer to maximize the commercial potential of the recording at the expense of aesthetic or other considerations. In the end, though, the *musical* fundamentals are the same: the producer is the privileged listener, mediating the relationship between the score, the performing artists and the processes and technologies of recording.

---

[1]   Some aspects of this chapter are based on work which has been published in Andrew Blake, 'Recording Practices and the Role of the Producer', in Nicholas Cook, Eric Clarke, Daniel Leech-Wilkinson and John Rink (eds), *The Cambridge Companion to Recorded Music* (Cambridge, 2009), pp. 36–62. I am grateful to the editors of that volume, and of this, for all their helpful input.

[2]   Internet posting by John Deacon (former director of British Phonograph Industry), accessed August 2005.

(Less often the classical producer has also mediated the rather more difficult relationship between the living composer, the performers and the technologies.) The producer's key task seemed to revolve around correcting mistakes, while prompting aesthetic decisions by the performers or engineers, and also prompting the sound engineer to produce a particular type of sound, aiming usually for what Colin Symes has called the 'best seat in the house' approach to sonic values – the attempt to make a recording which could be experienced in the living room as if the listener was in row 12 of the stalls seats at an actual concert.[3]

Through most of the twentieth century, classical recordings were sold as the expected companion of prestige domestic equipment for their reproduction: hi-fi. The target consumer of these expensive goods was affluent, male and middle-aged. Alongside this hardware of conspicuous consumption and precision-engineered response came the software, the music itself, sold as well-packaged and expensive high art for the amateur enthusiast. The best-known classical record producers were, perhaps unsurprisingly, the same sort of person as the target consumer: middle-class men who knew what they liked, and bestowed, in collaboration with journalists and consumers alike, the discourses of superior technical ability, taste and even genius, on the performers they recorded and listened to.

The result was a niche but profitable market. EMI had exploited the relative profitability of classical recordings during the first 50 years of recorded music by building Abbey Road studios, which were opened in 1931.[4] After the Second World War and the establishment of the vinyl LP, the profitability of classical records may have declined somewhat, but whatever was made from actual sales, the classical artists signed to these labels were amply rewarded – the star singers and conductors could make half a million pounds Sterling annually from recording royalties in the late 1950s / early 1960s.[5]

In other words, the classical record industry worked from the 1930s to the 1960s with enthusiastic autodidacts (representing the equally enthusiastic middle class listener) as producers, and artisan engineers to do the actual recording. Producers such as Walter Legge at EMI and John Culshaw at Decca had no formal degree-level musical training (though Culshaw's memoirs register the arrival of music graduates both as producers, and university-trained 'tonmeister' sound engineers, from the 1960s onwards).[6] Legge and Culshaw had been 'trained' not in performance or composition but in music appreciation. That is, through mainly

---

[3]   See Colin Symes, *Setting the Record Straight: a Material History of Classical Recording* (Middletown, CT, 2004), pp. 60–87.

[4]   S.A. Pandit, *From Making to Music: the History of Thorn EMI* (London, 1996), pp. 64–5.

[5]   John Culshaw, *Putting the Record Straight* (London, 1981), pp. 320–21.

[6]   See Culshaw, *Record Straight*, pp. 168; 282; 340–41; but cf. the words of more recent Decca producer Andrew Cornall: 'I don't think anyone ever decides to do classical music production as a career move. I know I didn't', quoted in Richard James Burgess, *The Art of Music Production* (2nd edn, London, 2001), p. 188.

informal means they had come to acquire knowledge and appreciation of an already existing repertoire of music composed by a small number of individuals who had lived in Europe in the eighteenth and nineteenth centuries, and they forthrightly agreed that this repertoire was the best of all music. This attitude tended to imply not just that pop, or jazz, were by definition inferior, but also that any *new* music, and especially music using or proposing new forms and techniques, was simply surplus to requirements.

What emerged in consequence of this conservatism in commercial classical music recording, was a star system – in which, much as in pop music before the 1960s, the 'stars' were in most cases not *composers* but *performers*, and these stars operated by endlessly repeating their interpretations of a museum-repertoire of this relatively small number of recognized 'masterpieces' from the eighteenth and nineteenth centuries. Associated with EMI, for example, were a number of technically gifted aesthetic perfectionists with relatively limited musical ambition which matched fairly precisely the tastes of those recording them and selling the results. Italian conductor Carlo Maria Giulini, a case in point, became a 'star conductor' in the early 1960s, making an incandescent recording of the Verdi Requiem in 1964 – which is still commercially available – and a small number of other relatively commercially successful recordings, which represented his entire conducting repertoire; he seemed to know very little music, or about music, apart from these few dozen pieces. No producer seems to have tried to persuade him into a more adventurous *modus operandi*, despite the ready audience for his recordings.

While radio music production in the UK could at times be defiantly modernist,[7] classical record production started and largely remained conservative in outlook, with conservative producers employed by conservative label heads and working, in the main, with conservative performers, all of whom shared a distaste for the new. John Culshaw's memoir notes Decca's reluctance to record Benjamin Britten's opera *Peter Grimes*. Culshaw had argued against his employers – successfully, in the end – that 'if we were to abandon so relatively conservative a modern composer we should rule out contemporary music altogether'.[8] (The 1960s rehabilitation of Mahler's music, which is often seen as a by-product of stereo, is also a by-product of this anti-modernism: in jumping on the Mahler bandwagon the record labels could record unfamiliar – in the early 1960s – twentieth-century music which was not dissonant, and might therefore be expected to sell reasonably well.[9] Which –

---

[7]   On BBC radio and modernism in the 1920s–30s see Jennifer Doctor, *The BBC and Ultra-Modern Music 1922–36: Shaping a Nation's Tastes* (Cambridge, 1999); and, from the 1960s, Sir William Glock, *Notes in Advance* (Oxford, 1991); Jennifer Doctor and David Wright (eds), *The Proms: A New History* (London, 2007).

[8]   Culshaw, *Record Straight*, p. 176. Benjamin Britten could indeed be the exception which proved the rule. It's worth noting that Legge was a personal friend of Britten, and also that Carlo Maria Giulini was also interested in Britten; his 1969 live recording of the *War Requiem* is regarded as among the best.

[9]   Culshaw was aware of this trick and didn't like it: *Record Straight*, p. 340.

championed through the record labels by a bevy of star conductors such as Otto Klemperer, Georg Solti, Bernard Haitink, Leonard Bernstein and in the end even Karajan – it did.)

Suvi Raj Grubb: A 'Typical' Classical Record Producer

Many classical record producers lacked even Culshaw's concern for the state of contemporary musical composition. An example of this aesthetic conservatism is Suvi Raj Grubb. A South Indian Christian who was born in Madras in 1917, Grubb was socialized into the Anglican Church music repertoire – while still working in India he was a church organist and choirmaster. From 1949 to 1953, he had a career in All-India Radio, ending as a producer, and on emigration to England in 1953 (alongside his wife, a doctor) he worked as a freelance producer with the BBC. He became a member of the amateur Philharmonia Chorus, which had first been established for conductor Otto Klemperer's 1957 recording of Ludwig van Beethoven's 9th Symphony with the Philharmonia Orchestra. Playing a voluntary role in the administration of the choir led to Grubb meeting with the founder (and in his own view at least, owner) of the Philharmonia Orchestra, Walter Legge, who at that point was chief classical producer for EMI. Grubb became Legge's assistant at EMI in 1960, then a full producer in 1964, with responsibility for a roster of star international artists including pianist and conductor Daniel Barenboim and violinist Itzhak Perlman.[10] He went on to play a key early role in the remastering of existing recordings. He retired in 1985, publishing an important memoir, *Music Makers on Record*, in the following year. Suvi Raj Grubb died in Pune, India, in 1999.[11]

The production of record companies' conservative values can be seen from Grubb's first encounter with Legge, who saw Richard Strauss and Jean Sibelius as the great twentieth-century composers. Before Legge offered him his assistant's job, Grubb had to answer 20 questions on aspects of the standard Austro-German repertoire in which Legge focused on the minutiae of opus and Köchel numbers, ending with the questions 'How many minor key piano concertos are there by

---

[10]   Some of the other EMI stars with whom Suvi Raj Grubb worked included conductor Klemperer, a refugee from Nazism who dealt mainly with Austro-German mainstream repertoire (and was among the pioneers of the Mahler revival); Daniel Barenboim's wife, the cellist Jacqueline du Pré, who also tended to the Austro-German mainstream, leavened by her well-known interpretation of the Elgar cello concerto; cellist, conductor and ambivalent Soviet citizen Mstislav Rostropovich, who regularly worked with contemporary composers; and André Previn, who was a jazz pianist and film composer as well as a classical conductor, and who occasionally made adventurous recordings, though it is worth noting that his 1978 version of Messiaen's *Turangalila* Symphony was not produced by Grubb.

[11]   The biographical details here are from Suvi Raj Grubb, *Music Makers on Record* (London, 1986), particularly pp. 36–40.

Mozart?',[12] and 'what are the instruments in Schubert's octet?'.[13] Grubb got them all right. None of the questions was on twentieth-century music, whether classical or otherwise, or on pre-eighteenth-century music, or for that matter on Indian music.

Those who tend (naively) to presume a direct correspondence between musical taste and personal and political attitudes would not find it too much of a surprise that Walter Legge's taste in an orthodox musical repertoire mapped onto his own behaviour, and that this included his inhabiting a somewhat dictatorial role as a record producer – both in preparing for recordings and in overseeing them. In fact Legge's autocratic methods in the rehearsal studio, recording studio and control room led eventually to a relationship-breaking row with the conductor Otto Klemperer during a rehearsal. This meant both the end of the Philharmonia Orchestra (which after a while re-formed as the New Philharmonia, now scared off from professional management, and run instead by a committee of orchestral members along the same cooperative lines as the London Symphony Orchestra), and the end of Legge's recording career. The row forced his resignation from EMI (who preferred to keep their star sellers on the roster rather than bolster the egos of producers), and therefore opened the way for Grubb's assumption of a more senior role within the organization.

Grubb may have been easier to get on with, but his unquestioning inheritance of Legge's values – their shared musical conservatism – is clear. Talking of working with the conductor and modernist composer Pierre Boulez on a recording of Bela Bartók's piano concertos with Daniel Barenboim as the soloist, he remarks 'I confessed to him at one point that I found very modern music a tough proposition.'[14] Such tastes are directly reflected in the outputs of Grubb's recording career. The 240 gramophone recordings he produced for EMI which are mentioned in the appendix to *Music Makers on Record* (this list is not claimed to be a complete discography) contain approximately 1000 individual pieces of music. Only 61 of these are twentieth century works, most of them being tonal music by composers such as Richard Strauss, Jean Sibelius, Claude Debussy, Maurice Ravel, Sergei Rachmaninov, Dmitri Shostakovich and Manuel de Falla; there's a smattering of music by Igor Stravinsky and Bartók; one piece each by Arnold Schoenberg and Alban Berg; and nothing by any living post-war modernist composer such as Boulez himself. The few important recordings of twentieth-century music supervised by Grubb included the original version of Shostakovich's opera *Lady Macbeth of Mtsensk*, conducted by Mstislav Rostropovich in 1972; the first recording of the completed version of Falla's opera *Atlantida*, conducted by Rafael Frühbeck de Burgos in 1976; and pianist John Ogdon's 1967 recording of the fearsomely long, technically difficult and musically eccentric piano concerto by Ferrucio Busoni, conducted by Daniell Revenaugh.

---

[12]   There are two: in D minor, K. 466 and C minor, K. 491.

[13]   The Schubert Octet is scored for clarinet, bassoon, horn, string quartet and double bass.

[14]   Grubb, *Music Makers*, p. 68.

Whatever the adventurousness or otherwise of the repertoire recorded by Grubb, his sonic ambition remained the same: attempting to simulate the experience of the listener in the expensive seats of the concert-hall or opera-house. Recording equipment was to be used principally as a register, but not as a conditioner or manipulator of sound, so the recording environment was considered vital. Both Decca and EMI tended to use the Kingsway Hall but not the lightweight Royal Festival Hall, which produced too little bass. Grubb imagined himself as that ideal listener – someone sitting dead centre in the expensive seats a dozen or so rows from the front. This isn't to say that he just let the engineer set up the microphones and control the balances, then looked at the score and listened for wrong notes and intonation errors. He occasionally allowed himself to bring out details of the music which might be lost in some concert halls. More adventurously, his aesthetic sometimes allowed for changes in balance and equalization during a recording session, to match his assessment of the temper of the different works being recorded; though it's worth noting that he did nothing as adventurous as his contemporary John Culshaw. While busily 'simulating' the opera stage in stereo for the Decca recording of Wagner's four *Ring* operas – and indeed that *Peter Grimes* which had so frightened Decca – Culshaw was happy to manipulate the basic sound in apparent mid performance, using equalization and reverberation when he thought the drama demanded it. He was equally happy to add noisy sound effects when it suited the drama – to the disgust of some of the singers and conductors involved.[15]

The extra clarity possible in stereo recordings meant higher fidelity to the actual sound being recorded, so Grubb's comments on stereo were positive. But about the quadraphonic experiment of the mid 1970s he was uniformly negative, explaining that when he mixed for quad he just replicated the stereo mix for the front channels at the back, with a little extra reverb.[16] Grubb also had a lifelong suspicion of multitrack recording techniques, arguing (presciently) that they gave too much power to the producer.[17]

Despite his suspicions, Grubb was in fact a virtuoso producer, able to deploy that extra power and use any and all technical procedures available – including multitracking – in order to simulate the perfect version of the music for the listener. *Music Makers on Record* acknowledges the use of a multitrack recorder to overdub Mstislav Rostropovich's cello in a recording of the Brahms double concerto. At the full recording session the cellist had been suffering from hearing difficulties after a flight in an unpressurised cabin, and the result had been a performance with uncharacteristically poor intonation.[18] More impressively, *Music Makers* also details the extraordinary process used to record Mozart's opera *Don Giovanni*

---

[15]   Ibid., p. 64; for Culshaw's work in the pioneer stereo studio recording of Wagner's *Ring* operas, see John Culshaw, *Ring Resounding* (London 1967).

[16]   Grubb, *Music Makers*, pp. 16–17.

[17]   Ibid., pp. 128–9.

[18]   Ibid., pp. 222–3.

in 1973. Conductor Daniel Barenboim wished to use the cast he had assembled for performances at that year's Edinburgh festival, and EMI duly contracted the singers and orchestra, hired a school hall just outside the city and began to record. But first the singer playing Don Giovanni (Roger Soyer), and subsequently the singer playing Zerlina, one of the Don's many love interests (Helen Donath), fell ill and were unable to sing, and in the end some of the music had to be recorded months later in London. Hectic work schedules meant that some 'duets' were recorded onto multitrack tape, with the duetting singers performing in turn rather than together – a technique which was commonly used in rock, but was at that time virtually unheard of in classical music. The final mix involved synchronizing a two-track stereo tape recorded in Edinburgh with one of two 8-track tapes, recorded in London using artificial reverberation to simulate the sound of the original school hall, and mixing the results on to a further 2-track tape. Needless to say the final result is worlds away from multitrack rock experiments: the listener hears the usual simulation of the live opera as experienced in the best seat in the house.[19]

This, then, is the careful, technically sophisticated but relatively unambitious sound-world of would-be high fidelity, the attempt to be faithful to the concert performance as perceived by the listener sitting in the stalls. It is the fundamental aesthetic position which still apparently drives the production of classical recordings (for instance, very few classical recordings in the SACD and DVD-Audio formats, which offer surround-sound capabilities well beyond those of the 1970s quadraphonic experiments, actually challenge the row-12 ideal). Despite this, Grubb's recordings were never in danger of being any such thing as a mere copy of an artist's work: while that Edinburgh *Don Giovanni* may be regarded as exceptional, recurrent throughout his memoir is the acknowledgement that recordings should never, unlike actual concert performances, contain poor intonation, wrong notes or distorted sound, and he and his engineers would always edit and splice the various takes to produce an 'ideal' performance. He would doubtless have employed to the full the current digital editing software which allows music to be cut and pasted with microtonal and micro-temporal accuracy way beyond the dreams of Grubb's tape-splicing world. But even without the ambivalent delights of digital editing, classical recording had already arrived by the late 1950s at a situation in which it is not a copy of a live performance, but a simulacrum produced by the careful editing of 'repeated takes', in the apt title of Michael Chanan's book: a vinyl record, CD or MP3 file is a 'copy' of itself, but not of a performance – there is no 'original' beyond the carefully edited master tape or its digital file equivalent.[20] The listener at home in the imagined row 12 was (and is) hearing an equally imaginary performance.

---

[19]   Ibid., pp. 145–54. The episode is discussed in Simon Trezise, 'The Recorded Document: Interpretation and Discography', in Cook et al., *Cambridge Companion*, pp. 206–7.

[20]   Michael Chanan, *Repeated Takes* (London 1995).

When he moved away from the front-line role of record production, Suvi Raj Grubb did not always merely try to reproduce what he was given (though the attempt to form a perfect simulation remained the same). The aesthetics of restoration provide interesting variations on the conservative theme. Older recordings, especially the many mono 'hi-fi' recordings made in the decade before the widespread adoption of stereo, were often remastered and repackaged as the music business grew in confidence during the 1960s (a procedure which was repeated *ad nauseam* in the CD era 20 years later), and the object was as often to enhance as to restore an original recording. Grubb's work in this regard was important. Many older recordings – from the heroic early twentieth-century era of Melba and Caruso onwards – had favoured the named artist's voice or solo instrument at the expense of the orchestra or accompanist, and in his remastering work for EMI Grubb often changed the balance (and as often produced pseudo-stereo), in another simulation of the ideal listening position in the concert hall or opera house.

For example, when in 1964 he remastered conductor Wilhelm Furtwängler's 1950 version of Richard Wagner's opera *Tristan und Isolde*, which had been produced by Legge, Grubb tried to restore the balance between orchestra and singers, using a fairly crude form of equalization:

> All I had to do to give the orchestra greater prominence was, judiciously, to emphasise electronically the frequencies above and below the range of the voices – and considering that a tuba starts from about 43 cycles per second and a piccolo can play notes of up to 4000 cycles per second ... a wide field was available [for comparison, the human voice is about low bass 65 to high soprano 1046].[21]

In doing this rebalancing, Grubb may well have been implicitly critiquing the musicality of Walter Legge's work. His refurbishment of acknowledged highlights of Legge's contribution to the history of recording such as that *Tristan*, the von Karajan recording of the Mozart horn concertos, with Dennis Brain as soloist, which was re-released in 1972, or the 1963 rendition of Mozart's opera *Cosi fan Tutte* conducted by Karl Böhm which was re-released in 1973, all involved such changes in the relationship of soloist and ensemble. At all events, well before Legge's death in 1979 the two were no longer on speaking terms; Legge's published writings, including those edited posthumously by his wife, the German soprano Elizabeth Schwarzkopf, make no mention of Grubb, or of any aspect of their long professional and personal relationship.[22]

---

[21]   Grubb, *Music Makers*, p. 113.

[22]   The absences can be found in two edited collections of Legge's writings: Elizabeth Schwarzkopf, *On and Off the Record: A Memoir of Walter Legge* (London, 1988); and Walter Legge, *Walter Legge: Words and Music*, ed. Alan Sanders (London, 1998). Grubb is actually named as Legge's assistant on p. 109 of *On and Off the Record*, but in an essay

The Politics of Classical Recording: An Anglo-Indian Angle

I have consistently used the discourse of conservatism in regarding Grubb's musical knowledge and aesthetics. But in producing what I identified at the start of the chapter as a paradigmatic sign of whiteness, mainstream repertoire classical music, and despite the relative absence of reflection on the politics of race – including his own ethnic identity and history – from his memoir, Grubb was also politically aware of these issues, as you would be if you were a brown-skinned person living in 1950s–80s Britain, whatever your previous experiences and views.[23]

Raising the issues of race, ethnicity and empire, takes us back to where Grubb first learned the repertoire of Western classical music, which was in many instances through records sold by Indian HMV, a label which also produced Bhaskar Menon, the very successful CEO of EMI Capitol Records – the EMI label's worldwide division – from 1978 to 1990.[24] We should also pause to remember that the foundation of the Philharmonia Orchestra may have been Legge's idea, but it was supported in large part by money given by the Maharajah of Mysore.[25] The Imperial India into which Grubb was born was not an exotic Other completely divorced from British culture, on which the Imperial rulers operated at arms' length; many middle class and aristocratic Indians, educated British-style or at actual British schools and universities, had adopted aspects of British culture with enthusiasm (and great skill, as the history of cricket amply demonstrates). It should not surprise, therefore, that post-imperial India produced leaders in many aspects of British, European and American culture and business.

Nonetheless the connections should not be made too glibly. Thinking about HMV in India might in turn take us back through the conservative repertoire embraced by Grubb to the arguments made in the early 1990s by Sara Suleri and others about the formation of the set of writings, values and responses organized as 'English Literature'.[26] Lord Macaulay's now infamous 'Minute' of 1835 on education in India had stated, among other things that:

> We must at present do our best to form a class who may be interpreters between
> us and the millions whom we govern, – a class of persons Indian in blood and
> colour, but English in tastes, in opinions, in morals and in intellect.[27]

---

by Edward Greenfield which pays tribute to Legge's work, 'The Autocrat of the Turntable'. There is no mention by Legge himself.

[23]   For a couple of exceptions see Grubb, *Music Makers*, pp. 46, 223.

[24]   Pandit, *Thorn EMI*, p. 83.

[25]   Schwarzkopf, *Off the Record*, pp. 95–6.

[26]   Sara Suleri, *The Rhetoric of English India* (Chicago, 1992).

[27]   [Online]. Available at: www.columbia.edu/itc/mealac/pritchett/00generallinks/ macaulay/txt_minute_education_1835.html. [accessed: 29 December 2009].

To this end, these middle-class Anglicized Indians must be educated in the literature – including fiction, science and philosophy – which Macaulay believed to be obviously superior to anything available in the existing learned languages used in India:

> I have read translations of the most celebrated Arabic and Sanscrit works. I have conversed, both here and at home, with men distinguished by their proficiency in the Eastern tongues. I am quite ready to take the oriental learning at the valuation of the orientalists themselves. I have never found one among them who could deny that a single shelf of a good European library was worth the whole native literature of India and Arabia.[28]

On this basis, Suleri suggests, the whole canon of writings and supporting critical apparatus that has become known, taught and reproduced as 'English Literature' was formed and promulgated *as an educational project* first in India before being transferred back to Britain, the heart of darkness itself.[29]

We might view the place of European classical music in India through a similar lens; but in the end the focus has to be rather different. Music was indeed packaged as an adjunct of the European library which Macaulay wished to promulgate; it was sold as such by HMV India from the early twentieth century. While less directly concerned with Englishness than what became English Literature, the values and repertoire of European classical music became available as part of the Anglicised Indian gentleman's education. The differences are subtle but acute. Music's relative abstraction, its distance from the political implying a lack of direct engagement with the imperial project, could make it seem as an acceptable face of imperialism – much as American popular music is valued today in realms which are massively hostile to other manifestations of American cultural and economic imperialism.

The music criticism of the Palestinian cultural critic Edward Said, for example, is qualitatively different to his literary criticism.[30] His responses to the music of Beethoven, Richard Strauss, Britten and even Wagner, while politically aware, are on the whole positive in tone, admiring of these composers' achievements without the sophisticated and deeply political qualifications of his responses to European

---

[28]   [Online]. Available at: www.columbia.edu/itc/mealac/pritchett/00generallinks/macaulay/txt_minute_education_1835.html. [accessed: 29 December 2009].

[29]   Suleri, *Rhetoric*, pp, 33–4, 64–6. Cf. the arguments about the importance of English Literature in the formation of an anti-colonial subjectivity in C.L.R. James, *Beyond a Boundary* (London, 1963).

[30]   Examples of Said's everyday musical criticism can be found in Edward Said, *Music at the Limits: Three Decades of Essays and Articles on Music* (London, 2008). More thoughtful and connected essays on music are to be found in Edward Said, *Musical Elaborations* (London, 1992); and Miriam C. Said, Edward Said and Michael Wood, *On Late Style: Music and Literature against the Grain* (London, 2007).

literary production, and with hardly any reference to music from elsewhere in the world or from outside the European classical canon. This attitude, which is strikingly similar to the mode of music appreciation expressed by Legge, Culshaw, Grubb et al. has produced some puzzlement (if not a hostile response) from Said's fellow cultural critics.[31] Similarly, the careers in Western music of Grubb, Bhaskar Menon, or the distinguished Indian conductor Zubin Mehta, are not normally taken to imply moral or political acquiescence in an oppressive Eurocentrism.[32]

Then again, we might need a different lens altogether. In a sense it could be argued that Menon, Mehta and Grubb's enthusiastic embrace of Western music is the obverse of the Indian impact on British music-making. In this regard it is important to note that Grubb was operating as an EMI producer at exactly the same time as a wave of cultural Indianization took place in Britain. This was arguably a positive form of Orientalism, valuing an imagined India of pacifist political leaders, esoteric philosophy, gently perfumed air and sublime music which accompanied the first wave of immigration to Britain from the Indian subcontinent – which took place, the Grub family included, from the mid 1950s. Some aspects of this positive response are very well known: George Harrison had sitar-playing lessons from Ravi Shankar, and all the Beatles, along with the Who's Pete Townshend and others, went to India for direct contact with the kind of 'guru chic' lampooned so well in Hanif Kureishi's 1990 novel *The Buddha of Suburbia*. Harrison's sitar playing, of course, adorns several Beatles songs, such as 'Norwegian Wood' and 'Within You without You'.

Less well remembered are the kinds of Orientalist music which were produced in consequence of late-60s British progressive rock musicians' encounter with this form of knowledge – by bands such as such as the Third Ear Band, East of Eden, and most comprehensively Quintessence, whose music and lyrics might be taken to have anticipated the pseudo-Hinduism of mid 1990s band Kula Shaker in much the same way as the Beatles' music 'anticipated' the songs of Oasis. While much of this music might be eminently forgettable, more perhaps should be known of Indian violinist John Mayer and West Indian alto saxophonist Joe Harriott's two late-1960s *Indo-Jazz Fusions* albums, whose deployment of forces from classical music (violin, harpsichord), jazz (the typical small group of sax/flute, trumpet, piano, bass, and drums) and Indian music (tabla, sitar, tanpura) provided roads to new ways of composing, performing and listening which even now remain to be fully explored. Suvi Raj Grubb's contribution to this moment – he supervised the recording of two pieces of Indian classical music – was a brief footnote to a recording career which was otherwise entirely spent in the Western classical mainstream.

---

[31]   Typically puzzled, though on the whole positive, responses to Said's music criticism can be found in, for example, www.lrb.co.uk/v28/n21/letters#letter8; http://forum.llc.ed.ac.uk/archive/03/matthes.pdf. [accessed: 29 December 2009].

[32]   Mehta's honest reflections on the contradictions of his career can be found in Zubin Mehta, *Zubin Mehta: A Memoir: The Score of My Life* (London 2008).

Scratching around in the general detritus of the worldwide web as part of the research for this chapter, I came across just a few indirect references to Grubb's political views. Clearly one or two of his former professional colleagues (all of whom were white and middle-class) thought of him as a dangerous Red. One very interesting anecdote supplied by such a former colleague is that he had introduced Daniel Barenboim – with whom he had a long and close working relationship – to Edward Said – whom he certainly knew.[33] If so we can see this possible meeting at Grubb's London apartment as leading eventually to Barenboim's founding, with Said's support, of the Divan orchestra, which performs mainstream repertoire classical music in the context of bridge-building between the Palestinian and Israeli communities, and which is therefore arguably the most politicized deployment of classical music since the second world war. At the time of writing the claim about the meeting needs factually verifying, as it differs from Barenboim and Said's own account that they first met in 1991 when Said was in London to deliver the Reith Lectures – Grubb was by this point in retirement in Spain.[34] However, even the fact that the claim has been made supports the idea that whatever his tastes in music, Grubb was politically aware in a way his EMI colleagues, inhabiting their privileged positions of bourgeois whiteness and simply re-inscribing those positions through their work in the record business, were not.

Given this political awareness, was Grubb's EMI career mere masquerade? Was Grubb like Salman Rushdie's character Saladin Chamcha (a voiceover artist whose apparently English accent conceals his Indian identity while he works in London, only for that identity to emerge forcefully as the novel's plot unfolds?).[35] We might say that Suvi Raj Grubb didn't add much to the aesthetics of the profession of classical music production. His ethnicity did not produce a distinctive sound-world, and in a way that's the point. Well before equal opportunities legislation, he was more than an equal, indeed a leading participant in the (re)production of a conservative musical discourse which has often been taken for granted as a marker of elite whiteness. But he wasn't white, he wasn't conservative, and he finally returned to India. To write comprehensively either of the history of recorded music in Britain or of the impact of Indian immigration on British culture (or both) we have to register Grubb's place as an expert inhabitant, and professional reproducer, of a conservative aesthetic position, largely learned in India, which was qualified by a radical political outlook partly learned in Britain. In the end, then, we can say '*That's* who "that black man over there" was, Herbert.'

---

[33]   See e.g. Michael Jansen, 'No conflicts in this bond', http://archive.deccanherald. com/deccanherald/nov23/artic6.asp [accessed: 30 December 2009].

[34]   The orthodox account is in Daniel Barenboim and Edward Said, *Parallels and Paradoxes: Explorations in Music and Society* (London, 2004).

[35]   Salman Rushdie, *The Satanic Verses* (London, 1988).

Chapter 13

The Place of the Producer in the Discourse of Rock

Simon Frith

At the beginning of his book, *Setting the Record Straight: A Material History of Classical Recording*, Colin Symes suggests that:

> Very few analyses and histories of music (save those dealing with its popular varieties) consider the impact of the phonograph, and where they do, the discussion is mostly perfunctory. This reflects an ongoing legacy, one at the very heart of music, that has on the one hand disparaged mechanized music, and on the other has restricted the ambit of musical analysis to matters of composition and performance.[1]

In this paper I want to deal with one particular 'popular variety' of music, rock, and to suggest that when rock was constructed discursively as a new kind of popular music in the late 1960s, the initial discussion of the role of recording in rock practice was, if not perfunctory, certainly somewhat grudging. Rock ideology also disparaged 'mechanized' music;[2] rock writers, too, tended to restrict critical analysis to matters of composition and performance.

There is a paradox here, of course. Rock, like other kinds of twentieth-century popular music but unlike classical music, was a record-based form. Rock criticism was rooted in the business of record reviewing; rock history is primarily written as a history of recordings.[3] But two of the points Symes makes about classical music discourse could also be applied to rock discourse. Symes describes how live performance was taken to provide the ideal musical experience that classical recording engineers sought to simulate for consumers: 'the discourse of the concert hall thus slowly emerged as the keystone discourse to which classical

[1]   Colin Symes, *Setting the Record Straight: A Material History of Classical Recording* (Middletowwn, CT: Wesleyan University Press, 2004), p. 2.

[2]   See Simon Frith, 'Art *vs* Technology: The Strange Case of Popular Music', *Media, Culture and Society*, vol. 8, no. 3 (1986): 263–80.

[3]   Simon Frith, 'Going critical: writing about recordings' in N. Cook, E. Clarke, D. Leech-Wilkinson and J. Rink (eds), *The Cambridge Companion to Recording* (Cambridge: Cambridge University Press, 2009), pp. 267–82.

recording should defer'.[4] But in rock, too, the ideal musical experience is the live concert[5] and, as I shall show, early rock critics judged recordings against a band's 'authentic' (that is, live) sound. And this relates to Symes' second point: the lack of credit given to producers in the classical music world. Symes shows how long it took for EMI and other major labels to include name credits for producers or engineers on record sleeves. The US music magazine, *High Fidelity*, started adding producer names to the basic product descriptions provided by its classical record reviews in 1977, but this is still not a universal reviewing practice in either classical or rock publications.[6]

In 1978 Charlie Gillett reflected on the absence of producers from the by now well-established field of rock criticism in these terms:

> In one sense, maybe it is right that the producers remain virtually anonymous; after all, it is the performers who take the risks of laying themselves open to the public, and who deserve whatever fame they can acquire. The successful producer is usually paid well for his efforts, and should not covet public recognition too. But producers are not simply ignored; there is often an undertone of suspicion and mistrust in music paper coverage of producers, resulting in a negative image of some kind of bureaucratic Svengali who makes the artist conform to his company's concept of commercialism. At best the producer is portrayed as a benevolent layabout who keeps the musicians supplied with booze or drugs, and does his best to keep the tapes rolling.[7]

I'm not sure that such attitudes have altogether changed in the 30 years since these words were written. Producers are no longer anonymous but critics still seem uneasy about their role and their work is often therefore effectively ignored. To cite a recent example (chosen because it is otherwise a rather good book), Dai Griffiths' study of Radiohead's *OK Computer*, has an interesting chapter on the general significance of recording for the rock aesthetic and pays meticulous attention to the sound of *OK Computer* itself, yet the person responsible for the album's production, Nigel Godrich, is mentioned only once, in a short list of well-known record producers.[8]

In this chapter, then, I want to explore the role of the producer in rock's understanding of how music on record works. I will begin by looking at the origins of rock ideology, at the emergence of rock criticism. My findings here

---

[4]   Symes, *Setting the Record Straight*, p. 49 – for further discussion of this point see the chapter by Andrew Blake in this book.

[5]   See, for example, Daniel Cavicchi, *Tramps Like Us: Music And Meaning Among Springsteen Fans* (Oxford: Oxford University Press, 1998).

[6]   Symes, *Setting the Record Straight*, pp. 135–6, 197.

[7]   Charlie Gillett, 'In Praise of the Professionals', in Charlie Gillett and Simon Frith (eds), *Rock File 5* (London: Panther, 1978), p. 21.

[8]   Dai Griffiths, *OK Computer* (New York: Continuum, 2004), p. 4.

are based on a survey of *The Rolling Stone Record Review*[9] (henceforth *RSRR*), a collection of the reviews published in *Rolling Stone* 1967–70, and a reading of the early writings of the pioneering US rock critics, Greil Marcus, Jon Landau and Robert Christgau, and the first books of the British rock writers Dave Laing, Nick Cohn and Charlie Gillett.[10] I also consulted Paul Taylor's comprehensive *Popular Music Since 1955: A Critical Guide to the Literature*.[11] Under his heading 'Record Production' are listed three 'how to' titles (by Craig Anderton, Will Connelly and Dennis Lambert); a book including 'some guidance on record mixing techniques' in amongst a broader account of 'how to make and sell your own record'; a 19-page 1966 pamphlet on 'the art of recording' by Shel Talmy; the book of the 1982 BBC radio series, *The Record Producers*; and a history of EMI's Abbey Road studios. The only producers listed in the largest part of Taylor's bibliography, 'Lives and Works', are John Hammond, George Martin and Phil Spector.[12]

In his 1972 book on Phil Spector, Richard Williams writes:

> By the end of the Sixties, most rock fans could give you the names of any number of important producers: Jimmy Miller (with the Rolling Stones), George Martin (with the Beatles), Kit Lambert (with the Who), the Holland brothers and Lamont Dozier (with Motown's Four Tops and the Supremes) and so on. It was important to know that Stephen Stills produced the Crosby Stills Nash and Young albums, and that Bob Krasnow's production techniques were a crucial factor in the sound of Captain Beefheart's *Strictly Personal* album. Production methods had an immense influence on the aesthetics of the music in question.[13]

But neither Kit Lambert's nor Bob Krasnow's names appear in the extensive index of *The Rolling Stone Record Review* and Stephen Stills is not mentioned as a record producer. Rather, the first finding from my content analysis was that in the late 1960s and early 1970s record producers were only discussed systematically

[9]   Editors of *Rolling Stone*, *The Rolling Stone Record Review* (New York: Pocket Books. 1971), hereafter *RSSR*.

[10]   Greil Marcus (ed.), *Rock and Roll Will Stand* (Boston: Beacon Press, 1969); Jon Landau, *It's Too Late To Stop Now: A Rock and Roll Journal* (San Francisco: Straight Arrow Books, 1972); Robert Christgau, *Any Old Way You Choose It: Rock and Other Pop Music, 1967–1973* (Baltimore: Penguin Books, 1973); Dave Laing, *The Sound of Our Time* (London: Sheed and Ward, 1969); Nik Cohn, *Rock From the Beginning* (New York: Stein and Day, 1969); Charlie Gillett, *The Sound of the City* (London: Sphere, 1971). Less systematically I also looked through all the other rock books from this period that I own, some of which are cited here; others simply confirmed my findings.

[11]   Paul Taylor, *Popular Music since 1955: A Critical Guide to the Literature* (Boston: G.K. Hall, 1985).

[12]   Taylor, *Popular Music since 1955*, pp. 112–14.

[13]   Richard Williams, *Out of his Head: The Sound of Phil Spector* (New York: Outerbridge and Lazard, 1972), p. 14.

as central to a record's sound, sensibility and/or success in reviews of African-American music and white teen pop. Most *Rolling Stone* reviews of black records do name their producers and white pop is almost exclusively discussed in terms of its producer/production styles. My second finding (following on) was that at this time record production was almost always understood as, first, that which makes an act or sound *commercial* (with the producer therefore understood as a kind of entrepreneur – this was the central argument in Charlie Gillett's *Sound of the City*, which was primarily about such producers) and, second, that which *standardizes* sounds or genres.

This, for example, is Jon Landau's 1968 *Rolling Stone* review of Stevie Wonder's *I Was Made to Love Her* and the Temptations' *With a Lot of Soul*:

> The [Wonder] album has all the worst characteristics of the Motown sound with only a very few of the saving graces. The whole thing has a blatantly manufactured quality to it typical of Motown's capacity to crank out albums without giving any thought to experimentation or expanding the range of its artists' capacities ... Unfortunately the Temptations' latest is a similarly manufactured job in which the distinctive qualities of this fine group are largely lost ... On the new album their distinctive style is obscured, the artefacts of Motown production predominate ... [14]

And this is Paul Gambaccini's 1970 description of a batch of British hit singles:

> They have some common characteristics. The writers and producers, all from the Tony Macaulay school, are more important than the performers, all second-string groups who in some cases don't exist outside of the studio and in others do little else more exciting than cut soft-drink commercials. Form is more important than substance.[15]

This was the context for writers' suspicion of producers' effects on rock bands. Here, for example, is David Gancher's positive review of Asylum Choir's *Look inside the Asylum Choir* in 1968:

> As rock becomes more and more a producer's medium, there has been a tendency for excitement and musical daring to fade away, filtered out by days and days spent in the studio. So many of the best groups – the Airplane, the Dead, Moby Grape – sound stifled and stuffed on record. The Asylum Choir's is a well produced album, but it has not lost *presence*; you can feel the music as well as hear it.[16]

---

[14] *RSRR*, p. 180.
[15] Ibid., p. 245.
[16] Ibid., p. 366.

And three views of The Beatles and The Rolling Stones. First, Ed Ward in 1969:

> The Beatles create a sound that could not possibly exist outside of a studio. Electronically altered voices go *la la la* in chorus, huge orchestras lay down lush textures, and the actual instruments played by the Beatles themselves are all but swallowed up in the process. Indeed, *Abbey Road* is the address of a studio in London. On the album, tape splices go whizzing by, and the ear strains to dissect layers of over-dubbing. For the first time they play with their new Moog, which disembodies and artificializes their sound. Too often the result is complicated instead of complex.
>
> In direct contrast with this we have the Stones. They all play real instruments and exactly at that. Additional instrumentation seems to be used only when there is no alternative and then it is kept to the minimum and mixed in unobtrusively. They, too, spend a lot of time remixing and overdubbing, but the end result is always credible – once can imagine little Stones performing in the speakers.[17]

Second John Mendelsohn in 1970:

> Well, it was too good to be true – somebody apparently just couldn't Let It Be, with the result that they put the load on their new friend P. Spector, who in turn whipped out his orchestra and choir and proceeded to turn several of the rough gems on the best Beatles album in ages into costume jewelry.[18]

And finally Jon Landau in 1968:

> The album [*Their Satanic Majesties Request*] is marred by poor production. In the past there has been a great gulf between the production styles of the Beatles and the Stones. The Beatles' production is often so 'perfect' that it sounds computerized. *Sgt. Pepper* really does sound like it took four months to make. The Stones have never gotten hung up on that kind of thing. There is far greater informality to their sound and they probably have recorded more mistakes than any other group in pop music … In the past such mistakes all made sense because it was part of the Stones' basic statement, their basic arrogant pose. With the shift in pose to something quite different, something nearly 'arty', the weak guitars and confused balance merely becomes annoying. Instead of tightening up the rudiments of their production, the Stones confuse the issue with their introduction into the instrumental track of countless studio gimmicks.[19]

The concerns expressed here reflect a suspicion that the studio is a setting for artifice while rock's appeal rests on its 'roughness', its use of 'real' instruments,

---

[17]   Ibid., pp. 24–5.

[18]   Ibid., p. 27.

[19]   Ibid., pp. 91–2.

its imperfections. In smoothing rock out, it hardly needs to be said, producers are taken to be doing what is commercially necessary. As Robert Christgau says of Carole King's hugely successful LP, *Tapestry*, 'then Lou Adler decided to produce her. The result goes down easy.'[20] For rock critics, in other words, the problem of production was at least in part a problem of commerce. As Dave Laing wrote:

> The key figures in the making of discs like [Neil] Sedaka's were no longer the songwriters or arrangers, but the producers and engineers attached to the recording studio. The sense of the disc as no more than a *record* of something else (a live performance) had been undermined, and the more experimental of pop musicians have not been slow to realize the significance of the autonomy of the disc. The fact that the impetus for some of the least commercially significant work in pop (indeed some of it has been deliberately anti-commercial) should have come from the very commercial need for novelty to make hit records in the early sixties, is yet another example of the way in which pop music ties together art and industry in a Gordian knot.[21]

The resulting problems for rock critics in dealing with production were most honestly articulated by Robert Christgau. In his reviews we find a clear expression of the struggle involved in differentiating rock from pop as a matter of aesthetic judgement, a struggle in which producers have an pivotal but paradoxical role: they are central to both what makes good pop good and bad rock bad. Compare Christgau's views of records by The Eagles (in 1972), Carly Simon (in 1973) and the Box Tops (in 1969). First the Eagles:

> It is no accidental irony that such hard-rock professionals convey their integrated vision of self-possession and pastoral cool by way of a dynamite corporate machine, including genius manager David Geffen and genius producer Glyn Johns. It is the custom of affluent liberals to let others do their dirty work – that way they can continue to protect the illusion that they are not harming a soul by doin' what they please ... The music, the lyrics, and the distribution machine are all suave and synthetic. Brilliant stuff – but false.[22]

Then Carly Simon:

> Since 'You're So Vain' is such a name-dropper's delight anyway, it is worth mentioning that its producer, Richard Perry, is married to the daughter of George Goldner, who in conjunction with producer Shadow Morton was responsible for both 'Leader of the Pack' and 'Society's Child'. Perry has specialized in bringing performers as diverse as Captain Beefheart, Tiny Tim, Theodore Bikel and Barbra

20   Ibid., p. 175.
21   Laing, *The Sound of Our Time*, pp. 112–13.
22   Christgau, *Any Old Way You Choose It*, pp. 268–9.

Streisand into the pop mainstream, and he's done just the same for Carly Simon … the song is a schlock masterpiece. It puts Ms Simon exactly in her place.[23]

And finally the Box Tops:

> A record I do hope you'll buy is *Super Hits* by the Box Tops, who epitomize everything that is best about produced groups and single records. The group's only asset is lead singer Alex Chilton, but with that one asset, producers Dan Penn and Spooner Oldham have achieved the highest kind of rock and roll, a music of such immediate appeal that I regard it as a litmus elimination for phony 'rock' fans. Each new instrument, each pause, works to build tension and qualify meaning, yet final control seems to fall not to critical intelligence but to some crazy kind of rapacious commercial instinct, an instinct that might seem pretentious if it weren't so busy being delighted with itself – Phil Spector with economy, sort of. If I sound delirious, it's because I have just listened to *Super Hits* after two weeks of Stones and Beatles, and it still knocks me out. Don't yawp at me about art, anybody – this is what it's all for.[24]

For other reviewers the producer's role in siding with record companies against artists is more straightforward. This is Greil Marcus on Van Morrison in 1969:

> I went to the Avalon Ballroom in San Francisco to hear Van Morrison perform with a stand-up bass player and a hornman. After a brilliant set in which he sang all of *Astral Weeks* as well as three songs from his previous record, we talked about the failure of *Blowin' Your Mind*.
>
> 'I've got a tape in Belfast with all my songs on that record done the way they're supposed to be done', he said. 'It's good and simple, doesn't come on heavy. "TB Sheets" isn't heavy. It's just quiet … It was the producer who did it, and that record company. They had to cover it all with the big electric guitar and the drums and the rest. It all came out wrong and they released it without my consent.' He said that with a gentleness that almost nullified the fact that the album had ever existed at all. *Blowin' Your Mind* had seemed like the pointless chaos of Morrison on his own – too much freedom – but it had been, once again, the bars of someone else's prison.[25]

From a rock perspective a good producer was not simply on the artist's side in such disputes but worked in general to realize the artist's vision (whether or not this made commercial sense). Producers were therefore praised when they were heard to pull something out of the performers rather than impose something on them. Ed Ward thus pays tribute to John Cale's 1969 production work on

---

[23]   Ibid., pp. 293–4.

[24]   Ibid., p. 82.

[25]   *RSRR*, p. 478.

The Stooges: he 'has squeezed everything he can out of them, and he has done a fine job',[26] while John Mendelsohn writes that 'Denny Cordell ... deserves a feverish round of applause for producing this album [Joe Cocker's 1969 *With a Little Help From My Friends*]. Cordell's success in fusing a consistently marvelous backing unit out of America's premier studio soul singers and England's most famous rock musicians and delicate egos cannot be exaggerated'.[27]

In one respect what we have here is the rock version of the ideology of 'the self-effacing producer' that Michael Jarrett has documented in jazz and country record production (see his chapter in this book) and that Charlie Gillett describes in R&B recording: the key producers were those 'who were able to bring out the best in singers without imposing themselves too demandingly onto the overall sound'.[28] But there are ways in which rock musicians (unlike jazz, country and R&B musicians, at least in this period) regarded the studio not just as the place where the essence of their music could be captured (or 'squeezed' out of them) by the craft of a self-effacing producer or engineer, but also where they could use the producer or engineer's technical skills and trickery to their own artistic ends. If recording was central to the emergence of rock as a new kind of music making, then suspicion of producers also involved a kind of turf war, an argument about who had *creative* authority in the recording process. Jon Landau remarked:

> It is often hard to know who to call an artist on a Motown record. No matter how much Sam Phillips did for Jerry Lee Lewis in the studio, no one has ever thought of calling a Jerry Lee Lewis record a Sam Phillips record. But was 'Baby Love' a Supremes record or a Holland and Dozier record? The only thing that can be said for sure is that the record wouldn't exist without either component.[29]

For rock musicians, by contrast, it was vitally important to their sense of what they were doing that they were the ones with the authority – in the studio as much as in live performance (and in time Motown artists were to be influenced by rock ideology in their increasingly fraught relations with their studio producers). In his infamous 1971 *Rolling Stone* interview John Lennon thus dismisses George Martin's contribution to the Beatles' work, mentioning him in passing alongside music publisher, Dick James, as just 'one of those people who think they made us. They didn't. I'd like to hear Dick James' music and I'd like to hear George Martin's music, please, just play me some.'[30] Lennon can perhaps be forgiven his irritation. Robert Christgau cites an article in *Time* magazine in 1967 (following the release of *Sgt. Pepper*) 'in which George Martin, the group's producer, who

---

26   Ibid., pp. 384–5.

27   Ibid., p. 371.

28   Gillett, *The Sound of the City*, p. 203.

29   Landau, *It's Too Late To Stop Now*, p. 145.

30   Jann S. Wenner and Joe Levy, *The Rolling Stone Interviews* (New York: Black Bay Books, 2007), p. 43.

has a degree in music and is thus permitted to be a genius, was singled out as the brains of the operation'.[31] And in his *Rolling Stone* interview, in 1974, Paul McCartney confirms the Beatles' dismay at such comments:

> The time we got offended, I'll tell you, was one of the reviews, I think about *Sgt Pepper* – one of the reviews said, 'This is George Martin's finest album.' We got shook; I mean, 'We don't mind him helping us, it's great, it's a great help, but it's not his album, folks, you know.' And there got to be a little bitterness over that.[32]

But Lennon was also using his interview to explain himself as the genius ('Yes, if there is such a thing as one, I am one.')[33] and we can read this interview now as the end point of the 1960s ideological shift from pop to rock (which the Beatles embodied), a shift which involved among other things a new understanding of musical creativity in the studio.[34] In the early to mid 1960s it was the performers who were regarded as uncreative, as malleable voices to which producers, writers, arrangers and engineers gave shape and texture.[35] Rock reversed this hierarchy, re-sited the source of creativity from the producers to the acts they were producing. Not all musicians felt the need to be as rude about their producers as Lennon (Paul Simon, for example, described his recording relationship with Art Garfunkel and engineer, Roy Halee, as a 'a three-way partnership').[36] and by 1975 even Lennon was admitting 'I'm a learner at production, although I've been at this business so long and I used to produce my own tracks with the help of George Martin and Paul McCartney and George Harrison and everybody else ... .'[37] Both Lennon and Simon are clear, however, that when it came to the crunch *they* were the creative wellsprings.

The early rock critics, listening to what came out of the studio but not often privy to what happened inside it, may soon have understood that record production/sound was something to be assessed but they were not always clear what it was they were assessing. Ed Ward writes of Laura Nyro's 'Up on the Roof' in 1970 that 'Laura's reading of this old classic is unbeatable, and the production by Felix Cavaliere and Arif Mardin is flawless',[38] and Jim Miller uses the same term when describing 'the engineering and production work' on the Beach Boys'

---

[31]   Christgau, *Any Old Way You Choose It*, p. 41.

[32]   Ben Fong Torres, *What's That Sound? The Contemporary Music Scene from the Pages of Rolling Stone* (New York: Doubleday Anchor, 1976), p. 25.

[33]   Wenner and Levy, *The Rolling Stone Interviews*, p. 61.

[34]   For another version of this story see Jan Butler's chapter on Brian Wilson in this book.

[35]   See Gordon Thompson, *Please Please Me: Sixties British Pop, Inside Out* (Oxford: Oxford University Press, 2008), chapter 6.

[36]   Fong Torres, *What's That Sound?*, p. 203.

[37]   Ibid., p. 63.

[38]   Ibid., p. 254.

1970 *Sunflower*: 'it's flawless, especially in view of the number of overdubs'.[39] Al Kooper writes of John Simon's production of the Band's 1968 *Music from the Big Pink*: 'The reason the album *sounds* so good is Simon. He is a perfectionist and has had to suffer the critical rap in the past for what has not been his error, but now he's vindicated.'[40] while, by contrast, John Mendelsohn calls Jimmy Page 'a very limited producer',[41] and Robert Christgau states flatly that Alex Hassilev 'can't produce'[42] and that Bob Johnston's production of Bob Dylan's *Self-Portrait* 'ranges from indifferent to awful'.[43] But it is not clear on what basis any of these judgements are made.

The one critic who did sometimes explain what producers did technically was Jon Landau. In his 1971 article, 'Engineering: What You Hear is What You Get', he wrote

> The engineer and remixer play a role as great as any individual musician in affecting the final sound. While in reviewing records it is often impossible to define precisely what one is hearing in engineering terms, a general awareness of the engineering and mixing function is essential to understanding contemporary music.[44]

And this approach is reflected in his more interesting reviews:

> But what is giving Charlie [Watts], and the record [*Between the Buttons*] as a whole, that extra push is the fact that [Andrew Loog] Oldham apparently decided that he really was going to produce this album. He has paid particular attention to Watts, with excellent results. The close-miked snare and hi-hat fit what's happening perfectly. The dry, lightly-echoed sound gives the record tremendous bite.[45]

---

[39]   Ibid., p. 326.

[40]   Ibid., p. 469.

[41]   Ibid., p. 6.

[42]   Christgau, *Any Old Way You Choose It*, p. 89.

[43]   Ibid., p. 204.

[44]   Landau, *It's Too Late To Stop Now*, p. 137.

[45]   Ibid., 67–8. John Burks, who was managing editor of *Rolling Stone* at the time, was not convinced of Landau's expertise here, however: 'He used to drive me nuts! We were copy-editing and weren't supposed to mess with Landau's stuff too much, and this guy, as far as I was concerned didn't know shit from shine-ola, didn't know how music was made. So everything he writes is speculative, and he doesn't know what he doesn't know. I'd been in recording studios when the Beach Boys were doing their stuff as a *Newsweek* correspondent, watching how their stuff was produced ... I'd been with Nancy Wilson, to a Cannonball Adderley recording date, Jefferson Airplane, so I'd been to jazz, pop and rock recording dates. And if you get to know the players and producers, you come to see what the process is.' (From an unpublished 2005 phone interview with Matt Brennan, to whom I am

What can we conclude from this survey of early rock criticism? First that rock critics were aware of the significance of the record as the object of their reviews. They routinely referred to sound qualities. But, second, that there was surprisingly little reference to producers or production in rock reviews (especially when compared to the reviews of R&B, soul and pop records). What's apparent is that the role of the producer was somewhat problematic for rock critics to assess so that, for example, producers were regularly seen to be the problem of bad records but rarely as essential to good ones.[46]

My point here, though, is not that rock critics somehow misunderstood or wilfully denied the realities of record-making. Rather I want to expand Dave Laing's 1969 point about recording as one way in which 'pop music ties together art and industry in a Gordian knot'. I would argue that *all* recorded music involves this Gordian knot: the recording studio is the place in which the relationship of art and industry is articulated, through the relationship of musicians and producers; it is the setting in which music – of all kinds – takes on commodity form. These relationships have changed over time, partly as an effect of technology (which shifts understanding of what can be done in the studio) and partly as an effect of ideology. Different musical worlds account for studio practices differently, involve different kinds of negotiation and hierarchies between composers, performers, producers and engineers. What concerns me, in other words, is the particular way in which rock both emerged from and helped shape a new understanding of studio practice in the second half of the 1960s.

As is clear from Albin Zak's chapter in this book, in the 1950s the recording studio became something more than the place in which a live-in-the-studio recording was made. The new technology of long-playing records and magnetic tape meant new creative possibilities, but these were understood differently in different music worlds. For the pop world, as Zak describes, the 1950s marked the rise of studio 'tricks': commercial pop records increasingly featured perceived 'gimmicks' as the emphasis was placed on a track's distinctive sounds (rather than reproductive clarity). It was thus easy enough for established popular musicians and critics to mock the new approaches to record production, to see producers 'creative' ideas as driven simply by the need to make a transitory impact in the market place. Tim Anderson quotes a *Billboard* story from as early as 1952 about the marketing of a Perry Como single in 'old' pop terms: 'No Gimmick! No Echo

---

grateful for this quote.) I suspect Burks' account here is less a comment on Landau's studio knowledge (or lack of it) than a reflection of *Rolling Stone's* own turf wars, the 'tension' Burks describes between the reporters and the critics, between descriptive and evaluative accounts of studio practice.

[46]   This is still commonplace in rock scholarship. In Peter Mills' recent book about Van Morrison, for example, Bert Berns' problematic contribution to Morrison's pop phase is discussed but the lengthy analysis of Astral Weeks makes no mention of producer Lewis Merenstein at all (Peter Mills, *Hymns to the Silence: Inside the Words and Music of Van Morrison* (New York: Continuum, 2010), pp. 88–94, 276–304).

Chamber! No One Playing 'Hot Triangle'!!!'[47] And it's obvious from contemporary reviews that rock'n'roll was just part of this gimmicky here-today-gone-tomorrow soundscape in which all pop records were regarded with suspicion – Stan Freberg thus parodied not just Elvis Presley's echo-laden 'Heartbreak Hotel' but also the faux/folk realism of Harry Belafonte's 'Banana Boat Song'.

In short, if, as Colin Symes argues, classical record producers used the new technology to perfect the simulation of the concert hall experience for the living room, pop producers sought to make novel sounds sellable or used new recording devices to dress up voices and instruments, giving them a radio or jukebox presence that was clearly not in any sense 'live'. Recording studio rather than concert hall sound was pop's aesthetic centre and this had implications for the way in which rock sought to establish its own distinctive non-pop aesthetic sensibility.

One way of thinking about this is to imagine how different musical history would have been if the Beatles' first single had been produced by Joe Meek[48] and Bob Dylan's *Highway 61 Revisited* had been produced by Phil Spector.[49] The issue here is not that Dylan and the Beatles had established live concert hall sounds that needed self-effacing production, but that they had *characteristic* sounds which were developed as significantly in the studio as on stage, sounds that needed a kind of collaborative creative process for which neither Meek nor Spector would have been obviously suited. In distinguishing rock from pop practice, in other words, we need to understand that what made rock music-making something new was the combination of collective creativity and sonic personality embodied in the new phenomenon of *the band*. In the classical world what happened in the studio was referred to an ideal way of listening to music; in the rock world it was referred to an ideal way of making music, to a particular experience of the creative process. This obviously drew on jazz but involved a new conception of musical identity that had its roots in the rise of a new kind of self-conscious youth culture. What's involved here (and the problems of making music the rock way in the studio) is well described in Alex Kapranos's reflections on ProTools, 'the blessing and the curse of modern recording' (his band being Franz Ferdinand):

> It's used to match everything up so it all sounds too perfect. Everything's built up, so the drummer will go in and play the snare, play the kick, and then those sounds will be placed onto the beat. It cheats the band, too: what gives the band its character is how you all play together, how you interact. It's how everyone doesn't fall on the beat in the same way that's interesting ...[50]

---

[47]   Tim J. Anderson, *Making Easy Listening: Material Culture and Postwar American Recording* (Minneapolis: University of Minnesota Press 2006), p. xvi.

[48]   Something Brian Epstein at one point tried to arrange. See John Repsch, *The Legendary Joe Meek: The Telstar Man* (London: Woodford House, 1989), pp. 189–90.

[49]   As Dylan apparently once suggested – see Clinton Heylin, *Behind the Shades* (London: Faber & Faber, 2011), p. 217.

[50]   *Guardian Weekend*, 1 October 2005, p. 18.

For early rock musicians (and rock critics), then, the question was how best could a producer enable them to create – experiment – in the studio through the collaborative process that defined the band's 'character'. One approach was for the producer to become, in effect, a member of the band – George Martin as the fifth Beatle, Jimmy Miller part of the Rolling Stones – and a new generation of record producers did indeed encourage and become part of a workplace in which, in producer Bob Johnston's words, 'everything was wide and scattered, open'.[51] (Such a new way of working was in part an effect of the amount of money that rock albums could generate – a quite new level of return for record companies.) Another approach, at least in music writers' understanding, was Gillett's 'benevolent layabout', simply keeping a band happy one way or another and letting the tapes roll. Clinton Heylin, for example, uses just this image in describing Bob Johnston's 'lack of creative input' into *Highway 61 Revisited*: 'Dylan once again found himself with another in-house producer, Bob Johnston. If he was looking for someone with greater imagination and technical expertise [than previous producer, Tom Wilson], he had fallen short. If he was looking for someone happy to roll tape, Johnston was his man.'[52]

The problem of such accounts is not simply that rolling the tape is an ideological rather than a technical description of what the producer actually did, but also that it ignores the fact that at the end of a recording session it is the producer who has responsibility for the product – the result of a creative process in a form fit for market. This is the respect in which the producer cannot be just another member of the band. The producer's job, to put this another way, is to put an end to the creative process. In his recent book on Van Morrison, Greil Marcus gives a fascinating account in these terms of producer Lewis Merenstein's contribution to *Astral Weeks*. In this case Merenstein initiated the creative process involved, bringing together the New York jazz players with whom Morrison was to work:

> They recorded live, Morrison saying nothing to the musicians in terms of banter or instruction, and saying everything in the cues of his chords, hesitations, lunges, silences and in those moments when he loosed himself from words and floated on his own air. But that's too simple. When you listen, you hear the musicians talking to each other; more than that you hear them hearing each other ...

> At its highest pitch, the album has become a collaboration between Morrison and [bassist, Richard] Davis, or a kind of conspiracy, one that takes advantage of the producer and the other musicians but excludes them from the real conversation – excludes them, but somehow not the listener ...

---

[51]   Quoted in Greil Marcus, *Like a Rolling Stone: Bob Dylan at the Crossroads* (London: Faber & Faber, 2005), p. 144.

[52]   Heylin, *Behind the Shades*, p. 217.

After the sessions were finished, Merenstein, with Morrison and the conductor Larry Fallon consulting, overdubbed strings and horn parts. Sometimes the songs are unimaginable without them, and the added sounds so layered into the original instruments as to be part of them, as on 'Sweet Thing'; sometimes they're gratuitous, especially the strings on 'Cypress Avenue' and the gypsy violin on 'Madame George', but after forty years they tune themselves out.[53]

And Marcus makes sense too of Bob Johnston's 'tape rolling' for Bob Dylan:

Johnston's sound is not merely whole, song by song the sound is not the same, but it is always a thing in itself. There is a glow that seems to come from inside the music. It's what Johnston called 'that mountainside sound', and nothing else explains that phrase as well as the final sound of 'Like A Rolling Stone'. As a single or on *Highway 61 Revisited*, mono or stereo, it has always sounded like Johnston to me.

'I don't remember, I don't remember', Johnston said when I asked him about the state of the master tape of 'Like A Rolling Stone' when he took over Bob Dylan's recordings. 'I got in there', he said after a while. 'I would do anything I wanted to do and I never told anybody about anything. I never tried to jack anybody around – I would just go, and play, and, say, "Is this okay?" And that's how it happened. But as far as credit, as far as what I did with it, I really couldn't tell you'. …

'I think you spotted what it is', Johnston said finally. 'I may have got in there and mixed that thing. I may have added to it. The thing that I tried to do – the first time I walked in with Dylan' … . 'I said, "Your voice has to come up." He said, "I don't like my voice. My voice is too goddam loud." And I'd say ok, and I'd turn it up a little bit, and he'd say' – and Johnson affects an effete clipped voice – 'My voice is too *loud*.'. Finally he quit saying that. My guess is he didn't want to fuck with me anymore, *but that's what I wanted*.[54]

Marcus's account of the 'Like a Rolling Stone' studio sessions is fascinating for two reasons. First, for the way it situates the record's producer, Bob Johnston, in an aesthetic argument. Marcus has been, I think, the most influential of all rock writers in suggesting the terms in which rock should be evaluated – certainly influential on other critics, but also on musicians. His approach is rooted in what I'd call pragmatic romanticism. From this perspective rock is a music that articulates an individual sense of being which – mysteriously – resonates with both history and audience; the critic's task is both to sense this mystery and to account for it, to show *how* it happens, in the collaborative and often accidental processes of music

53   Greil Marcus, *Listening to Van Morrison* (London: Faber & Faber, 2010), pp. 53–5.
54   Marcus, *Bob Dylan at the Crossroads*, pp. 142–4.

making and music listening. If producers were always implicitly involved in the rock story, their role is now being made explicit.

And this leads to my second point. *Astral Weeks* and 'Like a Rolling Stone' were crucial records for the emergence of rock as a new art form; they embodied the claims that rock was something new: a popular cultural form with serious artistic intentions, a commercial music that had to be understood in terms of individual expression. And they both involved music – sounds – which were created in the studio; both Bob Dylan and Van Morrison then developed live shows that reflect their studio-based sense of musical possibilities rather than vice versa (I've already quoted Marcus's review of Morrison's 1969 *Astral Weeks* live performance), just as Elvis Presley's original live act explored the performing possibilities of a band and sonic sensibility first articulated experimentally in Sun's studio. How can we reconcile this recording practice with rock's central commitment to the truth of live performance?

What emerges from a reading of early rock criticism is an argument that rock bands are involved in a process of *continuous* creation for which both stage and studio are key sites. If classical music recording represented an ideal of live performance and pop music was produced for radio, its live shows simulating its recorded sounds, rock was understood as a kind of work-in-progress in which the 'work' involved, the album, could be treated as a template for live exploration.[55] This explains, I believe, the uneasy place record producers occupy in rock scholarship. They are vital to one part of the story, to what happens in the studio, but not to another part, what happens on the road. It is unusual, for example, for a band's record producer to be its live sound engineer. In this respect rock record producers are seen as both more significant for rock as an art form than producers in jazz, folk or classical music, but less important for rock as a cultural project than producers in pop or dance music. The producer was both obdurately present in the music and readily ignored in the way that music was discussed.

---

[55] For jazz musicians, by contrast, a recording tends to be the end result of a period of live improvisation. They are reluctant to tour such 'old' material – see Simon Frith, 'Is Jazz Popular Music?', *Jazz Research Journal*, vol. 1, no. 1 (2007): 7–23.

Chapter 14

The Beach Boys' *Pet Sounds* and the Musicology of Record Production

Jan Butler

> If there was one person that I have to select as a living genius of pop music, I would choose Brian Wilson ... *Pet Sounds* must rank as one of the highest achievements in our genre.[1]

Musicologists are beginning to turn to the recording itself as an object of analysis, and to take seriously observations in other fields about the interactions of record production, aesthetic values, song writing and commercial concerns that jointly determine that object.[2] However, it is rare that these interactions be theorized per se, as a weighted ensemble of determinations that shape a recording and its reception; instead scholars have tended to focus on only one aspect, ignoring the relationships between them. This essay attempts such a weighted assessment, focusing on one of the most discussed albums in the history of pop music, namely The Beach Boys' *Pet Sounds* (1966).

The above quotation from George Martin, included in a celebratory box set of *Pet Sounds* in 1996, encapsulates the widely accepted view of Brian Wilson and *Pet Sounds* in the 2000s. The oft-told construction of Wilson as a genius usually follows a familiar narrative arc of the tragic artist: Brian Wilson, composer, producer, arranger and vocalist of The Beach Boys, revolutionized the world of popular music through his experiments with record production which resulted in *Pet Sounds* in 1966, inspiring the Beatles to revolutionize music further through *Sgt. Pepper*. Triumph then turned to tragedy as Wilson burned out and scrapped his next eagerly awaited album, *Smile* in 1967, then virtually disappeared from the music scene amidst tales of drugs and mental illness. Wilson eventually overcame his problems and returned triumphant once more to tour *Pet Sounds*

---

[1]   George Martin, producer of The Beatles, interviewed in 'The Making of Pet Sounds' booklet from *The Beach Boys: The Pet Sounds Sessions* (produced by Brian Wilson), 4 CD Box set, Capitol, 724383766222, 1996, p. 123.

[2]   See for example Theodore Gracyk's philosophical take on the aesthetics of rock, *Rhythm and Noise: An Aesthetics of Rock* (London, 1996), and Peter Wicke's more sociological approach in Peter Wicke, *Rock Music: Culture, Aesthetics and Sociology* (Cambridge: 1990).

live in 2000 and re-recorded and released *Smile* in 2004.[3] This narrative usually uses the creation of *Pet Sounds* in particular as evidence of Brian Wilson's genius, a recording that now regularly appears at or near the top of lists of the greatest rock albums ever recorded. However, the contemporary reception of *Pet Sounds* in 1966 differed sharply from this modern consensus, with reactions ranging from rejection to confusion and at times celebration.

In this essay, I consider the interrelated elements surrounding both the creation and reception of the album in 1966, arguing that the initial failure and later success of *Pet Sounds* depended not simply on properties of the recording itself but also on the institutional forces surrounding it. As will be demonstrated, the release of this particular recording coincided with a time of flux in the record industry, when a rapidly changing market caused the institutions surrounding the production and marketing of records to change, both in terms of allowing greater creative freedom to the producers (and later artists), and through the expansion of the methods used to reach the audience. The methods and technologies available to produce records, and the audience that popular music appealed to were also rapidly changing, with the established teen market for rock and roll making way for a new, 'hipper' rock audience looking for more complex sounds. The Beach Boys' *Pet Sounds* was released at the apex of this time of confusion in 1966, providing an excellent opportunity to explore how wider factors impact on record production.

Keith Negus concluded from his sociological study of the record industry in 1992 that the fundamental aim of all record company activity is to reduce the risk of a commercial failure when releasing a new recording into an unpredictable market. Negus argues that the main strategy used to cope with this inherent unpredictability is one of artist development, in which 'a range of record industry personnel contribute to the sounds and images of pop and mediate between artists and their potential audience' with the hope of creating a market for the resulting recordings.[4] However, this method of encouraging commercial success had yet to be established in 1966, when *Pet Sounds* was released. Studies carried out by Peterson and Berger in the 1970s[5] portray an industry in a state of confusion over effective methods to reach the rapidly fluctuating demands of the market from the early 1950s onwards, with the major American record companies at that time fighting the independents for market share. By 1963, a year after the Beach Boys

---

[3]   This narrative is often promulgated through media such as the feature-length documentary, *Beautiful Dreamer: Brian Wilson and the Story of Smile* (David Leaf, LSL Productions, 2004).

[4]   Keith Negus, *Producing Pop: Culture and Conflict in the Popular Music Industry* (London, 1992), p. 134.

[5]   Richard A. Peterson and David G. Berger, 'Entrepreneurship in Organisations: Evidence from the Popular Music industry', *Administrative Science Quarterly*, vol. 16, no. 1 (1971): 97–107; and Richard A. Peterson and David G. Berger, 'Cycles in Symbol Production: The Case of Popular Music', *American Sociological Review*, vol. 40, no. 2 (April 1975): 158–73.

had signed with the major label Capitol, the majors had managed to dominate the charts, holding the top three single slots for the first time in a decade.[6] The secret of the majors' success during this period of market turbulence was not artist development but instead, according to Peterson and Berger, a shift towards an entrepreneurial model of production. Record companies at this time were split into three divisions: manufacture, sales and promotion, and production. Manufacturing and sales and promotion remained relatively stable in varying market conditions, following similar procedures whatever recordings were produced. This left the production division as the main market-driven variable. The majors needed to create more innovative products in order to gain market share from the independents, and they did this by shifting towards a more loosely organized production sector which could adapt quickly to the rapidly changing market. The key to this adaptability was the entrepreneur producer. The entrepreneur producer was given freedom to organize the various specialists (engineers, artists, freelance backing musicians and so on) and equipment involved in making a recording, using new combinations of the available resources to create hit records. The success or failure of an entrepreneur producer's efforts was assessed according to a recording's movements in the charts and amount of airplay, and producers were hired or fired accordingly.[7] In other words, in the 1960s, rather than attempting to *create* markets through the more recent strategy of artist development, the majors depended on entrepreneur producers to try to *meet the demands of* a changing market in order to minimize the chance of a recording being a commercial failure.

Brian Wilson was one of the earliest recording artists to be allowed to act as an entrepreneurial producer, a position which he managed to attain because Capitol were pleased with the sales of The Beach Boys' first single and album releases in 1962, which Wilson had written, arranged and performed as part of the group. He immediately took advantage of his new role, persuading Capitol that he should be allowed to record in whichever local studio he wished to, instead of in Capitol's in-house studios that were designed to record big orchestral sounds.[8] This was unprecedented at that time, but Capitol trusted Wilson's instincts as an entrepreneurial producer and allowed him freedom to experiment with different studio sounds. Wilson, following the influence of Phil Spector, started 'to design the experience to be a record rather than just a song'.[9] In a few short months, the combination of Wilson gaining institutional freedom as entrepreneur producer, the individual creativity of Wilson, engineer Chuck Britz and the musicians used, and the use of different recording spaces and technology in the form of a three-track tape recorder and the 'high, bright sound' of the new recording studio at Western

---

[6]   Peterson and Berger, 'Cycles in Symbol Production', pp. 158–73, 167–8.

[7]   Peterson and Berger, 'Entrepreneurship in Organisations', pp. 97–107, 98–101.

[8]   Keith Badman, *The Beach Boys: The Definitive Diary of America's Greatest Band on Stage and in the Studio* (San Francisco, 2004), pp. 26–32.

[9]   Barney Hoskyns, *Waiting for the Sun: Strange Days, Weird Scenes and the Sound of Los Angeles* (London, 2003), p. 65.

Recorders,[10] resulted in the establishment of the distinctive Beach Boys sound, featuring 'double-tracked, meticulously synchronized harmony parts'.[11]

Capitol's faith in Wilson was well-founded as he dutifully recorded three albums and at least four singles every year until 1966, most of which at least charted in the Top 10, and which, in combination with sales of Beatles records, kept Capitol dominating the Top Three of the singles chart.[12] During this time, the recording technology available to Wilson became more advanced, as he gained access to four-track tape machines and eventually one of the first commercial eight-track machines at Columbia studios (Los Angeles) in 1965.[13] These increasingly powerful machines enabled Wilson to build up more complex mixes, and gave him more control over the sounds produced, enabling him to expand further the idea of designing records.

The success in 1964 of Wilson's label mates, The Beatles, increased the pressure on his record as an entrepreneur producer as he faced serious competition for his string of Top Ten Hits for the first time since the release of *Surfin' USA*. At the end of 1964, after a small breakdown, Wilson withdrew from touring to become primarily a recording artist, leaving the rest of The Beach Boys (including new member Bruce Johnston) to take his music around the world.[14] The absence of the Beach Boys encouraged Wilson to work with other musicians, giving him a new palette of sounds to develop further in the studio. He worked on new methods of arranging and mixing sounds through the early months of 1965, leading to the release of 'California Girls' in July of that year, which Wilson now pinpoints as the moment when he fully realized how to use the studio itself as an instrument.[15] The influence of The Beatles on Wilson also peaked in 1965 with the release of *Rubber Soul* which featured a range of unusual instrumentations that further inspired Wilson to experiment with new sounds and instruments.[16]

The genesis of *Pet Sounds* began toward the end of 1965, when Wilson decided to plan a new musical direction for the group. In a series of interviews in 1966, he described the motivation and initial ideas behind *Pet Sounds*:

> I wanted to move ahead in sounds and melodies and moods. For months I plotted and planned ... I sat either at a huge Spanish table looking out over the hills, just

---

[10]   A three-track tape recorder is one that will record three separate soundtracks onto one reel of tape, a four-track has four, an eight-track has eight, and so on. The three-track was the most advanced tape machine available in Los Angeles at this time.

[11]   Hoskyns, *Waiting*, p. 65.

[12]   Brad Elliott, *Surf's Up! The Beach Boys on Record 1961–1981* (London, 2003).

[13]   Badman, *The Beach Boys*, p. 87.

[14]   Ibid., pp. 75–9.

[15]   Howard Massey, *Behind the Glass: Top Record Producers Tell How They Craft the Hits* (San Francisco, 2000), p. 45.

[16]   Badman, *The Beach Boys*, p. 104.

thinking, or at the piano playing 'feels'. 'Feels' are musical ideas: riffs, bridges, fragments of themes, a phrase here and there.[17]

These 'feels' were built up into individual songs, which Wilson started to think of as consisting of multiple movements, like 'capsulised classical concertos',[18] which he could then mentally break down into 'precise little increments',[19] allowing him to 'deal with each instrument individually, stacking sounds one at a time'.[20] These instrumental parts could then be explained to each musician before being recorded in the studio. In keeping with his quest for a new direction for the Beach Boys, Brian also hired advertisement writer Tony Asher to write the lyrics for the album, which were introspective and based on the two men's memories and feelings about love.

Pet Sounds was recorded in 27 sessions spread over four months and using four different studios, each of which was selected for its distinctive sound, created through a combination of the physical design of each studio and the unique consoles and tape machines available. Wilson recorded the instrumental backing track first, usually in one session, using the best freelance session musicians then working in Hollywood. This use of session musicians instead of band members, and the wide range of instrumentalists used, including bass harmonica and the theremin, was almost unheard of in rock at this time. Wilson would work with musicians individually, singing or playing them the details of their part and experimenting with them to create the sound he wanted. He would then experiment with the whole ensemble, instructing them on their relative positions to their mikes, altering echo effects, which he recorded live, and further experimenting with details of rhythm and combinations of sounds before recording a take. He would then record several takes until he was completely happy with every detail of the backing track.

This method of experimenting in the studio and working with the musicians to help realize the sounds that he had imagined was unique at the time; a combination of mixing live and composing on the spot. He recorded the backing tracks on three- or four-track tape machines, depending on which studio he was in. This allowed him greater control over the balance of different instruments when he bounced them down to a single-track mono mix on another four-track recorder, or the eight-track recorder at Columbia studios, leaving the remaining three or seven tracks available for the vocals. Thus, the instrumental track was 'locked in' long before the Beach Boys came into the recording studio. The vocals also took a long time to record, with the Boys learning their parts when they arrived at the studio. The backing vocals were recorded with all the Beach Boys except Mike Love, who needed extra amplification, around one mike, and all the vocals, both lead and backing, were doubled for extra intensity of sound. The vocals

---

[17]   Quote in Charles, L. Granata, *Wouldn't it be Nice: Brian Wilson and the Making of the Beach Boys' Pet Sounds* (Chicago, 2003), pp. 72–3.

[18]   Ibid., p. 58.

[19]   Quoted in ibid., p. 61.

[20]   Ibid.

would then also be reduced down to one track and combined with the original instrumental track to create the mono master, which was then slightly compressed and equalized to give it a cohesive sound.[21] Due to Wilson's fragmentary use of the new multitrack technology, it was not until the final album was released that many of the performers on the record knew what the complete songs sounded like.

One particular song that exemplifies the result of the unusual recording techniques described above is the closing track of the album, 'Caroline, No', which was also released before the album was completed as the first Brian Wilson solo single, of which more below. The song is sung in the first person, and is addressing a girl called Caroline who has changed as she has grown older, losing her 'happy glow' and cutting off her long hair. It appears to be about lost innocence and the disillusionment that can come with time after the initial rush of love has passed – quite different subject matter from previous Beach Boys' hits. The song opens with an unusual percussive effect, created by playing an upside down plastic water cooler bottle, then feeding the sound through an echo chamber to create strong reverb. A gently undulating harpsichord and ukulele come in over a subtly syncopated bass line followed almost immediately by Brian Wilson's sweetly mournful lead vocal. The whole song was sped up to raise it by a semitone in order to make Brian's voice sound younger and sweeter than it really is. The melody line meanders with no clear distinction between verse and chorus, although it is in a basic strophic structure, with the refrain of 'Caroline, No' acting in place of a chorus. The lack of dense Beach Boy vocal harmony is very noticeable. The orchestration of the song becomes denser as it progresses, with the addition of guitars, saxophones, flute and bass flute. It ends with the full ensemble playing an instrumental version of the opening verse, and as this fades out, in an unprecedented move, the real-life sound of a passing train and Wilson's pet dogs wildly barking (created through a combination of a pre-recorded train and the dogs barking in the studio) fades in and out again to end the album.[22]

The completed album was very different from previous Beach Boys' material, and also sounded unlike any other rock album at that time. The album functioned as a coherent unit, rather than a collection of possible singles padded out with filler material, to the extent that some claim it was the first concept album. The subject matter was a direct contrast to the usual upbeat Beach Boy themes of high school and surfing, with lyrics that focus on a young lover's individual doubts and hopes and fears, and were the first in rock to feature the word 'God' in the title (in the song 'God Only Knows'), a decision that was considered to be risky at the time. As a result of these issues, Capitol executives were unhappy with the finished album. The sales department in particular were worried because the production,

[21]   For a detailed account of the recording of *Pet Sounds*, see ibid., pp. 115–81.

[22]   See *Pet Sounds Sessions*, Disc 1, track 13, Disc 2, tracks 1 and 2, and Disc 3, tracks 23 and 30 for various informative versions of 'Caroline, No' that aided this description, as well as the accompanying booklet, 'The Making of Pet Sounds' for details of the recording methods used.

style and subject matter were so different from the established sound of the Beach Boys, with their wholesome, 'fun in the sun' image. The album was nevertheless released in America on 16 May 1966. Unfortunately, despite some glowing reviews amongst American music critics, it was, by the Beach Boys' standards, a relative flop, peaking briefly at number 10 on the album chart on 2 July, and was the first Beach Boys record in three years not to reach gold record status.[23]

There are various theories amongst Beach Boys fans as to what might explain the initial commercial failure of *Pet Sounds*, ranging from conspiracy theories that Capitol was trying to sabotage the group's success to the idea that the world was just not ready yet for such a work of 'mighty genius'. However, it could be argued that the main problem for the Beach Boys' *Pet Sounds* was essentially one of marketing. By 1966, the band was an unusually long-established act, closely associated by the public with the Californian surf culture (despite the fact that only Dennis Wilson surfed) due to their song lyrics and visual portrayal. Gracyk argues that every new release issued by an established artist is listened to in terms of their previous releases and their established performing persona, which suggests that without marketing support, it is difficult for any established band to change direction and take their audience with them.[24] The Beach Boys in 1966 were one of the first groups to have a career that spanned more than a few years, and, unfortunately for the band, as the music scene developed from rock and roll to rock, there was no support system in place to help them to make the transition from teen rock band to hip rock group, despite their development musically. It seems likely that in attempting to make the transition without the appropriate institutional support, the band appeared to their existing fans to be betraying their previous surfing teen roots with their new more sombre direction, thus losing them record sales, but at the same time the weight of their established image and style prevented them from attracting a new 'hip' audience of people who would appreciate their progressive musical direction. Despite some recognition of the fact that the change in direction of the Beach Boys exemplified by *Pet Sounds* could cause a problem for record sales, Capitol executives simply hoped for the best and released the record based entirely on Wilson's track record as a successful entrepreneur producer, using established promotional techniques to support its release.

The way that the album was marketed in the US was typical of the time. However, in the 60s, it was usually the producer, not the sales and promotions employees, whose job it was to package a recording, to commission or design the sleeve and organize liner notes, and sometimes to introduce the recording to sympathetic DJs to ensure that it received enough airplay.[25] The promotion and sales department's job was then to take the finished product and ensure that it appeared on the radio and in record stores. In the case of *Pet Sounds*, as Wilson

---

[23]   Granata, pp. 186–8.

[24]   Gracyk, *Rhythm and Noise*, pp. 54–5.

[25]   Peterson and Berger, 'Entrepreneurship in Organisations', p. 100.

was the producer, the band themselves organized a cover for the album with a drab photo of the band with some goats on the front, and pictures of both Brian Wilson in the recording studio and the band on their recent tour of Japan on the back, which mainly show them wearing their distinctive surf-related striped shirt outfits. These images gave little indication of the new musical direction of the group.

According to research carried out by Hirsch, in the late 60s, recordings could only reach consumers through gate-keepers in the mass-media who received objects to promote from the record industry. At this time, before the establishment of a dedicated rock press, the main gate-keepers were radio programmers and DJs. These gate-keepers were the crucial audience that the promotion and sales department were aiming at, as record stores would usually only stock records that gained radio airplay.[26] Earlier research by Hirsch showed that a record company would only promote records to gate-keepers that they already expected to be hits, using techniques including full-page advertisements in the trade press and personal appearances by the recording artists to create anticipation and demand for releases.[27] *Pet Sounds* was treated this way, with promotional spots pre-recorded for radio stations by the Beach Boys advertising the new album and its singles, and full-page advertisements in *Billboard*, the main trade magazine in America at the time.[28] These adverts, however, gave no indication of the new sound or direction of the Beach Boys, instead depending on their successful established image and track record of teen hits. This can be seen in the promo spots, improvised by the Beach Boys, that were given to radio stations to promote the first single released from the album, 'Caroline, No', one example of which will be discussed here.

The promo spot opens with an old bar piano playing in the style of chase music from a silent film. Mike Love interrupts: 'Just a second, Bruce, hold it. Bruce … Bruce! Bruce, we want a little Top 40 sound for this thing …'. Bruce, who we presume was playing the piano, promptly switches to a more ragtime-influenced vaudeville playing style. Love continues, saying that he is speaking on behalf of all the Beach Boys and asking listeners to listen to Brian Wilson's 'Caroline, No'. This is followed by a triumphant cadence on the piano, over which someone shouts, 'Stop that Piano!'[29]

This and other promo spots for 'Caroline, No' are very similar in style to earlier Beach Boys promo spots, in which the band 'goof around' and depend on their names being recognized and the audience's previous familiarity with the group

---

[26]   Paul M. Hirsch, 'Processing Fads and Fashions: An Organisation-Set Analysis of Cultural Industry systems', *American Journal of Sociology*, vol. 77, no. 4 (January 1972): 639–59.

[27]   Paul M. Hirsch, *The Structure of the Popular Music Industry* (Ann Arbor, 1969), pp. 34–6.

[28]   Badman, *The Beach Boys*, pp. 131–4.

[29]   See *Pet Sounds Sessions*, Disc 3, track 12 for this promo.

rather than giving any indication of what the next single or album will be like.[30] As the new musical direction that 'Caroline No' represents is not even hinted at here, other than to suggest that it will be a sound suitable for the Top 40, it would be easy for DJs and consumers to assume from these spots that the up-coming single would be in the familiar Beach Boys style, with upbeat surf-oriented lyrics, vibrant vocal harmonies and traditional five-piece band backing (drums, guitars, bass and singers).

This single was the first indication that the Beach Boys' new sound was perhaps not going to be entirely successful, as it only reached number 32 in the charts. To compensate for this, Capitol rushed out the 'Sloop John B' single, which pre-dated *Pet Sounds* by six months and again gave little indication of the style of the upcoming album (although they did allegedly force Brian Wilson to include it on the *Pet Sounds* album after its success in the single charts, where it reached number two).[31] Capitol reacted to the relative failure of the *Pet Sounds* album as they had reacted to the failure of 'Caroline, No', by rushing out a new album that reflected the band's established style – the first *Best of the Beach Boys* album, released on 5 July 1966. The album soon outsold *Pet Sounds*, reaching number eight, and reached gold record status very quickly. The release of a 'Best of' album usually indicated the end of a band's career, and signalled a withdrawal of support from Capitol for new Beach Boys product.[32] This was entirely according to the norms of institutional organization at that time, where the only adaptable element was production. A record that did not sell was compensated for by one that probably would. The methods for marketing remained unchanged.

However, in Britain, *Pet Sounds* was a huge success. Crucially, this success was not generated by Capitol, who initially had no intention of giving *Pet Sounds* an international release. Instead, it was driven by Derek Taylor, ex-publicist of The Beatles, whom The Beach Boys had personally hired in March 1966 in order to, in Brian Wilson's words, 'take them to a new plateau'.[33] Using techniques closer to those described as artist development by Negus, Taylor and Bruce Johnston went to Britain with a copy of *Pet Sounds* on the day of its American release to create demand for the album and raise publicity for the upcoming Beach Boys UK tour. To do this, they arranged preview hearings of *Pet Sounds* for 'hip' British journalists and rock luminaries, including Lennon and McCartney of the Beatles, in their hotel room in London. This ensured that as many journalists as possible saw that as many 'hip' British musicians as possible were excited about the new Beach Boys album. These journalists then successfully created demand for the album by portraying Brian Wilson in particular as being a pop genius, and heralding the

---

[30] See *Pet Sounds Sessions*, Disc 3, track 25 for another example of a 'Caroline, No!' promo. Early examples of such promo spots can be found in the *The Beach Boys Good Vibrations: 30 years of the Beach Boys* 5 CD Box set, Capitol, C2077778129424, 1993.

[31] Granata, *Pet Sounds*, p. 187.

[32] *The Pet Sounds Sessions* accompanying booklet, pp. 18–19.

[33] Badman, *The Beach Boys*, p. 120.

album as the future of pop music.[34] Due to this demand, *Pet Sounds* was released to great acclaim in Britain on 27 June, 1966, where it soon shot to number two on the album chart and became one of the top five selling albums of 1966.

After the success of *Pet Sounds* in Britain, Capitol seemed to change their view of the album and, in the absence of a new Beach Boys single, decided to release a new single from it – 'Wouldn't it be nice' backed with 'God Only knows', released on 22 July. This quickly became a hit across the world, although it still only reached number eight in the US chart. In response, in order to create a market for the next Beach Boys release, Derek Taylor began his so-called 'Brian is a genius campaign', in which he used similar techniques to those he had in London, introducing Wilson and the Beach Boys to the local 'hip' intelligentsia of the LA scene. In particular, Taylor introduced Wilson and the band to David Anderle, a TV executive and artist who was later hired by Elektra Records. Anderle continued with the 'Brian is a genius' campaign, creating excitement about Wilson's latest work in the press, both music and national, and arranging for Wilson to be included as an example of a 'hip' rock musician in the 1967 documentary being made in 1966 by CBS about the emerging rock movement and its music, *Inside Pop: The Rock Revolution*.[35]

Meanwhile, work had started on the next Beach Boys album, which would be called *Smile*, and also continued on 'Good Vibrations', which had begun during the recording of *Pet Sounds*. Capitol records were still following the model of entrepreneurial producing, allowing Wilson creative freedom to work on his records as he wished, but executives had misgivings about the cost, which were high due to Wilson's developing compositional methods. Building on the 'feel' method that he had used during the making of *Pet Sounds*, 'Good Vibrations' was worked on in 22 sessions spread over six months, during which small sections were recorded and re-recorded, the track was continually composed and altered as it was created, and several trial mixes were made, considered and ultimately discarded before the final version was decided upon. Under the terms of being an entrepreneur producer, Wilson would only be allowed to continue with this level of creative freedom if he managed to turn his next record into a hit. 'Good Vibrations', then, was an important test case for Capitol, representing a huge financial gamble on an entrepreneur producer whose track record seemed to be faltering. It was released in the US on 10 October 1966, and soon peaked at number one across the world, causing Capitol to admit that they were wrong about the Beach Boys' new direction, and to once more back Wilson as an entrepreneurial producer as he continued his work on *Smile*. This was entirely in keeping with the ongoing entrepreneurial production system – if a producer could keep producing hits, they were given the freedom to continue creating product; if not, they were soon fired. The huge success of 'Good Vibrations' also suggests that Taylor's techniques of creating a market for Brian Wilson were having a positive effect, allowing the band to successfully reach new audiences before the institutional development of

---

[34] Ibid., pp. 134–9.

[35] Ibid., pp. 148–50.

the technique of artist development. This more positive view of the Beach Boys as rock auteurs soon ended after the non-release of *Smile* in 1967, however, as I have discussed elsewhere.[36]

The above discussion demonstrates that critical celebrations of *Pet Sounds* depended not simply on properties of the recording but also on the institutional forces shaping its initial reception. The release of this particular recording coincided with a time of flux in the record industry, with the established teen market for rock making way for a new, 'hip' intelligentsia. In America in particular, the institutional forces were not yet in place to allow acts such as the Beach Boys to successfully make the transition from 'square' surf band to 'hip' studio auteurs, although the rapturous reception of *Pet Sounds* in Britain suggests that these forces were perhaps already better developed elsewhere. *Pet Sounds*' later integration into a narrative of tragic genius and studio wizardry has also been enabled by these same institutional forces, now firmly entrenched in both countries. The release of the *Pet Sounds Sessions* box set not only demonstrates the undoubted mastery Wilson had of the technology at his disposal, but also indicates the success that the institutions have finally had of creating a market for this recording. Although this chapter would have been impossible to write without the box set that has emerged because of the album's later rapturous reception, my discussion suggests that it is only a historical overview that takes into account the various institutional and cultural concerns surrounding the album that can look beyond the marketing myths to give a more nuanced musicology of record production.

Discography

The Beach Boys, *Good Vibrations: 30 years of the Beach Boys*, 5 CD Box set, Capitol, C2077778129424, 1993.
The Beach Boys, *The Beach Boys: The Pet Sounds Sessions* (produced by Brian Wilson), 4 CD Box set, Capitol, 724383766222, 1996.
The Beach Boys, *Pet Sounds*, vinyl reissue, Capitol, SVLP 149, 1999.

Filmography

Beautiful Dreamer: Brian Wilson and the Story of Smile (David Leaf, LSL Productions, 2004).

---

[36] The events surrounding the Smile album are covered in depth in Jan Butler, *Record Production and the Construction of Authenticity in the Beach Boys and late-sixties American Rock*, PhD thesis, University of Nottingham, 2010, pp. 171–9, 205–9.

Chapter 15

Tubby's Dub Style: The Live Art of Record Production

Sean Williams

Methodology

In this chapter I use several different approaches including interviews, analysis of video footage, and transcription of audio recordings, but the primary focus of my research has been a material analysis of the technology used by King Tubby to produce records from 1972 to 1979 at 18 Dromilly Avenue, Kingston Jamaica. Since King Tubby's studio no longer exists in the form it took in the 1970s some of the technical details remain speculative. However, the MCI mixing desk, the centrepiece of his studio, currently resides in the collection of the Experience Music Project, Seattle, and I have been able to examine it in its current condition. In the absence of written records or film footage of King Tubby's own studio practice, I have used footage of one of his apprentices, Lloyd 'Prince Jammy' James, to work out some details of signal routing and performance practice within the Dromilly Avenue studio, but given the highly reflexive nature of this studio practice and the inevitable presence of feedback systems (both figurative and literal in the case of tape delay) some of the most valuable insights have come from recreations of the studio setup that I have made and incorporated into my own creative music practice.

Whilst the emphasis of this paper is on technical detail, it is essential that this research be considered within the wider ecological perspective as suggested by Bateson, and elaborated upon by Waters through the idea of the 'performance ecosystem'.[1] The feedback paths between use of particular tools and techniques, the personnel in the studio during the mix, the testing of the dub-plates on the sound-system at the dance, the queue of producers outside the studio waiting to have their recordings mixed, all exert influence on the way the music on the record sounds. Far from taking a technologically deterministic position, I believe that a close examination of the tools and techniques from a material perspective can provide useful information about how affordances were exploited, how limitations were overcome, and essentially how an alignment of Tubby's knowledge and expertise with the technology at his disposal not only shaped his own music but

[1]   S. Waters, 'Performance Ecosystems: Ecological Approaches to Musical Interaction', Electroacoustic Music Studies Network, De Montfort/Leicester, 2007.

also influenced the many different genres and styles of recorded music making across the world. This reflexive practice cannot be abstracted from the social and cultural environment within which it operated, and this paper therefore presents an analysis of the technological perspective in acknowledgement that this is only one part of a much more complicated story.

Introduction

Osbourne Ruddock (1941–89), otherwise known as King Tubby, is widely credited as being one of the most influential figures in the development of the style of music originating in Kingston Jamaica in the early 1970s known as Dub. Common recording practice in Kingston in the late 1960s and early 1970s was to record the backing track consisting of drums, bass, rhythm (guitar and organ) and horns onto four-track tape, and then to record the vocals at a separate 'voicing' session, often in another studio. This allowed producers to use the same backing track or 'rhythm' for several different singers and even to use different lyrics, and to mix the backing tracks accordingly. Another common format was to record drums, bass, rhythm (with horns on the same track), and vocals onto a four-track tape ready for mixing directly onto a mono or stereo master. King Tubby's small studio in the bedroom of the house at 18 Dromilly Avenue in the Waterhouse district of Kingston Jamaica was equipped only to mix these four-track tapes and occasionally to record vocalists (in the old bathroom) on top of these existing rhythms in voicing sessions. Except for one isolated report of Lee 'Scratch' Perry attempting to record drums in the tiny bathroom vocal-booth with a bass player sitting in the control room,[2] it was not equipped for full recording sessions. Whilst it is commonly accepted that the distinctive sound of records produced at studios such as Sun Studios, Abbey Road Studio 2, or Goldstar (Phil Spector's Wall of Sound) is the result of the specific combination of the acoustic recording space, the technology, the engineering skills, and quite often, the regular session musicians used, with Tubby's dub mixes we can eliminate the acoustic element and the musicians' influence as being anything more than generalized since he was mixing tapes originally recorded at many different studios by many different players. The two remaining constant elements therefore, that contribute to the distinctive sonic characteristics – the soundprint – of mixes made at Tubby's studio are the equipment used and the performance practice associated with the act of *mixing* as opposed to the original act of recording. It is worth noting that these elements are electrical and physical as opposed to being acoustic and physical, and therefore it is useful to think of King Tubby as an electronic music maker. Except for the occasional aforementioned voicing sessions, the only performers recorded at Tubby's studio were the engineers performing the mixes – King Tubby

---

[2]   M.E. Veal, *Soundscapes and Shattered Songs in Jamaican Reggae* (Middletown, CT: Wesleyan University Press, 2007), p. 148.

and his apprentices: Philip Smart, Lloyd 'Prince Jammy' James, Pat Kelly and Overton 'Scientist' Brown amongst others. Given the amount of transformation and reinterpretation that happens in Tubby's mixes and the dissimilarity between the song as recorded initially and Tubby's substantially altered mix of the song, the mixing desk and the associated effects devices and machinery must be thought of as Tubby's musical instrument, and defining this instrument and working out how it was played can provide a useful perspective for a critical analysis of King Tubby's dub style.

Tubby was originally an electrical engineer and crucially, in the mid 1960s, built and ran the celebrated *Tubby's Home Town Hi-Fi* sound system. Sound systems featuring DJs playing records as opposed to performances from live bands have been central to Jamaican dance music culture since the 1950s,[3] providing a nucleus for the outdoor dances and often being run as extensions to record businesses such as those operated by Duke Reid and Clement 'Coxone' Dodd. Tubby was an early adopter of transistor technology, using transistor amplifiers for the treble speakers, and valve amplifiers for the bass. He used steel horns for the treble speakers, suspending them from trees where possible, so as to project the high frequencies evenly across the dance floor.[4] This level of care and attention to sound quality won him many clients ordering amplifiers for their own sound systems, and Tubby's later incorporation of tape delay (and probably reverb) in his sound system controls for live spatial effects, increased the flow of orders. In order to make suitable crossovers and the very large transformers needed for his sound system, he had to wind his own, and this was a regular duty of his various apprentices, especially the more technically minded Overton 'Scientist' Brown.

Although *King Tubby's Home Town Hi-Fi* wasn't the largest sound system in Jamaica it was widely acknowledged as being the best sounding.[5] His intimate understanding of frequency ranges, filtering and speaker-response needed for designing and constructing sound systems for himself and his many customers, coupled with his attention to detail contributed to his extensive skills at cutting records as a mastering engineer. Bradley relates how other sound system operators such as Duke Reid and Coxsone Dodd would sometimes audition their dub-plates on Tubby's sound system rather than their own in order to hear them properly. This fastidiousness is indicative of the care taken in his practice both as a mastering engineer and as a creative 'dub organizer'.[6]

Recording the rhythms separately to the vocals allowed producers to release different versions of the same song, but Tubby was able to take this same rhythm and with or without using the vocal track, was able to make a mix that was so substantially different to the original that it could be released as the B-side of

---

[3] L. Bradley, *Bass Culture: When Reggae was King* (London: Viking, 2000).

[4] Ibid., p. 314.

[5] Bradley, *Bass Culture*, and Veal, *Jamaican Reggae*, pp. 314–21.

[6] 'Dub Organizer' is the title of a record produced by Lee 'Scratch' Perry, voiced (by Dillinger) and mixed at Tubby's studio containing the line: 'Tubby's are the dub organizer'.

the single, thereby removing the necessity for the producer to pay for recording a different track for that purpose. Not just an economic way to fill a B-side, if this dub mix was good enough it would become more popular than the A-side, and this soon led to the release of entire dub albums such as Lee Perry's *14 Dub Blackboard Jungle* (Upsetters, 1973) and Augustus Pablo's *King Tubby's Meets Rockers Uptown* (Yard Music, 1976), both of which heavily featured King Tubby's mixing skills. Once he started remixing – making dub versions – he was able to start making much more creative, performative decisions in the studio, and, once cut to a dub-plate, these versions could be played to, and tested on an audience using his own sound system within a matter of hours, allowing almost instant feedback and fine tuning of his mixes. Running the sound system was therefore a key factor in the evolution of his mixing style. Tubby's studio remained in high demand through the 1970s with Tubby eventually taking a back seat to focus more on the sound system part of the business, leaving the bulk of the mixing work to his apprentices. The popularity of dub reached a low point in the early 1980s and eventually the MCI mixing desk was replaced and, after being in the possession of Rodwell 'Blackbeard' Sinclair for some years, was purchased in January 2001 by the Experience Music Project in Seattle. King Tubby was murdered outside his home in February 1989.

Instruments

There are an astonishing number of stories and myths surrounding Tubby's equipment and unpicking these has been difficult. Putting together information from accounts by Bradley and Veal, various interviews with assistants, sleeve notes and other less formal sources, it appears that he was indeed using a homemade mixer, with no real multitrack capabilities, until the 1972 purchase, facilitated by Bunny Lee, of the old MCI mixing desk and Scully and Ampex 4-track tape machines from Byron Lee's Dynamic Sounds studios, formerly West Indies Recording Label (WIRL). This mixing desk was designed and built by Grover C. 'Jeep' Harned of Music Centre Incorporated (MCI) in the mid-to-late 1960s. At this time mixing desks were not available as off-the-shelf items and they were either produced in very small runs or were more often custom made and tailored to the requirements of individual recording studios. Makers would use a combination of self-designed and borrowed circuitry and would use stock items for the more mechanical elements such as VU meters and faders. MCI started making one of the first widely available production models known as the JH-400 series in 1973, but before this, each desk would have been almost unique. Because all the signals were routed through it and it occupied the central focus of the studio, this MCI desk is the most important tool and arguably had the biggest impact on Tubby's new sound and dub style. The desk, commonly and misleadingly referred to as a four-track mixer, has 12 input channels, each with gain, basic equalization (EQ), one auxiliary send and a channel fader. Four output buses are controlled by four

Painton-style quadrant faders,[7] there is a test-tone oscillator, monitor controls, a very early example of remote tape transport control, and a patchable high-pass filter. The patchbay built into the side of the desk allows access to the signal path at various points in the signal chain for each channel and bus as well as access to the high-pass filter. The main sound-transforming tools used by King Tubby are the high-pass filter, volume controls, reverberation and delay.

King Tubby's 'Big Knob' Filter

Tubby's so-called 'Big Knob' filter has 11 frequency steps from 70 Hz to 7.5 KHz[8] all accessible within 165 degrees of rotation, allowing extreme sweeps to be performed with ease. It is situated at the top right-hand corner of the master section and is operated by means of a 40 mm diameter control knob. The knobs for controlling almost all the other features such as EQ settings, auxiliary sends and so on are a smaller 30 mm, hence the name. High-pass filters are usually used to mitigate against proximity effect or to reduce low-frequency rumble, so the rationale behind the enormous frequency range exhibited here is initially unclear. On examining the desk at the Experience Music Project in Seattle, I discovered that the filter is a standard production model filter module made, like other components in the desk, by Altec, and not individually designed by Jeep Harned at all. This fits with Bob Olhsson's comments about Harned building a small number of custom desks from Altec and Langevin parts prior to launching the MCI JH-400 series desks.[9]

The hand of Art Davis hovers over the shared designs of many EQs and filters of this period by Altec, Langevin and Cinema Engineering and during the 1960s there were all sorts of arrangements, takeovers and relationships between these companies as well as Electrodyne. This particular filter, an Altec 9069b, is a passive inductor-based T-network filter, in the same family as the Langevin EQ255a (with which it shares identical frequency step values), and the Cinema Engineering 4031, and in the same class as the Urei 565 'Little Dipper', the Eckmiller HV-55, the Maihak W49 HörspielVerzerrer (radio play distorter) and other units by Danish firm NTP, Neumann, Siemens and the other German Broadcast companies. These devices comprise the class of *radiophonic* or *sound effects filters* typically used to simulate distant sound or spatial dislocation, voice mediated through radio or telephone, and other such spatial effects in radio and cinema sound design. The main characteristic of these filters, whether they are passive or active, is

---

[7]   Found on many BBC, EMI and other mixing desks from the mid-to-late twentieth century, these faders describe part of a circle rather than being linear tracking and work by means of stud contacts switching discreet resistors into the signal path rather than by the continuous conductive plastic or carbon tracks used in later designs. Harned's famous desk made for Criteria Studios in Miami exhibits quadrant faders on each channel.

[8]   70 Hz, 100 Hz, 150 Hz, 250 Hz, 500 Hz, 1 kHz, 2 kHz, 3 kHz, 5 kHz, 7.5 kHz.

[9]   B. Olhsson, *Mid 60's custom MCI consoles*. [Online]. Available at: http://recforums. prosoundweb.com/index.php/m/113753/0/ (2004). [accessed: 14 June 2011].

that they have stepped frequency selection. This precludes their use as dynamic performance instruments from a design point of view – indeed, the Maihak W49 has printed on it right above the frequency selectors 'Nür gerastete Stellungen benützen' [*only* use detented settings] – so it took a leap of imagination by people such as King Tubby and Karlheinz Stockhausen[10] to use such filters in this way. This perhaps explains why nobody at Dynamic Sounds made much use of the filter while the desk was there, and further supports the case against technological determinism. The stepped nature aligns it with a set-and-forget practice associated with traditional utility high-pass filters as usually found on input channels of mixing desks and microphone pre-amps.

His apprentices spent time winding transformers (and presumably inductors too) for the many sound system clients,[11] so Tubby's familiarity with crossovers and filters as part of his sound system work make it unsurprising that he began to experiment with this filter creatively very soon after acquiring the desk. Indeed, there are accounts of him using crossover networks with his previous homemade mixing desk to split a monophonic signal (from a record or tape) into different frequency bands, allowing him to remix a mono recording by being able to attenuate the bass, mid-range and treble independently, much like using kill-switches on some contemporary DJ mixers.

Prince Jammy recounts some details about the MCI mixer:

> It was a very unique board because it was custom built for Dynamic Sounds ...
> it had things that the modern boards nowadays don't really have, like a high-pass
> filter that made some squawky sounds when you change the frequency ... We
> would put any instrument through it – drums, bass, riddim, voices. That high-
> pass filter is what create (sic) the unique sound at Tubby's.[12]

Chris Lane refers to the filter as Tubby's 'secret weapon',[13] but acknowledges that it is but one of many techniques that form Tubby's style. The strongest characteristics of the filter's sound are the discreet steps, the clicks and crunches when the frequency is switched, and the phasing effect heard when filtered

---

[10]   Stockhausen made extensive use of the W49 in both composition and performance. For a comparative study of Stockhausen and King Tubby's use of stepped filters see S. Williams, 'Stockhausen meets King Tubby's: The Stepped Filter and Its Influence as a Musical Instrument on Two Different Styles of Music', in F. Weium and T. Boon (eds), *Artefacts: Studies in the History of Science and Technology: Vol. 8* (Washington, DC: Smithsonian Institution Scholarly Press, published in cooperation with Rowman and Littlefield Publishers, 2012).

[11]   Veal, *Soundscapes*, p. 132.

[12]   Ibid., p. 114.

[13]   C. Lane, 'A Musical Revolution', *Natty Dread: Le Magazine du Reggae*, vol. 19 (2003).

signals are mixed with the unfiltered originals. The most reasonable assumption is that signals were routed to the filter via one of the four output groups which is corroborated by this account from Bunny Lee:

> an' Tubby's studio did 'ave a ting weh you could a thin it, an' do all different kinda ting with it, right, – it's not even really equalization, the ting 'ave four push-up ting, when you push the one in the middle and 'ave it up and down, with the ting, it create some mad sound, like you hear all some knife a cut thru'.[14]

The 'ting ... in the middle' refers to one of the four bus faders and supports the idea that it was used as the filter send. Sending the whole mix through the high-pass filter would not result in audible phasing of the signal, but by sending the signal via a bus it would be possible to mix the filtered sound with the dry sound and this would make the phase differences around the cut-off frequency audible. This effect explains the occasional references to Tubby using a phaser.

In the context of a mono mix the high-pass filter is an extremely useful spatialization tool in a different way than delay or reverb. Being familiar with the crossover frequencies for his sound system amplifiers, Tubby would have been keenly aware of what filter settings to use to separate some sounds so that they were only projected through the suspended horns. Manipulating the filter control would then physically move the sound vertically through the dancefloor, and adding reverb and delay would create an enormous range of spatio-temporal effects.

Faders

Another key performance detail is the shape of the fader caps. They are the round 'Rolo' style, much used by Langevin and Altec, which make for a more tactile control over the volume, and in the absence of mute switches the feel of the faders would have been all the more important since they were used heavily throughout a mix, and often moved very quickly with precise timing to immediately cut or reintroduce a sound. It is hard to quantify the contribution of the fader design to Tubby's mixing style, but, as the key interface between the musician and the music, this must be taken into account, as should the linear scale of the fader, marked in regularly spaced 5 dB units, thus differing from contemporary faders which exhibit a more sensitive area around 0 dB as well as the ability to increase gain typically by 10 dB. A qualitative analysis must be approached by acquiring some original Langevin faders and incorporating them into a performance practice but at this point I am yet to locate any with which to experiment.

There are many stories of Tubby replacing the faders on his mixing desk, but I found no clear evidence of any customization unless the entire top panel has been

---

[14]   O. Ruddock, *Dub Gone Crazy* (Manchester: Blood And Fire, 1994), sleeve notes.

replaced and re-engraved, which is highly unlikely. All the visible controls match the legend exactly and the only evidence that I could find in support of the idea that the faders could have been replaced was a slight variation in the shape of the two bolt-heads used to secure each channel fader to the fascia. All the other bolts are countersunk flat-headed bolts, but these are slightly round headed.

However, the fader caps are the red 'Rolo' shaped Langevin/Altec style, consistent with the fader modules themselves, and the legend stamped into the one-piece surface of the desk matches the scale of the fascia supplied with the Langevin faders available at the time. Even the layout of the fader module and EQ module for each channel mirrors the layout of the closely related Electrodyne channel strips of the 1960s and the whole channel layout is remarkably similar to the Electrodyne ACC-1204 console, so if Tubby did replace the faders they were either a like-for-like replacement, or he was very lucky to find a different variety that fitted exactly. It is conceivable that he could have replaced older stepped attenuators/faders with continuous faders from the same manufacturer. Either way, they are clearly consistent with the desk being built by Harned from parts manufactured either by Altec, Langevin, or Electrodyne, and there is no evidence at all for Tubby having replaced rotary potentiometers with linear faders on this desk. The fader stories may well relate to modifications carried out on his previous homemade mixer but that is beyond the scope of this paper to ascertain. The quadrant faders on the buses are similar to those used on Harned's MCI desk built slightly earlier for Criteria Studios in Florida and a similar desk built for King Studios. The coloured caps, red, blue, green, and white, correspond to the coloured legend indicating the bus output connectors at the rear of the desk, so it is unlikely that these have ever been replaced either with anything but like-for-like substitutes.

Reverberation

The other main elements in the mix are reverberation (reverb) and delay. Reverb was routed via the single auxiliary send, accessed for each channel by a rotary control immediately above each channel fader, to a Fisher K-10 Spacexpander – an American valve driven spring reverberation unit designed for the domestic hi-fi market to 'simulate the echoes of a well-designed auditorium'.[15] Several accounts report that this unit was heavily modified by Tubby, but experimentation has so far only revealed that muting one of the two springs in the reverb tank produces a sound closer to that heard on the records. The inputs and outputs on a Fisher K-10 are unbalanced RCA/phono sockets, and on inspecting the desk I found two cables with RCA/phono plugs hanging out of the back with the other ends hard wired into the inside of the desk. Since the tape machines and the other outboard equipment would have been connected via XLR or ¼" jack connectors, this increases the

---

[15]   A. Fisher, *The Fisher K-10 Dynamic Spacexpander Reverberation Unit: Operating Instructions and Warranty* (USA: Fisher Radio Corporation, 1967), p. 14.

probability that these RCA/phono plugs might have been used for connecting the K-10. This would suggest at least some level of modification to the send source or return destination of the reverb signal within the desk, but exactly what remains a mystery. Many of Tubby's records feature the spring tank being dropped or knocked, and this is such a harsh sound in relation to the normal reverb levels that it strongly suggests the use of compression, probably on the main output of the mixer. Tubby's dub of John Holt's 'A Quiet Place', entitled 'A Noisy Place' featured on *King Tubby's In Fine Style* is a classic example of this often used trick. Since compression is a standard tool used for mastering and mixing, it would be highly unusual for Tubby's studio not to have the option of using compression on individual tracks or across the whole mix.

Delay

Given that there were two four-track tape machines in the studio, I have asked several experienced engineers and technicians including Graham Hinton (EMS, SSL Amek) and Steve Albini (Electrical Audio) which they would have used for playback and which for delay, and the universal answer has been to use the Ampex for playback and the Scully for delay. Chris Lane's recollections of the studio support this assumption, so I believe that delay was achieved using the Scully 4-track, but in the absence of a second auxiliary send, each channel was routed to an additional output bus, which fed the tape-delay input post-channel-fader. In such a setup, the signal is recorded onto the tape with the record head and immediately played back via the playback head with the delay time being the distance between the record and playback heads divided by the tape speed. With one bus used for the main mix and one used for the filter, this left two possible buses for delay, and in the video clip of Prince Jammy performing two dub mixes in Tubby's studio from the film *Deep Roots Music* (Johnson and Pines 1982), you can see Jammy (who is not using the high-pass filter and therefore has three available delay send buses) using three channels for drum delay and voice and guitar delay respectively. The tape outputs were returned on their own channels and these channels were also routed back to the respective tape delay output-bus as well as to the master output, thus enabling both delay level and feedback to be controlled for each delay channel by that channel fader alone. In the absence of the limitation of only one auxiliary send it is usual to have two separate controls for delay feedback and delay level. Having incorporated Tubby's limitation of one control for both parameters into my own practice for some live performances, I found it to be extremely effective because it freed up one hand which could then control other parameters.

Chris Lane recounted to me of his visit in 1977 that whilst he and Dave Hendley were having some tracks mixed by Prince Jammy, they asked him to make a faster delay by switching playback speed of the delay machine from 7.5 ips to 15 ips thereby halving the delay time. Lane relates that Jammy 'wasn't best pleased about this 17 year old kid interfering with his mixing style' (interview with the author 2009) but that they had not used the faster tape speed before and would try it and see if it sounded good. Lane told me how he heard the faster delay used on a few records after that visit but it doesn't appear to have been used much. It is, however, used to striking effect on 'Tubby's Dub Song' from Dave Hendley's *King Tubby's In Fine Style* compilation. It might have been possible to vari-speed the Scully machine but I have not noticed this effect in any output from Tubby's studio yet. The significance of this fixed delay time is that it influences interpretation and criticism of the rhythmic qualities arising from the use of delay in some tunes. Veal attributes the double-speed drum track in Yabby You's 'Fire Fire Dub' to a conscious decision,[16] but given the technical limitations of just two different delay-times, perhaps this effect is achieved less by design more by serendipity with the delay time accidentally being in sync with the track tempo. Either way, it still relies on Tubby's musical sense to make the decision about whether to use it in this context or not, and being able to recognize and make creative use of such an effect is a familiar technique relied upon by improvising musicians in all genres.

It is clear that although limited in features, the equipment Tubby was using was generally of very high quality indeed.

Performance Practice

The wear patterns on the desk, coupled with the footage of Prince Jammy at the controls suggest that inputs from the four-track tape were on channels 7 to 10, and delay returns were on channels 1 and 2 and possibly 3, with filter return possibly on channel 11 or 12. Such an arrangement allows for a central mixing position with the four main channels accessible by both hands, delay channels operated by the left hand, and filtering by the right, with both hands able to access the reverb sends. What is striking about the footage of Jammy is the economy of movement and the agility with which the controls are manipulated. This is something more than an engineer carrying out a technical exercise at a mixing desk – it is clearly a highly skilled musician performing with a musical instrument. The limitation of only four tape channels is a liberating constraint that allowed more focus on the effects manipulation, more careful performance on the channel volume faders, and greater flexibility for one performer to structure the mix as a whole.

Sixteen-track, and later 24-track, recording, which became the standard in most professional studios in the 1970s, would easily confront the performer with a paralysis of choice and it is perhaps no accident that the increased number of tracks adopted in later years coincided with a change of quality in dub production, not necessarily for the better. The MCI mixing desk is only 90 cm wide which allows the engineer to reach all controls easily without moving around. Not only is there a danger of paralysis of choice when working on a larger mixing desk, but the extreme width of many large format SSL desks with 48-plus channels and

16   Veal, *Soundscapes*, pp. 121–2.

their unhelpful ergonomics make the act of mixing far less intuitive and physically more demanding; parallax error in channel selection and different parameters being too far apart are two obvious problems of larger consoles not exhibited by the MCI desk.

For me, the most exciting physical evidence of performance practice are the aforementioned wear patterns on the surface of the desk, particularly around the filter control, with clearly visible traces of thumb, fingers and the palm of the right hand indicating heavy usage. It brings to mind the Fender signature series of guitars such as, Andy Summers' Telecaster and Jaco Pastorius' Jazz Bass and, in the absence of any film footage of Tubby himself, provides the clearest visible evidence of Tubby's performance practice.

Tubby's feel is sometimes ascribed to his love of jazz,[17] and the improvisatory nature of his mixes supports this theory. To quote Bunny Lee: 'if he mix the same tune a dozen times you will have twelve different version'.[18] Tubby fixes his improvisations in the form of records, and he draws on a number of structural, spatial, rhythmic and timbral techniques to stamp his identity onto each version. In 'Rebel Dance' at around bar 33, he uses the clicks and crunches as the filter is switched between frequency steps to punctuate and augment the rhythm with a triplet feel. This would not be possible with a continuously variable synthesizer filter but it is also clear that it is not simply technological determinism at work here either. To use Stephen Hill's expression, it is the *alignment*[19] of Tubby's tacit knowledge of electronics coupled with his musicality and the affordance of the instrument characterized by the clicks and steps, which combine in his practice and which make it unique and which allows him to make significant musical changes to a tune's internal rhythm. An argument can be made that tape delay is also used to restructure rhythm and to create cross rhythms, but in performance terms this is perhaps less deliberately controllable and is certainly less performative since the delay time is limited to one of two values whereas the filter can be stepped between its 10 frequency steps at will to create precisely timed rhythmic interventions. It is sometimes difficult to distinguish between Tubby's and Jammy's mixes but this can be partly explained by remembering that Jammy was Tubby's apprentice and that repeat business for the studio revolved around a house style. Rather than the technology solely determining this style, it is more plausible to assume that social and economic factors would have encouraged the convergence of each engineer's mixing style *within* the framework of limitations and affordances set by the available technological configurations. It is beyond the scope of this paper to analyse the different mixing styles of Tubby, Jammy, Scientist and the other apprentices, but such a study could build on the research presented in this paper

---

[17]   Ibid., p. 117.

[18]   Bradley, *Bass Culture*, p. 316.

[19]   S. Hill, *The Tragedy of Technology: Human Liberation Versus Domination in the Late Twentieth Century* (London: Pluto, 1988).

and explore the preferences and refinements of each engineer's practice within the ecological context of a common set of tools and instruments.

On examining the instruments, and in particular the mixing desk, although most were of very high quality, it is clear that Tubby had to deal with and overcome severe limitations, and while it is certainly the case that some of the equipment lent itself to being used in a particular way, it was Tubby's expertise and creative imagination that exploited the affordances of these elements and combined them into a single musical instrument enabling the production of such inventive and enduring music. A grasp of these technical characteristics and limitations is essential for a complete musicological analysis of Tubby's creative music practice. This material research cannot be used in isolation from the social, cultural and economic conditions centred around King Tubby's studio in the 1970s but offers as much detail as possible from a technical perspective in order to contribute to a deeper understanding of the performance ecosystem in which King Tubby's music evolved.

Acknowledgements

I would like to thank John Seman at The Experience Music Project, Seattle, for granting me access to examine King Tubby's mixing desk and Chris Lane for the interview.

Discography

Pablo, Augustus. *King Tubby's Meets Rockers Uptown*. (Yard Music 1976) RLP001.

Ruddock, O. 'Rebel Dance' on *King Tubby's Special 1973–1976*. (Trojan 1973–6) TRLD409.

Ruddock, O. (Compiled by Dave Hendley). *King Tubby's In Fine Style*. (Trojan 2004) TJDDD063.

Ruddock, O. *Dub Gone Crazy*. (Blood And Fire Ltd. 1994) BAFCD002.

Upsetters. (Produced by Lee 'Scratch' Perry). *14 Dub Blackboard Jungle*. (Upsetters 1973) LUXXCD004.

Chapter 16

Recording the Revolution: 50 Years of Music Studios in Revolutionary Cuba

Jan Fairley and Alexandrine Boudreault-Fournier

Introduction

In 2010 the Spanish singer Amparo Sánchez released a new record called Tucson-Havana.[1] Photographs in the glossy CD booklet are dominated by Sánchez and musicians in the pre-Revolutionary EGREM studios in Central Havana made famous by the Buena Vista Social Club.[2] Indeed a guest for one song *La Parrandita de los Santos* is none other than veteran singer Omara Portuondo, the only women associated with the all-male Buena Vista collective. The message is clear: it is a pilgrimage to these studios even if the music itself has few discernible Cuban characteristics and only a couple of guest Cuban musicians.

The Central Havana EGREM (Empresa de Grabación y Ediciones Musicales/ Recording Studios and Music Publishing Enterprise) studios have become 'holy ground'. Here unexpectedly a multi-million selling disc made by World Circuit, a small independent UK company, changed the face and fortunes of Cuban music at the end of the twentieth century. Yet the studio's cultural capital pre-dates Buena Vista, famous as the place where visiting US artists like Nat King Cole recorded from the 1940s onwards when they belonged to Panart Records. Since the Buena Vista Social Club phenomenon the EGREM studios have become famous by association similar to London's Abbey Road because of The Beatles and Detroit's Hitsville USA studios for Tamla Motown. Like an old church whose walls are soaked in prayer, hymns and incense, the wooden walls of the EGREM studios with their warm acoustic and slightly dilapidated state are seemingly saturated in previous music made there and the presence of those who made it. It offers an

---

[1]   Amparo Sánchez, Tucson-Havana, WRASS257.

[2]   For an account of the studios in the context of the orchestra and their work with UK producer Nick Gold and US guitarist Ry Cooder, Cuban producer Juan de Marcos González, see Jan Fairley, 'The Rejuvenating Power of the Buena Vista Social Club', *Samples*, Jahrgang 8; the German online publication of Arbeitskreis Studium Populärer Musik (ASPM) ed. Ralf von Appen, André Doehring, Dietrich Helms and Thomas Phleps. [Online]. Available at: http: //aspm.ni.lo-net2.de/samples-archiv/Samples8/fairley.pdf [accessed: 15 April 2011].

indefinable, intangible, value-added cultural capital, a quality that is perceived by non-Cuban 'foreign' artists and producers as 'affecting' their recordings.

In much the same way as Sánchez, UK DJ Gilles Peterson, funded by Havana Club International purveyor of Cuban rum, recently went to these studios in Havana and recorded a host of cutting edge Cuban musicians of the moment:

> I got the call to go to Havana a year ago. A trip to Cuba in September 2008 to check out the new generation of Havana based artists ... I had literally only just stepped out of the cinema having watched the Che movie ... would I find anything going on outside of Buena Vista, rumba and reggaeton? ... come the spring of 2009 I was preparing for a 5-day Egrem Studio love-in ... What a week we had in this iconic spot ...[3]

With the help of vanguard pianist Roberto Fonseca (offering continuity as replacement pianist for Rúben González for the Buena Vista Social Club upon the latter's infirmity), Peterson continues the mythology of authenticity and quasi-colonial discourses established by the Buena Vista Social Club project, to the extent of taking photos and small films of himself in the studio as the 'discoverer' of burgeoning 'new' talent (not linked to the EGREM studios beforehand) in this sacred place.

In contrast, if you ask Cuban musicians where they would like to record if they have the money, they would almost certainly never choose these run-down EGREM studios in Central Havana. Depending on their budget, they might opt for the state-of-the-art Abdala air-conditioned studios with a bar, satellite TV and other luxuries; or the re-furbished uptown EGREM Miramar studios (or in Oriente province, the EGREM Siboney studios in Santiago de Cuba); or the updated studios of the Cinematographic Institute ICAIC; or they might ask musician Silvio Rodríguez if they could use his small Ojalá studios; or those attached to the Pablo Milanés Foundation. Or they would build their own studios in their own homes like musician-producer Lucia Huergo in her parents' old home near Havana's Zoo; or Edesio Alejandro and Juan de Marcos González in their small living rooms in Alamar. Many such smaller studios are often used by others through the system of reciprocity, the favour friendship networks that keep Cuban society going.

These contrasting preferences echo two music recording trends that emerged in Cuba in the 1990s: one for consumption outside the country iconically represented by the Buena Vista Social Club project, a music that mined 'authentic' romantic tropes of a pre-Revolutionary repertoire; another on the island itself where many other modern musics linked to pertinent everyday life concerns are constantly emerging, some as part of an official 'alternative' scene recognized by the state system, others unofficial, 'underground' and relatively clandestine in people's

---

[3]   Gilles Peterson in the Foreword to the CD booklet *Gilles Peterson presents Havana Cultura New Cuban Sound*, BW00D038CD.

bedrooms.[4] We provide two case studies to illustrate how contemporary musicians have responded to their desire to record new musics in a charged ideological context. Lyng Chang's To'Mezclao studios in the spare bedroom of his small flat up two flights of stairs opposite the bakery in Havana's Calle Ayestaran and Kiki, based in Sueño, a comfortable neighbourhood in Santiago de Cuba.

These two case studies further illustrate that the contemporary Cuban period is characterized by the coexistence of underground and official networks of music production. During the dramatic 1990s economic crisis officially called the 'Special Period in time of peace',[5] the country was forced to open up economically, rules and laws changed drastically as a pragmatic mixed economy was adopted which changed music production on the island. In this chapter we use this 1990s watershed of the opening up of Cuba to transnationalism and entrepreneurship to position the art of recording in relation to the parameters of *cubanidad*.

Producing *Cubanidad*

We use the site of music recording to explore the concept of *cubanidad*, a term used by Cubans to define the indefinable – what it means to be Cuban – and more specifically, how *cubanidad* is expressed through the production and recording of music. Fernando Ortíz, Cuba's early twentieth-century ethnologist, defined *cubanidad* as 'the quality of the Cuban person' and 'a condition of the soul' that embraces 'the particular quality of Cuban culture'.[6] Music and the creation of new styles has always been an essential identity marker. This essence of 'being Cuban' rooted in nationalist sentiments has been seminal on the island.

Post-1959 Cuban nationalism was embedded in revolutionary ideology and history. Throughout the revolution, being Cuban has involved being loyal to the efforts of the revolution acting in the socialist interests of its people. In many ways Fidel Castro (whose first name literally means loyal) and the memory of Ché

---

[4] For a discussion of Cuban music in the Special Period 1990s see Jan Fairley, '"Ay Dios Ampárame" (O God Protect Me); Music in Cuba during the 1990s, the Special Period', in K. Dawe (ed.), *Island Musics* (Oxford: Berg, 2004); Vincenzo Perna, *Timba: The Sound of the Cuban Crisis* (Farnham: Ashgate, 2005); A. Hernández-Reguant, 'Havana's Timba: A Macho Sound for Black Sex', in K.M. Clark and D.A. Thomas (eds), *Globalization and Race* (Durham: Duke University Press, 2006), pp. 249–78; for Cuban music since 1959 see Robin D. Moore, *Music and Revolution, Cultural Change in Socialist Cuba* Berkeley: University of California Press, 2006); G. Baker, 'Mala Bitza Social Klu: "underground", "alternative" and "commercial" in Havana hip hop', *Popular Music*, vol. 31, no. 1 (2012), addresses slippage in usage and meaning of these terms.

[5] See Fairley, 'Ay Dios Ampárame'; Perna, *Timba*; A. Hernández-Reguant, *Cuba in the Special Period: Culture and Ideology in the 1990s* (New York: Palgrave Macmillan, 2009).

[6] Fernando Ortíz in Renée Clémentine Lucien, preface by Françoise Moulin Civil, *Résistance et cubanité* (Paris: L'Harmattan 2006), p. 15.

Guevara embody heroic ideals of valiant struggle and sacrifice for the greater good embracing moral rather than material incentives, as part of the everyday. While there may be elements of a patriarchal double-bind, many Cubans whatever their ambivalences and ambiguities voice loyalty to the sovereignty of the island and its history, often vociferously proud to be Cuban and proud of their flag. At the same time despite the 50-year-plus official US blockade of the island and a constant US–Cuban polemic many Cubans feel an affinity for US culture, while some have family sending economic support from the diaspora.

This means that *cubanidad* is a complex beast. Although transnational influences have always existed in Cuba – overtly pre-1959, more covertly post-1959 – the cultural politics that gradually developed on the island after the 1959 Revolution have meant that everything created had to fall within established revolutionary parameters. The nomination of Abel Prieto, a poet and writer of the 1960s generation and previous president of UNEAC (the Writers and Artists Union), as the head of the ministry of culture in 1997 was a strong sign of rejuvenation, opening and revaluation of the significance of the 1960s period.[7] Soon after taking office, faithful to his long haired style,[8] Abel Prieto institutionally recognized rock and rap as authentic forms of Cuban artistic expression.

The struggles and achievements of the generation represented by Prieto during the 1960s and 1970s have paved the way for the present cultural politics of twenty-first-century Cuba. A tension between the kind of culture revolutionary Cuba should produce, the role of culture and who can make it lay at the heart of this period.

We approach *cubanidad* thereby as imbuing every aspect of creative life, how one expresses oneself as a Cuban and how far one may go in doing so. To this end, we are interested in how, in contemporary Cuba, alternative recording sites provide different readings of what it is to create and produce music 'made in Cuba'. We contextualize these sites historically and in relation to the current Cuban context, providing a complex picture of how politics, ideology and nationalism intermesh with creativity within shifting economic and political models of governance.[9]

---

[7]   Arturo García Hernández, 'Interview with Abel Prieto, Cuban Minister of Culture', Mexico's *La Jornada*, February 2007. [Online]. Available at: http: //embacu.cubaminrex. cu/Portals/7/Interview.doc [accessed: 26 April 2011].

[8]   In the 1960s longhaired men were often forced to cut their hair in accordance with 'revolutionary social hygiene' policy. Some denounced this policy as a form of repression against alternative behaviour. See for instance Ian Lumsden, *Machos, Maricones, and Gays: Cuba and Homosexuality* (Philadelphia: Temple University Press, 1996).

[9]   While conscious of the danger of falling into an essentialist vision of *cubanidad*, our intention is to explore this complex term in the context of sites of music recording. Our account in no way provides a definitive discussion of *cubanidad* or the myriad of ways Cuban 'essence' is expressed.

Cultural Politics of Music Making

It has been argued that from a Western, cultural-capitalist perspective, there are two polar ways of understanding cultural production in the nation-state.[10] In the first, popular culture is simply left to the market. In contrast, the second position favours the *dirigiste* role of the state, what Toby Miller and George Yúdice label 'command culture'.[11] In this context, the state has a central role in the promotion, funding and implementation of specific cultural policies because the market is of secondary importance, either non-existent or highly regulated by the state. Within a command culture, however, there are a broad variety of methods and strategies that influence the creation of a diversified realm of cultural policies.[12] For instance, the Russian and Cuban revolutions had different perspectives on how to approach and promote a national culture, although Marxist-Leninist principles influenced both.[13] Furthermore, traditional socialist realism has never existed in Cuba. Exclusions were justified because 'newer' music had to 'earn' its place in the internal market, which implies a market governed by radio and live performance as well as fitting with broad ideological ideas that informed cultural policy.[14]

Under this model, Cuba stands as a 'command' type of culture, in which the market and other organizations (for example, NGOs) are in large part regulated by state authorities.[15] Yet it is true that since the Special Period, the Cuban state has negotiated the challenges of globalization with 'linkages to direct foreign investment of equal magnitude to what aid from socialist countries had been'.[16] It is also clear that despite economic dependence, Cuba never followed any strict Soviet models.

In such a context, those musicians not recognized by or unable to enter the dominant system for varying reasons find themselves marginalized within the official system. In such a context, the notions of 'underground' and 'commercial' acquire distinct meanings to those in Europe and North America. Joaquín Borges-Triana defines 'underground' as a scene that represents a variance or an *alternative*

---

[10] Toby Miller and George Yúdice, *Cultural Policy* (London: Sage Publications, 2002).

[11] Miller and Yúdice, *Cultural Policy*.

[12] Stefan Toepler, 'From Communism to Civil Society? The Arts and the Nonprofit Sector in Central and Eastern Europe', *Journal of Arts Management, Law, and Society*, vol. 30, no. 1 (2000): 7–18.

[13] See Peter Manuel, 'Marxism, Nationalism and Popular Music in Revolutionary Cuba', *Popular Music*, vol. 6, no. 2 (1987): 161–78. We would like to stress that the size of Cuba, the Caribbean locality, the colonial history and the personality of its revolution make it very different from Chinese and Russian particular revolutionary contexts.

[14] On social realism, see the interview with Abel Prieto by García Hernández.

[15] Miller and Yúdice, *Cultural Policy*.

[16] Randy Martin, 'Beyond Privatization? The Art and Society of Labor, Citizenship, and Consumerism', *Social Text*, vol. 17, no. 2 (1999): 35–48, 40.

to the 'official thought' [*pensamiento oficial*] in Cuba.[17] Even if Borges-Triana does not provide a concise explanation of what distinguishes 'underground' from 'alternative', it is understood that they both refer to spaces, genres and artists that are not included in the dominant music scene that is, the state owned industries.

State authorities tolerate 'underground' expressions as long as they do not transgress unwritten cultural politics, guidelines and revolutionary norms and values. In other words, pockets of unofficial artistic trends are tolerated as long as they do not contravene the revolution's approach to culture and arts. For instance, musicians are allowed to 'own' their studios as long as they do not dedicate this space to commercialization and profit making. Once inside the social network, musicians know who owns what: exchanges and contracts are common both amongst Cuban and between them and foreign musicians in a culture defined by reciprocity, exchange and favour between and within networks.

The commercialization of culture reflects ideologies embedded in the socialist ideal of creation and arts. As Cuban musicians evolve in this context, many express a 'morality of commercialization', which is embodied by a formal focus and concern for social causes. Many successful musicians attempt to maintain the fragile balance between commercial success and morality as making and accumulating money unofficially can be perceived as a 'crime' in Cuba[18] and does indeed create problematic ideological dilemmas. There is an underlying ideal that if a musician supports the Revolution then commercialism is outside their set of choices as culture should be free for all to benefit from. This reserved approach to commercialism is not limited to musicians and can be observed in other spheres of Cuban life.[19]

The emergence of home studios among musicians and the population at large in the 1990s contributes to the development of underground sectors of cultural activity. On the whole, the official authorities tolerate such alternative spaces of creation as long as owners play the revolutionary game and do not behave in dissident fashion. The following three sections offer a concise representation of Cuban music recording history.[20]

---

[17]   Joaquín Borges-Triana, *Concierto Cubano finisecular: para un estudio de la música cubana alternativa* (Habana: Editorial Universitaria, 2008), p. 41. Joaquín Borges-Triana is a Cuban scholar journalist.

[18]   Interview with Kiki, reggaeton producer, January 2010, Santiago de Cuba. We recognize that the term 'crime' is exaggerated, yet it is used as such to express the fact that there is an element of risk and 'fear' as Cubans are regularly imprisoned for contravening rules regarding illegal sales of merchandise and other illicit activities.

[19]   For commercial versus social implication balance in community project development through religion and tourism see Adrian H. Hearn, 'Afro-Cuban Religions and Social Welfare: Consequences of Commercial Development in Havana', *Human Organization*, vol. 63, no. 1 (2004): 78–87.

[20]   We thank Antoni Kapcia for discussion regarding the problematic nature of defining historical periods: what fits one aspect (for example economy) will not necessarily fit another (for example culture or foreign policy) (email: 13 May 2010).

The Blockade: Music Production and Recording from 1959 to the 1990s

The immediate post-1959 period was a transition period for the revolution having finally overthrown the Batista dictatorship by audacious methods and heroic acts which immediately cemented themselves as ideologically defining and iconic characteristics for the future. Fidel Castro and Ché Guevara (who promised 'revolución con pachanga' (a dance craze of the time)) publicly and privately sought backers in the USA but found no support for the revolutionaries' desire to run the island independently.[21] Opting ultimately for the backing of the Soviet Union, this alliance further impacted on the Cold War era. Liaison with the USSR meant periods of internal tension within Cuba, particularly in the late 1960s as different political and cultural visions fought for space and hegemony. In the interim US-owned nightclubs and hotels were nationalized: they had previously practised apartheid, allowing black musicians to entertain white clients while refusing the same musicians access.[22] The media was nationalized including radio stations and recording companies like Panart Records, founded in 1943 and which owned studios, pressed records and distributed foreign labels.

Cultural activity shifted from entertaining US tourists to playing music for Cuban people at open-air concerts, community centres, schools and colleges. Radio was the main means of production and consumption of music, with programmes dedicated to a broad spectrum of genres with musicians playing live in various radio studios like CMCJ.

The late 1960s and early 1970s (latterly officially 1971–76) is referred to as the 'Grey Five' showing the location of culture within a force field of ideological philosophies.[23] The period witnessed internal conflict between bureaucrats and artists as to how revolutionary culture should be defined, with a small group of powerful bureaucrats repressing and censoring following perceived Soviet-influenced notions of what revolutionary culture could and should not be. This period witnessed harsh repression and censorship. At the same time there was artistic struggle against this with debates and discussion centring on concepts of the 'new man' with attendant international cultural activities to foster dialogue

---

[21]   Jan Fairley, 'Cuba: 50 Years since the Revolution', *Songlines* [UK magazine] (2009), pp. 27–30.

[22]   See Cuba's black national poet Nicolas Guillén's poem *Tengo*, parodied by *timba* orchestra La Charanga Habanera as *El temba* (1996); Fairley, 'Ay Dios Ampárame', p. 92; Robin D. Moore, *Nationalizing Blackness: Afrocubanismo and Artistic Revolution in Havana, 1920–1940* (Pittsburgh: University of Pittsburgh Press, 1998); see also Mikhail Kalatozov's 1963–64 film *Soy Cuba* (I Am Cuba), produced by ICAIC-MOSFILM DVD Mr Bongo Films UK 2009.

[23]   Anna Szemere, *Up from the Underground: The Culture of Rock Music in Postcolonialist Hungary* (Pennsylvania: Penn State University Press, 2001), p. 25.

with progressive forces in Latin America and beyond emanating from Cuba's new intellectual power house Casa de las Americas.[24]

The first 'alternative' usage of studios emerged within the state system through initiatives taken during the 'grey period' between Haydée Santamaría, founding director of Casa de las Americas[25] who had supported the *guerrillas* in the Sierra Maestra, and Alfredo Guevara, president of the Cinematographic Institute ICAIC (Instituto Cubano de Artes Industriales Cinematográficas (both members of inner revolutionary circles)). In 1969/70 a loose group of musicians who became known as the Grupo Experimental Sonora de ICAIC (GESI) were brought together to work as a collective, their remit to work with various film directors composing soundtracks for new ICAIC films.[26]

The collective included two iconoclastic singers, one of whom, Pablo Milanés, had been incarcerated for 'bohemianism' alongside others held for 'homosexuality' in an UMAP (Unidad Mílitar de Ayuda a la Produción/ Military Production Unit or Forced Labour Camp) in the countryside near Camagüey.[27] The other, Silvio Rodríguez, had been harassed and censored when given media space and, like others of his generation, was perceived as dubious. Few anticipated that Milanés and Rodríguez would become key figures in defining revolutionary culture and seminal composers of the Spanish-speaking word in the second half of the twentieth century.

GESI met daily on the second floor of the Vedado ICAIC building, dividing their time between composing, recording and acquiring practical and theoretical music skills. Working with Cuba's leading figures including classical guitarist-composer-conductor Leo Brouwer[28] they were exposed to international material

---

[24]   OLAS, an acronym that also means 'waves', was a series of meetings intended to help move Cuba out of its cold war isolation and reforge links with the continent.

[25]   This account is based on various interviews with Silvio Rodríguez, notably 29 October 1999; Pablo Milanés, April 1999; Pablo Menendez, 26 April 1999; Omara Portuondo, June 2005; Sara González, June 2005.

[26]   Members and associates of GESI were initially Silvio Rodríguez, Pablo Milanés, Noel Nicola, Eduardo Ramos and Sergio Vitier. They were joined by Leonardo Acosta, Emiliano Salvador, Leonginaldo Pimentel and Pablo Menéndez; then Sara González and Amaury Perez. Musicians Norberto Carrillo, Genaro C. Caturla, Lucas de la Guardia, Amado del Rosario also played on GESI discs.

[27]   See Tomás Gutiérrez Alea and Juan Carlos Tabío's 1994 Cuban-Mexican film *Fresa y Chocolate* based on Senal Paz's short story *El Lobo, el bosque y el hombre nuevo* (The Wolf, The Forest and the New Man) the first public acknowledgment of the existence of these camps and Milanés' and others' experiences. In her 1999 book *Pablo Milanés* (Havana: Letras Cubanas, 1999), musicologist Clara Díaz makes the camp sound like a voluntary camp to which Milanés took his guitar. In 2000 Diaz admitted she self-censored feeling it was imprudent even in 1999 to write about that reality as Milanés, in discussion with her about the biography did not mention it (interview 26 November 2000, Havana).

[28]   Interview with Pablo Menendez, Playa, Havana, 26 April 1999. Many existing popular musicians took rudimentary music classes as part of professionalization for salaried status.

notably courtesy of a 1968 visit by Guevara to Brazil from where he brought back Tropicalia and MPB discs as well as US alternative rock for collective listening. Paid subsistence salaries, they composed songs for film and documentary soundtracks.[29] Significantly they composed their own songs which were later edited and released as a series of GESI discs in the 1980s by EGREM on a sub label called 'Areito'.[30]

GESI had access to the film institute studio (a converted 1950s TV studio) with low-level mono technology. ICAIC sound engineer Jerónimo Labrada, with second-wave collective member Pablo Menendez (son of US singer activist Barbara Dane of Paredon Records who has lived in Cuba from 1967) took charge of the recording side. Menendez describes GESI as a 'think tank'. Another participant with hindsight described GESI as dedicated to renovation of popular music with Brazilian MPB as a model, while 'resisting the penetration of the US music industry'.[31] What is certain is GESI offered a safe space for sharing ideas and pursuing creativity until 'they kicked us out at night'. Those involved composed music for a host of projects between 1969 and 1978, considering themselves as 'self-defined revolutionaries … patriotic … rebels, questioning'.[32]

While there is no space here to map its extraordinary history, musicians associated with GESI became part of the nascent *nueva trova* and trans-continental *nueva canción* movement.[33] Official legitimization within Cuba's cultural system through an island-wide youth movement was necessary[34] and November 1972 saw musicians associated with the movement recognized as cultural workers by the Ministry of Culture and state salaried with attendant requirements (rehearsing,

---

[29]   The disc 25 años de Cine Cubano Revolución Grupo Experimentación Sonora vol. 1 includes songs for a host of revolutionary initiatives including CDR (the all-important grass roots neighbourhood Committees for Defence of the Revolution).

[30]   Areito being the names for songs associated with indigenous Caribbean Taíno peoples.

[31]   See Leonardos Acosta's sleeve notes for the disc 25 años de Cine Cubano Revolución, Grupo Experimentación Sonora, vol. 1. LD-4175.

[32]   S. Rodríguez, *Canciones del Mar* (Havana: Ediciones Ojalá en colaboración con Casa de las Americas, 1996), p. 10.

[33]   For an early account of the *nueva trova* movement see R. Benmayor, 'La "Nueva Trova": New Cuban Song', *Latin American Music Review*, vol. 2, no. 1 (1981): 11–44; Clara Díaz, *Silvio Rodríguez* (Havana: Letras Cubanas, 1993); Díaz, *Pablo Milanés*; A. López Sánchez, *La canción de la Nueva Trova* (Havana: Atril Producciones Abdala, 2001); for *nueva cancion* and *nueva trova* see Jan Fairley, 'Annotated bibliography of Latin American popular music with particular reference to Chile and to *nueva canción.*' *Popular Music* vol.5 (1985) pp. 305, 310, 316.

[34]   The M.N.T (Movimiento la Nueva Trova) linked to the Brigada 'Hemanos Saíz' de Música one of the main cultural infrastructures in the twentieth as well as the twenty-first century. See LP *La canción, una arma de la revolución* Egrem LD3464.

playing to a cross-section of Cuban society, touring, and so on).[35] Significantly it gave the musicians access to EGREM recording facilities with later release of their own recording projects[36] which came to define the music of the Revolution as one counter to the Soviet socialist realist models. Rather guitar-based songs with polysemic metaphorical lyrics created by musicians who favoured jeans, and admired The Beatles and 'western' popular music triumphed.

The *cubanidad* expressed by these musicians was totally new and despite hostility from cultural bureaucrats, they moved from being marginal to alternative to official, prompting the joke that they went from being 'banned' in the 1960s to 'obligatory' in the relatively prosperous 1980s. Their zeitgeist music pirated on cassette off the island distributed through informal often politically linked continental networks, without any major company, transnational distribution or marketing, made Rodríguez and Milanés the most influential singers of their generation in the Hispanic world. Thus the initiative of Guevara, Santa María and others to provide a space for a revolutionary culture representing the creative concerns of a new generation of artists paid off, redefining the cultural politics of the Revolution and of the Spanish speaking world in the 1970s and 1980s, providing seminal songs for a future generation of Latin musicians.

The state EGREM label released a broad, eclectic catalogue across genre and region, its own vision inhibited by scarce resources and limited budget. Limited studio access was coupled with scarcity of all production materials (tape, pressing facilities, cardboard for album covers and so on). Still records were produced, supplied to radio and sold quickly through EGREM shops. Radio, live performance and TV were the main means of mediation and distribution as few ordinary Cubans owned hardware to play records or cassettes (even in the twenty-first century many Cuban musicians record and deliver tape straight to radio stations). Technology was a limited import into Cuba in the 1960s and 1970s; although by the 1980s it was available into discreetly 'hidden' dollar shops these were accessible only to Cubans who earned a percentage of their earnings in foreign currency.

The scarcity of recording possibilities must be coupled with the fact that certain musics were not officially recognized and thus effectively prohibited or defined as underground. This changed as the cultural flow of musicians on and off the island increased in the 1980s and 1990s with consequent purchase and availability of independently owned technology brought back to the island. Cubans abroad brought technology home with them on visits and left it behind when they left. In tandem personal, private ownership of technology was fuelled as tourism increased fostering relationships between Cubans and non-Cubans. Without claiming that technology can freely enter Cuba without restriction, we highlight that the

---

[35]   GESI toured the island with a truck and basic equipment: Menendez remembers at first that no one had heard of them and in places like Banes asked them to sing Mexican popular songs.

[36]   Some linked to Spanish recording companies like Fonomusic where their work was released.

technological means to produce and record music became more available on the island after the 1990s. This means recording in Cuba did not augment because of state initiatives, but because of an expansion of home production.[37] Therefore, we argue that a considerable increase of access to technology by different layers of the population has contributed to the emergence of a myriad of tendencies which complicate and enrich definitions of *cubanidad*.

The 1990s: Building of First Major Studios since the Revolution and Musicians' Home Recording Studios

By 1994 the dramatic changes of the Special Period saw Cuba legally and structurally open up to transnational influences.[38] Most specifically Cuba adopted a mixed economy, nicknamed 'capisol' by many on the street.[39] As a consequence, rules and laws changed significantly allowing foreign companies to operate independently inside the country, enabling Cuban musicians to become self-employed professionals and to make their own contractual agreements with foreign labels independent of state control and to travel abroad for work.[40] At the same time as state structures in Cuba changed, small Cuban *empresas* or businesses were allowed to work 'independently' within the state. This encouraged the founding of entrepreneurial recording labels like Bis Music (under Cuba's first women producers including Caridad Diez, one of the initiators in 1997 of Cubadisco, the Cuban music industry fair, and now its executive director). Despite those major changes and although there are now many enterprises run on this entrepreneurial model within the state, the Cuban economy remains centrally planned as quasi-capitalist structures are incorporated under state control.[41]

During this period key new studios were built through initiatives taken by *nueva trova* musicians Rodríguez and Milanés who had earned a substantial amount of money for the Cuban economy from the popularity of their compositions throughout the Spanish-speaking world. Rodríguez initiated the building of the first major studios in Cuba since the Revolution. This multiplication of studios gave new freedom to existing Cuban musicians. Smaller studios have been used by a new young generation, such as those known as the Interactivo collective,

---

[37] Robin D. Moore, *Music and Revolution, Cultural Change in Socialist Cuba* (Berkeley: University of California Press, 2006), p. 233.

[38] See P. Perez Sarduy and J. Stubbs, *AfroCuba: An Anthology of Cuban Writing on Race, Politics and Culture* (Melbourne: Ocean Press /LAB, 1993); Hernández-Reguant, *Cuba in the Special Period*.

[39] A play on words meaning capitalism in the sun/under socialism; interview with Jose Luís Cortés, leader NG La Banda, see Fairley, 'Ay Dios Ampárame'.

[40] Fairley, 'Ay Dios Ampárame', pp. 80–81.

[41] Bert Hoffman and Laurence Whitehead, 'Cuban Exceptionalism Revisited', GIGA Research Unit: Institute for Ibero-American Studies. Working Paper no. 28, 2006, p. 14.

involving Yusa, Roberto Carcasses and Telmary, whose music has different transnational aesthetics and who have established transnational working links.

Abdala

The Abdala studios, named in honour of a literary work of Cuban intellectual icon and independence hero José Martí, were built in Miramar, Havana, at no. 318 Calle 32 on the corner of 5th Avenue in the mid 1990s, opening officially on 25 May 1998.[42] Silvio Rodríguez had earned 'una buen cantidad de dinero' ('a good deal of money') performing and selling TV rights for a significant post-dictatorship concert in 1990 in Chile with Cuban jazz group Irakere led by Chucho Valdés. Upon his return he negotiated through the Ministry of Culture to self-administrate the money to realize the first purpose-built, acoustically architect designed, state-of-the-art recording studios since the Revolution with facilities to record large and small ensembles to attract international musicians to the island and meet the needs of Cuban musicians. To increase funds Rodríguez toured for several subsequent years with Grupo Diákara. Upon completion the studios were incorporated as part of the major state CIMEX Corporation. The studios were designed following visits to studios outside Cuba, including London's Abbey Road studios and Peter Gabriel's Real World Studios. Abdala links internationally to UK studios through membership of the APRS, the Association of Professional Recording Services.

In 1994 the project was delayed by 'Special Period' stringencies when a shortage of oil resulted in chronic shortages of electricity bringing cement production to a halt. Abdala's completion in 1998 was a key part of a dynamic vision of a modern music infrastructure for the island when the country was in the grip of its worst economic crisis since the revolution.

With a total studio area of 2,150 m² including gardens, Abdala has three different-sized studios: one 153 m² with a live area capable of taking a symphony orchestra and three isolation cabins for soloists; a MIDI studio 8.8 m²; a smaller recording studio for rehearsal; mastering and tape restoration facilities (with pro-tools); analogue, digital copying and tape dubbing facilities; two solid-state logic mixing consoles; instruments for hire including a Steinway concert and baby grand pianos; and facilities for cassette duplication.[43] Abdala has a music research and documentation centre and a small library headed up by a resident musicologist. Its hospitality facilities include a snack bar with satellite television, and a shop selling instruments and musical accessories. The whole inside area is air-conditioned, a

---

[42]   This account is based on a visit to Ojalá and Abdala Studios, April 1999 (20–28), interview with Silvio Rodríguez, Ojalá and Teresa Torres Páez, Manager Abdala, 29 October 1999.

[43]   The EGREM, Miramar studios which opened in April 1998 were also constructed with sound engineering advice and equipment from UK and operates as a private, self-financing business within the state, built with state loans; covering costs with a margin of profit returned to the state. Interview with manager EGREM Miramar, 23 April 1999.

luxury in Cuba found only in certain hotels. Abdala has its own record label with sub labels like Rodríguez's own Unicornio label and also produces discs for artists associated with the *nueva trova* movement. A majority of Abdala technical and recording staff are music graduates who, along with those of the Ojalá studios are all state employees. Its equipment is kept in tip-top condition and its facilities are competitively priced. It meets the challenge of maintaining equipment without direct sponsorship from international companies despite the difficulties of the Special Period and the continuing blockade.

While the US blockade ensures it is no international hub, it is a beacon for modernity in difficult times and though it is not possible to associate any specific watershed productions with Abdala, it has attracted non-Cuban musicians like Cape Verde's Cesaria Evora (whose French record company rosta includes Cuban artists). Ironically the Abdala studios were completed just as the downtown EGREM studios they superseded were being 'rediscovered' for the world by Buena Vista Social Club.

Ojalá

The Ojalá studios, run by Silvio Rodríguez and named after one of his iconic songs, were built in 1994–95. When the Abdala studios project stalled in 1994, Rodríguez converted a residential property (allocated and owned by the state) with two back buildings in Calle 98A a residential side street in Playa into a small studio, taking advantage of the fact that state building workers were free to work on smaller projects. A large upstairs room was converted into the main studio with a recording desk in the room next door linked by a glass window. As with Abdala, engineering advice and equipment was sourced through the UK.

These studios are used for Rodríguez's own recordings; those of associates including other top-flight Cuban musicians such as Chucho Valdés, Omara Portuondo; and those without funds who ask for support. Subsidy for those without funds comes from renting out the studios to those with financial backing from outside Cuba to cover studio costs, maintenance and the work of musicians without funds, which Rodríguez estimates as 60 per cent of studio usage.[44] Rodríguez and a staff of seven plus engineer are paid state salaries. His personal funds are boosted by taxed foreign author's rights and royalties paid in foreign currency. Author's rights paid in Cuban pesos are used for project funds. Rodríguez's Ojalá label, linked to Abdala, is funded by Rodríguez's discs sold within Cuba. Foreign disc sale remuneration is paid into a special fund for Cuban cultural projects.

---

[44] Edesio Alejandro disc *Black Angel* thanks 'Dios y Silvio Rodríguez ...'; SR reports EA had the studios for unlimited time/'sin limité de tiempo'.

Pablo Milanés Foundation

At the same time that Rodríguez built Ojalá studios, Pablo Milanés built studios in a large old house in Calle 11 in Vedado. Both musicians in the spirit of the times had negotiated with the state to invest money earned abroad in music business infrastructure. Milanés differed by calling his studios the Fundación Pablo Milanés, that is, independent of state control. Whereas Rodríguez used state employees and administrative procedures for his projects, Milanés wanted to be able to decide who worked for him and who recorded there (including non-officially recognized musicians): an approach that he admitted in 1999 was 'too advanced' for Cuba. His foundation challenged the culture ministry's status quo, embroiling the foundation in administrative red tape to such a degree that eventually in frustration he closed it through a public statement released to the press.[45] Since then Milanés has spent a lot of time outside Cuba in Mexico and Spain; and while in latter years he returns home more often, he has made statements abroad that challenge the government's cultural policy.

Since the Foundation's official closure the studios, known as Estudio PM Records, have been used with Milanés' permission by different musicians, many of them of the generation of his daughter, the singer Haydée Milanés. They include Yusa who recorded her groundbreaking debut eponymous album there with producer Pável Urquiza.[46] The *cubanidad* expressed here is best described as a shift in the *nueva trova* traditions forged in tandem with transcontinental political networks in favour of one influenced by Brazilian and Spanish cutting-edge music by a generation fighting to stay living at home with creative time working abroad.

Increased access to technology via these new studios has professionalized the music infrastructure. Successful musicians acquired technology and built their own recording spaces. They further allowed younger musicians to use their equipment, providing the means for more recordings in a difficult economic period.

The Underground Scene: A Glimpse of Two Studios in the Years 2000

As the state's intervention in cultural affairs remained strong even after the 1990s, the term 'underground' is understood as 'not fully integrated into the official system'. Yet, the two following case studies illustrate that the notion of 'underground' can acquire various meanings. In other words, 'underground' studios are not positioned equally in relation to the state. Different factors such as the music genre(s) produced and the musicians associated with the studios directly influence the way 'underground' is defined and lived by those implicated.

---

[45] This account is based on an interview with Pablo Milanés April 1999; see also Jan Fairley, 'The Dark Side of the Island', *Guardian*, 20 May 1999, S2, pp. 12–13.

[46] *Yusa*, Tumi Music TUMI112, 2002; interviews with Yusa, Havana; Roberto Carcasses, Ojos de Brujo; Telmary, and so on.

To'Mezclao

To'Mezclao's name, taken from the Spanish phrase 'todo mezclado' meaning 'all mixed together' is a clear indicator of their music, a fusion of popular styles, dominated by transnational Latin and Caribbean rhythms from *cumbia, merengue*, salsa, *reggaeton, bachata*, rap and hip-hop to Cuban son, *songo*, rumba and other fusions.[47] A seven-piece band with its ears and eyes turned towards the commercial zeitgeist, like many in Cuba their objective is success on and off the island. The brainchild of Lyng Chang, born into a Cuban-Chinese family in eastern Cuba where his grandfather was the founder of Radio Manzanillo, the band organize and work out of Chang's flat in the neighbourhood behind the Plaza de la Revolución.

In through a street door up two steep flights of stairs through a covering metal grated door and front door, the main living room has large flight cases containing the band's equipment stored against an inner wall while the spare bedroom measuring 4 metres by 4 metres has been made into a studio. The studio, complete with Cuban flag on the wall, is equipped with a compact Yamaha mixing console, AKG 414 CK 91 and Newmann TLM microphones, including the classic 1945s RCA microphone allegedly used by Fidel Castro and Ché Guevara for their triumphal broadcast shortly after the revolutionaries seized power. Chang studied radio and TV production at the Instituto Superior del Arte (ISA). He spent from 1990 until 2006 working for two of Cuban radio stations, Radio Rebelde and Radio Taíno.

Chang got into the music business partly through meeting Mo Fini, owner of UK-based TUMI Records, one of the independent international companies that established itself in Cuba in the early 1990s when the mixed economy enabled them to license EGREM archive material for compilations, record discs by Cuban artists and maintain offices on the island. To'Mezclao were signed by TUMI when they were formed by Chang. This gives them an infrastructural backing for production, recording and touring outside Cuba. Chang came to Havana where he worked in various capacities on TUMI projects. He began presenting a daily show De 5 a 7 (from 5 to 7) for the bi-lingual tourist targeted Radio Taíno and a weekly Saturday night music video show Saturday on Cuba's main channel Cubavisión.

With his valuable cultural and social capital accrued through working in the Cuban media and for TUMI, Chang founded the band in 2007 with official permission from the Institute of Music which allocated the band to the state management Empresa Adolfo Guzmán. Thus the band is institutionally recognized which gives access to official state media and the possibility of touring inside and outside the country. At the same time signed by TUMI they have an infrastructural backing for production, recording and touring.

The band had various initial line-ups before settling with six men and two women with a multiracial image all with versatile abilities that enable them to

---

[47]   Interviews by Jan Fairley with To'Mezclao in June 2005 and September 2010; see also Philip Sweeney, 'An Exceptionally Clever Bastard', *Songlines* [UK magazine], (March 2009), pp. 44–5.

cover as wide a range of music as possible, often pulling together multiple styles in one piece. The band includes black reggaeton-rapper 'La Crema' who came from Manzanillo from Candido Fabré's top orchestra, alongside lead vocalist Yoandri Castro 'El conejo'. Unusual for Cuban orchestras the keyboard player is Yusi González, a female graduate of the Amadeo Roldán Conservatory, Cuba's top music school and former keyboardist with David Álvarez' group Juego de Manos. Married to Chang (together they have a son), her sister Yoaniky González is the flautist and second female member of the group.

The band follows classic Cuban discipline, rehearsing long hours and touring regularly. As an official group they work within the state system, fulfilling formal and informal obligations, touring and doing their share of official events such as the Pina Colada Festival of fusion music. At the same time their creativity is fuelled with the knowledge that they have an outlet to the wider world, thereby creating music with national and transnational audiences in mind.

Chang is a talented, disciplined, well-organized producer who has acquired many technological skills on the job through trial and error, and with advice from such contacts as Cuban soundtrack composer Edesio Alejandro. Chang records the group on an Apple Mac Computer using Pro-tools and digital performer software and digi-design and Edirol hardware. Chang edits films the band makes of themselves with a Mac Laptop and a mini DV Cannon XM1 (using locales like the roof of their home building), supplying them direct for Cuban television consumption while also uploading them onto You Tube.

In the case of To'Mezclao, *cubanidad* would be defined as Cuban-Latin pop made by a self-driven group of Cubans working as an independent unit within the state with support from TUMI, UK. While producing music for a young, island wide Cuban audience through live performance and the Cuban media their trans-continental sound and keen instinct for a commercial transnational sound put them in a special category. Through the vision and cultural capital of Chang they enjoy the best of both worlds: they complement the present scene (creating commercial sounding youth music) while having a direct line out of the country giving them access to the latest in technology as well as exposure to non-Cuban aesthetics discourses. They bridge the two music recording trends outlined originally as having emerged in Cuba in the 1990s, deliberately creating music that they hope will appeal to internal and external markets.

Kiki Reggaeton Recording Studio

In Santiago de Cuba, there are approximately 10 underground recording studios that work with artists who cannot be recorded by Siboney (EGREM), the sole official studio in the region. Out of the 10, 6 concentrate on 'urban music', a commonly used taxonomy to refer to underground rap and reggaeton music. The other studios, which are technologically more sophisticated, record dance and traditional music. Professional musicians who tour abroad own the best-equipped studios in the city, among them, Kiki Valera, eldest son of the Familia Valera

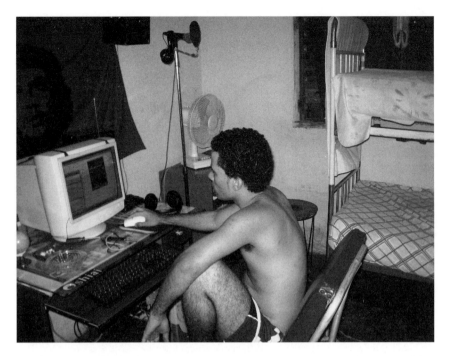

Figure 16.1   Kiki in his bedroom studio, Santiago de Cuba, photo by Alexandrine
Boudreault-Fournier

Miranda's director, a group associated with the revival of traditional son who have
been featured in key films and had discs put out on Smithsonian and European
World Music labels (see Figure 16.1).

These 10 studios are considered illicit to one degree or another and unofficial
as they work in parallel to the state system of music recording.[48] In other words,
Kiki's studio is perceived as underground. Despite the fears of many of these studio
owners that they might be abruptly shut down by the authorities for reasons of
censorship or other reasons to do with ideological control, as yet such an occasion
has not arisen. On the contrary, the apparent conviviality of Siboney with these
home-based studios suggests a developing tolerance towards alternative music
production houses.

Kiki Production Inc (different from Kiki Valera despite their shared name)
is one of the six illicit studios producing urban music in Santiago de Cuba. A
few features distinguish Kiki's studio from To'Mezclao's. First Kiki is a self-
taught sound engineer and he is not a professional musician. Before he began

[48]   See Alexandrine Boudreault-Fournier, 'Positioning the New Reggaeton Stars in
Cuba: From Home-Based Recording Studios to Alternative Narratives', *Journal of Latin
American and Caribbean Anthropology*, vol. 13, no. 2 (2008): 337–61.

to spend most of his time producing music, Kiki was a rapper in a group called Magia Negra. He began to play with recording programmes (using Reason and Frutyloops software) on a Pentium 3 computer. Kiki first produced music for his own group and later for friends. The EGREM Siboney studio records very few urban music groups to this day, Marca Registrada being one of the exceptions.[49] This has in turn motivated many producers to record underground rappers and reggaetoneros in unofficial studios, including Kiki's studio.

Kiki's work rapidly expanded at the beginning of the 2000s, when the reggaeton craze really took off. As Kiki's production shifted from underground rap to reggaeton, his reputation among the hip-hip movement in eastern Cuba significantly rose. Kiki rapidly became one of the best-known urban music producers in Santiago and the surrounding provinces.

Kiki's clientele is the second most important feature that differentiates his studio from that of To'Mezclao. Kiki deals with young male musicians who dream of succeeding commercially but who have limited knowledge of music. Therefore, through collaborating with these young reggaetoneros, Kiki aims at producing music for pleasure and *canciones de exito* (successful songs). Yet *exito* does not imply quality, as Kiki explains:

> ... young fellows don't even notice if your recording is of good or bad quality. What they want is to have fun. If the background track is catchy, you have a hit, no matter if the recording is good or bad.[50]

Thanks to his foreign friends and contacts with young foreigners studying in Santiago,[51] Kiki's bedroom has recently been transformed into a two-room recording studio built entirely of industrial cement. The space is tiny, but he does not need more room, as he does not record acoustic instruments ...[52] Kiki creates the percussive, usually electronically produced backing tracks and then records the voices of reggaetoneros and backing vocals. In as little as two days, he can meet up with the artist, agree on the song's aesthetics, create the background track, and complete the voice recording and sound mixing. Kiki maintains that:

---

[49]   Interview with Jorge Pujals, music producer Siboney studio, EGREM headquarters, Santiago de Cuba, 4 October 2005.

[50]   Interview with Kiki, Santiago de Cuba, January 2010.

[51]   Thousands of young people from Latin America and Africa are fully funded by the Cuban state to study in Cuba.

[52]   See also Wayne Marshall, 'From Música Negra to Reggaeton Latino: The Cultural Politics of Nation, Migration and Commercialization', in Raquel Z. Rivera, Wayne Marshall and Deborah Pacini Hernandez (eds), *Reggaeton* (Durham: Duke University Press, 2009), pp. 19–79.

> Our production has little quality because we do not own the proper technology. Yet, this limitation provides a special aesthetic for what we produce. You really feel that it comes from the street, that it is underground.[53]

Kiki and other producers of urban music from Santiago de Cuba are consciously involved in the production of a 'cheap' sound used as an identity marker for immediate consumption. Tracks are exchanged and distributed through home-burnt CDs, flash memory sticks and other devices which contribute to the rapid spread of a freshly baked *canción de exito*. When asked if he would accept work in Siboney, Kiki's response was: 'Siboney is the best equipped studio in eastern Cuba … [but] why would I work there, if I have more freedom to do whatever I want at home?' Indeed, Kiki plays numerous roles: he decides with whom he wants to work, sets his prices and is the artistic manager of all projects. Although Kiki works alone, his discourse is typical and endemic among young urban producers who have acquired a level of freedom in owning their own recording studio. They are directly implicated in alternative ways of producing music and in the creation of sounds directly emerging from the streets.

Conclusion

On 20 September 2009, new cultural ground was broken when the international 'Paz sin fronteras' concert was held in Havana's Revolution Square organized from outside the country by Colombian superstar singer Juanes in tandem with the Cuban Institute of Music.[54] Although Juanes declared that he wanted to invite some of the newer Cuban hip-hop and reggaeton musicians to take part, this did not happen and the more cutting edge side of the island's music scene was represented by Orishas and X Alfonso, musicians with international success working with or accepted by the Cuban system (although Orishas had earlier been underground rappers). In his final thanks to the world after an exhilarating and emotional finale to over a million people in the square itself and untold millions watching elsewhere on TV in South America and Spain, Juanes name-checked a list of people including Los Aldeanos, a controversial underground rap group from Havana who produce and record their music and video clips at home. The name of this group was not lost on many present as Aldo, one of the group's members, had been taken into custody and some of his personal effects temporarily confiscated, notably his lap top computer.

Los Aldeanos' songs tell pertinent everyday stories. However, unlike *nueva trova* who use metaphor allowing for multiple interpretation, and 1990s *timba*

---

[53]   Interview with Kiki, Santiago de Cuba, January 2010.

[54]   See Jan Fairley, 'Backpage … from Havana, Cuba. Jan Fairley Reports from the second Peace without Borders concert in Havana', in *Songlines* [magazine UK] (November/December 2009), p. 120.

dance groups who subverted topical material ironically and parodically by fusing sexual with political double entendre, Los Aldeanos' songs include overt social critiques concerning basic inequalities. In the direct tones of hip-hop they sing to an audience among marginal barrios who find in their material a new 'truth'. Rap hits home in ways other music with its different levels of meaning does not. This means while all the studios mentioned in this article manage to survive, they do so because the material they produce does not subvert or challenge the status quo.[55] There is no clandestine culture or music in Cuba and the state has a history of reining in citizens including musicians who overstep the mark.[56] The Los Aldeanos anecdote shows that if home-produced music does go too far in its message about discrepancies in everyday life in Cuba, notably social inequality and freedom of expression, the authorities will do their best to silence that freedom of expression that technological democracy has seized. Therefore, positive and peaceful relationships with state officials rely on the respect of established parameters that cannot be transgressed. This is true for musicians who also play the role of recording producers.

The existence of multiple recording studios in Cuba, whether official, alternative or underground, represents distinct networks, which relate differently to the dominant system. They are either fully integrated, working in parallel or in Los Aldeanos' case, in a liminal world in which they create a resistance music. More specifically, the various EGREM studios correspond to official sites of recording as they maintain direct relationships with the ministry of culture. It becomes more nuanced and complex when we look at the relationship between home studios such as those of To'Mezclao and Kiki, which maintain relations with state institutions to different degrees. State authorities recognize To'Mezclao's studio but it would be optimistic to think that all of its activities are officially acknowledged. Therefore, some of its activities could be characterized as underground. Kiki's studio is also underground, but underground because local cultural authorities do not officially recognize its existence. Yet it is not illicit, as until now its production has not openly subverted official discourses, in contrast to Los Aldeanos. These nuanced differences remind us that the position of such studios in relation to official music recording networks is extremely flexible as the type of production, the people involved and the messages transmitted influence the nature of their relationship with official structures. Yet, there is still risk involved.

Ultimately most of the studios mentioned in this chapter were put together thanks to the determination of musicians whose desire was to possess control over their artistic production and consequently of its commercialization. We argue that this reflects an attitude of struggle (*luchar*) and survival (*sobrevivir*, typically expressed by the saying 'no es fácil'), two words current in Cuban street conversation that infuse the nature of *cubanidad* itself. The various types

---

[55] For various incidents of censorship around *timba* dance music see Fairley, 'Ay Dios Ampárame'.

[56] Fairley, 'Ay Dios Ampárame', p. 87.

of recording sites all contribute to redefining the relationship between state institutions and alternative ways of producing artistic products. This underlines the fact that such spaces and actors shape cultural policies, implying that they are involved in the artistic and ideological renovation of Cuban history. Rather than a top-down model of state intervention in cultural affairs, we suggest that dialectical and dynamic exchanges between different actors, including artists, bureaucrats, producers, and even foreigners, act as motors of change and have influenced Cuban revolutionary culture since the beginning of the 1960s.

However, the Aldeanos case is revealing of a somewhat cyclical pattern in Cuban cultural politics. According to the famous Cuban blogger Yoani Sánchez, Silvio Rodríguez was influential in negotiating the liberation of Aldo – from the Aldeanos rap group – during his incarceration just as Alfredo Guevara, Haydée Santamaría and others helped him and his generation out in the 1960s. Rodríguez's diplomatic intervention to defend a young commentator expressing perceptions perceived as dissident through music in 2010 is a timely reminder that the relation between creators and cultural politics are embedded into cycles which, even if expressed differently, seem to repeat themselves through Cuban history.

Interlude 3

Comments and Commentaries by Industry Professionals and Producers

Richard James Burgess

Simon Zagorski-Thomas: *Why is it important that students get to hear from both industry people and academics when studying production?*

The large, high-end studio complexes of the past 50 years, with their highly trained engineers and constant flow of diverse projects and producers, provided a thorough training in the studio arts. With the closing of most of these studios and the consequent collapse of the apprenticeship system it has become increasingly difficult to get a broad-based education in the recording arts purely through work experience. This has created a need for formal university and college training and, fortunately, many experienced engineers and producers are now teaching in these programmes. Understanding a wider perspective such as that now taught in academia is important because different methods of production tend to prevail at certain times in specific locations. A person entering the production field who only learns from a working professional may get a valuable but narrow perspective when it comes to learning essential skills. A more inclusive overview of the art and science can enable students to identify the skills they need to embark on a career suited to their natural abilities, and affinities. Production techniques are constantly evolving and the person who develops a comprehensive skill-set is better situated to adapt to new trends. On the other hand, experienced producers share some characteristics with old soldiers – they know how to stay alive in challenging circumstances – so, observing experienced working professionals is an invaluable complement to a comprehensive education.

Simon Zagorski-Thomas: *Do you think that academic research about production can help the industry – and, if so, how?*

The art, craft and business of production have become very sophisticated and specialized; for example, country, hip-hop, rock, dance, pop and metal producers use distinctly different methods that can all result in a charting record and substantial sales. Niche styles of music such as jazz, world and folk each employ their own approaches to recording. Individual preferences abound: analogue, hi-resolution digital, multitrack, stereo, surround sound, all samples and soft-synths, in-the-box, production deals, label deals, freelance, staff producer at a label and so on. Given this fragmented state of the process, academic research on production can help the industry understand not only the musical and technical but also the business and legal differences and needs. Industry magazines, word of mouth and a limited number of books have previously been the main sources for this information but academia can offer a more rigorous and systematic analysis. Practices commonplace in one sphere if documented, evaluated and classified can be used or adapted for another. With the cyclical nature of the music industry, methods that have fallen out of favour may, with minor modifications, become the norm again. Cataloguing, preserving, analysing and disseminating disparate modus operandi, from musical to legal, ensures they are available to anyone who wishes to learn them.

Maureen Droney

Simon Zagorski-Thomas: *What do you think is the value of studying case studies of iconic (or other) productions? How does that kind of research help students?*

It is of huge value. Music is the art that is most in touch with human emotion. Iconic productions, hit songs, music that resonates with a wide cross section of people – how can we not want to delve into this and try to figure out what it is that makes these productions connect in such a universal way?

Simon Zagorski-Thomas: *In the same vein, what do you think can be done to encourage contemporary producers and musicians to share their stories and experiences with academics?*

Ask them! In my years working as a journalist, I interviewed a great number of producer and engineers. Those who work behind the scenes, like producers and engineers, are usually very willing to share their thoughts, opinions and experiences. They are not asked as often as artists are to divulge these things, and very often are eager to communicate about the projects they've worked on.

Simon Zagorski-Thomas: *We've got case studies looking at a 1950s–60s classical producer (Suvi Raj Grubb), Brian Wilson and Pet Sounds, King Tubby's dub reggae style and modern Cuban hip-hop: obviously this is only a sample but do you think there are producers, musical styles or eras that are in danger of being ignored and lost?*

Any and all of those. Plus, the San Francisco bands of the '60s, Memphis soul, New Orleans roots music, Mexican Narcocorrido, Seattle grunge, French dance music, the folk rock of the '70s in Los Angeles, gay disco in San Francisco, TexMex, there are endless styles and eras to research. A lot has been documented, but there is always more to discover. For example, what makes a 'scene' develop in a certain area? That is a question that has always fascinated me.

Jerry Boys

Generally I thought Jan Butler's chapter on the Beach Boys (Chapter 14 this volume) was an interesting piece of writing. I wouldn't have minded a bit more information about how it was made, if it was possible. It's such a seminal record in terms of record production. At the time, along with *Sgt. Pepper*, they were both mind-blowing records. They just did things in the studio that no one else had done before.

I don't think that you can get away from the fact that Brian Wilson was a bit crazy and on all sorts of drugs, which was part of the reason that he did what he did. That's also part of the genius – that the drugs and the weirdness are part of what makes the record and if hadn't been like that he wouldn't have made those records. *Pet Sounds* is quite strange – but they're very beautiful and I love the record. From what I remember of the time, he was very insecure and couldn't deal with the public acclaim and the business side of it and that's why he got into the drugs, as a sort of escape – as still happens today – but it also allowed him to free his genius. Of course their position as a very successful band gave them the freedom, as Jan Butler mentions, to be exploratory and experimental at a time when record companies still perceived themselves as the people who told you what to do.

History's a dangerous thing really – it's only ever someone's version of what happened. But all the factual things in the article ring true to me. I can't say I know that they're true but they *feel* true and some of them are backed up with things I knew at the time or have found out since. I wouldn't have minded knowing a bit more detail about how they recorded things – you know, microphones and equipment types of things.

In my personal opinion, Jan Fairley and Alexandrine Boudreault-Fournier's chapter on Cuban music (Chapter 16 this volume) doesn't quite do what the title says – a lot of it is about people recording today and the political aspect of how it's changed with the revolution. It doesn't spread across the last 50 years evenly. It's mainly talking about people I don't know about – but in my limited experience the young Cuban musicians are making slightly Cuban-esque versions of the music young musicians are making everywhere. They've all got into the same technology and so on. They still manage to bring this type of Cuban energy to the music that a lot of other people don't – but with modern technology. It didn't have enough musical history for me – who did what, when and where they did it. I would have said it could have started in the 1940s as well when Arsenio Rodríguez started recording because I think that's the beginning of Cuban music, in a recording sense, becoming something different and exploratory. In his era he was quite a man and his stuff was quite unlike anything that was being done by Cubans at the time. Maybe other people who are more into the politics of that kind of situation would find it more interesting – and to be fair it was mainly talking about things I didn't really know about or only peripherally.

Mike Howlett

Record producers devise many different schemes to overcome an artist's discomfort. I learned several techniques from engineers who had worked with other producers, for example, building a sort of room out of studio screens and covering the whole structure with blankets so the artist has a private space to perform, unseen by the control room. One producer friend[1] told me that he found certain artists liked to decorate the studio with cloth hangings and use low lighting and candles to create an atmosphere of mystery.

Paul D. Miller

Simon Zagorski-Thomas: *What do you think can be done to encourage contemporary producers and musicians to share their stories and experiences with academics?*

They will share whatever they do. That's what music is about.

Simon Zagorski-Thomas: *There's an obvious under-representation of black music and musicians in this area (and popular music studies in general).*

Yeah, it's kind of weird that there are not that many black academics focused on sound tech issues. I'm not quite sure what that's about. I consider myself more of an artist than technologist, so I'm not sure where to go with that question. But it is a strange phenomenon.

There is a kind of narrow bandwidth to the book's subject matter. All creativity is just a reflection of an internal process of thought that has been externalized. Once we get into digital media, it just becomes a kind of hyper-mirror of all sorts of things that we thought wouldn't be a synchronized reflection. The image and sound track of history has always been non-synchronous. Events were documented after the 'fact'.

So too with audio recordings – they were documents of an acoustic event that has already happened. I think that you are now seeing everything as a simultaneous event, happening 'all at once'. I guess it's kind of eerie how correct McLuhan was when he wrote 'A commercial society whose members are essentially ascetic and indifferent in social ritual has to be provided with blueprints and specifications for evoking the right tone for every occasion.[2]

---

[1]   Steve Power, co-producer with Guy Chambers, of Robbie Williams.

[2]   Marshall McLuhan, *The Mechanical Bride: Folklore of Industrial Man* (New York: The Vanguard Press, 1951) p. 51.

Katia Isakoff

As an executive committee member of the Association on the Art of Record Production (ASARP) one of my primary objectives over the years has been to help bridge the gap between professional practitioners and academic researchers in this field. Much progress has been made and, as Jan Butler outlines in her chapter: 'Musicologists are beginning to take the recording seriously as an object of analysis, and to take seriously observations in other fields about the interactions of record production, aesthetics, composition and commerce that determine that object.' However, there remains a dichotomy between the two and this can come into play when conducting case study research. Although it is beyond the scope of this interlude to explore this dichotomy in any great detail, I would like to offer some observations regarding the challenges one might encounter as a researcher when interviewing practitioners and conducting case-study work. As Allan Moore rightly points out in his chapter (Chapter 7 this volume), this is an interpretive discipline.

In 1974 *Rolling Stone* magazine featured a discussion between David Bowie and William S. Burroughs that touched on the subject of journalistic interpretation and portrayal of artistic endeavours.[3] Bowie started by declaring, '... I don't want to get other people playing with what they think that I'm trying to do. I don't like to read things that people write about me. I'd rather read what kids have to say about me, because it's not their profession to do that.' Burroughs responded, 'They try to categorize you. They want to see their picture of you and if they don't see their picture of you they're very upset.' Bowie also went on to admit, 'I change my mind a lot. I usually don't agree with what I say very much. I'm an awful liar' to which Burroughs replied, 'I am too.' Although Bowie and Burroughs are not commenting on the merits of academic research there are parallels to be drawn and this should give pause for thought when determining the level of accuracy and reliability of the information gathered and interpreted. Many practitioners are naturally protective of some areas of what it is they 'do'. This does not usually stem from a lack of willingness to share knowledge and experience, but rather, that the practitioner may be reticent and guarded for fear that the extent to which analyses, deconstruction and scrutiny of one's body of work and process would need to take place – the question of 'why' might lead to a fracture of the intuitive self ... the 'mystique'. Participants may indeed mislead or lie. I have witnessed a researcher suffer a tough time during a Q&A session at a conference in which a group of visiting international musicians proclaimed the researcher's findings to be wholly inaccurate. It transpired they knew the participants/band very well and later confided that the participants had reported that midway through the field study they had grown frustrated with

3   Craig Copetas, 'Beat Godfather Meets Glitter Mainman', *Rolling Stone Magazine* (28 February 1974). [Online]. Available at: www.teenagewildlife.com/Appearances/ Press/1974/0228/rsinterview [accessed: 2 April 2011].

the researcher's presence, which they had found to be too intrusive, and the questions lacking. Apparently, they entertained themselves by embellishing the truth and fabricating stories in response to a researcher deemed to be trying, as Burroughs remarked, to 'categorize' and project 'their picture'. We have seen an increased number of practitioners involved in education and research, some of whom have undertaken their own doctoral research, the results of which can offer profound and unique insight. Practice-led and practice-based research is of particular interest as it provides common ground for practitioners and researchers to meet and collaborate. To borrow from Sullivan[4] '… it is evident in the histories of ideas that those instances that breach accepted practices and make use of creative and critical approaches contribute in a profound way to our store of knowledge and understanding. This is the legacy of what artist-researchers have to offer'.

Tony Platt

Katia Isakoff: *Engineer and Producer Tony Platt is a veteran practitioner and despite being unconvinced about the perceived value of research conducted in particular areas of this field, he remains a keen supporter of education and research and offers the following comments and advice on the subject*:

I have no problem with the concept of research – in fact, why would I? Research is an essential part of social, technological and creative evolution. Of course I can see that when faced with an industry that is so serendipitous and such a quirky collaboration between creativity and technology the temptation to find some kind of 'key' to how it works must be overwhelming. The fact is that what makes music (and working with music) so enjoyable is the total lack of predictability. My problem is with the kind of research being undertaken. I feel a large part of it is somewhat self-indulgent and contributes little to the music industry in a wider sense. Spending hours trying to evaluate why or how a particular artist, engineer or producer achieved a particular result benefits no one and in fact is pretty near impossible because there are too many variables to allow a proper scientific evaluation.

What the industry could do with is some solid research into evaluating new business models and alternative ways for practitioners to make a living in it. This would be extremely worthwhile and probably open up much more important insight into the way many creative industries function.

You asked what 'tips' I can offer about how researchers should approach practitioners:

---

⁴   G. Sullivan, 'Methodological Dilemmas and the Possibility of Interpretation', *Working Papers in Art and Design*, 5 (2008). [Online]. Available at: http://sitem.herts.ac.uk/artdes_research/papers/wpades/vol5/gsfull.html [accessed: 2 April 2011].

1.   Interview is better than questionnaire – generally it takes so long to respond in writing most producers will just never get around to it.
2.   Do your research about the questions! So many times I am asked questions that have been asked before and the full answer is already on file somewhere.
3.   Make sure the questions make sense – too many times I have been asked questions that show a worrying lack of understanding on the topic in the first place.

Phil Harding

Katia Isakoff: *What makes a record producer agree to talk to other people about their daily practices in the recording studio?*

Usually the first time will be an interview for an audio tech magazine or maybe an invitation to talk to students about studio techniques. Demonstrating those techniques in a college or university studio will generally be an easier solution as that will be a familiar environment to the producer rather than the daunting task of talking to an audience in a lecture theatre. For me it was a studio masterclass at LIPA in 1998 that drew me into a world of 'passing on my practices' or realizing that there needs to be some linkage between industry and education. I soon realized that the daily tasks that I take for granted, like setting up for a mix and common equalization techniques, are the subject of fascination to the student entering the world of commercial recording and mixing.

Afterword

As a textbook, this collection of essays was designed to be an introduction to the study of recording. As editors we assumed that many of the book's readers would be thinking about the issues discussed here for the first time. We hope that readers now have a better knowledge of the history of recording, a better appreciation of the variety of methods with which recording can be studied, and a better understanding of the cultural, technological and aesthetic issues thereby raised. But there is one point that we should, finally, make explicitly. The essays in this book challenge the assumption that there is music and there is recording, something done to music. Our argument – the starting point for the Art of Record Production – is that recording is itself a way of music-making. It is not something done *to* music but a process in which sound becomes music. Recording is, indeed, the process through which the music that most of us listen to most of the time is created in the first place.

Simon Frith
Simon Zagorski-Thomas
April 2011

Bibliography

Ackerman, P., 'Diversified Sphere of American Music at Peak Influence', *Billboard* (29 April, 1957), p. 21.

'Adventures in Sound', *Popular Mechanics* (September, 1952), p. 216.

AES Historical Committee, *'When Vinyl Ruled': An Exhibit by the AES Historical Committee*. [Online]. Available at: www.aes.org/aeshc/docs/mtgschedules/109 conv2000/109th-vinyl-report-1.html

Aldous, D.W., *The 'SIMPLAT' Sound Recording Disc and Supplement* (London: V.G. Manufacturing Co. *c.*1939).

Aldous, D.W., 'Letter to the Editor', *Wireless World*, vol. 47, no. 10 (1941): 270.

Aldous, D.W., *Manual of Direct Disc Recording* (London: Bernards Publishers, 1944).

Alten, S., *Audio in Media* (Belmont: Wadsworth Publishing, 2002).

Anderson, T.J., *Making Easy Listening: Material Culture and Postwar American Recording* (Minneapolis: University of Minnesota Press, 2006).

Anon 1: www.amazon.com/gp/product/B00000IMYT/002–9794229–0633631?v =glanceandn=5174 [accessed: 9 June 2001].

Anon 2: www.furia.com/page.cgi?type=twasandid=twas0231 [accessed: 9 June 2001].

Anon 3: www.villagevoice.com/music/9918,weisbard,5320,22.html [accessed: 9 June 2001].

Anon 4: www.rollingstone.com/artists/benfolds/albums/album/178578/rid/62128 63/?rnd=1140538083125andhas-player=trueandversion=6.0.12.857 [accessed: 9 June 2001].

Anon 5: www.benfoldsfive.com/thesongs.html [accessed: 9 June 2001].

Badman, K., *The Beach Boys: The Definitive Diary of America's Greatest Band on Stage and in the Studio* (San Francisco: Backbeat Books, 2004).

Baker, G., 'Mala Bitza Social Klu: "underground", "alternative" and "commercial" in Havana hip hop', *Popular Music*, vol. 31, no. 1 (2012).

Bakhtin, M., *The Dialogic Imagination: Four Essays*, ed. M. Holquist, trans. C. Emerson and M. Holquist (Austin and London: University of Texas Press, 1981).

Barenboim, D. and Said, E., *Parallels and Paradoxes: Explorations in Music and Society* (London: Vintage 2004).

Barnes, K., *Rolling Stone Magazine* review of the Yes *Relayer* album in 1975 in *Phonograph Record*. [Online]. Available at: www.rocksbackpages.com/article. html?ArticleID=6852 and www.rocksbackpages.com/article.html?ArticleID =6881.

Barthes, R., 'The Death of the Author', in S. Heath (ed. and trans.), *Image, Music, Text* (New York: Noonday Press, 1977), pp. 142–53.

Bastick, T., *Intuition: How We Think and Act* (Chichester: John Wiley and Sons, 1982).

Bates, E., 'Mixing for *Parlak* and Bowing for a *Büyük Ses*: The Aesthetics of Arranged Traditional Music in Turkey', *Ethnomusicology*, vol. 54, no. 1 (2010): 81–105.

Bateson, G., *Steps to an Ecology of Mind: Collected Essays in Anthropology, Psychiatry, Evolution, and Epistemology* (London: Intertext, 1972).

Batten, J., *Joe Batten's Book: The Story of Sound Recording* (London: Rockliff, 1956).

Bayless, J., 'Innovations in Studio Design and Construction in the Capitol Tower Recording Studios,' *Journal of the Audio Engineering Society* (April 1957): 75–6.

Bayley, A. (ed.), *Recorded Music: Performance, Culture and Technology* (Cambridge: Cambridge University Press, 2009).

BBC Recording Training Manual (London: British Broadcasting Corporation, 1950), pp. 49–83.

Becker, H., *Art Worlds* (Los Angeles: University of California Press, 1982).

Begun, S.J. and Wolf, S.K., 'On Synthetic Reverberation', in M. Camras (ed.), *Magnetic Tape Recording* (New York: Van Nostrand Reinhold Company, 1985).

Behncke, B., 'Liederkranz Hall: The World's Best Recording Studio?'. [Online]. Available at: http://vjm.biz/new_page_3.htm [accessed: 9 September 2007]

Benmayor, R., 'La "Nueva Trova": New Cuban Song', *Latin American Music Review*, vol. 2, no. 1 (1981): 11–44.

Best, G.M., 'Improvements in Playback Disk Recording', *Journal of Motion Picture Engineering*, vol. 25, no. 2 (1935): 109–16.

Biel, M., 'The History of Instantaneous Recording and the Development of the Recording Studio Industry: Part One', handout at the Annual Conference of the Association for Recorded Sound Collections, Nashville, Tennessee, 1 May 1997.

Biel, M., 'The History of Instantaneous Recording and the Development of the Recording Studio Industry: Part Two', handout at the Annual Conference of the Association for Recorded Sound Collections, Syracuse, New York, 22 May 1998.

Biel, M., 'The Introduction of Instantaneous (direct) Disc Recording in America', handout at the Annual Conference of the International Association of Sound and Audiovisual Archives, Vienna, Austria, 21 September 1999.

Blake, A., 'Recording Practices and the Role of the Producer', in N. Cook, E. Clarke, D. Leech-Wilkinson and J. Rink, (eds), *The Cambridge Companion to Recorded Music* (Cambridge: Cambridge University Press, 2009), pp. 36–62.

Blauert, J., *Spatial Hearing: the psychophysics of human sound localization*, trans. J.S. Allen (Cambridge, MA: MIT Press, 1983).

Blaukopf, K., 'Space in Electronic Music', *Music and Technology* (New York: Unipub, 1971).

Boden, M., *The Creative Mind: Myths and Mechanisms* (2nd edn, London: Routledge, 2004).

Borges-Triana, J., *Concierto Cubano finisecular: para un estudio de la música cubana alternativa* (Habana: Editorial Universitaria, 2008).

Borwick, J., *Loudspeaker and Headphone Handbook* (3rd edn, Oxford: Focal Press, 2001).

Boudreault-Fournier, A., 'Positioning the New Reggaetón Stars in Cuba: From Home-Based Recording Studios to Alternative Narratives', *Journal of Latin American and Caribbean Anthropology*, vol. 13, no. 2 (2008): 337–61.

Bourdieu, P., *Outline of a Theory of Practice* (Cambridge: Cambridge University Press, 1977).

Bourdieu, P., *The Logic of Practice* (Cambridge: Polity Press, 1990).

Bourdieu, P., *Field of Cultural Production*, ed. R. Johnson (New York: Columbia University Press, 1993).

Bourdieu, P., *The Rules of Art: Genesis and Structure of the Literary Field* (Cambridge: Polity Press, 1996).

Bowden, S. and Offer, A., 'Household Appliances and the Use of Time: The United States and Britain since the 1920s', *Economic History Review*, New Series, vol. 47, no. 4 (1994): 725–48.

Bowman, R., *Soulsville USA: The Story of Stax Records* (New York City: Schirmer Books, 1997).

Bradley, L., *Bass Culture: When Reggae was King* (London: Viking, 2000).

Braun, H.-J. (ed.), *Music and Technology in the Twentieth Century* (Baltimore: Johns Hopkins University Press, 2002).

Briggs, G.A. (ed.), *Audio Biographies* (Idle, Bradford: Wharfedale Wireless Works, 1961).

Briggs, J., 'A Look at Commercial High Fidelity', *New York Times* (22 November, 1953), X43.

Brock-Nannestad, G., 'The Lacquer Disc for Immediate Playback: Professional Recording and Home Recording from the 1920s to the 1950s', presented at Art of Record Production, Second Annual Conference, Edinburgh, 8–10 September 2006.

Brooks, T., *Lost Sounds: Blacks and the Birth of the Recording Industry, 1890–1919* (Urbana: University of Illinois Press, 2004).

Burgess, R., *The Art of Record Production* (London: Omnibus Press, 1997; 2nd edn, 2001).

Butler, J., *Record Production and the Construction of Authenticity in the Beach Boys and late-sixties American Rock*, PhD thesis, University of Nottingham (2010).

Carlton, J., 'Columbia Profits Jumped 850 per cent in 1946; Industry Dough Swirls for Majors,' *Billboard* (29 March, 1947), p. 16.

Case, A., *Sound FX: Unlocking the Creative Potential of Recording Studio Effects* (Boston: Focal Press, 2007).

Case, J., *Instantaneous Recordings*, in F. Hoffmann (ed.), *Encyclopedia of Recorded Sound*, vol. 1 (2nd edn, New York and London: Routledge, 2005), pp. 519–20.

Cavicchi, D., *Tramps Like Us: Music And Meaning Among Springsteen Fans* (Oxford: Oxford University Press, 1998).

Chanan, M., *Repeated Takes: A Short History of Recording and its Effects on Music* (London: Verso, 1995).

Christgau, R., *Any Old Way You Choose It: Rock and Other Pop Music, 1967–1973* (Baltimore: Penguin Books, 1973).

Clarke, E., *Ways of Listening: An Ecological Approach to the Perception of Musical Meaning* (Oxford: Oxford University Press, 2005).

Cogan, J. and Clark, W. (eds), *Temples of Sound: Inside the Great Recording Studios* (San Francisco: Chronicle Books, 2003).

Cohen, M., Interview with Queen in March 1976 in *Phonograph Record*. [Online]. Available at: www.rocksbackpages.com/article.html?ArticleID=6852 and www.rocksbackpages.com/article.html?ArticleID=6881.

Cohn, N., *Rock from the Beginning* (New York: Stein and Day, 1969).

Cook, D.A., *A History of Narrative Film* (4th edn, New York: W.W. Norton, 2004).

Cook, N., Clarke, E., Leech-Wilkinson, D. and Rink, J. (eds), *The Cambridge Companion to Recorded Music* (Cambridge: Cambridge University Press, 2009).

Copetas, C., 'Beat Godfather Meets Glitter Mainman', *Rolling Stone Magazine* (28 February 1974). [Online]. Available at: www.teenagewildlife.com/Appearances/Press/1974/0228/rsinterview [accessed: 2 April 2011].

Crosby, B. and Martin, P., *Call Me Lucky: Bing Crosby's Own Story* (New York: Da Capo Press, 1953).

Csikszentmihalyi, M., 'Society, Culture and Person: A Systems View of Creativity', in R. Sternberg (ed.), *The Nature of Creativity: Contemporary Psychological Perspectives* (New York: Cambridge University Press, 1988).

Csikszentmihalyi, M., *Creativity: Flow and the Psychology of Discovery and Invention* (New York: Harper Collins, 1997).

Csikszentmihalyi, M., 'Implications of a Systems Perspective for the Study of Creativity', in R. Sternberg (ed.), *Handbook of Creativity* (Cambridge: Cambridge University Press, 1999).

Culshaw, J., *Ring Resounding* (London: Secker and Warburg, 1967).

Culshaw, J., *Putting the Record Straight* (London: Secker and Warburg, 1981).

Daley, D., 'Producer Billy Sherrill: Brilliant Career of a Nashville Legend' in *Mix*, vol. 26, no. 8 (2002).

Daudt, W., *Praktische Erfahrungen bei der Selbstaufnahme von Schallplatten*, Funktechnische Monatshefte 4 (1933): 177–81.

Day, T., *A Century of Recorded Music: Listening to Musical History* (New Haven: Yale University Press, 2000).

Derrida, J., *Speech and Phenomena and Other Essays on Husserl's Theory of Signs*, trans. D.B. Allison (Evanston, IL: Northwestern University Press, 1973).

Díaz, C., *Silvio Rodríguez* (Havana: Letras Cubanas, 1993).

Díaz, C., *Pablo Milanés* (Havana: Letras Cubanas, 1999).

Dockwray, R. and Moore, A.F., 'The Establishment of the Virtual Performance Space in Rock, *Twentieth Century Music*, vol. 5, no. 2 (2009): 63–85.

Dockwray, R. and Moore, A.F., 'Configuring the Sound-Box, 1965–72', *Popular Music*, vol. 29, no. 2 (2010): 181–97.

Doctor, J., *The BBC and Ultra-Modern Music 1922–36: Shaping a Nation's Tastes* (Cambridge: Cambridge University Press, 1999).

Doctor, J. and Wright, D. (eds), *The Proms: A New History* (London: Thames and Hudson, 2007).

Dolan, R.E., *Music in Modern Media: Techniques in Tape, Disc and Film Recording, Motion Picture and Television Scoring and Electronic Music* (New York: G. Schirmer, 1967).

Doyle, P., *Echo and Reverb: Fabricating Space in Popular Music Recording, 1900–1960* (Middletown, CT: Wesleyan University Press, 2005).

Droney, M., *Mix Masters: Platinum Engineers Reveal Their Secrets for Success* (Berklee: Berklee Press, 2003).

Elliott, B., *Surf's Up! The Beach Boys on Record 1961–1981* (London: Helter Skelter Publishing, 2003).

Eton, C., 'Tops … for the Juke Box', *High Fidelity* (1:2, 1951), p. 62.

Emerick, G. with Massey, H., *Here, There and Everywhere: My Life Recording the Music of the Beatles* (New York: Gotham Books, 2006).

Everett, W., *The Foundations of Rock: From Blue Suede Shoes to Suite Judy Blue Eyes* (Oxford: Oxford University Press, 2009).

Fairley, J., 'Annotated bibliography of Latin American popular music with particular reference to Chile and to *nueva canción.*' *Popular Music* vol. 5 (1985): 305–56.

Fairley, J., 'The Dark Side of the Island', *Guardian*, 20 May 1999, S2, pp. 12–13.

Fairley, J., '"Ay Dios Ampárame" (O God Protect Me); Music in Cuba during the 1990s, the Special Period', in K. Dawe (ed.), *Island Musics* (Oxford: Berg, 2004), pp. 77–97.

Fairley, J., 'Backpage … from Havana, Cuba. Jan Fairley Reports from the Second Peace without Borders Concert in Havana', *Songlines* [UK magazine] (November/December 2009), p. 120.

Fairley, J., 'Cuba: 50 Years Since The Revolution', *Songlines* [UK magazine] (2009), pp. 27–30.

Fairley, J., 'The Rejuvenating Power of the Buena Vista Social Club', *Samples*, Jahrgang 8 (German online publication of Arbeitskreis Studium Populärer Musik (ASPM), ed. R. von Appen, A. Doehring, D. Helms and T. Phleps (2009)). [Online]. Available at: http: //aspm.ni.lo-net2.de/samples-archiv/ Samples8/fairley.pdf [accessed: 15 April 2011].

Fauconnier, G. and Turner, M., *The Way We Think: Conceptual Blending and the Mind's Hidden Complexities* (New York: Basic Books, 2002).

Fisher, A., *The Fisher K-10 Dynamic Spacexpander Reverberation Unit: Operating Instructions and Warranty* (USA: Fisher Radio Corporation, 1967).

Fitzgerald, J., 'Down into the Fire: A Case Study of a Popular Music Recording Session', *Perfect Beat: The Pacific Journal of Research into Contemporary Music and Popular Culture*, vol. 5, no. 3 (1996): 63–77.

Fong Torres, B., *What's That Sound? The Contemporary Music Scene from the Pages of Rolling Stone* (New York: Doubleday Anchor, 1976).

Fowler, C., 'As the Editor Sees It', *High Fidelity* (Summer 1951), p. 8.

Fox, T., *In the Groove: The People behind the Music* (New York: St. Martin's Press, 1986).

Frerk, W., *Selbstaufnahme von Schallplatten: Eine Anleitung für Phono- und Tonfilm-Amateure* (Berlin: Photokino-Verlag; 1st edn 1932, 2nd edn 1935, 3rd edn 1939).

Frith, S., 'Art *vs* Technology: The Strange Case of Popular Music', *Media, Culture and Society*, vol. 8, no. 3 (1986): 263–80.

Frith, S., 'Is Jazz Popular Music?', *Jazz Research Journal*, vol. 1, no. 1 (2007): 7–23.

Frith, S., 'Going critical: writing about recordings' in N. Cook, E. Clarke, D. Leech-Wilkinson and J. Rink (eds), *The Cambridge Companion to Recording* (Cambridge: Cambridge University Press, 2009), pp. 267–82.

Gaisberg, F.W., *The Music Goes Round* (New York: Arno Press, 1942; reprint, 1977).

García Hernández, A., 'Interview with Abel Prieto, Cuban Minister of Culture', Mexico's *La Jornada*, February 2007. [Online]. Available at: http: //embacu. cubaminrex.cu/Portals/7/Interview.doc [accessed: 26 April 2011].

Gaydon, H.A., *The Art and Science of the Gramophone and Electrical Recording up to Date* (2nd edn, London: Dunlop and Co, 1928).

Gelatt, R., *The Fabulous Phonograph: From Edison to Stereo* (rev. edn, New York: Appleton-Century, 1965).

Gibson, D., *The Art of Mixing* (2nd edn, Boston: Course Technology, 2005).

Gillett, C., *The Sound of the City* (London: Sphere, 1971).

Gillett, C., 'In Praise of the Professionals', in C. Gillett and S. Frith (eds), *Rock File 5* (London: Panther, 1978).

Gillett, C., *Making Tracks: The Story of Atlantic Records* (London: Souvenir Press, 1988).

Glock, Sir W., *Notes in Advance* (Oxford: Oxford University Press, 1991).

Gracyk, T., *Rhythm and Noise: An Aesthetics of Rock* (London: Duke University Press, 1996).

Gracyk, T., with Frank Hoffman, *Popular American Recording Pioneers, 1895–1925* (New York: Haworth Press, 2000).

Granata, C.L., *Sessions with Sinatra: Frank Sinatra and the Art of Recording* (Chicago: A Cappella Books, 1999).

Granata, C.L., *Wouldn't it be Nice: Brian Wilson and the Making of the Beach Boys' Pet Sounds* (Chicago: A Capella Books, 2003).

Green, A., '"New" Music Biz Faces the Crossroads', *Variety* (6 January, 1954), p. 225.

Green, L., Jr., and Dunbar, J.Y., 'Recording Studio Acoustics,' *Journal of the Acoustical Society of America*, 19 (May 1947): 413.

Greene, P.D. and Porcello, T. (eds), *Wired for Sound: Engineering Technologies in Sonic Cultures* (Middletown, CN: Wesleyan University Press, 2005).

Griffiths, D., *OK Computer* (New York: Continuum, 2004).

Grubb, S.R., *Music Makers on Record* (London: Hamish Hamilton, 1986).

Guralnick, P., *Last Train to Memphis: The Rise of Elvis Presley* (Boston: Little, Brown and Company, 1994).

Hall, E., *The Hidden Dimension* (Garden City, NY: Anchor Books, 1966).

Hammond, J., with Townsend, I., *On Record: An Autobiography* (New York: Summit Books, 1977).

Harvith, J. and Harvith, S.E. (eds), *Edison, Musicians, and the Phonograph: A Century in Retrospect* (New York: Greenwood Press, 1987).

Hearn, A.H., 'Afro-Cuban Religions and Social Welfare: Consequences of Commercial Development in Havana', *Human Organization*, vol. 63, no. 1 (2004): 78–87.

Hennion, A., 'An Intermediary between Production and Consumption: The Producer of Popular Music', *Science Technology and Human Values*, vol. 14, no. 4 (1989): 400–424.

Hennion, A., 'The Production of Success: An Antimusicology of the Pop Song', in S. Frith and A. Goodwin (eds), *On Record* (New York: Pantheon Books, 1990), pp. 185–206.

Henshaw, L., 'Rock-'N'-Roll Swamps '56 Music Scene', *Melody Maker* (15 December, 1956), p. 21.

Hernández-Reguant, A., 'Havana's Timba: A Macho Sound for Black Sex', in K.M. Clark and D.A. Thomas (eds), *Globalization and Race* (Durham: Duke University Press, 2006), pp. 249–78.

Hernández-Reguant, A., *Cuba in the Special Period: Culture and Ideology in the 1990s* (New York: Palgrave Macmillan, 2009).

Hertsgaard, M., *A Day in the Life: The Music and Artistry of the Beatles* (New York: Delacorte Press, 1995).

Hesmondhalgh, D. and Negus, K. (eds), *Popular Music Studies* (London: Arnold, 2002).

Heylin, C., *Behind the Shades* (London: Faber & Faber, 2011).

Hill, S., *The Tragedy of Technology: Human Liberation versus Domination in the Late Twentieth Century* (London: Pluto, 1988).

Hirsch, P.M., *The Structure of the Popular Music Industry* (Ann Arbor: Survey Research Center, University of Michigan, 1969).

Hirsch, P.M., 'Processing Fads and Fashions: An Organisation-Set Analysis of Cultural Industry Systems', *American Journal of Sociology*, vol. 77, no. 4 (1972): 639–59.

History of Manhattan Center. [Online]. Available at: www.mcstudios.com/about-mc-studios/mc-studio-history.php [accessed: 21 August 2009].

Hoffman, B. and Whitehead, L., 'Cuban Exceptionalism Revisited', GIGA Research Unit: Institute for Ibero-American Studies, Working Paper no. 28, 2006.

Holman, T., *Surround Sound: Up and Running* (2nd edn, Boston: Focal Press, 2008).

Hoskyns, B., *Waiting for the Sun: Strange Days, Weird Scenes and the Sound of Los Angeles* (London: Penguin, 2003).

James, C.L.R., *Beyond a Boundary* (London: Serpent's Tail, 2000).

Jarrett, M., 'Cutting Sides: Jazz Record Producers and Improvisation', in D. Fischlin and A. Heble (eds), *The Other Side of Nowhere: Jazz, Improvisation, and Communities in Dialogue* (Middletown, CT: Wesleyan University Press, 2004).

Johnson, H. and Pines, J., *Reggae: Deep Roots Music* (London (Film), 1982).

Johnson, M., *The Body in the Mind: The Bodily Basis of Meaning, Imagination and Reason* (Chicago: Chicago University Press, 1987).

Kahn, A., *Kind of Blue: The Making of the Miles Davis Masterpiece* (New York: Da Capo Press, 2000).

Katz, B., *Mastering Audio: The Art and the Science* (Oxford: Focal Press, 2002).

Katz, D., *People Funny Boy* (Edinburgh: Payback Press, 2000).

Katz, M., *Capturing Sound: How Technology Has Changed Music* (Berkeley: University of California Press, 2004).

Kazmierczak, A., 'Hitting the Big Time in the Australian Rock Scene', *Arts Online*. [Online]. Available at: www.abc.net.au/arts/music/stroies/s913325.htm [accessed: 3 June 2003].

Kealy, E., 'From Craft to Art: The Case of Sound Mixers and Popular Music', *Sociology of Work and Occupations*, vol. 6, no. 1 (1979): 3–29.

Kealy, E., 'From Craft to Art: The Case of Sound Mixers and Popular Music', reproduced in S. Frith and A. Goodwin (eds), *On Record: Rock, Pop and the Written Word* (London: Routledge, 1990).

Keep, A., 'Does "Creative Abuse" Drive Developments in Record Production?', Proceedings of the First Art of Record Production Conference, University of Westminster, London, 2005. [Online]. Available at: www.artofrecordproduction.com/content/view/141/ [accessed: 26 April 2011].

Keightley, K., '"Turn It Down!" She Shrieked: Gender, Domestic Space, and High Fidelity, 1948–59', *Popular Music*, vol. 15, no. 2 (1996): 149–77.

Kenney, W.H., *Recorded Music in American Life: The Phonograph and Popular Memory, 1890–1945* (New York: Oxford University Press, 1999).

Kluth, H., *Jeder sein eigener Schallplattenfabrikant* (Berlin: Weidmannsche Buchhandlung, 1932; 1st edn, January; 2nd edn, April).

Kostelanetz, A., in collaboration with G. Hammond, *Echoes: Memoirs of Andre Kostelanetz* (New York: Harcourt Brace Jovanovich, 1981).

Kraft, J.P., *Stage to Studio: Musicians and the Sound Revolution, 1890–1950* (Baltimore: Johns Hopkins University Press, 1996).

Kureishi, H., *The Buddha of Suburbia* (London: Faber, 1990).

Lacasse, S., 'Persona, Emotions and Technology: The Phonographic Staging of the Popular Music Voice', Proceedings of the 2005 Art of Record Production Conference. [Online]. Available at: www.artofrecordproduction.com [accessed: 19 June 2012].

Laing, D., *The Sound of Our Time* (London: Sheed and Ward, 1969).

Lakoff, G., *Women, Fire, and Dangerous Things* (Chicago: Chicago University Press, 1987).

Lakoff, G. and Johnson, M., *Metaphors We Live By* (Chicago: Chicago University Press, 1980).

Landau, J., *It's Too Late to Stop Now: A Rock and Roll Journal* (San Francisco: Straight Arrow Books, 1972).

Lane, C., 'A Musical Revolution', *Natty Dread: Le Magazine du Reggae*, vol. 19 (2003).

Lanza, J., *Elevator Music: A Surreal History of Muzak, Easy Listening, and Other Moodsong* (Ann Arbor: University of Michigan Press, 2004).

LaRue, J., *Guidelines for Style Analysis* (2nd edn, Detroit: Harmonie Park Press, 1996).

Lastra, J., *Sound Technology and the American Cinema: Perception, Representation, Modernity* (New York: Columbia University Press, 2000).

LeBel, C.J., 'Recent Improvements in Recording', *Electronics*, vol. 13 (September 1940): 33–5, 79–81.

Legge, W., *Walter Legge: Words and Music*, ed. A. Sanders (London: Gerald Duckworth, 1998).

Levitin, D., 'John Fogerty Interview', *Audio Magazine* (January 1998). [Online]. Available at: http: //cm.stanford.edu/~levitin/JOHN_FOGERTY.htm [accessed: 24 June 2007].

Levitin, D.J., *This is Your Brain on Music: The Science of Human Obsession* (New York: Dutton, 2006).

Lewisohn, M., *The Beatles Recording Sessions* (New York: Harmony Books, 1988).

Liebler, V.J., 'A Record Is Born!' *Columbia Record*, (1959), p. 4

Linz, H.-D., *Gramophone Needle Tins: History and Catalogue with Current Valuations* (Regenstauf: Battenberg, 2006), p. 206.

López Sánchez, A., *La Canción de la Nueva Trova* (Havana: Atril Producciones Abdala, 2001).

Lovett, W.A., Eckes, A.E. and Brinkman, R.L., *U.S. Trade Policy: History, Theory, and the WTO* (Armonk, NY: M.E. Sharpe, 2004).

Lumsden, I., *Machos, Maricones, and Gays: Cuba and Homosexuality* (Philadelphia: Temple University Press, 1996).

McCluhan, M., *The Mechanical Bride: Folklore of Industrial Man* (New York: The Vanguard Press, 1951).

McIntyre, P., 'Creativity and Cultural Production: A Study of Contemporary Western Popular Music Songwriting' (unpublished PhD thesis, Macquarie University, Sydney, 2004).

McIntyre, P., 'Paul McCartney and the Creation of Yesterday: The Systems Model in Operation', *Popular Music*, vol. 25, no. 2 (2006): 201–19.

McIntyre, P., 'Copyright and Creativity: Changing Paradigms and the Implications for Intellectual Property and the Music Industry', *Media International Australia Incorporating Cultural Policy*, vol. 123 (2007): 82–94.

McIntyre, P. and Paton, B., 'The Mastering Process and the Systems Model of Creativity', *Perfect Beat: the Pacific Journal of Research into Contemporary Music and Popular Culture*, vol. 8, no. 4 (2007): 64–81.

Madler, M.R., 'Recording Studios Growing Silent: Closures Hit Industry', *San Fernando Valley Business Journal* (23 October 2006). [Online]. Available at: http: //goliath.ecnext.com/coms2/gi_0199–6061675/Recording–studios–growing–silent–closures.html#abstract [accessed: 2 July 2008].

Manuel, P., 'Marxism, Nationalism and Popular Music in Revolutionary Cuba', *Popular Music*, vol. 6, no. 2 (1987): 161–78.

Marcus, G. (ed.), *Rock and Roll Will Stand* (Boston: Beacon Press, 1969).

Marcus, G., *Like a Rolling Stone: Bob Dylan at the Crossroads* (London: Faber & Faber, 2005).

Marcus, G., *Listening to Van Morrison* (London: Faber & Faber, 2010).

Marshall, W., 'From Música Negra to Reggaeton Latino: The Cultural Politics of Nation, Migration and Commercialization', in R.Z. Rivera, W. Marshall and D.P. Hernandez (eds), *Reggaeton* (Durham: Duke University Press, 2009), pp. 19–79.

Martin, G. (ed.), *Making Music: The Essential Guide to Writing, Performing and Recording* (London: Pan, 1983).

Martin, R., 'Beyond Privatization? The Art and Society of Labor, Citizenship, and Consumerism', *Social Text*, vol. 17, no. 2 (1999): 35–48.

Massey, H., *Behind the Glass: Top Record Producers Tell How They Craft the Hits* (San Francisco: Backbeat Books, 2000).

Mehta, Z., *Zubin Mehta: A Memoir: The Score of My Life* (London: Amadeus Press, 2008).

Meintjes, L., *Sound of Africa! Making Music Zulu in a South African Studio* (Durham NC: Duke University Press, 2003).

Miller, T. and Yúdice, G., *Cultural Policy* (London: Sage Publications, 2002).

Mills, P., *Hymns to the Silence: Inside the Words and Music of Van Morrison* (New York: Continuum, 2010).

Monson, I., *Saying Something: Jazz Improvisation and Interaction* (Chicago, IL: University of Chicago Press, 1996).

Moore, A.F., *Rock: The Primary Text: Developing a Musicology of Rock* (2nd edn, Aldershot: Ashgate, 2001).

Moore, A.F., 'The Persona/Environment Relation in Recorded Song', *Music Theory Online*, vol. 11, no. 4 (October 2005).

Moore, A.F., 'The Act You've Known for All These Years: A Re-Encounter with Sgt. Pepper', in O. Julien (ed.), *Sgt. Pepper: It Was Forty Years Ago Today* (Farnham: Ashgate, 2008), pp. 139–46.

Moore, A.F., 'Interpretation: So What?', in D.B. Scott (ed.), *Research Companion to Popular Musicology* (Farnham: Ashgate, 2009), pp. 411–25.

Moore, A.F., 'Where is Here?: An Issue of Deictic Projection in Recorded Song', *Journal of the Royal Musical Association*, vol. 135, no. 1 (2010): 145–82.

Moore, A.F., 'One Way of Feeling: Contextualizing a Hermeneutics of Spatialization', in S. Hawkins (ed.), *Festschrift for Derek Scott* (Farnham: Ashgate, 2012).

Moore, A.F. and Dockwray, R., 'The Establishment of the Virtual Performance Space in Rock', *Twentieth-Century Music*, vol. 5, no. 2 (2009): 63–85.

Moore, A.F., Schmidt, P. and Dockwray, R., 'A Hermeneutics of Spatialization for Recorded Song', *Twentieth-Century Music*, vol. 6 (2009).

Moore, B.C.J., *An Introduction to the Psychology of Hearing* (5th edn, Oxford: Elsevier Academic Press, 2004).

Moore, R.D., *Nationalizing Blackness: Afrocubanismo and Artistic Revolution in Havana, 1920–1940* (Pittsburgh: University of Pittsburgh Press, 1998).

Moore, R.D., *Music and Revolution, Cultural Change in Socialist Cuba* (Berkeley: University of California Press, 2006).

Moorefield, V., *The Producer as Composer: Shaping the Sounds of Popular Music* (Cambridge, MA: MIT Press, 2005).

Morse, E.M., 'Terrible Thing Is Happening to Singers! Everybody Shouts', *Down Beat* (19 November, 1952), p. 2.

Moulton, D., *Total Recording: The Complete Guide to Audio Production and Engineering* (Sherman Oaks, CA: KIQ Production, 2000).

Moylan, W., *An Analytical System for Electronic Music* (Ann Arbor, MI: University Microfilms, 1983).

Moylan, W., 'The Aural Analysis of the Spatial Relationships of Sound Sources as Found in Two-Channel Common Practice', 81st Convention of the Audio Engineering Society, Los Angeles, November, 1986.

Moylan, W., *The Art of Recording: The Creative Resources of Music Production and Audio* (New York: Van Nostrand Reinhold, 1992).

Moylan, W., *Understanding and Crafting the Mix: The Art of Recording* (2nd edn, Boston: Focal Press, 2007).

Music Directory Canada (Toronto: CM Books, 1983, 1986, 1990, 1997, 2001, 2007).

Negus, K., *Producing Pop: Culture and Conflict in the Popular Music Industry* (London: Arnold, 1992).

Negus, K. and Pickering, M., *Creativity, Communication and Cultural Value* (London: Sage, 2004).

Nesper, E., *Nimm Schallplatten selber auf!* (Stuttgart: Franckh'sche Verlagshandlung, 1932).

Nixon, G.M., 'Recording Studio 3A', *Broadcast News*, 46 (September 1947), p. 33.

Olhsson, B., *Mid 60s custom MCI Consoles*. [Online]. Available at: http://recforums.prosoundweb.com/index.php/m/113753/0/ [accessed: 14 February 2011].

Olsen, E., Verna, P. and Wolff, C., *The Encyclopedia of Record Producers* (New York: Billboard Books, 1999).

Ortíz, F., in R.C. Lucien and F.M. Civil, *Résistance et cubanité* (Paris: L'Harmattan, 2006).

Pandit, S.A., *From Making to Music: The History of Thorn EMI* (London: Hodder & Stoughton, 1996).

Perez Sarduy, P. and Stubbs, J., *AfroCuba: An Anthology of Cuban Writing on Race, Politics and Culture* (Melbourne: Ocean Press /LAB, 1993).

Perna, V., *Timba: The Sound of the Cuban Crisis* (Farnham: Ashgate, 2005).

Peterson, R.A. and Berger, D.G., 'Entrepreneurship in Organisations: Evidence from the Popular Music Industry', *Administrative Science Quarterly*, vol. 16, no. 1 (1971): 97–107.

Peterson, R.A. and Berger, D.G., 'Cycles in Symbol Production: The Case of Popular Music', *American Sociological Review*, vol. 40, no. 2 (April, 1975): 158–73.

Pope, R., *Creativity: Theory, History, Practice* (New York: Routledge, 2005).

Porcello, T., *Sonic Artistry: Music, Discourse and Technology in the Sound Recording Studio* (unpublished PhD thesis, University of Texas, Austin, 1996).

PRESTO Instantaneous Sound Recording Equipment and Discs (New York: Presto Recording Corporation, 1940).

Priore, D., *Smile: The Official Story of Brian Wilson's Lost Masterpiece* (London: Sanctuary Publishing, 2005).

Pruter, R., *Doowop: The Chicago Scene* (Urbana, IL: University of Illinois Press, 1996).

Ramone, P. and Granata, C.L., *Making Records: The Scenes Behind the Music* (New York: Hyperion, 2007).

Ray, R.B., 'The Automatic Auteur: or, A Certain Tendency in Film Criticism', in J. Braddock and S. Hock (eds), *Directed by Allen Smithee* (Minneapolis: University of Minnesota Press, 2001), pp. 51–75.

Read, O., *The Recording and Reproduction of Sound: A Complete Reference Manual on Audio for the Professional and the Amateur* (2nd edn, Indianapolis: Howard W. Sams, 1952).

Read, O. and Welch, W.L., *From Tin Foil to Stereo: Evolution of the Phonograph* (2nd edn, Indianapolis: Howard W. Sams, 1976).

Repsch, J., *The Legendary Joe Meek: The Telstar Man* (London: Woodford House, 1989).

Rice, R., 'Profiles: The Fractured Oboist', *New Yorker* (6 June, 1953), p. 46.

Ricoeur, P., *Interpretation Theory: Discourse and the Surplus of Meaning* (Forth Worth: Texas Christian University Press, 1976).

Rodríguez, S., *Canciones del Mar (*Havana: Ediciones Ojalá en colaboración con Casa de las Americas, 1996).

Rolling Stone, The Rolling Stone Record Review (New York: Pocket Books, 1971).

Rolontz, B., 'High Fidelity Record Firms' Magic Phrase', *Billboard* (27 March, 1954), p. 37.

Rothenberg, A. and Hausmann, C. (eds), *The Creativity Question* (Durham: Duke University Press, 1976).

Ruddock, O., *Dub Gone Crazy* (Manchester: Blood And Fire, 1994).

Rumsey, F., 'Spatial Quality Evaluation for Reproduced Sound: Terminology, Meaning, and a Scene-Based Paradigm', *Journal of the Audio Engineering Society*, vol. 50, no. 9 (2002): 651–66.

Rushdie, S., *The Satanic Verses* (London: The Consortium, 1988).

Said, E., *Musical Elaborations* (London: Vintage, 1992).

Said, E., *Music at the Limits: Three Decades of Essays and Articles on Music* (London: Bloomsbury, 2008).

Said, M.C., Said, E. and Wood, M., *On Late Style: Music and Literature Against the Grain* (London: Vintage, 2007).

Salem, J.M., *The Late Great Johnny Ace and the Transition from R&B to Rock 'n' Roll* (Urbana, IL: University of Illinois Press, 1999).

Salsman, E., 'Where Sound Sounds Best' (orig. pub. March 1961), in R.S. Clark (ed.), *High Fidelity's Silver Anniversary Treasury* (Great Barrington, MA: Wyeth Press, 1976), p. 301.

Sanjek, R. and Sanjek, D., *Pennies from Heaven: The American Popular Music Business in the Twentieth Century* (New York: Da Capo Press, 1996).

Sawyer, K., *Explaining Creativity: The Science of Human Innovation* (Oxford: Oxford University Press, 2006).

Schaeffer, P., *Traité Des Objets Musicaux: Essai Interdisciplines* (Paris: Éditions de Seuil, 1966).

Schafer, R.M., *Soundscape: Our Environment and the Tuning of the World* (New York: Alfred A. Knopf, 1977).

Schmidt Horning, S., 'Chasing Sound: The Culture and Technology of Recording Studios in America, 1877–1977' (unpublished PhD thesis, Case Western Reserve University, 2002).

Schmidt Horning, S., 'Engineering the Performance: Recording Engineers, Tacit Knowledge and the Art of Controlling Sound', *Social Studies of Science*, vol. 34, no. 5 (2004): 703–31.

Schmidt Horning, S., 'Recording: The Search for the Sound', in A. Millard (ed.), *The Electric Guitar: A History of an American Icon* (Baltimore: Johns Hopkins University Press, 2004).

Schon, D., *The Reflective Practitioner: How Professionals Think in Action* (New York: Basic Books, 1983).

Schwandt, E., *Technik der Schallplatten-Heimaufnahme*, Funk-Bastler, vol. 36, no. 4 (1931): 561–5.

Schwarzkopf, E., *On and Off the Record: A Memoir of Walter Legge* (London: Faber, 1982).

Shaughnessy, M.A., *Les Paul: An American Original* (New York: William Morrow, 1993).

Shea, W., 'The Role and Function of Technology in American Popular Music, 1945–1964' (unpublished PhD thesis, University of Michigan, 1990).

Shuker, R., *Understanding Popular Music* (London: Routledge, 2001).

Simons, D., *Studio Stories* (San Francisco: Backbeat Books, 2004).

Simonton, D.K., 'Creative Cultures, Nations and Civilisations: Strategies and Results', in P. Paulus and B. Nijstad (eds), *Group Creativity: Innovation Through Collaboration* (Oxford: Oxford University Press, 2003), pp. 304–25.

Somer, J., 'Popular Recording: or, The Sound That Never Was,' *HiFi/Stereo Review* 16 (May 1966): 54–8.

Sternberg, R. (ed.), *Handbook of Creativity* (Cambridge: Cambridge University Press, 1999).

Sterne, J., *The Audible Past: Cultural Origins of Sound Reproduction* (Durham, NC: Duke University Press, 2003).

Stewart, A., 'Of Mikes and Men: Old Studios Fall Silent,' *Washington Post*, 20 March 2005.

Suisman, D., *Selling Sounds: The Commercial Revolution in American Music* (Cambridge, MA: Harvard University Press, 2009).

Suleri, S., *The Rhetoric of English India* (Chicago: Chicago University Press, 1992).

Sullivan, G., 'Methodological Dilemmas and the Possibility of Interpretation', *Working Papers in Art and Design*, 5 (2008). [Online]. Available : http://sitem.herts.ac.uk/artdes_research/papers/wpades/vol5/gsfull.html [accessed: 2 April 2011].

Sutton, A., *Recording the Twenties: The Evolution of the American Recording Industry, 1920–29* (Denver, CO: Mainspring Press, 2008).

Sweeney, P., 'An Exceptionally Clever Bastard', *Songlines* [UK magazine], (March 2009) pp. 44–5.

Symes, C., *Setting the Record Straight: A Material History of Classical Recording* (Middletown, CT: Wesleyan University Press, 2004).

Szemere, A., *Up From the Underground: The Culture of Rock Music in Postcolonialist Hungary* (Pennsylvania: Penn State University Press, 2001).

Tagg, P., *Introductory Notes to the Semiotics of Music*. [Online]. Available at: www.tagg.org/xpdfs/semiotug.pdf [accessed: 9 June 2009].

Taubman, H.'High Fidelity in American Life', *New York Times* (22 November, 1953), X39.

Taylor, P., *Popular Music since 1955: A Critical Guide to the Literature* (Boston: G.K. Hall, 1985).

Taylor, T., *Strange Sounds: Music, Technology and Culture* (New York: Routledge, 2001).

Tenney, J., *Meta – Hodos and META Meta – Hodos* (Oakland, CA: Frog Peak Music, 1986).

Théberge, Paul, 'The Network Studio: Historical and Technological Paths to a New Ideal in Music Making', *Social Studies of Science*, vol. 34, no. 5 (2004): 759–81.

Théberge, P., 'Everyday Fandom: Fan Clubs, Blogging, and the Quotidian Rhythms of the Internet', *Canadian Journal of Communication*, vol. 30, no. 4 (2005): 485–502.

Thompson, E., *The Soundscape of Modernity: Architectural Acoustics and the Culture of Listening in America, 1900–1933* (Cambridge, MA: MIT Press, 2002).

Thompson, G., *Please Please Me: Sixties British Pop, Inside Out* (Oxford: Oxford University Press, 2008).

Thorens brochure, *Memophone: Ihr Heimstudio*, trans. G. Brock-Nannestad (Ste. Croix, Switzerland: H. Thorens *c.*1939).

Toepler, S., 'From Communism to Civil Society? The Arts and the Nonprofit Sector in Central and Eastern Europe', *Journal of Arts Management, Law, and Society*, vol. 30, no. 1 (2000): 7–18.

Toynbee, J., *Making Popular Music: Musicians, Creativity and Institutions* (London: Arnold, 2000).

Tracy, J., 'Les Paul', *Down Beat* (20 April, 1951), p. 15.

Trezise, S., 'The Recorded Document: Interpretation and Discography', in Cook et al. (eds), *The Cambridge Companion to Recorded Music* (Cambridge: Cambridge University Press, 2009).

Ulanov, B., 'Mitch the Goose Man', *Metronome* (July 1950), p. 34.

US Census Bureau, *Economic Census 2002: NAICS 51224, Sound Recording Industries: 2002* (Washington: US Department of Commerce, November 2004).

US Census Bureau, *Economic Census 2007: NAICS 51224, Sound Recording Industries, Preliminary Report* (Washington: US Department of Commerce, February 2010).

Veal, M.E., *Soundscapes and Shattered Songs in Jamaican Reggae* (Middletown, CT: Wesleyan University Press, 2007).

Warner, T., *Pop Music: Technology and Creativity: Trevor Horn and the Digital Revolution* (Aldershot: Ashgate, 2003).

Waters, S., 'Performance Ecosystems: Ecological Approaches to Musical Interaction', Electroacoustic Music Studies Network, De Montfort/Leicester, 2007.

Watts, A., *Cecil E. Watts: Pioneer of Direct Disc Recording* (privately published, 1972).

Weisberg, R., *Creativity: Understanding Innovation in Problem Solving, Science, Invention and the Arts* (Hoboken: John Wiley, 2006).

Wenner, J.S. and Levy, J., *The Rolling Stone Interviews* (New York: Black Bay Books, 2007).

Werner, C., *Up around the Bend: The Oral History of Creedence Clearwater Revival* (New York: Avon Books, 1988).

Wexler, J. and Ritz, D., *Rhythm and the Blues: A Life in American Music* (New York: St. Martin's Press, 1993).

White, W.B., 'Aspects of Sound Recording: 1 – The Echo Difficulty', *Talking Machine World* (15 July 1920), p. 159.

White, J.D., *Comprehensive Musical Analysis* (Lanham, MD and Oxford: Scarecrow Press, 1994).

Wicke, P., *Rock Music: Culture, Aesthetics, and Sociology*, trans. R. Fogg (Cambridge: Cambridge University Press, 1990).

Williams, A., 'Divide and Conquer: Power, Role Formation and Conflict in Recording Studio Architecture', *Journal of the Art of Record Production*, vol. 1, no. 1 (2007).

Williams, R., *Out of His Head: The Sound of Phil Spector* (New York: Outerbridge and Lazard, 1972).

Williams, S., 'Stockhausen meets King Tubby's: The Stepped Filter and Its Influence as a Musical Instrument on Two Different Styles of Music', in F. Weium and T. Boon (eds), *Artefacts: Studies in the History of Science and Technology: Vol. 8* (Washington, DC: Smithsonian Institution Scholarly Press, published in cooperation with Rowman and Littlefield Publishers, 2011).

Wilson, J.S., 'Creative Jazz', *New York Times* (Apr 5, 1953), X9.

Wilson, J.S., 'How No-Talent Singers Get "Talent"', *New York Times* (21 June, 1959), SM16.

Wolff, J., *The Social Production of Art* (London: Macmillan, 1981).

Zagorski-Thomas, S., 'The Musicology of Record Production', *Twentieth-Century Music*, vol. 4, no. 2 (2008): 189–207.

Zak, A.J. III, *The Poetics of Rock: Cutting Tracks, Making Records* (Berkeley: California University Press, 2001).

Zak, A.J. III, 'Editorial', *Journal of the Art of Record Production*, vol. 1, no. 2 (2007). [Online]. Available at: www.artofrecordproduction.com/component/option,com_docman/task,doc_view/gid,52/ [accessed: 1 November 2007].

Zbikowski, L., Conceptualising Music: Cognitive Structure, Theory, and Analysis (Oxford: Oxford University Press, 2002).

Index